The Craft of the Psychodynamic Case Study

A Practical Guide

Aner Govrin

Routledge
Taylor & Francis Group

LONDON AND NEW YORK

Designed cover image: Getty Images

First published 2026
by Routledge
4 Park Square, Milton Park, Abingdon, Oxon OX14 4RN

and by Routledge
605 Third Avenue, New York, NY 10158

Routledge is an imprint of the Taylor & Francis Group, an informa business

British Library Cataloguing-in-Publication Data
A catalogue record for this book is available from the British Library

ISBN: 978-1-032-88587-2 (hbk)
ISBN: 978-1-032-88585-8 (pbk)
ISBN: 978-1-003-53857-8 (ebk)

DOI: 10.4324/9781003538578

Typeset in Sabon LT Pro
by Apex CoVantage, LLC

'The Craft of the Psychodynamic Case Study: A Practical Guide' is an essential companion for any clinician looking to transform therapeutic experience into a compelling narrative. With a perfect blend of theoretical insight and hands-on guidance, Aner Govrin leads readers through the art of writing psychoanalytic case studies, drawing from diverse schools of thought—from Klein to Kohut to the relational approach. More than just a manual, this book delves into the emotional and creative challenges of case writing, introducing the concept of 'responsible creativity'—a way to harness imagination ethically while staying true to clinical reality. It also dares to ask: Could therapy be captured not just in words, but through art, film, or dance? This fresh perspective expands how we communicate the depth of our work. Writing a case isn't just documentation; it's a second analysis, unlocking new layers of understanding. I strongly recommend this book as an indispensable resource for anyone eager to refine their clinical voice, break through creative barriers, and bring the richness of the therapeutic experience to life on the page.'

Giuseppe Civitarese, *author of* The Limits of Interpretation: Essays on Bion and Field Theory, London, 2025

'This comprehensive, accessible guide fills a yawning gap in the clinical literature: psychotherapists have long needed a framework for writing evocatively about their patients. Aner Govrin walks them through the daunting challenge of capturing in words all that a patient has conveyed through verbal description, imagery, dreams, body language, emotional expression, and behavior. The book belongs in the libraries of all students of psychoanalysis and psychodynamic therapy and on the desks of all experienced practitioners who want to write about individuality in treatment.'

Nancy McWilliams, *PhD, ABPP, Visiting Professor Emerita, Rutgers Graduate School of Applied and Professional Psychology*

'Virtually all forms of psychotherapy are, at one and the same time, procedures designed to relieve suffering and deeply personal relationships that engage the most intimate aspects of our shared humanity. Communicating what we do to colleagues and students, honoring the ambiguities that shape our work, capturing its ineffable edge, all the while protecting the privacy of our patients, has vexed clinicians forever. Aner Govrin's "Practical Guide" takes on this daunting task and accomplishes it. His book is required reading for anybody who thinks about writing about – or thinking about – our work, and that means anybody who practices psychotherapy.'

Jay Greenberg, *PhD, Training and Supervising Analyst, William Alanson White Institute, Recipient, 2015 Mary S. Sigourney Award for Outstanding Contribution to Psychoanalysis*

'When psychodynamic treatment concludes, practitioners continue their involvement in writing a case study. As study implies, they reconstruct the mental process undergone by both patient and therapist, not just their visible behavior. Aner Govrin animates the writing process for practitioners of all levels and theoretical orientations. Freud once said the psychodynamic case study resembled more a short story than science. Govrin, teaching the tradition in its modern incarnations, shows us why it must retain that form, while embodying one of the most exacting exercises anyone can undertake.'

Susan Sugarman, *Princeton University*

THE CRAFT OF THE PSYCHODYNAMIC CASE STUDY

The Craft of the Psychodynamic Case Study: A Practical Guide is the first comprehensive guide to help clinicians transform their therapeutic experiences into compelling, meaningful case narratives that honor both clinical truth and literary craft.

Every therapist faces the challenge of translating profound clinical experiences into coherent written case studies. This groundbreaking guide bridges a critical gap in professional training, offering practical tools for crafting compelling narratives while maintaining ethical boundaries and theoretical integrity. The book explores five major psychoanalytic approaches—Klein, Bion, Winnicott, Kohut, and Relational—each with specific writing strategies. Rich with clinical examples, it guides practitioners through diverse phenomena, from Klein's manic repair and envy, through Bion's alpha function and reverie, to relational self-disclosure. Readers learn to develop their narrative voice, structure long-term therapy into phases, write about transference and countertransference, and navigate confidentiality challenges.

More than a technical guide, this book revolutionizes how we think about case studies as creative non-fiction, introducing the concept of "responsible creativity" that empowers clinicians to move beyond formulaic reports. Perfect for psychodynamic psychotherapists and mental health practitioners at all levels writing cases for exams, publications, conferences, team presentations, or personal reflection.

Aner Govrin, PhD, is a psychoanalyst, philosopher, and clinical psychologist. He is the director of a doctoral program, "Psychoanalysis and Hermeneutics," at The Program for Hermeneutics & Cultural Studies, Bar-Ilan University. He is a Tel-Aviv Institute for Contemporary Psychoanalysis (TAICP) member and editor of the series Routledge Introductions to Contemporary Psychoanalysis.

COMPARATIVE PSYCHOANALYSIS BOOK SERIES

DAVID HENDERSON & JON MILLS
Series Editors

Comparative Psychoanalysis studies controversy and dialogue in psychoanalysis. Intellectual, personal, and institutional conflict are endemic to the history of psychoanalysis. Alongside this there are creative efforts to establish understanding and communication among differing perspectives. Comparative methodologies are encouraged among all schools of psychoanalysis regardless of topic, theoretical or clinical orientation, or application to the behavioral sciences and humanities including historical reassessments, conceptual clarification, clinical exploration, reflections on the future of applied psychoanalytic thought, and attempts to articulate the conditions for fruitful dialogue. All subject matters in the arts and humanities, philosophy, anthropology, cultural studies, and the human sciences are ripe for comparative investigation within the frameworks of theoretical, clinical, and applied psychoanalysis. As an inherently interdisciplinary field of study, psychoanalysis requires a robust understanding of comparative methodology. Controversial discussions and criticism are invited. In the spirit of pluralism, Comparative Psychoanalysis is open to any theoretical school in the history of the psychoanalytic movement that offers novel critique, integration, and important insights in comparative scholarship.

Titles in this series:

The Psychoanalytic Understanding of Consciousness, Free Will, Language, and Reason: What Makes Us Human? *By Robert Samuels*

Carl Jung and the Evolutionary Science: A New Vision for Analytical Psychology *By Gary Clark*

The Craft of the Psychodynamic Case Study: A Practical Guide *By Aner Govrin*

Contents

Acknowledgments   *xvii*

Introduction   **1**
The ideal case vs. real case: Bridging the gap in clinical writing—a
   meditation on the impossibility of representing therapeutic experience   3
The purpose of the book and how it is organized   4
How were the psychoanalytic schools chosen?   6
How to use this guide   7
References   8

Part 1   The essentials: Foundations of clinical writing   **9**

**1 The prelude to psychodynamic case studies: What to know
   before writing**   **11**
The psychodynamic case study as a creative nonfiction genre   11
The challenge   13
The hybrid nature of the genre of psychodynamic case studies   13
   First clinical example: Medical report style   14
   Second clinical example: Contemporary style   15
Responsible creativity   16
   The paradox of concealment and revelation   17
   The written case as a continuation of the therapeutic process   17
      Clinical example: Lost in translation   18

Notes	19
Recommended reading	20
References	21

2 Navigating the maze: Overcoming challenges of psychodynamic writing — **23**

Fear of criticism	23
Making sense of something messy	24
Losing the freedom of not knowing	25
Writing as a betrayal	26
Deconstructing and reconstructing: Tools and techniques for multilayered case study writing	27
Choosing the right patient for a case study	27
During or after: The temporal crossroads of case study writing	28
Writing a psychodynamic case report after treatment: Embracing memory's complexity	28
Creative destruction	29
A case study journal	30
Example of a case study journal: Associative notes on Sean	32
Getting help from colleagues	34
Reading case studies	34
Suggestions for to focused reading of psychodynamic case studies	37
Reading poetry	39
Using AI to write a case study	39
Mapping the case along "psychic truth" and "trauma healing"	41
Deciding when the case is complete	43
Why do case studies fail?	44
Recommended reading	45
References	45

3 The formal sections of a complete case study — **47**

Referral reasons	47
Background history	48
Psychodynamic formulations	50
Psychodynamic formulations by schools of thought	51
Psychodynamic formulation in Klein's theory	51
An example of using psychodynamic formulation according to Klein	53

Psychodynamic formulation in Bion's theory   55
   An example of psychodynamic formulation in
      Bion's theory   56
Psychodynamic formulation in Winnicott's theory   58
   Key elements in Winnicott's psychodynamic formulation   58
   An example of a psychodynamic formulation in
      Winnicott's theory   58
Psychodynamic formulation in self psychology   60
   An example of psychodynamic formulation in
      self psychology   62
The course of treatment   64
   Division of the course of treatment into phases   64
      Writing on themes or shifts   67
      Writing on each session   67
      Dividing treatment chronologically   68
      Writing about the silences: A note on "dead" periods   70
      Demonstrating the evolution of therapy through dreams   73
   Plot axes   74
      The pendulum of treatment: Navigating the tension between
        growth and resistance   74
      Crises   75
      Distrust-Honeymoon-Crisis-Resolution: The most common
        plot structure in psychodynamic case studies   76
   Case studies evolving through interpretations   80
      Clinical example of a case study evolving through interpretations   81
The termination phase   82
   Excerpts from endings of three canonical case studies   82
   Myths and realities of termination   83
   Non-mutual endings   83
   Thoughts on writing treatment endings   83
   Presenting the treatment achievements in a nuanced way   84
      Clinical example: A balanced description of therapeutic
        achievements   85
The discussion section   86
   Example of discussion section   87
Writing a psychodynamic case report for child patients   88
   Key elements in writing child case studies   89
Recommended reading   90
References   91

4 The therapist as storyteller: Weaving clinical wisdom into narrative art — **93**

Narration — 93
  Direct quotes or third-person narration? — 94
  Tenses — 95
  Profanity, dirty talk — 96
  Omniscience — 97
Style — 98
  Choosing the writing style — 99
  The value of humor in psychodynamic case studies — 103
The opening paragraphs — 103
  Sigmund Freud from "Studies in Hysteria," 1895 — 104
  Sue Grand from "The Reproduction of Evil" (2002) — 105
  Christopher Bollas from "When the Sun Bursts: The Enigma of Schizophrenia," 2015 — 105
Characterizing the Patient — 106
  Clinical example — 109
Selecting a pseudonym for the patient — 110
External appearance and behavior: Attire, demeanor, and movement — 111
The symphony of communication — 112
  Communication: First example — 113
  Communication: Second example — 114
Avoiding clichés — 114
Using "as if," "as though," and "one might have thought" — 116
  Examples — 116
Using metaphors — 116
From punctuation to precision — 118
Read your text out loud — 118
Recommended reading — 118
References — 119

5 Confidentiality strategies — **121**

Glen Gabbard's strategies to secure confidentiality — 122
  Disguise — 123
    Thick disguise — 123
    Clinical example — 124
    Considerations for disguise — 124
    Thin disguise — 125
    Exaggerated disguise-not advisable — 125
  Consent — 126
    Using the case study to advance the treatment — 126

Recommended reading   128
References   129

Part 2   The specifics   **131**
From Klein to relational: A journey through five psychoanalytic
   landscapes   131
References   132

6 A case study in the spirit of Melanie Klein   **133**
The greatest challenges   133
Related concepts   134
Therapeutic atmosphere   135
Therapy goal   135
Capturing transformation: Writing about change in Klein's
   framework   136
   Clinical example   136
Betty Joseph: Here and now, instead of breast and penis   137
   What causes change?   139
      Clinical example   139
Contemporary Kleinian therapists: Irma Brenman Pick   140
   Clinical example   141
Demonstrations of clinical phenomena   142
   Negative therapeutic reaction and envy   142
      Clinical example   142
   Manic defenses   143
   Clinical example   143
   Splitting   144
      Clinical example   144
   Harsh superego: Clinical example   144
   Symbolic equation   146
      Clinical example   146
   Reparation   146
      Clinical example   147
   Manic reparation   147
      Clinical example   148
Understanding the Oedipal triangle in clinical writing:
   Britton's contemporary view   148
Termination phase in a Kleinian orientation   150
   Clinical example   150
Suggestions for writing a case study based on Klein's theory   151
   Exploration of "general childhood situations"   152
   Transference and interpretation   153

Patient's response 154
Countertransference 154
Notes 155
Recommended reading 155
Five exemplary case studies of Kleinian theory 156
References 157

7 A case study in the spirit of Wilfred Bion **159**
The greatest challenges 159
Related concepts 161
Therapeutic atmosphere 161
Therapy goal 161
Capturing transformation: Writing about change in Bion's
framework 162
Demonstrations of clinical phenomena 162
Container/contained 162
Clinical example 163
Alpha function 164
Clinical example: Alpha function in mother-toddler
relationship 164
Clinical example: Parental failure of alpha function 165
The therapist's transformative dream 165
Clinical example 166
Development of the container within the analytic field
(Antonino Ferro; 2018, Civitarese, 2022) 167
Attacks on linking 168
Clinical example 169
The state of NO-THING 169
Clinical example 170
Catastrophic change 170
Clinical example 171
Selected fact 172
Clinical example 173
Bion's concept of psychic growth 175
Psychic growth: First clinical example 175
Psychic growth: Second clinical example 176
Termination phase in a Bionian orientation 176
Clinical example 177
Suggestions for writing a case study based on Bion's theory 177
Dream-like memory analysis 177
Basic approach to documentation 178

The SCREAM framework   179
Documenting core processes   179
    Field perspective   179
    Container/contained relationship   179
    Beta element transformation   180
    Selected facts   180
Working with memory and desire   180
    Suppression of desire   180
    Handling memory   180
The therapist's development   180
    Personal growth and learning   180
    Maintaining perspective   181
Writing style and technique   181
    Narrative approach   181
    Handling uncertainty   181
Recommended reading   181
    Five exemplary Bionian case studies   182
References   183

8 A case study in the spirit of Donald Winnicott   185
The greatest challenges   185
Related concepts   186
Therapeutic atmosphere   186
Therapy goal   187
Capturing transformation: Writing about change in
    Winnicott's framework   187
Demonstrations of clinical phenomena   188
    Unobtrusive presence   188
        Clinical example 188
    Hate in the countertransference   189
        Clinical example 189
    Preferring silence over interpretation   190
        Clinical example 190
    Regression   190
        Clinical example 191
    Fear of breakdown   192
        Clinical example 193
    Playfulness and creativity in therapy   194
        Clinical example 194
    Use of an object   194
        Clinical example 195

The termination phase in Winnicott's approach 196
  Clinical example 197
Suggestions for writing a case study based on Winnicott's
  theory 198
  Emphasize the holding environment 198
  Highlight experiential therapy 198
  Explore true and false self dynamics 199
  Regression to dependence 199
  Course of treatment 199
  Atmosphere and non-verbal communication 200
Recommended reading 200
  Five exemplary Winnicottian case studies 200
References 202

9 A case study in the spirit of Heinz Kohut 203
The greatest challenges 203
Related concepts 204
Therapeutic atmosphere 204
Therapy goal 204
Capturing transformation: Writing about change in Kohut's
  framework 205
Relational self psychology 205
  Clinical example 206
Self psychology and the spiritual dimension 208
  Clinical example 208
Demonstrations of clinical phenomena 210
  Transmuting internalization 210
    Clinical example 210
  Self disorder in the preemergent phase (self-structure) 212
    Clinical example 213
  Consolidations disorder (disturbances in selfobject experience) 214
    Clinical example 214
  Life curve disorders (disturbances of self experience) 216
    Clinical example 216
  Selfobject transference 217
    Clinical example 217
  Fragmented self 219
    Clinical example 219
  Sexualization as defense 220
    Clinical example 220

The termination phase in Kohut's theory   221
    Clinical example   222
Suggestions for writing a psychodynamic case study based
    on Kohut's self psychology   223
    Mapping selfobject needs   223
    Transmuting internalization: From dependence to autonomy   224
    Narcissistic expressions in therapy   224
    Fragmentation and emptiness: Encountering the fragmented self   224
    Empathic attunement: A bridge between two worlds   225
    Optimal frustration   225
    The therapeutic relationship as a corrective selfobject   225
    Signs of progress: A view of the changing self   226
Recommended reading   226
    Five exemplary self psychology case studies   226
References   227

10 A case study in the spirit of the relational approach   229
The relational revolution: Transforming psychodynamic case studies   229
The greatest challenges   231
Related concepts   233
Therapeutic atmosphere   234
Therapy goal   234
Capturing transformation: Writing about change in the relational framework 235
Demonstrations of clinical phenomena   235
    Enactment   235
        Clinical example   237
    The therapist's subjectivity   241
        Clinical example   242
    Conflict and negative feelings   242
        Clinical example   243
    Mutual recognition   244
        Clinical example   245
    Self-disclosure   246
        First clinical example   246
        Second clinical example: Self-disclosure in bad taste   247
    Dissociation   247
        Clinical example   248
Gender and race issues   249
    First clinical example   249
    Second clinical example   250

Termination in the relational approach 251
    Clinical example 252
Suggestions for writing a case study based on the relational approach 254
Recommended reading 257
    Five exemplary relational case studies 258
References 259

11 Concluding remarks: The clinical case comes alive through art **261**
    References 263

Index *264*

Acknowledgments

I am deeply grateful to Analu Verbin, Ilana Shalit, and Aviel Oren, who read the book's chapters and provided detailed feedback that significantly improved the manuscript. Their thorough review and insightful comments were invaluable to developing this work.

Special thanks to Rina Lazar, Tair Caspi, and Jill Salberg for their important contributions to this project, particularly for their thoughtful feedback on early drafts and their invaluable insights about the challenges of translating clinical work into written narratives.

I would also like to express my gratitude to the clinicians who consulted with me at various stages of their case writing process. Their experiences and challenges in clinical writing have taught me a great deal and helped shape my understanding of the complexities of crafting psychodynamic case studies.

Introduction

3 AM. The computer screen glows in the darkness, its cursor blinking accusingly on an empty document. Another therapist sits before it, attempting to translate two years of therapeutic work into a coherent case study. She knows everything but she doesn't know how to express anything. The words simply refuse to flow. She finds out that she had been too enchanted by those fleeting moments to discern the deeper currents that surged beneath their surface, until the act of writing demanded she confront the intricate labyrinth of meaning she had so blithely traversed.

The internal censorship committee is in full session tonight: there's the vulnerable child within who trembles at the thought of criticism, the echo of a dismissive supervisor from training years, the towering figures of psychoanalytic literature whose ghostly presence seems to mock every attempted sentence, and the ever-vigilant psychoanalytic police, ready to strike down any creative thought that strays from theoretical orthodoxy.

This scene repeats itself across the globe. The intern preparing their first case presentation for a peer group; the therapist completing a case study for their training program; the newly qualified clinician crafting a psychodynamic treatment summary for a patient's file; the experienced analyst hoping to share a particularly fascinating therapy journey—too many find themselves frozen before the blank page, caught between the urgency to share their clinical wisdom and the paralyzing fear of doing it wrong.

The sense of inadequacy in capturing the therapeutic experience is universal, yet it points to something profound about our field. The very struggle to translate the ineffable qualities of human connection into written language lies at the heart of psychodynamic work. Perhaps this is why writing about our clinical work feels simultaneously essential and impossible. Think about your own experience for a moment. What case comes to mind—the one that taught you the most, challenged you the deepest, transformed both you and your patient? Now imagine writing about it. What emotions arise? What holds you back?

The obstacles are numerous and complex. Beyond the internal critics and fears of external judgment, therapists grapple with significant ethical concerns regarding their patients'

DOI: 10.4324/9781003538578-1

wellbeing. They may feel they are exploiting their patients' trust and experiences for personal or professional gain, whether for passing an exam or publishing a paper.

When thinking about clinicians who want to write case studies, we are reminded of students in the Hogwarts School of Witchcraft and Wizardry, from the Harry Potter books. Similar to a young student waving his wand, trying to transform a cup into a bird while fearing failure, clinicians also struggle to take the familiar raw material of therapy and transform it into . . . something else. Both groups require courage and daring to break boundaries, expose their vulnerability to criticism, and step out of their comfort zone.

To write a case study, you will need to rise above the ground, like a wizard student freeing himself from gravity, and gain a broader perspective. Rising above the ground allows the therapist to escape the narrow and intimate angle of the therapeutic experience, and see the therapeutic process with a broader, more complex, and deeper view. This is an opportunity to connect the private and the universal, between the specific moments of the therapeutic encounter and the broader picture of the human change process. Just as a wizard student needs to rise above the ground to see the complete landscape, so too does the clinician need to "rise" above the initial layer of experience to expose the deep and hidden meanings of the therapeutic process.

Rising above the ground resembles an artistic act that creates something from nothing. Similar to a painter gazing at a gray and ordinary landscape and discovering worlds of color and light, or like a writer taking a simple moment in life and shaping it into a moving narrative structure, the clinician is required to transform reality through its representation. This is a thought alchemy, where the everyday experience—therapeutic and human—elevates beyond its direct reality. This rising is not an escape, but rather the opposite: it is a deeper look, capable of exposing the hidden layers, the profound meanings lurking beneath the surface. It is an act of creation, where reality is taken, examined, and presented anew—not as it is, but as it can be understood, illuminated, and empowered.

Like a young wizard at Hogwarts standing before their first broomstick, many therapists possess all the necessary tools but haven't yet learned to fly. The analogy extends further—just as magic requires both innate ability and technical skill, writing compelling case studies demands both clinical wisdom and literary craft. And like learning to fly, it requires the courage to leave the ground despite the fear of falling: audacity, always audacity.

*

I wrote my first psychodynamic case in the early 1990s as part of the exam every clinical psychologist must pass after completing their internship. The patient was an architecture student—a brilliant but highly anxious young man with megalomaniac and paranoid tendencies. He would enter the room silently with a blank expression, then suddenly break into an unsettling wide smile. Or, at the end of the session, he would shake my hand enthusiastically for an extended period, then go to the sink to wash his hands. He overwhelmed me, making the creation of a space for thinking and reflection complex. I found it challenging to convey what I felt in writing. Every sentence seemed forced and artificial, and I found myself dazzled with questions: How do you condense two years of therapy into ten pages? How can you write about your many failures and impasses? How do you construct the plot? Should you write in third person or first person? And most importantly, how do you translate sensory experiences, emotions, nuances, and complexities that are not conceptualized into written text?

From the exam itself, I remember one thing vividly. The examiner quoted a statement I had made, claiming that I found the patient had oral sadistic tendencies. She asked me, "How do you know he had such tendencies? Did he bite you?" This amused her and the entire examining panel, and I, of course, out of embarrassment and a desire to please, joined in their laughter. It was then that I also realized how a written case can sometimes appear amusing and even absurd in the seriousness with which it takes itself.

The experience taught me something crucial about case writing—it's not just about documenting what happened; it's about telling a story.

Since that first case study, numerous clinicians have sought my guidance on writing their own case narratives. Some were preparing for final certification, others aiming to publish at conferences or in journals. They grappled with a multitude of anxieties and technical challenges that went far beyond mere writing mechanics.

Their questions revealed deep professional vulnerabilities: How to choose a patient whose story illuminates broader clinical insights? How to protect patient confidentiality while maintaining narrative authenticity? Each consultation uncovered layers of uncertainty about representation, theoretical framing, and professional exposure.

The fear wasn't just about writing competence, but about revealing their unique clinical approach. Would their distinctive therapeutic style be understood or judged? Could they capture the nuanced, often ineffable moments of psychological transformation?

The need for a comprehensive guide emerged organically from these conversations not as a prescriptive manual, but as a compassionate companion to clinicians navigating the challenging terrain between clinical experience and written representation.

THE IDEAL CASE VS. REAL CASE: BRIDGING THE GAP IN CLINICAL WRITING—A MEDITATION ON THE IMPOSSIBILITY OF REPRESENTING THERAPEUTIC EXPERIENCE

The clinician-writer inevitably confronts a sobering realization: the written case will never truly resemble the actual clinical case. For many clinicians, this becomes the first major obstacle in their path to writing.

When you sit down to write a clinical case, you're haunted by two visions: the **Case** with a capital "C"—that idealized text that would perfectly capture the essence of your therapeutic work—and the actual **case** you manage to write on paper. The Case exists in your mind as a perfect crystallization of clinical wisdom, a complete representation that would convey not just what happened but the full meaning of the therapeutic journey. It would capture every nuance, every subtle shift, every unspoken understanding between you and your patient (for a detailed discussion, see Chapter 1).

But then there's the case—the one you actually write. As soon as you begin typing, the gap between these two versions widens. The Case in your mind contains multitudes: simultaneous layers of meaning, complex interpersonal dynamics, moments of profound understanding that seemed to transcend language. Despite your best efforts, the case on your computer screen can only capture these elements sequentially, partially, through the limited medium of words.

The Case promises a complete understanding—it would show not just what happened in therapy but why it mattered, not just the sequence of events but their deeper significance. It would reveal both the particular truth of this specific therapeutic relationship, and universal insights about human nature. But the case you're able to write inevitably falls short. It becomes a series of selected moments, a necessarily incomplete representation, a map rather than the territory itself.

This understanding can be liberating. When you recognize that no written case can ever fully capture the Case in your mind, you're freed from the impossible standard of perfect representation. Instead, you can focus on writing cases that, while acknowledging their limitations, still contribute valuable insights to our collective understanding of therapeutic work.

*

The challenge of bridging the gap between Case and case makes the need for practical guidance on case study writing all the more pressing.

In the vast library of psychoanalytic literature, case studies are abundant. While there are several textbooks and guides teaching clinicians how to write psychodynamic formulations and diagnoses, there is a curious absence of resources teaching the art of case study writing itself.

Writing case studies is often not part of therapists' training (Stuart, 2024). Traditionally, clinicians have learned through personal supervision, reading existing cases, and consulting with colleagues—methods that have evolved to fill the training void.

The absence of writing training stems from the common, yet mistaken, opinion that it's unnecessary. Since Freud's time, the written case has been perceived as a medical report describing the treatment and its results. Just as doctors do not undergo training to write a "Discharge letter" or "Clinical summary" but fill in the fixed format according to pre-written headings, psychoanalytic training institutes throughout the generations did not see a need for writing training. This perception persists today, highlighting the profound connection between psychoanalysis and the medical profession—a link that remains deeply ingrained in our collective unconsciousness.

THE PURPOSE OF THE BOOK AND HOW IT IS ORGANIZED

This guide offers a flexible framework for both emerging and experienced clinicians. It provides structure without constraining creativity, serving as a catalyst for clinical writing that allows individual wisdom to shine through.

For novice writers, the guide offers practical navigation: ethical considerations around confidentiality, strategies for balancing clinical detail with narrative engagement, and techniques for effective storytelling.

For seasoned clinicians, the guide presents an opportunity to reflect on established writing practices, potentially challenging comfortable patterns and introducing fresh narrative approaches.

The guide's purpose extends far beyond merely teaching techniques for writing psychodynamic case studies. It's designed to provoke thought, illuminate the complexities of psychoanalytic writing, and stimulate unconscious creative processes. It aims to help you think about the case and examine broader philosophical and clinical questions. For instance, to what extent is the written case faithful to the actual case? What is lost in the translation of therapy into a written case? What makes the case study part of the creative nonfiction genre? How should the creativity you demonstrate in writing your case study be responsibly deployed?

The goal of these questions is to help you see the case in a broader perspective through the act of writing. By engaging with these deeper inquiries, you are participating in a broader dialogue about the nature of therapeutic work, the challenges of representation, and the complex relationship between experience and language.

This book is divided into two parts.

"Part 1: "The Essentials—foundations of clinical writing"" provides the foundational knowledge every clinician needs before putting pen to paper. It covers critical aspects such as maintaining confidentiality, navigating the challenges of writing, understanding the case study genre, and learning the fundamental techniques of representation and narrative construction.

"Chapter 1: The prelude to psychodynamic case studies: What to know before writing" will help you recognize and master the rules of the case study genre: creative nonfiction. It will also encourage you to adopt a mindset of "responsible creativity," a concept I coined to explain one of the major challenges in writing case descriptions: how to be creative—allowing imagination to flourish and expressing your literary abilities—all while remaining faithful to your experiential truth and that of the patient.

"Chapter 2 Navigating the maze: Overcoming challenges of psychodynamic writing" discusses the intricate challenges of writing a case, such as making sense of something messy and losing the freedom of not knowing. This chapter equips clinicians with several practical suggestions to assist in writing the case study, such as reading poetry, studying case studies, maintaining a patient journal, and more.

"Chapter 3: The formal sections of a complete case study" details the structural elements, including reasons for referral, background history, psychodynamic formulations, the course of treatment, and discussion.

"Chapter 4: The therapist as storyteller: Weaving clinical wisdom into narrative art " discusses the treatment phase: the course of treatment, dividing the course of treatment into phases, narrative style, the opening paragraph, plot axes, the termination phase, and presenting treatment achievements and discussion.

"Chapter 5: Confidentiality issues" explores strategies for maintaining patient privacy through proper disguise and consent procedures.

"Part 2: The specifics: From Klein to relational: A journey through five psychoanalytic landscapes" helps clinicians understand how to craft a case study through the lens of five psychoanalytic theories:

Chapter 6: A case study in the spirit of Melanie Klein.

Chapter 7: A case study in the spirit of Wilfred Bion.

Chapter 8: A case study in the spirit of Donald Winnicott.

Chapter 9: A case study in the spirit of Heinz Kohut and self psychology.

Chapter 10: A case study in the spirit of the relational approach.

Each chapter in part two describes:

- The greatest challenges in writing a case study in the specific school
- The therapeutic atmosphere
- Related concepts
- Therapy goal
- Capturing transformation: Writing about change
- Demonstrations of clinical phenomena
- Suggestions for writing a case study

Each chapter throughout the book concludes with recommended reading.

Throughout this guide, I use numerous clinical examples and case descriptions to illustrate different aspects of case formulation and writing. **Unless otherwise specified, all examples and cases are fictional and do not represent actual patients.** In creating the fictional therapeutic cases for this book, I employed various creative methods. Real patient dreams were modified significantly, keeping only their basic narrative structure while changing the specific details and symbols. Brief moments from actual therapy sessions were transformed and expanded—for instance, a patient's angry "goodbye" became an elaborate story about an angry patient who overturned a plant in my clinic. Similarly, when a colleague shared her experience of sexual tension with a patient, this evolved into a complete seduction narrative where the patient casually removed her shirt, supposedly due to heat, revealing her chest. A character from a short story could also serve as inspiration for a fictional patient.

These composite vignettes feature patients of diverse ages, genders, cultures, and sexual orientations, reflecting the rich variety of individuals we encounter in clinical practice. This approach allows for detailed exploration of clinical writing techniques while ensuring no actual therapeutic relationships are compromised.

HOW WERE THE PSYCHOANALYTIC SCHOOLS CHOSEN?

I've known since I was an intern that when I'm with Kleinian analysts, I feel more Kleinian, and when I'm with relational therapists, I feel more relational—these theoretical approaches are different homes between which I comfortably move, creating a dialogic space within my psychoanalytic world.

My selection, therefore, is highly personal. I included what I have studied, what I have been engaged with for years, what I love, and what I integrate into my own therapeutic practice. Each of them is like an old friend accompanying me along the way—Klein, so precise, with her penetrating gaze into the sources of aggression and hatred; Bion with his dark, enigmatic language, forcing you to become a partner in his text; Winnicott, the life-loving optimist with the complexity within the simplicity of his writing; Kohut, whose writing touches and resonates with humanity, with a deep understanding of empathy and narcissistic needs; and the boundary-breaking relational approach, always challenging with the importance of the therapist's subjectivity.

I have not covered Jungian therapy, Lacanian analysis, classical Freudian psychoanalysis, or attachment-based therapy, to name just a few. Each of these omitted approaches has its own rich tradition and unique contributions to the field, and they deserve equal attention and exploration. The psychoanalytic community would greatly benefit from similar in-depth examinations of case studies from these perspectives.

*

The guide's central advantage is helping clinicians develop a distinctive, professional narrative voice that authentically captures therapeutic experiences while maintaining theoretical integrity, clinical truth, and ethical boundaries.

HOW TO USE THIS GUIDE

This guide is intentionally designed as a modular resource, recognizing that each clinician's writing journey is unique. You do not need to read the chapters sequentially. Instead, approach this guide as a flexible toolkit from which you can select the most relevant tools for your specific writing needs and developmental stage.

Experienced clinicians might jump directly to chapters addressing advanced narrative techniques or exploring complex theoretical integrations. Those new to case writing may find more value in foundational chapters about structure, ethical considerations, and basic writing strategies.

Each chapter is crafted to stand independently, allowing you to:

- Select chapters most relevant to your current writing challenges
- Return to specific sections as your writing skills evolve
- Use the guide as a reference manual rather than a linear textbook
- Adapt recommendations to your personal writing style and clinical approach.

Some chapters might resonate immediately, while others may become meaningful at different points in your professional development.

The modular design acknowledges that clinical writing is a deeply personal craft. Your unique clinical voice, theoretical orientation, and narrative intuition are paramount. This guide aims to support and refine those individual capacities, not to standardize or constrain them.

Feel free to explore, skip, return, and reimagine.

Although the book provides practical tools and advice, it will not be enough on its own. Samuel Johnson once said, "What is written without effort is read without pleasure." The great challenge of putting a therapeutic case into writing and finding words and meaning for therapeutic work requires tireless emotional, creative, and cognitive effort and considerable time resources.

This profound personal journey of writing reminds us of a fundamental truth about the writing process itself. As Ogden (2024) writes, "Everyone who takes his or her writing seriously is a writer. A writer is a person who writes, not a person who publishes. To try to write like someone else is to destroy what is unique to my own experience, my way of talking, my way of thinking, my way of writing, my way of being" (p. 194).

And Civitarese (2024) suggests that psychoanalytic writing inherently becomes both autobiography and fiction—precisely, the fiction of autobiography or of theory (p. 436).

And one last thing. This guide is intentionally rich with suggestions and techniques, but it's essential to understand that you are not expected to absorb or apply every single suggestion. These strategies are meant to illuminate your path, not to overwhelm or constrain you. Your natural clinical sensibilities and intuitive understanding should remain the primary compass in writing a case study. Treat this guide as a kind of walking partner, accompanying you through the complex terrain of clinical narrative, gently whispering alongside you as you navigate challenging questions like: How do I capture the depth of a therapeutic relationship? How can I authentically represent the intricate emotional landscapes of my clinical work?

The abundance of guidance is designed to expand your thinking and offer creative possibilities, not to create a sense of pressure or inadequacy. Trust your clinical instincts, use what resonates with you, and let your genuine therapeutic insights guide your writing. The most compelling case writing emerges when clinicians can write while flowing with their feelings, creative unconscious, and clinical insights. I aim to support that profound, deeply personal process of clinical narrative creation.

REFERENCES

Civitarese, G. (2024). Flashes in a Moment of Danger: On the Autobiographical Essence of Psychoanalytic Writing in Adrienne Harris's Essay "You Must Remember This". *Psychoanalytic Dialogues 34*, 434–437.

Ogden, T. H. (n.d.). A letter to a young writer. *Parapraxis*. https://www.parapraxismagazine.com/articles/letter-to-a-young-writer

Stuart, J. (2024). "No Mortal Can Keep a Secret": Reading Freud's Cases as Preparation for Candidates' First Efforts to Write About Their Patients. *Psychoanalytic Inquiry, 44*(3), 194–209.

PART 1

The essentials

Foundations of clinical writing

....

The chapters that follow provide a comprehensive toolkit that addresses both the technical requirements and the creative challenges inherent in translating the therapeutic experience to the written page.

My hope is that by the end of this section you will have developed a solid foundation of knowledge in both the technical and creative-literary aspects of psychodynamic writing, enabling you to produce clinically grounded case descriptions that will contribute meaningfully to the psychoanalytic community.

DOI: 10.4324/9781003538578-2

CHAPTER 1

The prelude to psychodynamic case studies

What to know before writing

....

Before we delve into the writing process itself, a preliminary step is necessary. The first thing to understand is that the psychodynamic case study belongs to a genre known as creative nonfiction, a form of writing with its own unique characteristics and demands. Like any genre, it grants freedom to writers but also imposes limitations. Therefore, the upcoming chapter is theoretical and aims to consider the genre of case studies before approaching the task of writing one.

THE PSYCHODYNAMIC CASE STUDY AS A CREATIVE NONFICTION GENRE

Consider an Agatha Christie mystery: strangers gather in an isolated mansion, a murder occurs, and the investigation begins. Who committed the crime, when, and why? The detective methodically interviews each suspect before dramatically revealing the killer's identity, motive, and method in the climactic finale (Govrin, 2025). Psychodynamic case studies follow their own narrative conventions. Two people meet regularly in a clinical room furnished with chairs or a couch, with tissues nearby. One is the therapist who owns the space, while the other is the patient seeking help. Through 50-minute sessions, the patient shares psychological struggles, and the therapist applies psychoanalytic understanding. The story unfolds through the patient's life history and the transformative therapeutic moments that emerge. Every case study shares these structural elements. Viewing psychodynamic case presentations as a distinct literary genre—with its own patterns and rules, like any other narrative form—opens new possibilities for clinical writing. Understanding these genre principles can help clinicians develop more expressive approaches to documenting their work, enhancing reader engagement while remaining true to the authentic therapeutic experience.

Psychodynamic case studies occupy a fascinating and often debated literary landscape. Are they factual accounts, medical reports, or something else entirely? This book argues that the case study history has always been shaped by its in-between-ness. It represents a unique hybrid genre, a sophisticated form of creative nonfiction that blends the precision of medical reporting with the evocative power of storytelling. Like memoirs, biographies, and

DOI: 10.4324/9781003538578-3

historical novels, psychodynamic case studies portray a reality that, while rooted in lived experience, is not claimed to be a mirror image of objective truth. Analysts don't fabricate details but use their imagination and writing skills to elicit the reader's identification with the therapeutic processes. A well-written case transcends the limitations of dry reporting and creates a more lasting impression than any simple recitation of facts.

Imagination is, in fact, the driving force behind exceptional case studies. It breathes life into complex dynamics that would otherwise remain hidden. Without the power of imagination, a written case remains merely a pale shadow of the rich and intricate therapeutic experience that occurred in reality.

The last decade has witnessed a significant flourishing of personal nonfiction literature—memoirs, autobiographies, and life stories—both in local and global contexts. This phenomenon is linked, among other factors, to the ongoing erosion of objective truth's status in modern society. It is interesting to observe a parallel trend developing in the field of clinical documentation, where psychoanalytic case studies are gradually transforming toward more personal and subjective expression.

In the therapeutic space, where an ethic of "objective" and detached documentation once prevailed, there is now an increasing willingness among therapists to reveal their inner worlds, acknowledge their emotional involvement, and present their personal perspectives as integral parts of the therapeutic process and its understanding. This shift reflects a growing recognition that every case study is actually a narrative shaped by the therapist's subjective experience, not merely a neutral documentation of therapeutic facts. However, this trend is not without risks. An overemphasis on subjectivity may lead to clinical narcissism, where the therapist and their experiences become the focus of the story instead of the patient. The challenge facing contemporary case-study writers is to find a subtle balance between acknowledging subjectivity and maintaining a therapeutic perspective that respects both the patient and the therapeutic process.

This inherent blending of facts and creativity prompts important questions. How much creative license is permissible? Where is the line between legitimate artistic rendering and the fabrication of unknowable details? The very nature of the term "creative nonfiction" highlights this tension; creative writing inherently involves the construction of imagined realities, whereas nonfiction, by definition, does not. Yet, as even celebrated biographies demonstrate—with their narrative arcs, compelling characterizations, and evocative prose—the boundary between these two can be fluid and surprisingly productive.

Here's a powerful opening from Walter Isaacson's (2007) biography of Einstein:

> When Albert Einstein was five years old, his father showed him a pocket compass. For the young boy, it was a revelation. What hidden force could make the needle always point north? The magnetic field was invisible, yet it could influence objects in the physical world. This sparked a lifelong fascination with invisible forces. As Einstein later wrote, "Something deeply hidden had to be behind things."

Isaacson had the historical fact of Einstein being shown a compass by his father and Einstein's later quote about hidden things. However, he had no direct access to young Einstein's thoughts or immediate reactions. The vivid details about it being "a revelation" and the questions running through the boy's mind are the biographer's creative reconstruction, an educated imagining based on what we know about Einstein's later development and writings. This shows how biographers must sometimes bridge factual gaps with careful, informed speculation while maintaining historical authenticity.

The psychodynamic case-study writer must bridge the gap between documented facts and deeper psychological truths. The writer engages in what we might call **"responsible creativity"** —using their professional knowledge, understanding of human psychology, and narrative skill to flesh out the documented moments into a fuller story that rings true while maintaining fidelity to the core facts.

This book explores these fascinating intersections, examining how the unique characteristics of psychodynamic case writing allow for both therapeutic insight and the use of our creative thought to convey our understanding of the human condition.

THE CHALLENGE

The psychodynamic case study is a curious beast born from the marriage of medical reporting and creative storytelling. It's as if William Osler (1892)—often called the "Father of Modern Medicine," who was known for his meticulous clinical observations and medical case reports representing the scientific medical tradition—and Ernest Hemingway decided to collaborate, each bringing their distinct strengths to the table. Your challenge is honoring both traditions while finding your voice within this framework.

As you embark on your own case study, think of yourself as a translator, tasked with rendering the language of the unconscious into compelling prose. Case studies require balancing clinical fidelity with narrative coherence—remaining true to what occurred while shaping it into meaningful communication. Too literal a rendering obscures significance; too much artistic license risks distorting clinical reality. Like a skilled translator, you must remain faithful to the therapeutic encounter's essence while creating an engaging and illuminating narrative. Your clinical training provides the foundation for accuracy, but your creative instinct and playful understanding will transform clinical observations into a vivid, insightful account. The greatest satisfaction in writing a case will come when you find something to say about it that turns out exactly as you wanted to write it.

> Can a written case study be more compelling and insightful than the actual therapeutic experience it recounts? The answer is yes. This reminds me of a telling anecdote: my father was walking with his grandchildren when a passerby remarked, "What beautiful children!" my father replied, "Wait until you see their photos!" Sometimes, the representation can surpass what it represents. Just as a masterful translation of a poem can capture and even enhance the nuances and emotional resonance of the original, a well-crafted case study transforms the raw clinical experience into a vibrant narrative that reveals layers of meaning and understanding that might not have been fully apparent during the actual therapy.

THE HYBRID NATURE OF THE GENRE OF PSYCHODYNAMIC CASE STUDIES

On the medical side, your case study needs the bones of a solid clinical report. You'll include the essential facts: patient demographics, presenting problems, psychodynamic formulation, and course of treatment. These elements provide the necessary structure, ensuring your narrative remains grounded in professional practice. Think of them as the scaffolding that supports your more creative endeavors.

But here's where it gets interesting. Unlike a standard medical report, you're not just listing symptoms and interventions. You're crafting a story. This is where the literary elements come into play. You're not just writing about a patient; you're introducing a character. Your therapy room becomes a stage, and the therapeutic relationship unfolds like a plot.

At this point, we're moving from the dyad to the triad. A new player, the reader, enters the scene. And this reader isn't a private confidant like your best friend but an entire community of professionals who might read your case. From now on, everything you write will be in dialogue with them, considering what they understand, whether they're moved, whether they'll see the case as you do, whether they'll grasp the emotional experience. Your patient might also be among your readers, a challenge we will address in Chapter 5. Your writing now must resonate with their professional knowledge, engage their clinical curiosity and evoke their empathy while maintaining the integrity of your therapeutic insights and the patient's privacy.

Consider, for example, how might you describe your patient's entrance into your office. A straightforward report might note, "32-year-old female presents with symptoms of depression." But in a psychodynamic case study, you have the freedom to write, "Ann's shoulders slumped as she sank into the chair, her eyes darting around the room before finally meeting mine with a mix of defiance and despair."

This literary approach doesn't just make for more engaging reading. It actually provides a fuller, more nuanced clinical picture. By describing Ann's body language and the quality of her eye contact, you're conveying important diagnostic information in a way that brings the reader into the room with you.

Let's examine how these elements come together by examining two approaches to the same clinical encounter.

Here are two illustrations of a similar therapeutic scene during a first analytic meeting:

First clinical example: Medical report style

"Amanda, who describes herself as a professional and socially successful career woman, complains of a fear of heights, expressing her difficulty participating in mountain hikes or climbing a ladder. She also fears collapse and loss of control. Shifts between self-confidence and extreme panic attacks are reflected in tremors and stutter. Panic attacks occur when the patient lies on the couch and stops at the end of the meeting."

Written in a sparse style, the first vignette is typical of the classical period: it sticks to the facts, is communicated dryly, and is recounted in the third person. The "I" of the therapist is absent, and so there is no description of his feelings and responses. Throughout the text, the narrator never connects emotionally with their subject—not once do they attempt to see the world through her eyes or find within themselves the capacity to understand her experience truly.

The traditional approach to psychodynamic case writing, deeply influenced by the medical model and scientific aspirations of early psychoanalysis, champions a kind of literary self-effacement. The tone is very much as seen from overhead, disengaged and observational.

According to this view, the clinician's writing style should be like a perfectly transparent window—allowing readers to see directly into the consulting room without being distracted by the glass itself. The clinician-writer is warned: "Don't show off; avoid drawing unnecessary attention to yourself." Just as a therapist talking too much in session might prevent the patient's material from emerging, it's argued that an overly prominent writing style might obscure the clinical phenomena. Like someone chattering through a movie, a conspicuous authorial presence is seen as an unwelcome distraction from the real show—the patient's story and the therapeutic process.[1]

Yet this doctrine of stylistic invisibility and separateness, with its insistence that "less is more" and its elevation of clarity above all other virtues, contains its own paradox. Many of the most celebrated "purely clinical" case studies—from Karl Abraham's "A Short Study of the Development of the Libido" (1927) to Otto Fenichel's case reports (1945)—reveal, upon closer examination, highly distinctive voices and careful literary crafting. Their supposed transparency is itself a style, and their clinical objectivity is a carefully constructed pose. The fantasy of pure clinical prose, untainted by personal style, is perhaps just that—a fantasy, as elusive as the dream of the perfectly neutral analyst that an earlier generation of clinicians pursued. This is why even the most "objective" case studies are never truly style-free. They are, rather, written in a style that aims to create the illusion of objectivity—a literary achievement in its own right. The belief that we can somehow extract pure clinical content from the "distortions" of writing style is as misguided as thinking we can observe the therapeutic process without being part of it. In both cases, the observer and their mode of observation are inextricably part of what is being observed. In striving to be invisible as authors, we risk becoming invisible as therapists, missing the crucial truth that our subjectivity isn't a contamination of the clinical process but an essential instrument of our work.

Second clinical example: Contemporary style

"Amanda radiated self-confidence. Introducing herself as a successful career woman and an amateur hiker, she said she functioned extremely well in her social, professional, and family life. She sought therapy to overcome her fear of heights, to be able to climb a ladder at home or go on mountain hikes with her partner. She also reported difficult feelings threatening to take over at any moment, involving a loss of control. She spoke of these feelings somewhat inappropriately, as if she was observing someone else, slightly amused. I felt indifferent to her distress. I couldn't quite connect.

But there was a dramatic change once Amanda lay down on the couch. She started to tremble and hardly managed to mutter some unclear words. Suddenly, I encountered a split-off aspect that was much less contained than the presentation of herself she offered before lying down. That was an extremely disturbing experience for me. I didn't know what to do. I had to get a quick hold of what was happening. Another shock came at the end of the meeting: Amanda got up abruptly, her energy suddenly restored, and bounced back, in the blink of an eye, into her self-contained and cheerful persona."

The second vignette consists of more than facts; it presents a story about facts. In many ways, his text is a fuller description and, therefore, more faithful to the therapy than the factual, dry representation.

> For me, there are two kinds of case studies: those "at rest" and those "in action". The difference between a case study "at rest" and one "in action" is that the former presents static facts and data, while the latter brings to life the dynamic process of thinking and the experience itself.

The purpose of a well-written case is to portray not a thought, but a mind thinking. The talented writer of a case study knows that an idea separated from the act of experiencing it is not the idea that was experienced. The warmth and passion that accompanied the idea as it formed are a necessary part of its truth.

This blending of clinical precision with personal narrative raises an important question: When did this transformation begin? When did the therapist's emotions, needs, and experiences become central characters in case narratives?

While therapists have always written about their feelings towards patients—evident in Freud's work and certainly in Ferenczi's writings—it was the relational revolution that transformed this occasional practice into a systematic approach (Govrin, 2019). However, it's crucial to note that personal, literary writing styles predated the relational approach. Clinicians like Michael Eigen wrote in deeply personal, confessional literary styles as early as the 1970s, long before relational approaches emerged. Similarly, Herbert Searles employed intimate, self-revealing narrative techniques well before the relational turn. The relational approach systematized and legitimized this more personal, reflexive *mode of case writing*.

I will explore these nuanced historical developments in greater depth in Chapter 10 when I deal with writing cases inspired by the relational approach.

This fragile balance between personal disclosure and clinical responsibility leads us to consider the concept of "responsible creativity."

RESPONSIBLE CREATIVITY

Unlike memoir writers and writers of historical novels, we are responsible to the professional community and their patients. We operate within a body of knowledge aimed at alleviating the mental suffering of patients. Our main goal is to develop understandings and interventions that will help patients. We don't have the creative freedom that a memoir writer has. We write not for artistic or aesthetic purposes but to enrich the psychoanalytic knowledge. How can we ensure we're doing it right?

To address these concerns, it's crucial to understand the concept of "responsible creativity," which attempts to bridge the gap between writing and creativity on one hand, and our ethics as therapists on the other.

Consider the following example describing a sad patient: "Her sorrow was like a dark cloud that followed her everywhere, obscuring the sunlight of her life."

While this metaphor is vivid, you need to ask yourself if it truly captures the patient's unique experience or if it merely showcases your literary flair. Using such a generalized metaphor risks minimizing the individual's distinct emotional state. Don't write just to please or impress the reader, and never ever abandon your own therapeutic experience and your experience as a therapist. Remember, your focus should be on representing both the patient's voice and your own therapeutic experience authentically.

Responsible creativity in case writing requires a subtle equilibrium. We must harness our literary skills to bring the therapeutic encounter to life while maintaining our ethical obligations to our patients and profession. This means being judicious in using literary devices, ensuring that they illuminate the clinical material rather than overshadow it.

As the writer of a clinical case study you must persuade your reader that you are a reliable clinician and that readers can trust your account.

The paradox of concealment and revelation

The dilemma of disguising a patient's identity constitutes a fertile paradox at the heart of clinical writing. In the ethical act of concealing identifying details, we are invited, almost involuntarily, into the realm of creation. The moment we bestow a pseudonym upon a patient, alter their profession, or redesign their family constellation, we cross the delicate boundary between documentation and fiction.

Here, a dangerous epistemological temptation opens before us: if we are permitted to rewrite the patient's external biography, why stop there? The inventions need not be grand falsehoods—they often begin as small, almost imperceptible lies. Perhaps we add a minor detail to their childhood story, slightly modify their response to our intervention, or fabricate a moment of insight that never actually occurred. The boundary between disguise and invention is frighteningly thin, and if we've breached one boundary—why not breach them all? Why not invent an entirely new therapeutic history, one that better serves the narrative we've chosen to present?

The temptation to invent not just a new patient, but also a new therapy—more elegant, coherent, and impressive than the raw reality—is immense. It is more comfortable to present a patient whose progress aligns with our favorite theory, or one whose responses reflect the therapist we wish to be, rather than who we truly are.

Responsible creativity demands rigorous internal discipline. We must distinguish between changes that serve the duty of confidentiality and changes that serve our professional narcissism. Every fictional act must be examined by the crucial question: Does it bring us closer to the emotional truth of the therapeutic encounter, or does it distance us from it?

The profound paradox is that the necessity to conceal may lead to deeper revelation. The need to find metaphors, images, and alternative narrative structures can open a window to new understandings. When we deliberate on how to describe the patient without exposing them, we may discover additional layers in our understanding of them.

Confidentiality, then, is not merely an obstacle to overcome, but an invitation to a complex dialogue between concealment and revelation, between reality and fiction, between ethics and aesthetics—a dialogue that, at its best, leads to a deeper and more precise clinical truth.

The written case as a continuation of the therapeutic process

When writing a case study after therapy concludes, the clinician primarily engages with the internalized patient—their mental representation of the individual—rather than the actual person. What becomes especially important at this stage is recognizing what is lost when translating the lived therapeutic experience into written form. These gaps and omissions aren't simply technical limitations—they often contain crucial information about the therapeutic relationship itself, potentially revealing unconscious processes, countertransference reactions, or relationship aspects too nuanced to capture in standard clinical language.

The writing process has become an extension of clinical work, though, now, it is without the patient's actual presence to provide reality checks. During this process, the internalized patient continues to evolve and become more complex, primarily through the lens of the therapist's internal world. This evolution isn't necessarily a departure from truth but represents a different kind of truth—one emerging from deep reflection on the therapeutic experience.

When clinicians struggle to capture certain aspects of the therapeutic relationship in writing, these difficulties often point to significant dynamics. The moments where therapists find themselves unable to adequately describe an interaction or feeling become valuable clinical data themselves. These "translation losses" between lived experience and written word can illuminate previously invisible aspects of the therapeutic relationship.

This understanding carries important implications for case study writing. Clinicians should remain aware that their written accounts represent a complex interplay between their actual patient experiences and their ongoing internal work with the internalized patient. Special attention should be given to areas where words seem inadequate or where certain experiences resist straightforward description.

From this perspective, the gap between the described patient and the actual patient becomes not just an inevitable limitation but a potentially rich space for professional growth and theoretical advancement. Grappling with these gaps and attempting to bridge them can lead to deeper insights into both the specific case and the therapeutic process as a whole. The development of the internalized patient through the writing process mirrors how creative ideas evolve through responsible implementation, with each iteration potentially revealing new layers of understanding while maintaining professional integrity.

Clinical example: Lost in translation

After Ruth finished writing her case study about Megan, she was delighted with it. After all, she had presented what she considered a therapeutic success: a woman with borderline personality disorder, without stable employment and with a high turnover of partners, completed many years of therapy with improvements in all areas of her life. With Ruth's help, Megan found a stable and fulfilling job and had been in a relationship for a long time. Megan's ability to manage her abandonment anxieties and regulate her emotions without outbursts or breakdowns had grown extraordinarily.

However, a recent dream deeply troubled Ruth. In the dream, she and Megan were walking arm-in-arm down the street. Megan needed to urinate and didn't care about doing it on the street in front of everyone. Ruth screamed at her and asked her to find a bathroom. But to Ruth's astonishment, Megan squatted down and urinated in front of all the passersby. Ruth's dream seemed to highlight what she had omitted from her case study. The act of Megan urinating in public, despite Ruth's protests, might symbolize the ways in which the patient had "violated" Ruth's professional boundaries during therapy or how Ruth felt "soiled" or overwhelmed by the patient's emotional outbursts at times. This omission from the case study suggests that Ruth may have sanitized her account, focusing on the positive outcome while neglecting the messier, more challenging aspects of the therapeutic process.

Ruth's realization about the omission of the conflict between her and Megan led her to understand the extent to which she had repressed the intensity of her anger towards Megan. Following her dream and subsequent insight, Ruth revisited her case study, deliberately integrating the moments of tension, countertransference, and emotional complexity she had previously sanitized. She added nuanced sections describing her struggles with Megan's boundary violations, her own feelings of frustration and occasional professional exhaustion, and the nonlinear nature of therapeutic progress.

What made Ruth's approach particularly creative yet responsible was her decision to revise her case study while maintaining professional boundaries. She didn't simply add dramatic elements for effect, but rather thoughtfully integrated previously omitted aspects of the therapeutic relationship—her countertransference, moments of tension, and professional challenges. Her creative process involved finding appropriate clinical language to describe these difficult experiences while respecting both her own and Megan's dignity.

SEVERAL GUIDELINES FOR CLINICIANS TO MAINTAIN RESPONSIBLE CREATIVITY

1. Prioritize authenticity over drama: focus on capturing the true essence of the therapeutic relationship and process, rather than embellishing for dramatic effect. Use your creative skills to illuminate the subtle nuances and complexities of therapy, not to create sensationalized narratives.

2. Use creative tension responsibly: when you feel creatively inspired to write dramatically about certain therapeutic moments, pause to examine whether this impulse serves clinical understanding or personal gratification. Channel this creative energy into deepening professional insights rather than seeking emotional release.

3. Examine omissions and gaps: sometimes, the areas where therapists strive to be particularly creative are precisely the places where there may be a therapeutic failure or something the therapist is trying to suppress or hide. This effort to creatively navigate challenging topics can signal underlying issues or blind spots that deserve attention. By recognizing these gaps, therapists can gain valuable insights into their own processes and improve their practice.

4. Transform creative resistance into insight: when you find yourself resistant to writing about certain aspects of the therapy, use creative writing techniques to explore this resistance rather than avoid it. Your creative blocks might reveal important countertransference issues that need examination.

NOTES

1 This approach reached its apex in Bernstein's (2008) attempt to standardize clinical writing through a rigid three-part structure that artificially separated the analyst's experiences from their theoretical formulations and reflections about the process (for an objection to this view see also Young-Bruehl, 2008).

RECOMMENDED READING

Analytic writing as a form of fiction, by Thomas Ogden. *Journal of the American Psychoanalytic Association 69*, 221–223, 2021.

Ogden's article "Analytic writing as a form of fiction" (2021) is a groundbreaking contribution to understanding the craft of psychodynamic case writing. He revolutionizes our perspective by arguing that clinical case writing is inherently a form of creative fiction—not in the sense of fabrication, but as an artistic endeavor to capture the lived truth of the therapeutic encounter.

Clinical case studies in psychoanalytic and psychodynamic treatment, by Jochem Willemsen, Elena Della Rosa & Sue Kegerreis. *Frontiers in Psychology.* 8, 108, 2017. doi: 10.3389/fpsyg.2017.00108

This paper summarizes how the case study method is being applied in different schools of psychoanalysis and clarifies the unique strengths of this method and areas for improvement.

On the word's work, by Giuseppe Civitarese. *Journal of the American Psychoanalytic Association 70*, 1235–1238, 2022.

The essay explores the unique nature of psychoanalytic writing, focusing on how style and content merge to create meaningful clinical narratives. The author argues that psychoanalytic writing has a distinct "literary" quality in its ability to create worlds, where style is not secondary to logical argumentation but rather completes the conceptual framework. This is beautifully captured in his words:

> Style is not spurious or secondary to logical argumentation. When style happily marries concepts, it completes them in the same way a perception coordinates fluidly with body movements and vice versa. (p. 1236)

What makes this essay particularly valuable for clinicians learning to write case descriptions is Civitarese's insight into the special relationship between clinical practice and writing. He emphasizes that psychoanalytic writing must evoke emotions while maintaining theoretical rigor, citing how authors like Freud, Klein, and Winnicott achieved this through their distinctive styles. The author illustrates this through the metaphor of Orpheus and Eurydice, suggesting that writing, like psychoanalysis itself, is an attempt to bring something from the darkness into light, even knowing that complete illumination may be impossible. This perspective helps clinicians understand that effective case writing is not just about documenting facts, but about capturing the alive, emotional quality of the therapeutic encounter.

Four domains of experience in the therapeutic discourse, by Wilma Bucci. *Psychoanalytic Inquiry 27*, 617–639, 2007.

This article, authored by Wilma Bucci, from Adelphi University and the Derner Institute, presents a novel approach to case report writing that prioritizes scientific rigor and empirical methods.

Bucci's proposed method involves recording therapy sessions, analyzing them using multiple perspectives (the analyst's immediate impressions, clinical consultants' evaluations, and objective measures), and comparing these analyses to identify patterns and factors influencing treatment. This method will be of great value to researchers and clinicians alike, particularly those interested in empirical psychoanalysis.

Finding words: How the process and products of psychoanalytic writing can channel the therapeutic action of the very treatment it sets out to describe, by Rachel Altstein. *Psychoanalytic Perspectives 13*, 51–70, 2016.

The article provides valuable insights into how writing about clinical work can serve as more than just documentation—it can be a therapeutic tool that reveals unconscious dynamics in both therapist and patient. As stated in the article: "Finding words in the literal sense is the bridge between the act of writing—the sitting and the waiting for words to come—and therapeutic action in analysis." (p. 58)

Writing in psychoanalysis, by Editors: Emma Piccioli, Pier Luigi Rossi, & Antonio Alberto Semi. Karnac Books, 1996.

The book's practical value for clinicians is significantly enhanced by its thorough examination of the writing process itself. Patrick Mahony, in his chapter "Psychoanalysis—the writing cure," argues persuasively that Freud's self-analysis was essentially a "writing cure," emphasizing the crucial role of writing in Freud's self-discovery and the development of psychoanalysis. Mahony's analysis draws on Freud's own writings and correspondence, particularly his letters to Wilhelm Fliess, providing compelling evidence for his thesis.

Other contributors explore various aspects of the writing process, such as Henning Paikin's analysis of the transition "From analytic dialogue to published text," highlighting the challenges of representing the dynamic, intersubjective nature of the analytic encounter in the static form of written communication. Antonio Alberto Semi's chapter, "Writing in Psychoanalysis," offers a historical perspective, tracing the evolution of writing's role in psychoanalysis and considering the symbolic implications of writing, drawing on both Greek and Jewish traditions. The book is full of insights on the importance of clarity, precision, and attention to form and structure in psychoanalytic writing, providing readers with practical strategies for improving their own writing.

REFERENCES

Abraham, K. (1927). *Selected papers on psychoanalysis.* Hogarth Press and the Institute of Psycho-Analysis. (Routledge) https://doi.org/10.4324/9780429479854

Altstein, R. (2016). Finding words: How the process and products of psychoanalytic writing can channel the therapeutic action of the very treatment it sets out to describe. *Psychoanalytic Perspectives, 13*(1), 51–70. https://doi.org/10.1080/1551806X.2015.1108175

Bernstein, S. B. (2008). Writing about the Psychoanalytic Process. *Psychoanalytic Inquiry 28*, 433–449.

Bucci, W. (2007). Four domains of experience in the therapeutic discourse. *Psychoanalytic Inquiry, 27*(5), 617–639. https://doi.org/10.1080/07351690701468157

Civitarese, G. (2022). On the Word's Work. *Journal of the American Psychoanalytic Association, 70*(6), 1235–1238.

Fenichel, O. (1945). *The psychoanalytic theory of neurosis.* W. W. Norton & Company.

Govrin, A. (2019). Facts and sensibilities: What is a psychoanalytic innovation? *Frontiers in Psychology, 10*, 1781. https://doi.org/10.3389/fpsyg.2019.01781

Govrin, A. (2025) Responsible Creativity: Combining Clinical Report and Literary Writing in the Psychodynamic Case Study. *Psychoanalytic Psychotherapy, 39*, 20–39.

Isaacson, W. (2007). *Einstein: His life and universe.* Simon & Schuster.

Mahony, P. J. (1996). Psychoanalysis—the writing cure. In E. Piccioli, P. L. Rossi, & A. A. Semi (Eds.), *Writing in psychoanalysis* (pp. 3–20). Karnac Books.

Ogden, T. H. (2021). Analytic writing as a form of fiction. *Journal of the American Psychoanalytic Association, 69*(2), 221–223.

Osler, W. (1892). *The principles and practice of medicine: Designed for the use of practitioners and students of medicine.* D. Appleton and Company.

Paikin, H. (1996). From analytic dialogue to published text. In E. Piccioli, P. L. Rossi, & A. A. Semi (Eds.), *Writing in psychoanalysis* (pp. 37–52). Karnac Books.

Piccioli, E., Rossi, P. L., & Semi, A. A. (Eds.). (1996). *Writing in psychoanalysis.* Karnac Books.

Young-Bruehl, E. (2008). Discussion. *Psychoanalytic Inquiry, 28*, 518–526.

Willemsen, J., Della Rosa, E., & Kegerreis, S. (2017). Clinical case studies in psychoanalytic and psychodynamic treatment. *Frontiers in Psychology, 8*, 108.

CHAPTER 2

Navigating the maze

Overcoming challenges of psychodynamic writing

....

The psychodynamic case study serves multiple masters: the patient, whose story is revealed and translated; the therapy itself, which requires representation and conceptualization; the reader, awaiting discovery and understanding; the psychoanalytic community, seeking theoretical resonance; and the canonical literature, maintaining an ongoing dialogue. In its role as a multi-tasking "servant," it navigates conflicting loyalties, unresolved tensions, and opposing demands, thereby exposing the full complexity of its creation.

FEAR OF CRITICISM

Ronald Britton (1998) astutely observes:

> Publication anxiety is ubiquitous and has two sources. One is fear of rejection by the primary intended audience. The other is fear of recrimination by affiliated colleagues and possible exile from them. I think that a profound fear of rejection by the primary intended listener in its most serious form leads to an inability to conceptualize or, in lesser states of inhibition, produces an inability to write. (p. 199)

The act of writing a case study represents a seismic shift for many therapists. You move from the protected, intimate space of the therapy room to the public arena of professional discourse. Suddenly, you're not just the wise, empathetic listener; you're the one seeking validation, exposed and vulnerable to the judgment of your peers. Moreover, committing your work to paper feels irrevocable. Unlike the fluid, interactive nature of oral case presentations, a written study seems etched in stone. Unlike spoken words that dissolve into air, written case studies stand as permanent testimony—their indelible nature, resistant to erasure or revision, can paralyze even seasoned clinicians who understand that what they write today will echo through professional

DOI: 10.4324/9781003538578-4

memory forever. As Paikin (1996) notes, "The written word is in the nature of an oracle: it is separated from its author, and the paradox is that although the written word is dead, it lives an 'eternal' life of its own, because it will survive even if it is disproved!" (p. 49). Some therapists believe that if a case study isn't brilliant and incomparable to any other, they should abandon it. This is both an ambitious and simplistic approach. It rests on the implicit assumption that they possess extraordinary ability, and if this exceptional talent doesn't manifest in a case study of absolute originality and value, they should set aside their pen and avoid writing altogether. This demand for complete differentiation misses the essence of clinical work. The singularity of each case, if we adhere to such a concept at all, stems from the way each therapist dwells within the clinical magma from which they draw inspiration and immerse their experience. Absolute distinction is a difficult and perhaps impossible task, and certainly not necessary. The case studies we write are never entirely new; they reveal the traces and patterns from which the clinician draws from professional tradition to express their personal and professional voice. When a therapist describes their work, they internalize the voices of their teachers and supervisors, processing them in their authentic way. A good enough case study isn't one without comparison, but one that successfully reflects the human encounter that took place in the therapy room, with all its complex layers and emotional subtleties woven between therapist and patient. The approach that prefers absolute differentiation forgets that the very movement between reliance on tradition and personal expression is what gives clinical writing its depth and value—just as the patient moves between dependence and independence on the path to discovering their true self.

Another issue is fear of the "psychoanalytic police," a metaphorical term for the harsh, judgmental superego that therapists often internalize during their psychoanalytic training. This internal critic represents the collective voice of their mentors, supervisors, and the theoretical framework they've been taught to adhere to. It acts as a psychological watchdog, constantly monitoring their thoughts, interpretations, and writings to ensure they conform to the "correct" psychoanalytic doctrine. Consider a true story I heard from a colleague: Sofia, a young psychologist, was grappling with a significant challenge as she prepared to write a case study for her institute's training committee. As a self-psychologist amid a prominent community of object relational and Kleinian practitioners, she faced a dilemma: she could either remain true to her Kohutian approach and risk rejection, or compromise her principles to satisfy her evaluators. Ultimately, Sofia chose the latter option, opting to downplay her Kohutian techniques while emphasizing object relations in her discussion. Though her decision was pragmatic in the context of her professional environment, it left her with lingering regrets about her authenticity and the potential impact on her patient. Sofia realized that by not fully representing her approach, she might have missed an opportunity to advocate for the therapeutic methods she believed in. One should see writing psychodynamic case studies as a hurdle race toward an additional measure of freedom, a release from theoretical constraints and from the critical eye of the superego within and the community without, toward expressing a personal and unique voice. Easier said than done! But when it succeeds, there is a great sense of freedom, like a child feels when the class bully has gone away.

MAKING SENSE OF SOMETHING MESSY

No case can be fully written. Not only is it impossible to provide all the raw data, but it also inevitably passes through the perspective, selectivity, and interpretation of the clinician. Every clinical case study is shaped by editorial choices—what to include, what to omit, and how to organize the narrative. The very act of transforming lived experience and complex inner worlds into narrative form means that the case is, at best, a constructed representation rather than a complete record. The written case can be compared to the game of Mikado: from the chaotic scatter of colorful plastic sticks, one must patiently and carefully select, stick by stick, to create a new order. Authors typically present therapy as a collection of dramatic moments, neglecting to highlight the many sessions in which "gray" and undramatic therapeutic work was done. To maintain the living drama, the actual therapy is narrated in jumps and skips over large time intervals, like short videos that show a flower opening over two days or a day-long movement of clouds racing across the sky. The many hours omitted from the text are also important to the therapy, with essential, invaluable work accomplished during them as well. Yadlin-Gadot (2023) describes the writer Marie Cardinal, whose analysis resembled a thick book: "Patient leafing through its thousands of empty pages reveals four or five sentences that changed her life. Is not the power of these derived from the thousands of pages whose emptiness was written with love and effort by the analytic couple?"

The work of editing and trimming can deter many therapists. Presenting the reader with a complete and coherent therapeutic thread, isolating its components, and showing a sequence of continuity and plot development involves tremendous effort and unravels the living texture of the therapeutic relationship. I discuss this challenge extensively in Chapter 3. This process of distillation inevitably sacrifices some of the richness and complexity of the actual therapeutic experience. It is the necessary violence of creation, the pruning that allows the true shape of the work to emerge. Yet, in this act of shaping, something of the living, breathing reality of the therapeutic encounter is inevitably lost. Yadlin-Gadot's insight reminds us that the true power of therapy, like that of great literature, often lies in what remains unsaid, in the spaces between words. This is hard to convey in a written case.

LOSING THE FREEDOM OF NOT KNOWING

For a moment, let us consider the peculiar anxiety that grips therapists as they approach the task of committing their cases to paper. This is not merely the writer's familiar struggle with the blank page, but a more fundamental tension between the nature of therapeutic insight and the demands of narrative exposition. Therapists sit down to write about those moments of deep insight and significant change in therapy—instances where both therapist and patient seem to touch something profound. Yet, as they begin to record these moments, they realize they have been too easily satisfied with what these instances appear to convey. Now, they are compelled to think deeply about what these moments truly mean.

The most profound psychic changes occur beneath the threshold of consciousness, invisible to both analyst and analysand (Bollas, 1987). This notion strikes at the heart of our understanding of the therapeutic process, challenging our faith in the primacy of conscious knowledge. It's as if the therapist is being asked to map the contours of an invisible landscape, to describe the subtle shifts of tectonic plates that take place far beneath the surface of observable behavior.

Nina Coltart's (1992) assertion that "we do not know what we are doing" (p. 2) in our "impossible profession" might initially strike us as a kind of therapeutic nihilism. Yet it is, in fact, a profound acknowledgment of the mystery at the heart of our profession.

Bion's advice to forget everything one knows about the patient and approach each session as if it were the first speaks to a radical openness to experience that starkly contrasts with the demands of the written case.

The ongoing therapeutic relationship allows for—indeed, requires—a certain comfort with ambiguity. The therapist need not weave every observation into a grand tapestry of explanation, need not resolve every contradiction or trace the genealogy of every symptom. This openness to uncertainty, this willingness to dwell in the realm of the unknown, is perhaps the therapist's most valuable tool.

Keats wrote about "Negative Capabilities" when a man is capable of being in uncertainties, mysteries, doubts, without any irritable reaching after fact and reason (Li, 2009).

Yet the written case demands an entirely different approach. The act of writing inherently requires structure, coherence, and some degree of resolution. This transition from the fluid, open-ended nature of the therapeutic relationship to the fixed, explicatory nature of the written text can feel like a kind of closing off of possibilities that contradict the very essence of the psychoanalytic stance.

The case study, after all, is written not for the patient but for the reader—that unseen presence who hovers at the therapist's shoulder as they write, demanding clarity, explanation, and understanding. The reader wants to understand, and the writer must comply with the reader's wishes. This is the agreement between writers and readers.

In this light, the therapist's anxiety about writing becomes a reflection of a deeper tension within the therapeutic enterprise itself. The challenge, then, is not simply to write well but to find a form of writing that can somehow honor both the mystery of the therapeutic encounter and the reader's desire for understanding—a task that pushes against the very limits of what language can accomplish.

> Have you ever seen a case study that states: "When she entered the room, something occurred between us that I cannot put into words, explain, understand, let alone convey in writing"? In fact, there is no reason why clinicians shouldn't write this way.

Writing as a betrayal

Another significant barrier to case writing arises from the inherent tension between the intimacy of the therapeutic environment and the public nature of case studies. This reluctance touches on something deeper than mere professional anxiety; it confronts us with the possibility that we are betraying our patients' trust. When we write about our patients, we share intimate moments that belong exclusively to the therapeutic dyad. This act of sharing, especially without the patient's explicit consent, carries the weight of betrayal. While we disguise identifying details to protect confidentiality, this disguise also conceals our transgression. Even in cases of consent, the element of betrayal still exists. We alter the patient's identity, transforming them into someone else, stripping away their basic identifying features, and in this sense, we deny their name, identity, occupation, and sometimes even their age and family status—all for the sake of publishing for anonymous readers who were not part of the treatment.

I have outlined several key challenges therapists face when attempting to write case studies. It's important to note that while the guide offers a nuanced exploration of these challenges, it does not provide simple solutions to these intricate problems. In the next section, I will present several suggestions to facilitate the writing and creative process. These suggestions will indirectly address the difficulties described, offering practical approaches to navigate the complex terrain of case study writing.

DECONSTRUCTING AND RECONSTRUCTING: TOOLS AND TECHNIQUES FOR MULTILAYERED CASE STUDY WRITING

Choosing the right patient for a case study

When approaching an academic presentation or professional evaluation, the temptation is to showcase a case study that demonstrates clinical success and captures intellectual intrigue. Yet, beneath the surface of professional requirements lies a deeper inquiry: with which patient do I want to embark on a profound and intricate writing journey, one that might take me months or perhaps years to complete? To whom should I make this investment?

This question delves into the heart of what transforms a case study from a mere clinical report into a profound exploration of the therapeutic process. Here are some considerations:

Transformative cases—choose a patient whose treatment journey has significantly impacted you as a therapist. These cases often provide the richest material for reflection and insight. For instance, consider a patient who reacted with intense hostility whenever the therapist offered even a slightly different perspective. Any interpretation that didn't completely echo the patient's view was perceived as a personal attack. Traditional empathetic approaches fell short, forcing the therapist to develop more nuanced strategies to help the patient tolerate psychological differences and build emotional flexibility.

Select a case that still evokes strong emotions or curiosity. Your continued engagement with the material will fuel the writing process. For example, consider a case involving a patient with a rare and complex trauma response—a survivor of a cult who developed an extraordinary psychological splitting mechanism. The patient's internal world was so fragmented that they simultaneously held contradictory narratives about their experience, creating a psychological landscape where truth and delusion continuously negotiated boundaries. The therapist found themselves drawn into a labyrinthine therapeutic journey that challenged fundamental assumptions about memory, identity, and psychological resilience.

Patients whose cases left you with lingering questions or uncertainties can also be excellent subjects, as the writing process may help you find new perspectives or understanding, such as a patient whose sudden withdrawal from therapy left the therapist questioning the lasting impact of their sessions on the client's self-esteem and overall progress.

Also, consider whether the case represents a **particular therapeutic approach**, challenge, or population that you feel is important to share with the professional community. For example, a therapist from an Eastern European country, who came from a Catholic community, shared their experience of working with a Jewish patient. This case highlighted the challenges and nuances of navigating cultural and religious differences in therapy, emphasizing the importance of understanding diverse backgrounds to foster a more inclusive therapeutic environment.

It's important that you feel free not to write about patients who are too difficult or whose treatment was too complicated for you. I know therapists who started writing something and then told themselves: this is not for me, I can't handle this, it's beyond my capabilities. It's like a traveler standing before a narrow, dangerous road with an abyss below and saying, I'm not trying to drive there.

During or after: The temporal crossroads of case study writing

Another significant issue is the timing of writing a case study—during ongoing treatment or after its completion. This represents a crucial decision point with substantial implications. Writing during treatment allows for capturing emotional processes and observations in real-time, potentially enhancing the ongoing treatment through insights gained during the writing process. However, this approach can make it challenging to maintain perspective on the overall therapeutic arc, as it becomes difficult to view therapy as a process with a beginning, middle, and end from an outside perspective.

Writing a case study about a patient who is still in therapy is often inadvisable. It can sometimes lead to the therapist engaging in an enactment, as the therapist may feel stuck on an unresolved issue, experience a crisis in therapy, or feel anxious, frustrated, or highly tense. While writing may alleviate some of that tension and provide a sense of resolution, it can also become a way to avoid directly confronting the actual issues with the patient during sessions and supervision.

Writing after treatment completion allows for viewing the complete therapeutic journey with its outcomes and turning points, alongside a better perspective on what was truly significant. It facilitates fuller processing of countertransference and identification of missed opportunities. However, this approach comes with its own challenges, including memory limitations and the risk of constructing an overly tidy narrative that doesn't capture the true complexity of the therapeutic process.

A recommended method is to adopt a hybrid approach: taking detailed notes during treatment but waiting until after completion to craft the full case description. This strategy combines the benefits of immediate observation with retrospective understanding while potentially minimizing the drawbacks of each approach. Ultimately, the choice depends on several factors, including the purpose of the writing, the specific characteristics of the case, and the writer's own learning goals. What's most important is maintaining awareness of how the timing of writing can influence both the therapeutic process and the resulting case description.

Writing a psychodynamic case report after treatment:
Embracing memory's complexity

When reconstructing a psychodynamic case study after therapy has ended, clinicians must grapple with the inherent fluidity of memory. Memories of sessions are not passive recordings but imaginative reconstructions shaped by the therapist's subjective lens. Certain moments—vivid emotions, pivotal exchanges, or unresolved tensions—may surface effortlessly, while others remain frustratingly elusive, as if retreating further the harder we strive to recall them. This selective recall reflects the brain's tendency to prioritize information that aligns with narrative coherence or emotional salience. Rather than viewing gaps as failures, therapists can acknowledge that forgetting is a natural byproduct of cognitive processes that filter and prioritize data to construct meaning. The act of writing, then, becomes an exercise in humility: accepting that the "story" of therapy is not a factual ledger but a living tapestry woven from fragments, inferences, and the therapist's own unconscious dynamics.

Forgetting and distortion, while potential pitfalls, also offer insights into the case's deeper currents. What resists retrieval often signifies unresolved themes, countertransference patterns, or defensive blind spots. For instance, a therapist's ongoing focus on a patient's anger while overlooking moments of vulnerability might reveal their own discomfort with fragility. By reframing gaps as invitations for reflection, clinicians can explore why certain details feel urgent to retain and others fade. The case report thus transforms into a dialogue between recollection and interpretation, where the therapist's selective memory illuminates both the patient's inner world and their own psychic participation in the process. Embracing this dynamic tension allows the report to evolve into a tool for ongoing clinical insight—one that honors the messy, nonlinear truth of therapy while striving for ethical and theoretical integrity.

Creative destruction

In the writing process, you may find yourself writing things that surprise you—things you didn't intend to write beforehand, which weren't revealed to you during supervision or in prior reflections on the case. It's not that you meant to discuss one aspect of the therapy and ended up addressing something entirely different; rather, there is a continuous peeling away of layers that leads to new and surprising revelations. For this to happen, something must be dismantled.

You might think that a case merely requires connection—to link theory with the case, to weave different treatment periods into a single narrative, to connect the discussion with the content of the case. However, there's an additional consideration. To make these connections, you must also do what Bollas calls "cracking up" (1995). Bollas describes the process of creative destruction in Freud's approach to dreams. According to Bollas, Freud's explanation of dream interpretation features a dialectical process of deconstruction and connection. The work of the unconscious gathers seemingly disparate ideas through condensation, creating the original dream content. When the patient is asked to free associate to the dream, they effectively deconstruct this condensation. Freud emphasized that in this process, the patient disperses the manifest content of the dream.

Both processes—bringing together and cracking up—are crucial features of the unconscious and form its dialectic. Each time a condensation is produced, its richness in meaning ensures that it will break apart during later elaborations. Free association is described as "creative destruction," breaking apart clear unities of thought and permitting new ideas to surface and develop.

This process is vital for personal freedom, preventing consciousness from becoming a form of ideational incarceration. The more intense the psychic experience, the less permanent its registration in consciousness, as the ideas that emerge from it soon give rise to a multitude of further and divergent thoughts.

The therapeutic process should be approached similarly to a dream, allowing for creative writing that reveals its otherness. Writing a case is a dynamic interplay of creation and destruction, connection and deconstruction, which enables the discovery of new and deeper meanings of psychic content.

The therapeutic journey has been solidified through years of treatment and supervision. To write about it deeply and creatively, the therapist must step outside their comfort zone, where they believe they understand the case in a specific way. All of this must be deconstructed to be reconstructed differently in the written case.

As the clinician "destroys" their initial understanding, they create space for new connections and interpretations to emerge. This destruction does not negate previous insights but rather opens up new avenues for understanding the therapeutic process. The resulting case study is likely to be richer, more insightful, and potentially more valuable for both the writer and the reader.

However, this process does not occur in isolation through conscious thought. It needs to happen unconsciously, akin to dream work.

There are several techniques that therapists can use to facilitate this process of deconstruction and reconstruction:

1. Visual representation: creating visual representations of the case can help dismantle linear thinking and reveal unexpected links.
2. Metaphor exploration: identifying and exploring metaphors related to the case can uncover deeper meanings and alternative interpretations.
3. Artistic expression: utilizing art, such as drawing or sculpting, to represent aspects of the case can tap into non-verbal understanding and generate new insights.
4. Dialogue writing: composing imaginary dialogues between different aspects of the case (e.g., between the patient's self-states or between the therapist and patient) can uncover hidden dynamics.
5. Meditation or mindfulness practices can help clear the mind and allow new connections to organically emerge.
6. Peer discussion groups: engaging in open-ended discussions about cases with colleagues can present fresh perspectives and challenge established interpretations.

A case study journal

"I will never forget that moment of terror," said the king, "I will never, ever forget." "Of course you will forget," replied the queen, "if you don't write on a note." This exchange from "Alice in Wonderland" aptly captures another recommendation for clinicians grappling with case study writing. The practice of maintaining detailed notes is essential, as memory alone cannot be trusted to preserve the nuanced details that make case formulation valuable.

One of the primary challenges in writing a case is the overwhelming familiarity with the patient. After countless hours spent in therapy sessions and supervision, it may feel as though all possible angles have been explored. A case study journal is intended to "crack up" the familiarity to construct something new by starting a free-associative flow through writing a therapy journal.

The journal weaves together elements from your daily life with your therapeutic case, creating a flow of free associations that leads to new lines of thought. Like a journey visiting different places, this process allows you to break down and reassemble the case in novel ways.

This approach lets the therapist break free from fixed interpretations and discover new layers of meaning in the therapeutic process. A journal might also help you overcome writer's block and foster creativity.

Begin by dedicating a notebook specifically to your case study, labeling it "Case study diary—not for publication." This private space frees you from the constraints of polished prose or sophisticated phrasing. Instead, it becomes a sanctuary for raw, unfiltered thoughts and impressions. Write from your imagination, heart, and senses, allowing a strong emanation to develop naturally.

The goal is to tap into a stream of consciousness that, by its very nature, may be scrambled, associative, and incoherent. This seemingly chaotic flow can form the foundation for a rich and insightful case description. Capture thoughts and associations as they arise throughout your day, often appearing unexpectedly in the most mundane moments. Dreams, fleeting images, shapes, landscapes, smells, isolated words, poetic fragments, or snippets of conversation—all are worthy of inclusion in your diary.

Keep your notebook close at hand, ready to record these ephemeral insights wherever you go. Place it by your bedside to capture dreams upon waking. You'll soon discover that the mere presence of this notebook stimulates your mind to engage more deeply with the case. Seemingly unrelated experiences—other therapy sessions, casual conversations, street sounds, or a stunning vista—may suddenly reveal profound connections to your case study.

Resist the urge to review your notebook too frequently. Allow time to pass between readings, encouraging movement, creation, and continued emanation rather than fixating on a single idea. Think of your notebook as a kaleidoscope, where each new rotation reveals a fresh configuration of colors and shapes.

In this era of digital convenience, which medium should we choose for our therapeutic journaling? While most of us have grown accustomed to typing on computers or smartphones, there's particular value in maintaining your therapeutic journal in longhand. Though perhaps less convenient, the physical act of handwriting serves the deconstruction process in unique ways. When we write by hand, we're forced to slow down, allowing more time for reflection and association. The physicality of handwriting engages different neural pathways than typing, potentially accessing memories and insights that might remain dormant when using digital tools.

Finally, this journaling approach highlights a fundamental truth about case writing: it is not a focused task to be "cracked" but rather a lengthy process that demands time, reflection, and deep engagement. Case writing resembles a journey of discovery more than a destination to reach. The journal acts as a companion in this extended process, allowing ideas to develop organically, insights to emerge gradually, and understanding to deepen over time. This slow, contemplative approach sharply contrasts with our culture's emphasis on immediate productivity and quick results. By accepting and embracing the time-intensive nature of case writing, we create space for genuine insight and meaningful synthesis of our clinical experiences.

Example of a case study journal: Associative notes on Sean

Monday: On my way home, I encounter a construction site that catches my eye. A structure caught in deep transition—neither fully demolished nor yet built. Exposed walls, a staircase leading nowhere, electrical wires dangling like open veins. I stop, struck by an insight—this is the very internal configuration of Sean himself. Not merely fragmented, but simultaneously undergoing processes of demolition and reconstruction. Like this building, he lacks a protective outer layer, exposed to external influences; his internal architecture visible to all, vulnerable, revealing the improvisations and shortcuts in his development. And yet, there exists potential for something whole, if only he could complete the rebuilding process.

Tuesday: During today's session with Michael, another patient his typical passivity was constricting as usual. But while he laid out the familiar content, something else drew me in—the depth beneath his words. His stories meander like underground rivers, saturated with meaning. Thus, I found myself making an involuntary comparison with Sean, who speaks as if reading from a pre-prepared script—flat text, without dimension, as clear as medication instructions and equally lifeless. The difference is sharp enough to be troubling. Is this truly about Sean, or perhaps about where I meet him? Maybe Sean comes to therapy with the structure I saw yesterday—half-demolished, half-under-construction—and I'm focusing on the ruins instead of the scaffolding?

Wednesday: In the evening, my seven-year-old son Eitan burst into tears after playing soccer. "I always lose," he sobbed. "Always, always, always." I found myself facing a mirror image of Sean with his dichotomous language—"I'll never have," "I always fail," "Everyone hates me." Yet, the difference cuts deep: in my son's eyes I saw the living pain of defeat, while Sean's eyes always remain dry, almost neutral, as if the actual pain has been shifted elsewhere, hidden. Is this what holds Sean's scaffolding together—this dissociation, because the real pain is unbearable?

Thursday: I overheard an argument on the street, a male voice cutting through the air: "You always do this!" with an accusatory tone that seemed copy-pasted from my last session with Sean. A moment later, the woman responded in a soft voice, "I'm sorry it seems that way to you. I'm trying to help." I lingered at the street corner, listening. How can a conciliatory response neutralize confrontation? Did her gentleness penetrate through his armor of suspicion? If so—this is precisely the experience Sean lacks: an encounter with softness that holds his anger without falling apart or counterattacking. Even I, in our sessions, sometimes respond to his accusations with a professional wall, fortifying myself behind therapeutic questions instead of offering that stable gentleness I just witnessed.

Friday: I returned to reading Kernberg on borderline personality organization, and found Sean between the lines—a description so precise that I felt uncomfortable, as if the pages themselves were reading him instead of me. I returned to thinking about the building-in-process I saw on Monday. Kernberg writes about "non-integration of self and other images" and that's exactly what I saw—stairs without exits, walls that don't meet ceilings, rooms unconnected to each other. Are the slowly emerging structure and my deeper understanding of Kernberg's text part of the same process, where I'm constructing Sean within me, and perhaps, in parallel, he is constructing himself in the therapy room?

Saturday: I went to an abstract art exhibition and lingered before a painting that initially appeared as if the artist had simply poured liquid paint onto the canvas without prior planning. But after several moments, I began to see patterns, recurring lines, an internal rhythm. Just like Sean's "chaos"—what first seems like random outbursts of anger or despair actually contains a hidden structure, a dark internal logic. And perhaps I'm wrong about his "superficiality"? Maybe it's just my reading habit, like someone looking at an abstract painting without seeing its complexity? An abstract painting won't immediately reveal its secrets. Have I been patient enough, or will I eventually see the order within Sean's mess?

Sunday: Dream: I meet a baby who wants ice cream, decide to buy him some. His mother warns me to protect him with my life. I enter a maze, confident I can navigate it, but quickly become lost, as does the baby. I exit the maze alone, guilty. I wake with the thought that Sean is the baby I lost, his vulnerable and hungry part that pleaded with me for something nourishing, sweet . . . and so I trace back my thoughts to the observation I made on Wednesday—about the difference between my son's vulnerable tears and Sean's dry eyes. The baby in the maze is the part I haven't found, the part whose hunger I didn't know how to listen to or protect. The maze is my theoretical understanding—seems safe and comprehensible to me, but misses the essential.

Monday: In a team meeting, Amir, one of the other psychologists, shares his difficulty with a patient he describes as "classic borderline." I feel discomfort crawling up my spine, like approaching an unpleasant truth. It takes me back to the building-and-demolition experience I saw a week ago. Amir speaks as if that patient is a fixed, finished structure—"classic borderline" like a still photograph, not like a film still in the making. Have I reduced Sean to that same static image? Have I ignored the scaffolding and focused on the ruins, forgotten the future in favor of the present? This is an ontological error—treating Sean as if he is what he is, instead of what he is in the process of becoming.

Tuesday: A bird flies repeatedly against my office window, collides with the glass, and returns. I think of Winnicott's description of "false self," that facade a person constructs in order to survive. Sean constantly chases after a reflection, an ideal image of himself—like a desperate search for something that isn't his. But unlike the bird, Sean's reflection changes frequently; it's not a fixed image but a fluid figure. And I understand—the crumbling facade of the building, his dry eyes, his flat speech, all these are scaffolding around a false self that can no longer exist, but the true self hasn't yet crystallized either. He's stuck in this in-between space, like a bird repeatedly hitting glass, returning wounded but ready to try again—that's Sean with his relationships, with his aspirations, with himself.

Wednesday: Dream: I write in a notebook and fill all its pages, yet somehow, it remains empty. I cannot understand how. I wake with a sense of warning—that despite all the associations and insights from the past two weeks, I may still miss Sean's true essence. After all, the insights I've gathered so far come from the initial observation of the half-demolished building and my thoughts about the lack of integration in his life. However, all the images and comparisons—with my son, with the woman on the street, with the bird, with the abstract art—reflect my perspective, the story I'm telling about Sean. The dream warns me: do I really know Sean, or just my version of him? Or perhaps, in the very effort to understand, I might change what I'm trying to comprehend?

Getting help from colleagues

Another effective strategy to breathe new life into the writing process is to seek feedback from colleagues even before starting the actual writing. Engaging with others in the initial stages of the writing process can inspire new understandings, deepen existing insights, and provide fresh angles for analysis. While it is natural to share your case study draft with close colleagues and supervisors familiar with your work, there is immense value in obtaining feedback from professionals outside your immediate circle. Constructive feedback from those not deeply enmeshed in your specific clinical context can reveal blind spots, challenge ingrained assumptions, and introduce innovative ways of conceptualizing the therapeutic material.

Therapists often gravitate toward colleagues who share their theoretical orientation. For instance, a Kleinian therapist might seek feedback from other Kleinians, while a self-psychologist might turn to Kohutian practitioners. This approach has its merits, as peers within the same tradition are well-versed in the specific language, methods, and goals of treatment. However, there is significant value in seeking feedback from therapists with different approaches. Open-minded colleagues from diverse backgrounds can offer fresh perspectives that challenge preconceived notions. Disagreements can lead to fruitful dialogues and new insights, allowing therapists to understand the path they chose and those they did not take. Consider the example of a self-psychologist providing feedback to a Kleinian therapist. The self-psychologist suggests that moments of silence during the patient's anxiety may have left the patient feeling alone, reminiscent of neglectful parents. While the Kleinian therapist acknowledges this perspective, it reminds her of the Kleinian stance toward reassurance. According to Klein (2017), patients possess an unconscious awareness of the quality of their analysis. Patients unconsciously appreciate when a therapist resists being drawn into fulfilling surface-level desires and instead maintains a stance focused on the analytical work. She argued that this steadfast commitment to the analytic process, rather than acquiescing to the patient's more immediate wants, represents the patient's best chance for genuine therapeutic progress and healing. However, she also recalls instances where her interpretations effectively calmed the patient's anxiety. The interpretation connected something that previously evoked anxiety with the ability to bear that anxiety, containing within it a reassuring element.

Thus, through the self psychology therapist, the Kleinian therapist—the case study author—becomes more aware of her attitude toward the issue of soothing the patient. The self psychology perspective contributes to a more complete and complex understanding of the Kleinian viewpoint.

Reading case studies

Archaeologists have their Rosetta Stone, historians their medieval manuscripts, natural scientists their fossils, and art historians their masterpieces. We psychodynamic psychotherapists have none of these grand artifacts. Our treasure is the case study.

Freud's case studies of Dora, the Wolf Man, and Little Hans; Winnicott's accounts of his work with Piggle; Klein's detailed observations of young Richard—these bridge the temporal distances between us and them. Through these case studies, we have formed personal connections with them. Thanks to these writings, our relationships with them resemble those we have with our living colleagues. The case studies bridge the gaps across time and space. They breathe life into those who have long departed from this world.

These case studies are not just our heritage—they are our teachers, our guides in the art of clinical writing. Tell me your favorite case study's author, and I will tell you who you are: Freud—Do you prefer elegant, literary prose that weaves between scientific observation and storytelling? Klein—Are you drawn to dense, technical writing that prioritizes interpretive depth over stylistic flourish? Bion—Do you value writing that intentionally challenges readers, using obscurity to provoke deeper thinking? Eigen—Do you lean toward bold, metaphorical language that captures raw emotional experiences? Ogden—Do you appreciate precise, lyrical prose that balances clinical insight with poetic sensibility?

Each time we sit down to craft a case study, we are, in a sense, entering into a dialogue with these masters. We are both students and colleagues, learning from their wisdom while striving to contribute our own unique voices to the ongoing conversation of psychoanalytic thought.

> If you want to write a case study, you must do one thing above all others: read many case studies. There is no other way, no shortcuts.

Every case study you read has something else to teach, even if it is badly written.

Through reading, we begin to internalize the principles of the genre. We observe how skilled authors weave coherent narratives from the tangled threads of therapeutic experience, how they craft beginnings and endings, how they describe pivotal moments, and how they imbue their writing with suspense and intrigue (on using Freud's Hans and Dora to teach clinical case writing see Stuart, 2024).

I want to show you two examples of skilled and creative case study writers to see what we can learn from them.

In the psychodynamic case study, the devil is in the details. Just as a novelist brings a scene to life through carefully chosen observations, the therapist illuminates the treatment through seemingly minor but revealing moments.

First, pay attention to Thomas Ogden's (1999) opening of a case:

> From my consulting room I could hear Ms S, a woman in her late thirties, close the door to the bathroom in my office suite. In the twelve years that we had been working together in a five-session-per-week analysis, it was only in the previous year or so that Ms S had begun occasionally to use the office bathroom.(p. 982)

Ogden continues:

> As I waited for her, I recalled an event that had occurred five or six years earlier when on leaving the bathroom, Ms S had realized that she had failed to button some of the many buttons on her trousers. In reality, there was no danger of them falling down, but she experienced intense feelings of embarrassment when she noticed the unfastened buttons. (p. 982)

Ogden told Ms. S that she might have felt the bathroom was a place where both she and the therapist were undressed (although at different times), and it may have felt as if they had been undressed together in that small room.

After the bathroom incident, the patient withdrew emotionally in a profound way for several months, creating a gap between her and the therapist.

In Ogden's case, a simple act—the use of a bathroom—becomes a portal into the patient's psyche, a moment pregnant with meaning. It's a beautiful detail, capturing Ogden as an author with a talent for beautiful details. The restroom, that most private of spaces, becomes a rich source of psychodynamic material when it intrudes into the therapeutic setting. Consider the patient who uses the facilities but neglects to flush, leaving behind corporeal evidence like some primal marking of territory. This act—deliberate or unconscious—speaks volumes about boundary issues, passive aggression, or perhaps a deep-seated need to be seen, truly seen, in all his messy humanity.

Then there's the patient who confesses, in a moment of free association, to always running the tap while urinating—a sonic camouflage to mask the sound of his most basic bodily function. This reveals a profound anxiety about being heard, about the exposure inherent in therapy. It raises questions: what vulnerabilities is he so desperately trying to conceal?

Lastly, picture the patient who religiously empties his bladder before each session, driven by a fear of interruption, of breaking the therapeutic flow. This seemingly innocuous habit reveals a rigid need for control, an anxiety about bodily needs intruding on the mental space of analysis. It begs the question: what else is he trying to "empty out" before he enters the room?

These restroom-related vignettes, trivial as they might seem, offer windows into the patient's psyche. They bring to the surface issues of shame, control, dependency, and the fundamental human struggle with our animal nature in the face of our higher aspirations. In noting and exploring these moments, the therapist creates a story—one that acknowledges the full, embodied humanity of the therapeutic encounter.

Ogden teaches us that every facet, no matter how seemingly trivial, holds the potential to be the key that unlocks the essence of the whole. Thus, we are compelled to examine with care, for the revelatory phrase or telling gesture might emerge from the most unexpected quarter, suddenly bringing clarity to the previously obscure.

Consider another example: Ronald Britton's (1998) approach to depicting "pleasant, polite, ordinary patients" reveals the hidden complexities of seemingly uncomplicated cases:

> They are the healthiest members of their families. They have relatively equable temperaments and, in both life and analysis, they are easygoing . . . Analysis can provide these people with an excellent opportunity to blame themselves in a quiet way that suits them well. (p. 85)

Britton astutely observes that these patients are "not often brought for supervision, unlike those regarded as 'difficult' cases, who are brought in large numbers" (p. 85). He then adds:

> It requires an effort by the analyst to do anything other than be pleased with apparent progress and gratefully accept calm seas after the choppy waters experienced in most of the other sessions of the day. (p. 85)

Here's an interesting intervention by Britton to a pleasing patient:

> 'Here, also, you invest everything in me; that is, you credit me with more than you have in the way of a good opinion of me. When you idealize me like that, you feel favored and

welcome. This relieves you of your apprehensions about me and our relationship. When you lose the idea that I am good and you are well off, fortunate, and favored, I think you are exposed to a sudden sharp discomfort, a fleeting painful doubt about me.'

In response to this intervention, the patient recalls a story about two students who died from gas poisoning in an apartment due to the landlord's negligence in not fixing a gas leak (there's also a gas heater operating in Britton's room).

Finally, as if compelled by a demon, the patient admits that he thinks Britton is a sadist.

The power of this case lies in the transformation the patient undergoes. A patient who appears outwardly agreeable, good-natured, and adaptable, encounters, with the help of therapy, his haunted and paranoid inner world. This transformation is linked to the therapist's understanding, who allowed himself to move out of the zone of safety and comfort that the patient offered to confront the rigid defenses that Klein so aptly described.

Britton teaches us that a compelling case study must always employ "hermeneutics of trust" and "hermeneutics of suspicion" at the same time. Even when written from perspectives that don't explicitly emphasize uncovering the unconscious, the case should illuminate how the therapist engages not merely with the facade the patient chooses to present but with the patient's "otherness"—that unconscious realm the patient conceals due to anxieties, conflicts, and hidden desires. While Kleinian approaches specialize in this type of communication with the patient's hidden self, every case study benefits from exploring this tension. The narrative should oscillate between what the patient willingly reveals and what they struggle to keep hidden.

Both writers exemplify the art of finding profundity in the seemingly ordinary, creating narratives that reveal the invisible architecture of transference relations. They remind us that the strength of a case study often lies not in dramatic events but in the ability to highlight the subtle, under-the-radar moments that constitute the true substance of therapy.

> You can read case studies simply for enjoyment, allowing your unconscious to absorb them and be impressed, making this impression accessible to you when writing. Alternatively, you can also read them when you are learning directly and intentionally.

Suggestions for to focused reading of psychodynamic case studies

When approaching reading a case study with the aim of improving your clinical writing skills, concentrate on three key areas:

1. Narrative structure and flow

    a. Opening and closing: how does the author introduce the patient and conclude the case? Is there symmetry between the beginning and end?

    b. Therapeutic movement: how are breakthrough moments, setbacks, and the overall therapeutic journey mapped out? What creates pacing and maintains reader interest?

    c. Structural coherence: how does the author navigate between chronological and thematic organization?

2. The therapist's voice and presence

   a. Subjective transparency: to what extent does the therapist reveal their emotional processes and countertransference?
   b. Professional authenticity: how does the author balance personal voice, professional perspective, and the patient's voice?
   c. Handling uncertainty: does the author acknowledge moments of doubt, errors, or unresolved aspects?

3. Integration of theory and practice

   a. Theoretical framework: what approaches guide the author, and how seamlessly are they woven into the clinical material?
   b. Clinical innovation: does the author provide fresh theoretical insights or challenge existing concepts through their case analysis?
   c. Balance: is there a healthy proportion between theoretical discussion and actual clinical experience?

Remember: you don't need to examine all aspects in every case study. Focus on elements that resonate with your interests and allow your mind to process the information creatively in ways that suit your developing style.

*

Reading case studies from the psychoanalytic canon often evokes complex emotions in clinicians. On one hand, encountering these masterpieces inspires and elevates clinical practice to new heights. On the other hand, these brilliant descriptions may instill deep feelings of inadequacy and self-doubt.

Who among us hasn't felt that subtle sting of unfavorable comparison between our work and those polished masterpieces? Examining the classic cases of Freud, Klein, or Winnicott can turn into a rather unflattering reflection of our own work—highlighting the flaws and shortcomings we perceive in our clinical and writing skills.

Such reading might trigger a paradoxical response: the more we become engrossed in these wonderful texts, the stronger our resistance to learning from professional literature grows. What irony! The very sources meant to nourish and enrich our work become sources of pain and distance.

How can we prevent this natural professional envy from paralyzing us? One approach is to view it as an opportunity for focused learning. Instead of drowning in broad comparisons, we can identify specific aspects that particularly impress us in our favorite case descriptions. What exactly captivated us? Was it the sharp insight? The surprising metaphor? The presentation of therapeutic dialogue? By isolating these elements, we can ask ourselves how to incorporate similar approaches into our work.

Sharing these feelings in a peer group or supervision also serves as a powerful antidote. We often discover that what seemed like a unique personal failure is, in fact, a universal experience among clinicians. Collegial discourse transforms these burdensome feelings into raw material for professional growth.

And if you find yourself paralyzed before a blank page, hypnotized by reverence for those intellectual giants to the point where you can't write a single word (we've all been there), perhaps it's the perfect time for a conversation with your analyst. Don't have one currently? Here's a golden opportunity to return to the couch! Note the amusing irony: resistance to writing psychoanalytic cases itself becomes premier psychoanalytic material.

At the end of the day, understanding that our unique perspectives and accumulated professional experiences give us an authentic and crucial voice in psychoanalytic discourse is key. Each of us sees and experiences the therapeutic encounter in a way no one else can. And that's precisely why our voices are essential.

In chapters six through ten, you'll find abundant suggestions for reading case studies from different schools, representing various approaches and writing styles. Perhaps this diversity will illustrate that there is no single correct way to write, thus freeing you to develop your own unique style.

Reading poetry

Poetry offers psychodynamic case study writers a unique lens for understanding and articulating therapeutic experiences. Like therapists, poets engage in the delicate art of translating ineffable human experiences into language that can be shared and understood.

Consider Marion Milner's (2010) illuminating example: while writing about a patient, she discovered that fragments of poetry lingering in her mind were not mere distractions but crucial connective elements bridging her raw clinical observations with deeper psychoanalytic understanding. Initially dismissing these poetic associations, she came to recognize them as vital interpretive tools that helped her comprehend the therapeutic process more profoundly.

The poet's economy of language offers another critical lesson: selecting precise words that evoke entire emotional landscapes. A well-crafted case study, like a poem, can make readers feel the contours of a therapeutic journey, not just intellectually understand it.

Furthermore, poetry reminds us of language's limitations. As Amos Oz (in Yeshurun, 2016, p198) noted, language can be a "formalin" that preserves moments at the cost of their living essence. The challenge for case study writers is to use words that breathe, capturing the fluidity of human experience without reducing it to rigid categorizations.

By embracing a poetic sensibility, case study writers can create narratives that are not merely clinical documents but profound explorations of human transformation.

Writing a psychodynamic case study is a meticulous and largely conscious act that passes ideas, emotions, and clinical observations through an extremely fine filter, refining them repeatedly until the words that express them achieve an absolute necessity and inevitability. Only those elements that can withstand this rigorous mental process, passing through the sieve of clinical relevance, should remain in the final text.

Using AI to write a case study

AI language models are rapidly evolving and transforming various aspects of mental health care and clinical practice. This technological advancement is creating new opportunities and challenges for therapists in their work, particularly in writing case studies and documentation.

Increasingly, therapists who seek my guidance on writing case studies have already experimented with AI tools. They arrive not with blank pages but with rough drafts shaped through conversations with AI assistants.

Like the early days of computer programming, when coding seemed like an arcane art accessible only to the technically gifted, writing psychodynamic case studies has long been perceived as the domain of the naturally eloquent. Many skilled clinicians, despite their deep clinical understanding and rich therapeutic experiences, have shied away from documenting their work, feeling they lack the literary talent to do justice to the complexity of their cases.

However, AI is beginning to transform and expand access to this process. Today, AI tools cannot independently generate meaningful case studies from raw clinical data. They are prone to clichés and banal metaphors. Their attempts at creating complete case narratives remain shallow, lacking the nuanced understanding of psychodynamic processes and the authentic voice that makes a case study compelling. In short, at least today (December 2024), you cannot simply feed session notes into an AI application and expect it to produce a thoughtful clinical narrative.

Instead, AI is emerging as a sophisticated writing partner, a kind of literary centaur where human clinical wisdom meets artificial intelligence's linguistic capabilities. Think of it as having an endlessly patient writing coach available at any hour, one that can help restructure paragraphs, suggest alternative phrasings, or explore different ways to present your complex clinical material. The key lies in knowing how to engage with these tools effectively.

Success requires breaking the writing process into manageable components. You might ask the AI to help articulate a specific transference pattern, explore different ways to present a crucial therapeutic turning point, or refine your description of a particular intervention. The more precise your prompts, the more useful the AI's contributions will be. You need to specify your theoretical orientation, preferred writing style, and the particular aspects of the case you want to highlight.

Consider how chess evolved after computers became unbeatable opponents. Rather than killing the game, AI transformed it, creating new ways to learn, practice, and improve. Similarly, AI tools are poised to enrich rather than replace the art of case writing. They may encourage more clinicians to document their work, knowing they have an efficient writing assistant at their disposal. The field could see an explosion of case studies from voices previously silenced by writing anxiety.

Notably, using AI effectively for case writing still requires substantial clinical experience and understanding. At least today, a novice therapist cannot guide the AI as effectively as a seasoned clinician, just as a beginner chess player cannot make the best use of chess engines.

While AI's drive toward coherence and clarity can be valuable, it risks sanitizing the raw, often messy reality of clinical work and oversimplifying the ambiguities inherent in psychodynamic practice. The key lies in using AI to enhance rather than replace the clinician's own process of discovery and articulation.

I did a small experiment and gave the AI the concept of Bion's NO-THING to work with. It revealed both its potential and significant limitations in psychodynamic writing. While the AI demonstrated competence in structuring theoretical frameworks and organizing narrative flow, it struggled with the profound complexity of Bionian theory. The AI effectively helped connect theoretical concepts with clinical material and maintain structural consistency. However, it repeatedly failed to capture the nuanced, paradoxical nature of Bion's ideas. Its interpretations tended to be reductive, missing the sophisticated epistemological implications of experiencing NO-THING as a fundamental psychological capacity. Most critically, the AI couldn't authentically represent the subtle clinical atmosphere of working with a patient who lacks the capacity for absence. Its suggestions often relied on traditional diagnostic categories, missing the unique phenomenological quality of such clinical encounters. The AI's tendency toward verbose, clichéd writing that required extensive editing was a significant drawback. Despite these limitations, the collaboration showed that AI can be a useful writing partner when carefully guided, serving as a structural tool that requires human sophistication to transform clinical writing from mere description to deep psychological insight. The key is to leverage AI's organizational strengths while maintaining a vigilant, nuanced, human interpretation of complex psychoanalytic concepts.

The potential long-term risk of AI in clinical settings goes beyond mere technological substitution. What we may witness is a gradual recalibration of therapeutic expectations where patients increasingly value efficiency, predictability, and algorithmic precision over the nuanced, sometimes messy human elements of care. As AI systems become more sophisticated in simulating empathy and therapeutic responses, patients might begin to prefer these interactions that lack judgment, fatigue, or personal bias, potentially diminishing their tolerance for the natural limitations of human therapists.

This transformation could fundamentally alter the therapeutic relationship in subtle but profound ways. Rather than AI becoming more human-like in its approach to therapy, humans might instead adapt to a more mechanical conception of healing—one that prioritizes measurable outcomes, standardized protocols, and data-driven interventions over the deeply relational aspects of traditional therapy. The greatest threat may not be therapists losing their jobs to machines, but rather the erosion of our collective understanding of what constitutes meaningful therapeutic connection, as both providers and patients increasingly internalize values aligned with computational rather than human intelligence.

Mapping the case along "psychic truth" and "trauma healing"

I will now move on to another recommendation, this time within the conceptualization of psychoanalytic thinking: mapping the case along "psychic truth" or "trauma healing."

If AI struggled to capture the nuanced complexity of Bion's NO-THING concept, mapping a case study along the axes of psychic truth and trauma healing represents precisely the kind of sophisticated, multilayered clinical thinking that artificial intelligence can achieve only through carefully directed guidance.

These two axes have shaped psychoanalytic thought. They represent fundamentally different approaches to understanding and treating psychological distress, each with its own hermeneutic stance.

The psychic truth axis, rooted in the Freudian-Kleinian tradition, embodies a hermeneutics of suspicion—a tendency to see the patient's content as distortion, censorship, and concealment of psychic truth. This approach posits that psychological suffering results from the repression or denial of uncomfortable truths about oneself. The therapist focuses primarily on the patient's unwillingness or inability to recognize certain truths, viewing resistance as a defense against knowing. As Freud wrote on the neurotic, "The guilt [. . .] It is in you [. . .] look inward, look into your own depths, learn first and foremost to know yourself!" (Freud 1917, pp. 142–143).

In contrast, the trauma healing axis, exemplified by theorists like Ferenczi, Kohut, and Winnicott, operates through a hermeneutics of trust—a tendency to believe and validate the patient's emotional experience. This approach focuses on repairing psychological damage through the therapeutic relationship itself, with the analyst providing a safe, empathic environment for processing traumatic experiences. Here, resistance is viewed as a protective response that requires relational repair.

These different orientations reflect distinct therapeutic searchlights. Truth-focused therapists scan for distortions, repressions, and unconscious material, while trauma-focused therapists look for opportunities for emotional repair and corrective experiences. With Klein, interpretation is paramount; with Winnicott, it's the experience itself that matters.

The distinction becomes particularly clear in how each approach handles transference. In truth-focused work, transference is primarily a window into repressed material. In trauma healing, it becomes the very vehicle of repair, offering opportunities for corrective emotional experiences. While both approaches may ultimately serve both truth and healing, their emphasis and methodology differ significantly.

When I present this division to trauma-healing analysts, they tell me that they too are interested in truth—experiential and emotional truth. And when I present this division to analysts who search for unconscious truth, they tell me that they too are interested in healing trauma. They are all correct, of course. Despite the limitations and relative simplicity of this division, I find that it distinguishes between two types of listening and two types of case studies.

In psychoanalytic writing, while both dimensions—psychic truth and trauma healing— may be present, many therapists tend to emphasize one approach over the other, which is perfectly acceptable. While most therapists combine both approaches to some degree, they often have a primary orientation that shapes their clinical work. Your case writing will likely reflect this primary therapeutic orientation, revealing your theoretical foundations and clinical preferences. This doesn't mean you ignore the other dimension entirely, but rather that your work has a dominant focus that influences how you conceptualize and describe the therapeutic process.

In deep clinical writing, the therapist is invited to ask essential questions: to what extent did the discovery of psychic truth contribute to the patient's growth? And where were the beneficial transference relationships the central factor in healing? It is important to note that, as we will see, separating these two processes can be challenging.

The discovery of psychic truth aids the patient's growth when repressed content emerges into consciousness, leading to the integration of previously disconnected parts of the self and fostering a more complete and authentic picture of the internal experience. A patient who recognizes repressed impulses, wishes, and fears is liberated from the psychic energy tied up in repression and can channel it toward more creative and constructive endeavors. This process of recognition also enhances the capacity for mentalization—the ability to understand oneself and others in terms of mental states.

Conversely, creating a facilitating environment can support trauma healing in ways that can be deeper than cognitive insight alone. When the therapist creates a safe, predictable environment that responds to the patient's needs—contrasting with the original traumatic experiences—a holding environment is established. The patient experiences, vividly and tangibly, that they can trust others, that their feelings are acknowledged and contained, and that they are valued.

In meaningful therapy, it is likely that both positions—the quest for psychic truth and trauma healing—are present to some degree, even if the clinician predominantly favors one. Identifying moments where transitions occurred between these positions may reveal significant turning points in therapy, and precise clinical writing can effectively capture these transitions. Were there instances when the therapist realized that the pursuit of psychic truth had become overly intrusive, prompting a shift to a more containing approach for trauma healing? Conversely, were there times when containment and empathy fell short, necessitating a deeper exploration of repressed content?

Deciding when the case is complete

One final question remains to be answered: how will I know that the written case has reached its completion and it's time for me to release it into the world? The French poet Paul Valéry famously said, "A poem is never finished, only abandoned." The same could be said of case studies. There may never be a definitive moment of completion, but rather a point where you recognize that further tinkering would be an act of interference rather than improvement.

Consider the case study as a bonsai tree, the Japanese art of growing and shaping miniature trees in containers. Japanese artists nurture, prune, and shape the tree with meticulous care; each edit is like a careful trim of a branch, and each revision is like the gentle wiring that guides growth. Just as the bonsai artist must resist the urge to constantly adjust and reshape—knowing that over-pruning can damage the tree's vitality—the case-study writer must learn to recognize when further editing might diminish rather than enhance the work. The art lies in knowing when to step back and trust that your careful cultivation has created something that can now exist independently of your constant attention. Like a mature bonsai that has found its form, a completed case study achieves a kind of natural balance—not perfect, perhaps, but authentically itself. The moment of completion comes not when every possible adjustment has been made, but when the work has developed its own internal harmony, its own distinct character that can now sustain itself without your constant intervention.

Ultimately, knowing when to let go is an act of faith—faith in your craft, the story's ability to stand alone, and the readers' capacity to find meaning in your words. It's about trusting that the autonomy you've granted your case study will allow it to resonate in ways you may never have anticipated.

The moment of releasing the case study is also a moment of acceptance, a moment that embodies what Klein calls the "depressive position": you must come to terms with its imperfections, its partiality, its incompleteness. You must accept your longing for the case, for all that you didn't manage to describe or write, and for all the depths you didn't reach.

So, perhaps the question isn't "How do I know when I'm finished?" but rather, "When has my case study become its own entity, ready to engage with the world on its own terms?" Listen closely, and the story itself will whisper when it's time to let it fly.

Why do case studies fail?

We must confront an uncomfortable truth: many clinicians are simply poor writers. Despite significant investments of time and intellect, their case studies are often murky, messy, showy, vague, and filled with psychoanalytic jargon. Their potentially vibrant narratives ossify into rigid expositions that fail to capture the reader's imagination or illuminate the true nature of the therapeutic encounter.

I recall that in one of our graduating classes, which was anxiously preoccupied with passing the exam, a telling pattern emerged in their case reports: many cases became an endless procession of technical terminology; some impressive, most excessive, and almost none capable of revealing anything more truthful than the therapists' reluctance to expose their own vulnerability and uncertainty.

An Israeli poet, Harold Schimmel (Yeshurun, 2016), once said that many poems are written on a predetermined and unsurprising path. He compared these poems to a mechanical toy, you wind up the mechanism with a key, and the monkey drums on its drum, takes off its hat, dances, and stops. This is how some case descriptions appear. They follow a fixed pattern and established rules, striving to imitate a set template. Paradoxically, theoretical fluency can induce paralysis. Well-versed in psychoanalytic thought, therapists may find themselves trapped in an intellectual hall of mirrors, endlessly refracting observations through theory's prism. This hyper-awareness of conceptual frameworks can blind one to the raw, untheorized reality of the therapeutic encounter. In short, many written cases have more weight than energy.

The seductive allure of the "eureka moment" is perhaps most pernicious. Many case studies falter in their pursuit of a neat, satisfying narrative arc with a dramatic breakthrough. This quest for a cinematic denouement often distorts the therapeutic process, glossing over subtle, incremental shifts that constitute real change. Other cases are often written using either overly worn storytelling devices or boring conventionality.

While it's tempting to attribute these failures to a lack of literary skill or overreliance on psychoanalytic terminology, the deeper malady lies in a fundamental misalignment of the therapist's self in relation to their work. Too often, the therapist-turned-author approaches writing through what Winnicott might call a "false self." This false self, driven by fear of judgment or a desire to impress, acts as psychic censorship, filtering out raw, messy truths in favor of a polished but lifeless account.

> The false self blocks access to the therapist's unconscious creative wellspring—that abundant source of insight that nourishes their deepest clinical work. When this wellspring is blocked, the result is a case study that may be technically polished but lacks the flickering inner flame that breathes life into the clinical material.

Writing a case study is, at its core, an act of presence. Not a passive presence, but a pulsating, rich, multilayered presence. It requires a special kind of responsiveness from the therapist—one that is attuned to the materials arising from the therapeutic encounter and to the unique language developing between the two psyches operating in this space. This writing must be approached with genuine dedication and curiosity, along with inner flexibility and focused listening.

Textual richness is not an external decoration for the case description; rather, it is an essential quality reflecting the richness of the therapeutic encounter itself. It is inappropriate to transform the case study into a collection of theoretical taxidermy—dried bodies of ideas that have lost the life spirit that once pulsed through them. Likewise, it should not become an anthology of pressed flowers—quotations taken out of context, stripped of their original scent and vibrant color.

Meaningful clinical description does not teach fixed "examples" or "recipes" for treatment, nor does it offer a collection of ideas that have grown moldy with the passage of time. Instead, it presents the therapeutic encounter in its vitality and complexity, with its dissonances and resonances, with moments of closeness and distance, and with subtle nuances that sometimes escape the eye; yet within them lies the secret of the therapeutic process.

RECOMMENDED READING

What does the presentation of case material tell us about what actually happened in an analysis and how does it do this? by Dr. Dale Boesky, Dr. Elias Rocha Barros, and Dr. Catherine Chabert. *International Journal of Psychoanalysis 94*, 1129–1134, 2013.

These three papers explore whether the material strives to present an accurate description of the analytic encounter. What does accurate mean in a context where our emotional reactions and ways of listening are integral to the encounter? Participating in this controversy, Dr. Dale Boesky, Dr. Elias Rocha Barros, and Dr. Catherine Chabert each offer unique answers.

'The music of what happens' in poetry and psychoanalysis, by Thomas H. Ogden. *International Journal of Psychoanalysis 80*, 979–994, 1999.

The article examines the relationship between the way the author listens to the language of poetry and the way he and his patient communicate and listen to one another in psychoanalysis, emphasizing the importance of attending to the "music of what happens" rather than merely uncovering what lies beneath the surface. This article provides a thoughtful perspective on the nuances of language and listening in the therapeutic setting.

REFERENCES

Boesky, D., Barros, E. R., & Chabert, C. (2013). What does the presentation of case material tell us about what actually happened in an analysis and how does it do this? *International Journal of Psychoanalysis, 94*, 1129–1134.

Bollas, C. (1987). *The shadow of the object: Psychoanalysis of the unthought known.* Columbia University Press.

Bollas, C. (1995). *Cracking up: The work of unconscious experience* (1st ed.). Routledge.

Britton, R. (1998). *Belief and imagination: Explorations in psychoanalysis.* Routledge.

Coltart, N. (1992). *Slouching towards Bethlehem . . . and further psychoanalytic explorations.* Free Association Books.

Freud, S. (1917). A difficulty in the path of psychoanalysis. In J. Strachey (Ed. & Trans.), *The standard edition of the complete psychological works of Sigmund Freud* (Vol. 17, pp. 135–44). 1955. Hogarth Press.

Klein, M. (2017). *Lectures on technique by Melanie Klein: Edited with critical review by John Steiner.* Routledge.

Li, O. (2009). *Keats and negative capability.* Continuum International Publishing Group.

Ogden, T. H. (1999). 'The music of what happens' in poetry and psychoanalysis. *International Journal of Psychoanalysis, 80*, 979–994.

Paikin, H. (1996). From analytic dialogue to published text. In E. Piccioli, P. L. Rossi, & A. A. Semi (Eds.), *Writing in psychoanalysis* (Chapter 3, pp. 37–52). Karnac Books.

Phillips, A. (2010). Introduction. In M. Milner, *The hands of the living god: An account of a psycho-analytic treatment* (pp. xviii-xxxv). Routledge.

Stuart, J. (2024). "No mortal can keep a secret": Reading Freud's cases as preparation for candidates' first efforts to write about their patients. *Psychoanalytic Inquiry, 44*(3), 194–209.

Yadlin-Gadot, S. (2023). Living moments and intuition in countertransference: A discussion of Bion's essay "Notes on memory and desire." Annual Conference, Presenter: Dr. Gadi Ben Shahar.

Yeshurun, H. (2016). *How did you do it? Interviews with poets* (Hebrew). Hakibutz Hameuchad.

CHAPTER 3

The formal sections of a complete case study

....

This chapter presents a comprehensive framework for writing a psychodynamic case study, focusing on its most crucial components: referral reasons, background history, psychodynamic formulation, course of treatment, and discussion. Different training programs and institutes may emphasize varying aspects of case writing. The framework offered here is deliberately broad, allowing writers to adapt it to their specific training requirements while ensuring that no significant aspects of the case are overlooked.

REFERRAL REASONS

The "Referral reasons" section in a psychodynamic case study acts as the opening scene of a compelling narrative, setting the stage for the therapeutic journey ahead. This crucial component introduces the reader to the patient's world, capturing the essence of their distress and the circumstances that drove them to seek help.

It also marks the moment when the therapist's unconscious emotional response begins to awaken, as the initial words about the patient's suffering intersect with the therapist's inner world, laying the groundwork for a complex transferential-countertransferential relationship.

In writing this section, therapists should aim to present a concise yet vivid picture of the patient's presenting complaint. Using the patient's own words and carefully selected quotes can powerfully express their emotional state and perspective.

The "Referral reasons" section typically includes key demographic details such as the patient's name (using a pseudonym), age, and marital status. It succinctly outlines the primary complaints, their duration, and any specific events that led the patient to seek therapy. The length and frequency of treatment may also be noted.

What fascinates me about well-crafted referral reasons is how they can foreshadow the entire therapeutic journey to come.

DOI: 10.4324/9781003538578-5

Consider these examples from famous cases:
Klein (1961) on Richard:

Richard was ten years old when I began his analysis. His symptoms had developed to such an extent that it had become impossible for him to attend school after the age of eight, when the outbreak of the war in 1939 had increased his anxieties. He was very frightened of other children and this contributed to an increasing avoidance of going out by himself. Moreover, since about the age of four or five, a progressive inhibition of his faculties and interests had been causing great concern to his parents. In addition to these symptoms, he was very hypochondriacal and frequently subject to depressed moods. These difficulties showed themselves in his appearance, for he looked very worried and unhappy. At times, however—and this became striking during analytic sessions—his depression lifted, and then suddenly life and sparkle came into his eyes. (p. 13)

What a remarkable opening. I'm struck by how Klein masterfully combines clinical precision with literary artistry in just a few sentences. What I find particularly moving is the dramatic contrast in the text—from the extensive list of Richard's symptoms and difficulties to that single, powerful image of "life and sparkle" in his eyes.
Donald Winnicott (1986):

He came to analysis saying that he could not talk freely, that he had no small talk or imaginative or play capacity, and that he could not make a spontaneous gesture or get excited.(p. 18)

This is another brilliant text. The patient's self-description perfectly aligns with Winnicott's theoretical framework—the inability to talk freely, play, or make spontaneous gestures reads like a textbook definition of False Self-pathology. But what makes this so remarkable is that Winnicott allows the patient's own words to illustrate his theory, rather than imposing theoretical language. It's as if the patient walked in and presented exactly what Winnicott spent years theorizing about!

Everyone knows the old joke that Jungian patients dream Jungian dreams and Freudian patients dream Freudian dreams. It turns out this is true for referral reasons as well—patients seem to present themselves in ways that perfectly match their future analyst's theoretical framework! As we have said, the written case belongs to the genre of creative nonfiction: facts that pass through the filter of the writer's creativity.

BACKGROUND HISTORY

Almost every case study includes basic anamnestic details presented in a concise form. As this is not a detailed psychological report but a case description, include only details that contribute to the overall narrative and connect to later therapeutic processes. Important elements to consider are (not all are required):

1. Demographic information: age, gender, occupation, marital status, and cultural background.

2. Family history: parents, siblings, family dynamics, communication patterns, and attachment styles.
3. Developmental history: key milestones, significant events, and relationships shaping personality development. Note any abnormalities in crucial developmental points (e.g., breastfeeding, motor skills, language acquisition, toilet training).
4. Pregnancy and birth: any unique circumstances surrounding pregnancy or birth.
5. Educational and vocational history: academic achievements, challenges, career aspirations, work places, work-related stressors.
6. Psychosocial history: social support network, friendships, and leisure activities.
7. Medical history: relevant illnesses, disabilities, treatments, and medications. For mothers, include pregnancy and birth histories.
8. Psychiatric history: past diagnoses, treatments, hospitalizations, and responses to previous therapies.
9. Trauma history: acute and chronic stressors, including abuse, neglect, or exposure to violence.
10. Cultural and spiritual beliefs: background, values, and practices influencing worldview and attitudes towards mental health.
11. Current stressors and coping mechanisms: identify present challenges and the patient's adaptive and maladaptive coping strategies.

Example:

Jon, 15, is the son of Miranda (44, industrial and management engineer) and Alex (44, academic researcher), with a sister, 18 years old. His birth was planned but prolonged and painful. Jon had difficulties with breastfeeding, reflux, and sleep in infancy. While motor and language development were timely, he struggled with bedwetting until age 8 and has a stutter.

Socially isolated in kindergarten, he experienced bullying in early school years. Academically, he excels with the help of tutors. Jon is described as a people pleaser and a rigid perfectionist, with his parents concerned about his lack of interest in sexuality and potential ongoing social difficulties. Family dynamics reveal a warm but insecure mother, a controlling father with angry outbursts, and a dismissive relationship between parents. Treatment included weekly sessions for Jon and bi-weekly parental guidance over five years.

The advantage of this example stems from presenting a precise developmental sequence, identifying risk and resilience factors, and providing a broad environmental context that explains the origin of current problems and their implications. It provides focused detail on the current referral reason and expectations from treatment, thus forming an excellent basis for diagnosis and personalized treatment planning. The detailed background enables the professional to understand the complex set of factors that led to the current situation and to develop an appropriate treatment plan that addresses the root causes of the problems rather than just their symptoms.

Example of an inadequate referral reason:

Shira, 28, sought therapy due to relationship difficulties and feelings of anxiety. She works as an office manager at a high-tech company and lives in Tel Aviv. Shira is described as an intelligent, beautiful, and assertive woman at her workplace. She has been in a relationship with Ben for two years, but reports communication difficulties between them.

Shira describes her childhood as "fairly normal," and her parents are still married. She is the eldest of three children. Shira tends to be self-critical, likely due to the high expectations her parents have placed on her. She reports anxiety in social situations, especially at significant events. In my opinion, the anxiety stems from insecure attachment patterns she developed in her early childhood, when her father was very busy with work and her mother dealt with periods of changing moods.

Shira switched between several studies at different colleges until she focused on management. She reports difficulty sleeping at night and recent concentration problems. It's important to note that she consumes alcohol socially on weekends. She is interested in therapy to "feel better."

The shortcomings in this referral are:

1. **Lack of basic details**—there is no information about the age of onset of anxiety, significant events that led to the current situation, or previous medical/psychiatric history.
2. **Failure to distinguish between primary and secondary issues**—there are references to superficial details ("beautiful," "intelligent") but a lack of depth in substantive topics such as anxiety patterns, their impact on daily functioning, or information about previous coping attempts.
3. **Excessive interpretation by the therapist**—the sentence "In my opinion, the anxiety stems from insecure attachment patterns" presents an early interpretive conclusion without sufficient basis in the data.
4. **Vagueness and non-specific information**—descriptions like "fairly normal childhood" or "feel better" are too general and do not provide real insights.
5. **Lack of developmental sequence**—there is no apparent connection between life events, the development of difficulties, and the current situation.
6. **Imbalance in details**—there is information about social alcohol consumption (which may not be relevant) but lack of information about previous treatment history, current stressors, or coping mechanisms.

PSYCHODYNAMIC FORMULATIONS

A psychodynamic formulation is a comprehensive conceptualization of an individual's psychological difficulties, using psychodynamic principles to understand the underlying dynamics, conflicts, and developmental influences contributing to their symptoms and behaviors.

Unlike a diagnostic assessment that focuses on identifying specific mental health disorders, a psychodynamic formulation delves deeper into unconscious processes and relational patterns that shape psychological functioning.

Key components typically include:

1. Developmental history
2. Intrapsychic dynamics
3. Object relations

4. Transference and countertransference
5. Psychodynamic conflict
6. Ego functioning
7. Life context and stressors.

The difference between reporting life events and psychodynamic formulation is fundamental. While reporting describes facts and events as they are, psychodynamic formulation attempts to explain the deeper reasons and motivations behind a person's behaviors and emotions, connecting past events to the present and offering hypotheses about unconscious mental processes.

For example, a simple report might describe: "Mrs. Gampel, age 45, suffers from severe social anxiety. She avoids social gatherings and struggles to speak in public. As a child, her parents were highly critical of her."

In contrast, a psychodynamic formulation would propose: "The excessive criticism from Mrs. Gampel's parents during childhood likely caused her to develop a deep sense of insecurity and an unconscious fear of rejection, leading to her current social anxiety and avoidance of social situations."

> Psychodynamic formulation, while often presented as "objective," is fundamentally subjective, relying heavily on the therapist's intuition and theoretical orientation. The most productive stance is to view it not as absolute truth, but as a dynamic, evolving, working hypothesis that remains open to revision and the unique unfolding of each therapeutic relationship.

Psychodynamic formulations by schools of thought

Another way to create a dynamic formulation is to make it specific to a psychoanalytic theory. This specification makes sense because each psychoanalytic theory maps the human psyche differently, defines suffering and distress in various ways, and holds a distinct conception of transference relations.

Therefore, the formulation should vary according to the premises of the psychoanalytic theory. For example, depression in Freudian psychodynamic formulation can be understood as pathological identification with the hated aspect of an object that has been ambivalently loved and lost, and as an unconscious attempt to preserve the beloved aspect of the object, protect it, and deny its loss. A Kleinian psychodynamic formulation of depression will emphasize the unconscious fantasy that the patient's anger has eliminated or killed the beloved object (Klein, 1952). In a Winnicottian psychodynamic formulation, depression is viewed as the patient taking on and transforming his mother's depression with the unconscious aim of freeing her from her depression.

It's important to note that psychodynamic formulations often integrate multiple theoretical perspectives, as many clinical phenomena can be better understood through such combinations.

Psychodynamic formulation in Klein's theory

In constructing a Kleinian psychodynamic formulation, it is essential to address several key elements. First, unconscious fantasies are critical in shaping the psyche and influencing emotions and behaviors. These fantasies are not merely abstract thoughts; they are integral to the ego and mind, directly affecting mental states. The child's real distress, stemming from needs and frustrations, contributes to the content of these fantasies, shaped by their experiences with caregivers and the Oedipal dynamics involved. A significant aspect of Kleinian formulation is the concept of projective identification, which involves projecting aspects of oneself onto another individual. This mechanism can facilitate communication and integration, but it often leads to attempts to rid oneself of undesirable traits or to dominate others, blurring the lines between self and other. The formulation should illustrate how these physical experiences, laden with unconscious meanings, interact with external reality, resulting in various defense mechanisms.

KEY ELEMENTS IN KLEIN'S PSYCHODYNAMIC FORMULATION

1. **Unconscious fantasies**: emphasize the fundamental fantasies that shape the psyche. These fantasies about objects and their interrelations are viewed as the foundation of the ego and mind. Importantly, these unconscious fantasies are originally grounded in bodily experiences, illustrating the primary connection between body and psyche. They arise from the infant's earliest physical interactions—suckling, nursing, being held, gazing, urinating, and defecating—and gradually develop into more complex psychological structures.

2. **Kleinian positions and their balance**: assess the dominance of paranoid-schizoid or depressive positions in the patient's functioning. Consider their capacity for guilt and empathy, whether paranoid anxiety or depressive guilt predominates, and the nature of persecutory guilt. The balance between these positions significantly influences patients' ability to integrate experiences and relate to others.

3. **Death drive and envy**: assess the strength of the patient's inherent death drive and the intensity of envy. These fundamental forces shape the patient's internal world and influence their ability to form loving relationships versus succumbing to destructive impulses.

4. **Symbolization capacity**: examine the patient's ability to form symbols versus reliance on symbolic equations. This capacity is crucial for psychological development and the ability to process experience.

5. **Pathological organization**: identify and understand the nature of the patient's pathological organization, including how defensive structures may have become rigid and self-perpetuating.

6. **Recognition of otherness**: assess the patient's sensitivity to otherness and capacity for separateness. Consider their ability to tolerate dependency, accept input from outside, and maintain boundaries between self and other.

7. **Object relations**: explore how early experiences shape internal representations and current relational patterns, including the capacity for whole object relations.

8. **Defense mechanisms**: identify primitive defenses such as splitting, projection, and introjection, understanding their role in managing anxiety and maintaining psychic equilibrium.

9. **Projective identification**: recognize this as a central mechanism for managing internal conflicts and regulating emotions.

10. **Integration of experiences**: consider the patient's capacity to integrate good and bad aspects of self and others, particularly concerning their position on the paranoid-schizoid to depressive position continuum.

An example of using psychodynamic formulation according to Klein

I will demonstrate psychodynamic formulation based on a case study by Betty Joseph in her paper "An Aspect of the Repetition Compulsion" (1959). It should be noted that Joseph does not dedicate a subsection to "psychodynamic formulation" and does not mention this term at all. However, Joseph's detailed case allows us to create a psychodynamic formulation.

A's case reveals a life story filled with complex relationship dynamics that have accompanied her from childhood to adulthood, manifesting in every significant relationship in her life. From her childhood, A grew up in a poor home in northern England, where there was a sense of emotional deprivation. Her mother, while addressing the children's physical needs, was restless, never sitting with them, and sometimes even forgetting her during meals or events.

This neglect instilled in A a sense of emotional deprivation, alienation, and desire for independence.

Alongside the mother, a dominant presence emerged in the form of an orphaned older cousin who acted as a caretaker and household helper. This cousin was a dedicated figure, but A perceived her as a suffocating shadow, excessively clinging to her, to the extent that in her childhood, she would crawl after her throughout the house, although in adulthood she had no recollection of this at all. The relationship with the helper was ambivalent: on one hand, there was an intense need for her closeness; on the other hand, a feeling of suffocation and a desire to distance herself.

The relationship with her father was equally complex. The father, who was in a troubled relationship with the mother, showed an open preference for A, sought her proximity, and even wanted her to spend vacations with him. A felt great embarrassment in his presence, and her connection with him evoked mixed feelings of closeness and rejection. With her younger brother, a dynamic of control and dependence also developed: in her childhood, she controlled and confused him, feeling that her mother was not functioning adequately. Later, the brother became very dependent on her, to the point of repeatedly attempting to break into her room to gain her attention.

This pattern of relationships repeated itself outside the family as well: men in her life, whether partners, relatives, or professionals such as lawyers and doctors, tended to become strongly attached to her, developing dependence on her, while she mainly felt responsibility, burden, and sometimes pity toward them, but did not experience genuine love or desire. Every professional relationship quickly leaned toward closeness, sometimes beyond what was acceptable, as she felt guilty leaving a doctor or lawyer, believing they needed her—whether for professional or financial reasons. Here too, the pattern of being "irreplaceable" recurs, but it is always accompanied by a sense of burden, guilt, and emotional distance.

The relationship with the analyst reflects all these patterns: A presents herself as a different patient—mature, non-dependent, cooperative, and even helpful to the therapist—but in practice, at the unconscious level, she attempts to make the therapist dependent on her, just as she did with other professionals. She tends to disconnect feelings of dependence, affection, or longing, and instead rushes to interpret her own condition, as if she is the one treating herself and others. Here too, the struggle between the need for connection and closeness versus the fear of fusion, dependence, jealousy, and humiliation is evident.

Thus, throughout her life, A moves between figures who need her and figures she needs, but always grapples with the burden of dependence, emotion, and the possibility of loving and being loved. She experiences relationships as a burden, endangering either herself or the other, and thus repeatedly returns to the same patterns of distance, guilt, need, and control—patterns that create a closed circle of loneliness, unfulfilled dependence, and a constant sense of missed opportunity.

Psychodynamic formulation of Betty Joseph's patient

Presenting issues

A experiences profound anxieties related to dependence on primary objects, which arise from early encounters with competition, neglect, and emotional turmoil within the family. The experience of dependence evokes intense ambivalence, swinging between love and appreciation for others and deep-seated hatred and jealousy.

Early childhood experiences

A's early interactions were marked by a tumultuous family dynamic, characterized by emotional distance, neglect, and competition for parental attention. A's mother's neglect and her father's attempts to create a special bond instilled conflicting feelings of longing and resentment in A. This ambivalence towards primary objects, especially the mother, laid the foundation for A's complex relational patterns and defense mechanisms.

Defense mechanisms

A's defense mechanisms help manage the overwhelming anxieties associated with dependence and ambivalence. A adopts a pattern of one-sided dependency in relationships, striving to make others reliant on her before ultimately abandoning them. Through splitting, A separates aspects of herself and the object into opposing categories, projecting unwanted and hateful traits outward while internalizing an idealized, devoured object.

Projective identification

Projective identification occurs as A projects her dependency and neediness onto others, distancing herself from these feelings within herself. Through this mechanism, she sidesteps confronting her own vulnerable and needy parts by "placing" them in others. At the same time, she develops identification with an idealized and strong object, allowing her to maintain a sense of control while defending against feelings of vulnerability and dependency.

Envy and manic victory

A's defense mechanisms involve not only splitting and projection but also intense envy and manic triumph over objects. Her tendency to make others dependent on her, including her attempts with Joseph, represents a manic victory over the object—a means to control and devalue the object's importance while dealing with her own profound envy. Her envy towards Joseph surfaces in her efforts to establish a special analysis status and demonstrate her indispensability, similar to her behavior with other professionals. This pattern functions both as a defense against dependence and as an expression of unconscious envy towards the abilities of the good object. This unconscious envy and craving for manic triumph originate from her early experiences with a neglectful mother and seem to fuel her compulsive need to make others dependent on her, only to later reject them—a pattern that simultaneously conveys both her envy and her triumph over the object.

Psychodynamic formulation in Bion's theory

It's hard to imagine a greater contradiction than writing a psychodynamic formulation according to Bion. After all, this is precisely what Bion always opposed: formulating the patient according to a fixed psychoanalytic theory. Nevertheless, some therapists write Bionian case descriptions to complete their training, and they too need support. Psychodynamic formulation is also important for educational purposes; it can bring order and clarity to a complex theory that might sometimes seem messy.

A Bionian formulation might discuss the container/contained function and disrupted developmental processes due to the caregiver's inability to provide alpha function for the infant's beta elements. Additionally, it would consider the mother's difficulties during times of distress, anxiety, and fragmentation to envision or dream an image in which the bad, difficult, and confused fragmented elements evolve into a beneficial entity (reverie).

KEY ELEMENTS IN BION'S PSYCHODYNAMIC FORMULATION

1. **Container/contained function**: assess the patient's early experiences with maternal containment and how this has shaped their capacity for emotional regulation and meaning-making.
2. **Alpha function**: explore the extent to which the patient's caregiver was able to transform raw sensory data (beta elements) into thinkable content (alpha elements), and how this has influenced the patient's ability to process and metabolize emotional experiences.
3. **Reverie**: consider the caregiver's capacity for reverie—the ability to hold and transform the infant's projected anxieties and distress into manageable experiences.
4. **Thinking apparatus**: evaluate the patient's mental apparatus development for thinking thoughts and containing emotional experiences.
5. **Projective identification**: examine how the patient uses projective identification for communication and emotional regulation.
6. **Attacks on linking**: identify any patterns of attacking links between thoughts or between self and others to defend against psychic pain.
7. **Frustration**: evaluate the patient's capacity to tolerate frustration and absence, examining whether they can maintain psychological development in the face of "no breast" experiences or tend to evade frustration through omnipotent thinking and primitive defenses.
8. **Transformations**: assess the nature of the patient's psychic transformations—whether they are rigid (maintaining fixed beliefs), projective (attributing internal states to external objects), or hallucinatory (losing touch with reality through excessive projective mechanisms).
9. **Psychotic part of the personality**: consider the extent to which the psychotic part of the personality dominates the patient's functioning, including how much it interferes with reality testing, learning from experience, and the capacity for symbolic thinking. Consider whether this part operates as a background influence or actively controls the patient's mental life.

An example of psychodynamic formulation in Bion's theory

Sue's early childhood was characterized by emotional neglect from both parents. Her mother, focused on her career, abruptly weaned Sue at four months due to work-related travel. Left with a caregiver, Sue refused bottle-feeding and cried inconsolably for days, which set the stage for a pattern of emotional abandonment.

As Sue grew, her mother's self-absorption and frequent absences continued. For instance, on Sue's first day of school, her mother forgot to pick her up, leaving Sue alone for hours. Although her father was physically present, he was emotionally distant, often lost in his own world. When Sue tried to share her achievements, like winning a spelling bee, her father would nod absently without engaging.

This parental unavailability led Sue to develop a fragmented sense of self. She oscillated between feeling worthless and experiencing intense, uncontrollable anger. Without attuned caregivers to help her process these emotions, Sue struggled to understand and regulate her internal experiences.

To cope, Sue became overly attuned to others' needs, first her father's "neediness" and later those of friends and partners. This served as a defense against confronting her own unmet emotional needs. However, it left Sue feeling hollow and unseen, perpetuating a cycle of emotional deprivation. Beneath this compliant exterior lay a deep well of rage that would emerge in passive-aggressive behaviors and occasional explosive outbursts, particularly when she felt abandoned or dismissed.

In one particularly revealing session, Sue demonstrated a striking attack on linking when the therapist made an empathic connection between her current relationship patterns and her early maternal abandonment. Initially, Sue showed visible relief at being understood, even tearing up. However, this moment of connection was quickly followed by a violent outburst where she accused the therapist of "making things up" and "trying to create problems that aren't there." She then retreated into an emotional numbness, later describing feeling "empty and foggy." Sue's pattern of attacking understanding served as a defense against both the pain of early abandonment and the terror of genuine emotional contact in the present.

The lack of consistent, nurturing parental presence in Sue's formative years impaired her ability to develop a robust mental apparatus for processing feelings and thoughts. As a result, she often felt overwhelmed by her emotions, unable to make sense of them or use them as guides for navigating relationships and life challenges.

This formulation provides a framework for understanding Sue's psychological struggles while remaining open to the evolving nature of the therapeutic process, in line with Bion's emphasis on approaching each session without memory or desire.

Dynamic formulation of Sue's case in Bion's theory

Container/contained function

Sue experienced a significant failure in the container/contained function during the early stages of her life. Her mother, focused on her career, and her emotionally distant father failed to provide an adequate container for her difficult emotional contents. The sudden weaning at four months and prolonged crying demonstrate the environment's inability to contain her distress. Consequently, Sue developed a mental structure where she tries to be the container for others (e.g., attentiveness to her father's needs and later to friends and partners), yet lacks a container for her own emotions, leading to feelings of emptiness and unregulated outbursts.

Envy

Envy in Sue's mental life is expressed in a complex manner. While not explicitly mentioned, its traces emerge as hidden rage and anger, potentially rooted in envy of others' perceived emotional fulfillment. Her oscillation between worthlessness and intense anger reflects the internal dynamics of envy—desiring to destroy what she cannot attain (e.g., attention, love). In therapy, her attacks on the therapist's insights may stem from envy of his ability to give meaning to her experiences, a skill she feels she lacks.

Projective identification

Sue uses projective identification as a central defense and communication tool. She projects vulnerable, needy parts of herself onto others, positioning herself as the caregiver to avoid confronting her own unmet needs. In sessions, she projects aggression onto the therapist, accusing him of "making things up," while unconsciously undermining the emerging therapeutic connection. This mechanism non-verbally communicates her confusion, anger, and emptiness.

Reverie

The absence of reverie in Sue's life is stark. Her parents failed to metabolize her raw emotions into digestible forms. Her father's absent-minded acknowledgment of achievements and her mother's physical and emotional unavailability left Sue without processed emotional feedback. Consequently, she lacks the internal capacity for reverie—the ability to give meaning to experiences—leaving her with unprocessed pain that manifests as emptiness and haziness.

Alpha function

Sue's alpha function—transforming raw emotions (beta elements) into thinkable thoughts—is impaired. Early neglect, sudden weaning, and school abandonment disrupted her ability to process emotions. Unprocessed beta elements (pain, abandonment, rage) persist, fueling explosive reactions and abrupt emotional shifts, as observed in sessions where she transitions from relief to anger to numbness.

Attacks on linking

Sue exhibits attacks on linking, which serve as a defense against emotional connections. When the therapist linked her relationship patterns to early abandonment, she initially responded with relief and tears but swiftly attacked the insight, accusing him of fabrication. These attacks extend beyond therapy: she disrupts connections between life events, feelings, and relationships, retreating into "emptiness and haziness" to avoid confronting abandonment pain and the terror of genuine connection.

Thinking apparatus

Due to these functional failures, Sue lacks an effective thinking apparatus. She struggles to synthesize emotional experiences into coherent narratives, reacting based on raw feelings rather than processed thought. By attacking the therapist's interpretations, she rejects meaning-making, preserving protective emptiness but stifling her psychological growth.

Psychodynamic formulation in Winnicott's theory

In a psychodynamic formulation based on Winnicott's theory, special attention should be devoted to the period of infancy when mother and baby form a single psychological entity. This unified psychological space emerges through a delicate, continuous process of maternal adaptation, in which the mother's responsiveness gradually matches and anticipates the infant's evolving needs, creating a holding environment that facilitates psychological growth. It is crucial to focus on the development of the true self, the transitional object, and transitional phenomena. Additionally, the formulation should examine the infant's attacks on the mother and her survival, along with trauma and the fear of breakdown.

Key elements in Winnicott's psychodynamic formulation

1. **Primary maternal preoccupation:** consider how the patient's early experiences with maternal care may have influenced their sense of safety, security, and trust in relationships.
2. **Transitional objects and phenomena:** consider how the patient's early experiences with transitional objects, such as a cherished blanket or toy, reflect their capacity for creative and symbolic play, as well as their ability to navigate the boundary between inner and outer reality. Pay special attention to parental attitudes toward these objects—did they respect the child's attachment and private space, or did they intrude with comments, criticism, or attempts to control how the objects were used? Reflect on how parents' handling of transitional objects may have supported or undermined the development of a secure transitional space. Note instances where parents might have prematurely discarded objects, insisted on washing them against the child's wishes, or made disparaging remarks about the child's attachment.
3. **True self and false self:** explore the distinction between the patient's true self and false self. Assess how the patient's false self may be masking underlying feelings of vulnerability, insecurity, or emotional distress.
4. **Aggression:** explore whether the patient's caregivers were able to withstand aggressive impulses without retaliating or withdrawing and how this might have influenced the patient's ability to integrate aggression, develop object constancy, and form secure attachments.
5. **Transitional phenomena and creative expression:** consider how the patient's engagement with transitional phenomena, such as daydreaming, fantasy, and creative expression, reflects their capacity for symbolization and emotional processing. Explore how the patient uses creative outlets to cope with stress, regulate emotions, and explore their inner world.

An example of a psychodynamic formulation in Winnicott's theory

Helen suffered from severe depression for many years. She was born to replace a child who died of SIDS (Sudden Infant Death Syndrome) shortly after birth. Her mother was devastated by this experience, and her husband attempted to remedy the situation by getting her pregnant again as quickly as possible. Her mother responded to the fact that she had a daughter by trying to convince herself and her baby that she was actually a boy. We may view this as a failure in the mother's ability to mourn the loss of her infant son. As a result, this condition disturbed Helen's psychosexual development. To avoid rejecting her mother, who, in her fantasy, lost her love, she compromised by perceiving herself as a weirdo. It was not a conscious compromise, but she felt sexually isolated, neither a girl nor a boy at the same time. It created an insurmountable rupture in her mental structure. The mother's lack of interest in who she truly was led Helen to depression and attracted her to partners who showed little interest in her.

Psychodynamic formulation for Helen according to Winnicott's theory

Helen presents with severe depression stemming from early experiences of maternal rejection and denial of her true gender identity. Born as a substitute for a deceased infant, Helen was met with her mother's profound grief and inability to mourn properly. Her mother, overwhelmed by her loss, attempted to fill the void by quickly conceiving another child, hoping to replace the deceased infant. Helen's mother struggled to acknowledge her true gender, instead projecting her fantasies onto Helen, treating her as if she were a boy. This failure to recognize Helen's true self and gender identity created a deep sense of confusion and distress for Helen, leading to feelings of inadequacy and self-rejection.

Primary maternal preoccupation and holding environment

Helen faced a significant failure in primary maternal preoccupation, as her mother, consumed by unprocessed grief over her deceased son, treated her as a substitute for the lost child. However, Helen's ability to develop complex adaptive strategies suggests the presence of substantial internal coping resources. Despite the challenges, there may have been instances of good-enough attunement and holding, possibly from other family members or close individuals in her environment who provided islands of security and recognition. Helen's capacity to establish a meaningful therapeutic relationship in adulthood, despite her complicated childhood experiences, demonstrates a fundamental capacity for trust in relationships, likely bolstered by positive experiences during her development.

Transitional objects and transitional space

Although Helen's transitional space was compromised due to her mother's interference in her self-discovery process, it appears that she managed to maintain the beginnings of a potential space where she could explore, though in a limited fashion, certain aspects of her identity. Her self-definition as "strange" —while reflecting an internal rift—also indicates creativity and a unique solution to an impossible situation. She created a third category, a personal transitional space where she could exist without entirely sacrificing her true identity or fully surrendering to external demands. This ability to create an intermediate domain, even if limited, lays a groundwork that can be expanded in therapy into a richer and more playful transitional space.

True self and false self

Due to her need to adapt to her mother's expectations, Helen developed a pronounced false self. However, beneath layers of defense, her true self did not vanish completely but continued to exist in a disguised form. Her pursuit of therapy and her ability to experience depression (as opposed to complete emptiness or pseudo-happiness) suggest the presence of a true self-seeking acknowledgment. In therapy, moments arise when the true self breaks through the cracks in her defenses—during instances of emotional honesty, authentic anger, or flashes of genuine desire for change. Helen gradually demonstrates an increasing ability to recognize her true feelings and desires, especially in the safe space provided by therapy, indicating potential for growth and development.

Dealing with aggression and powerful emotions

Although Helen learned to suppress her aggressive feelings and direct them inward, her expressions of vitality and life drive continue to surface in her behavior. The creation of the "strange" category illustrates a certain assertiveness—a subtle and sophisticated refusal to fully submit to her mother's demands. Additionally, her choice to seek therapy signals a longing for change and an inner strength motivating her to pursue a better life. Throughout therapy, she begins to exhibit an increasing ability to express powerful emotions directly, including frustration, disappointment, and anger—first toward distant figures and eventually within the therapeutic relationship as well. This relationship with the therapist provides her, for the first time, a safe space to experience and express a wide range of emotions, including healthy aggression, without the fear of abandonment or rejection.

Transitional phenomena, creativity, and playfulness

Despite the challenges she faced in her development, Helen displays promising signs of being able to utilize transitional space and engage in playfulness within therapy. She begins to demonstrate a capability for wordplay, using metaphors, and creatively conceptualizing her experiences. Gradually, Helen discovers a growing interest in creative fields—perhaps writing, art, or music—that offer her channels for self-expression and emotional processing. The therapist recognizes originality and unconventional thinking in her, which were previously obscured by the need to conform and please. Her "strange" experience, once a source of suffering, starts to be seen as a potential source of unique insights and unconventional perspectives.

Within the therapeutic space, Helen gradually succeeds in utilizing the therapist-patient relationship as a transitional realm where she can "play" with different identities and ideas, explore new possibilities, and construct a more cohesive narrative of self. The positive transference relationship formed with the therapist serves as a secure container for this exploration, allowing her, for the first time, to experience a relationship in which she is seen, recognized, and valued for who she truly is, with all her complexities. Through this therapeutic process, there is a chance that Helen will succeed in bridging the gap between parts of her self and develop a more complete and authentic sense of identity.

Psychodynamic formulation in self psychology

A self psychology psychodynamic formulation focuses on understanding how early selfobject experiences shape personality development and psychopathology. This formulation examines how disruptions in mirroring, idealizing, and twinship experiences during critical developmental periods lead to specific deficits in self-structure, impacting an individual's ability for self-regulation, maintenance of self-esteem, and formation of relationships.

Such a formulation assesses the person's available selfobject functions by analyzing both their developmental history of selfobject relationships and current patterns of seeking and maintaining selfobject connections. It considers how early selfobject failures create particular vulnerabilities in self-cohesion, which can manifest as various forms of psychological distress, including fragmentation anxiety, narcissistic rage, or chronic feelings of emptiness and meaninglessness. This understanding informs therapeutic interventions designed to provide corrective selfobject experiences and support the development of more stable self-structures through transmuting internalization.

KEY ELEMENTS IN SELF PSYCHOLOGY PSYCHODYNAMIC FORMULATION

1. **Self and selfobjects:** focus on how the patient's sense of self has been shaped by early experiences with selfobjects, such as caregivers or significant others, and how these relationships influence their sense of identity, self-esteem, and self-cohesion.

2. **Selfobject needs:** identify the patient's selfobject needs, including mirroring, idealization, twinship, adversarial, and efficacy (Wolf, 1994). Explore how the patient seeks mirroring, idealization, and twinship from others to support their sense of self and regulate their self-esteem. Consider how deficits in selfobject experiences may contribute to feelings of insecurity, fragmentation, or narcissistic vulnerability.

3. **Transmuting internalization:** assess the patient's capacity for self-soothing, self-reflection, and self-regulation, reflecting the extent to which they have integrated positive selfobject functions into their internal psychological structure.

4. **Self-coherence and self-esteem regulation:** consider how the patient's self-cohesion and self-esteem regulation are influenced by their internalization of selfobject functions. Explore how deficits in self-cohesion may manifest as identity disturbances, self-doubt, or emotional dysregulation, while disruptions in self-esteem regulation may lead to feelings of inadequacy, shame, or grandiosity.

5. **Developmental arrests and narcissistic injuries:** Kohut emphasized the impact of developmental arrests and narcissistic injuries on psychological functioning. Identify any early relational traumas or disruptions in selfobject experiences that may have contributed to the patient's psychological vulnerabilities, such as abandonment, rejection, or invalidation.

6. **Transference and selfobject needs:** explore the patient's transference reactions and how they reflect unmet selfobject needs in the therapeutic relationship. Pay attention to the patient's expectations of the therapist as a selfobject, including desires for validation, understanding, and empathic attunement, as well as any disruptions in the therapeutic alliance related to deficits in selfobject experiences.

7. **Treatment goals and interventions:** based on the psychodynamic formulation, develop treatment goals and interventions that address the patient's selfobject needs, promote transmuting internalization, and foster self-cohesion and self-esteem regulation. Consider incorporating empathy, validation, and selfobject transferences into the therapeutic process to repair developmental deficits and facilitate psychological growth and integration.

An example of psychodynamic formulation in self psychology

Danny, now 35, grew up in an affluent suburb of Boston as the only child of high-achieving parents. His mother, Sarah, a prominent corporate lawyer, hailed from a family of academics who always emphasized intellectual pursuits. His father, a renowned neurosurgeon, was the son of Holocaust survivors, inheriting their unspoken trauma and relentless drive for success.

From an early age, Danny was cared for by a rotating cast of nannies. He has vivid memories of standing at the window, watching his parents' cars disappear down the driveway, feeling a mix of abandonment and determination to gain their approval. Danny excelled academically, consistently earning top grades, but his achievements were met with perfunctory praise from his parents. "That's expected of a Goldstein," his father would say, patting him on the shoulder without looking up from his medical journals.

Danny's childhood was marked by loneliness. He recalls spending countless hours in his room, meticulously building elaborate Lego structures—cities that bustled with imaginary lives to fill the quiet of his actual home. At school, he struggled to connect with peers. While other kids played at recess, Danny often sat alone, reading advanced books to impress his teachers and, by extension, his parents.

As a teenager, Danny's drive for perfection intensified. He captained the debate team, founded the school's mock trial club, and graduated as valedictorian. Yet, at his graduation party, he overheard his mother on the phone with a colleague, discussing a case while his father chatted with other parents about their children's accomplishments, never mentioning Danny's.

In college, Danny threw himself into his pre-law studies, hoping to finally win his mother's admiration. He joined a fraternity seeking the brotherly bonds he craved but felt like an outsider, unable to relax and form genuine connections. His first serious relationship in his junior year ended after six months when his girlfriend complained he was emotionally unavailable and a workaholic—traits he recognized from his parents but felt powerless to change.

Now a successful corporate lawyer himself, Danny's life mirrors his parents' in many ways. His apartment is immaculate but unlived-in, and his calendar is full of meetings and social engagements he attends out of obligation rather than joy. He's had a string of short-term relationships, each ending when partners got too close or demanded more emotional intimacy than he could provide.

Beneath his professional success lies a profound sense of emptiness and meaninglessness. Danny often finds himself absorbed in philosophical ruminations about the futility of existence, arguing that all human endeavors are ultimately pointless since everything ends in death. He frequently expresses the view that individual lives are like grains of sand in an infinite desert—insignificant and ultimately forgotten. These nihilistic thoughts have intensified recently, contributing to his growing sense of disconnection from his achievements and relationships.

Recently, Danny experienced a panic attack in the middle of an important client meeting. The incident shook him deeply, making him question his life choices and prompting him to seek therapy. As he sits in the therapist's office for the first time, he fidgets with his expensive watch—a gift from his parents for making partner—and struggles to articulate why he's there, unused to discussing his feelings or admitting any kind of vulnerability.

Psychodynamic formulation for Danny according to self psychology

Self and selfobjects

Danny's sense of self has been profoundly shaped by his early experiences with inconsistent and emotionally unavailable selfobjects (his parents). This has resulted in a fragmented self-structure, characterized by a facade of high achievement masking deep-seated insecurities. His identity is heavily tied to external accomplishments, reflecting poor self-cohesion and unstable self-esteem.

Selfobject needs

Danny exhibits significant unmet selfobject needs:

Mirroring: his constant striving for academic and professional excellence reflects an intense need for validation and admiration, unfulfilled by his parents' perfunctory praise and lack of acknowledgment of the non-academic aspects of his personality.

Idealization: Danny's choice of career mirrors his mother's, suggesting an attempt to maintain an idealized connection with her. His panic attack—which indicates a failure to self-regulate—suggests a specific deficit in the idealization need, which he seeks, perhaps through partnership (merging) in the law firm or even in law itself. Choosing a career identical to his mother's serves to evoke some mirroring from her, and perhaps a sense of twinship.

Twinship: his struggles with peer relationships and emotional intimacy indicate an unmet need for a sense of similarity and belonging.

Adversarial needs: Danny's inability to experience constructive opposition and healthy conflict is evident in his avoidance of genuine relationships and his panic when facing challenging client situations. His early environment, focused solely on achievement, provided no space for healthy opposition or constructive disagreement.

Efficacy needs: while Danny achieved external success, his sense of genuine agency and effectiveness is compromised, as shown by his feeling "powerless to change" his emotional patterns. His accomplishments stem more from compulsive achievement than from a genuine sense of efficacy and competence.

Transmuting internalization

Danny shows limited capacity for transmuting internalization. His reliance on external validation and achievement for self-worth indicates poor integration of self-soothing and self-esteem regulation functions. His panic attack during a client meeting suggests fragile internal structures for managing stress and anxiety.

Self-coherence and self-esteem regulation

Danny's self-cohesiveness is tenuous, manifesting in his emotional unavailability and workaholic tendencies—defenses against a fragile inner self. His self-esteem is precariously regulated through external achievements, indicating poor internalization of self-valuing functions. This is evident in his inability to derive genuine satisfaction from his accomplishments.

Developmental arrests and narcissistic injuries

Significant narcissistic injuries are evident from Danny's childhood experiences of emotional neglect and conditional approval. The consistent lack of attuned responsiveness from his parents likely led to developmental arrests in his capacity for emotional intimacy and self-regulation.

Transference and selfobject needs

In therapy, Danny may initially relate to the therapist as he did to his parents, seeking approval through "perfect" patient behavior. He may struggle with the therapist's empathic attunement, finding it unfamiliar and possibly threatening to his defensive structures. Mirroring transference is likely to be prominent, with Danny seeking validation and admiration from the therapist.

Treatment goals and interventions

- Providing empathic attunement to address Danny's unmet selfobject needs.
- Facilitating the development of more robust internal structures for self-soothing and self-esteem regulation.
- Helping Danny develop a more nuanced and integrated sense of self, less dependent on external validation.
- Exploring and working through his fears of emotional intimacy.
- Gradually interpreting his defensive structures while maintaining empathic connection.

Interventions should emphasize creating a holding environment that allows Danny to experience and internalize reliable mirroring and idealization. The therapist should be prepared for potential empathic failures and work through them as opportunities for repairing early narcissistic injuries.

THE COURSE OF TREATMENT

Division of the course of treatment into phases

Dividing long-term psychotherapy into distinct phases presents clinicians with a complex and challenging task. The act of segmenting therapy into periods is, in essence, an act of storytelling that seeks to impose order and meaning on a process that is often chaotic, nonlinear, and deeply personal. This narrative framing can be both illuminating and potentially misleading. While it may be tempting to impose a structured narrative onto the therapeutic process, such divisions can sometimes obscure the fluid and nonlinear nature of change. The therapeutic journey is rarely straightforward; phases may overlap, regress, or repeat in circular patterns, challenging our attempts to neatly categorize them.

Despite the difficulties, dividing therapy into phases can be valuable. It compels the author to examine positive developments and moments of crisis in the patient's life and relate them to turning points and changes within the treatment. This process can provide structure and clarity to the case study, making it more accessible to readers and the therapist.

Consider the approach of Marion Milner in her book "The Hands of the Living God: An Account of Psychoanalytic Treatment" (2010). Her patient, Susan, was a young schizophrenic woman in her early twenties who was treated by Marion Milner for almost 20 years (1943–1962). She suffered from severe psychosis, disconnection from reality, and an inability to form basic human relationships, often expressing herself through primitive drawings that became crucial to her therapeutic process and the book's documentation. Milner divided her treatment of Susan into five periods: Susan's Artistic Journey Through Phases of Recovery.

Phase One: Before the Beginning of Painting. During this phase, Susan is not yet painting. This period is characterized by descriptions of traumatic childhood experiences, feelings of lost self following ECT treatment, and sensations of emptiness and lack of identity. The central feature is her inability to express emotions or internal images, with Susan primarily engaged in verbal attempts to understand "what is missing" within her. This phase is defined by the absence of visual expression—painting has not yet emerged as a therapeutic tool.

Phase Two: The First Paintings (1950). In this phase, Susan begins to spontaneously create "doodles." Her artwork is filled with phallic symbols, demon imagery, distorted creatures, feces-babies, and sensations of physical and mental disintegration. The key characteristic is the use of drawing as a tool to express primitive anxieties, experiences of a fragmenting body, and the lack of boundaries between self and environment. This phase is identified by the emergence of painting as a primal, raw, unconscious tool—resulting in turbulent, crowded drawings lacking clear structure.

Phase Three: Symbol Formation and Boundary Work (1951–1957). During this period, recurring motifs appear, such as circles, spirals ("whorls"), shells, and winding lines. The spiral becomes a central symbol representing the search for containment and holding, as well as anxiety about fragmentation or loss of boundaries. The paintings begin to show more structure, repetition, and attempts to organize inner chaos. This phase is marked by the transition from chaotic scribbles to recurring symbols that express a dialectic between defense and collapse.

Phase Four: Emergence of Narrative and Engagement with Object Relations (1957–1958). In this phase, Susan's paintings feature images of water, ducks, landscapes, houses, mouths, and confrontations between figures. There is a shift toward exploring the meeting between inner and outer worlds, between self and other, and sometimes images of wounds, holes, or a "hole in the heart" appear. The characteristic feature is an attempt to recognize the possibility of mutual hurt, guilt, and desire for repair. This phase is defined by the appearance of visual narratives, distinct figures, and the beginnings of integration between parts of the self.

Phase Five: Processing Loss, Identity Formation, and Movement Toward Life in the World. In this stage, Susan's paintings feature images of transformation (such as curling hair, water, and the phoenix), engagement with death and rebirth, and a transition to symbols of breathing, primal pleasure, and taking root in the world. Susan confronts her mother's death, forms new relationships, and explores the possibility of living in the world beyond therapy. This phase is marked by the emergence of transformation imagery, acceptance of boundaries, and relative wholeness in both the paintings and their content.

Milner's ingenious division of Susan's treatment through her evolving relationship with drawing reveals psychoanalysis as a creative, nonlinear journey rather than a calendar-bound progression. By anchoring each therapeutic phase in Susan's artistic expression, Milner creates a structure that mirrors the organic unfolding of psychological growth—from fragmentation to integration.

This organizational choice accomplishes multiple aims with elegant efficiency. It elevates Susan's drawings from therapeutic tools to the very medium of healing, demonstrates how psychological change actually occurs (with its inevitable backs and forths), and positions Milner as an engaged participant in the transformative process.

Robert Stoller's "Sexual Excitement: Dynamics of Erotic Life" (1986) offers another compelling alternative to linear thinking. In "Sexual Excitement," Stoller provides a masterful lesson in how to structure a case study through the lens of fantasy rather than time. Taking his patient Belle's elaborate masturbation fantasy as his organizing principle, he crafts a narrative that spirals inward rather than marches forward. He views these fantasies—especially Belle's central erotic scene—as psychological scripts that embody conflicts, childhood traumas, and attempts to transform harmful experiences into psychological victories. Stoller analyzes Belle's fantasies not only as content but also as process: how they are constructed, changed, and decoded during therapy and how they function as mechanisms for resolving hidden psychological problems, as well as means for preserving secrecy, control, and satisfaction. He also addresses how these fantasies maintain tension between danger and safety, between the known and the hidden, and between trauma and repair—showing how Belle uses fantasy to convert anxiety into sexual excitement.

Through chapter titles like "The Underground Fantasy" and "Sadomasochism," Stoller peels back the layers of Belle's erotic imagination like an artful psychoanalytic origami master. What emerges is not merely a young woman's sexual daydreams, but a complex psychological story. Belle's fantasy life becomes a stage where childhood wounds are transformed into adult victories, with each scene carefully choreographed to repair the past.

The genius of Stoller's approach lies in showing us how a single fantasy can contain multitudes—from the depths of anality to the heights of exhibition. In doing so, he demonstrates that the shortest distance between trauma and healing isn't always a straight line—sometimes it's a dreamy detour through the erotic imagination.

What interests us is that Stoller's approach is unique because of its rejection of temporal constraints. By liberating the narrative from the tyranny of the clock, he allows Belle's fantasies to exist in a kind of eternal present, where childhood traumas and adult desires coexist in a state of perpetual dialogue. This method mirrors the very nature of the unconscious, where time bends and folds upon itself, and where a childhood memory can ignite an adult passion with the immediacy of a live wire.

According to John Forrester (2017), Stoller's approach to structuring Belle's case study in "Sexual Excitement" (1986) bears a striking resemblance to Freud's seminal work, particularly his analysis of the Wolf Man. In both Stoller's and Freud's cases, we see the analysis revolving around a singular, potent psychic formation—for Belle, her elaborate erotic daydream; for the Wolf Man, it was his iconic dream of the wolves. This technique of using a single, complex psychic product as the centerpiece of analysis has become, as Forrester notes, "the prototype of analytic understanding" (p. 72). It's a microcosm that, when fully explored, reveals the macrocosm of the patient's entire psychic life. Forrester's comparison highlights how this narrative strategy has evolved in psychoanalytic literature. From Freud's focus on trauma as the "original scene of psychoanalysis" to the dream becoming the "exemplary scene," we see analysts like Stoller applying this deep-dive approach to a variety of psychic phenomena, including complex sexual fantasies.

*

Ultimately, the division of a case study should serve as a map of the patient's inner landscape rather than as a timeline of events. It should breathe with the life of the therapy itself, pulsing with moments of connection, shadowed by periods of withdrawal, and punctuated by flashes of profound realization. Whether following Milner's milestone-based approach or Stoller's thematic exploration, the goal remains the same: to honor the complexity of the human psyche and the art of psychotherapy, offering not just a record of treatment, but a living document of transformation.

Here are several axes along which therapists tend to divide long-term therapy into periods:

Writing on themes or shifts

One axis is to identify major themes or shifts in the therapeutic journey. Use the verbatim notes you wrote or the notes you prepared for yourself during the treatment. Sometimes, you'll extract something from them, and it will jump out at you. These shifts serve as natural transition points between different phases of therapy and allow for a more fluid understanding of the patient's progression. These themes may encompass breakthrough moments, impactful life events, or shifts in the therapeutic relationship.

Transference and countertransference dynamics are crucial in dividing therapy into phases. The interplay between transference and countertransference dynamics profoundly shapes the trajectory of treatment. These dynamics, like shifting tides, may herald transformations within the patient's inner landscape or the therapeutic relationship itself, offering invaluable insights into the ever-evolving phases of therapy. By vigilantly monitoring these subtle currents, patterns and themes emerge, guiding the division of therapy into distinct periods.

An illustrative example can be found in Anne Alvarez's poignant case study, detailed in "Live Presence: Psychoanalytic Psychotherapy with Autistic Children, Borderline Children, Children Affected by Deprivation, and Victims of Abuse" (2005). As Alvarez chronicles the progression of Ruby's therapy, the chapter headings serve as signposts marking significant milestones in his journey towards healing and self-discovery. Titles such as "Plant Life and Wakes," "Waking Up," and "First Waking" paint a vivid picture of Ruby's gradual emergence from the cocoon of his condition.

Alvarez's meticulous attention to the nuances of their communication is evident as she describes her increasing vigilance in discerning between authentic expression and mere facade. Through her skillful navigation of the therapeutic terrain, Alvarez guides Ruby towards a deeper understanding of himself and the world around him. The journey towards "Becoming a Vertebrate" is a testament to Ruby's resilience and Alvarez's steadfast commitment to his growth. It is a narrative of hope, resilience, and the transformative power of human connection, beautifully captured in the pages of Alvarez's evocative case study.

Writing on each session

Few know that Melanie Klein (1961) documented 93 sessions with young Richard, while Winnicott (1986) recorded 18 sessions in "Holding and Interpretation." These meticulous accounts capture every interpretation, transference shift, and therapeutic intervention in remarkable detail.

While this approach might seem impractical for modern articles—demanding extensive time for documentation and overwhelming readers with details—its value for knowledge production is immense. By tracking each session, you create a comprehensive map of the therapeutic journey, revealing subtle patterns and changes that might otherwise remain hidden. This method captures the evolution of interpretations, the gradual shifts in the therapeutic relationship, and the precise moments when breakthrough insights occurred.

Consider adapting this method selectively—perhaps documenting certain phases of therapy in detail while maintaining broader summaries for others. This way, you preserve the richness of clinical observation while making it manageable in today's practice environment. Remember, Klein and Winnicott's detailed accounts continue to generate new insights decades later, suggesting that such comprehensive documentation, while challenging, serves as an invaluable repository of clinical wisdom.

Dividing treatment chronologically

When writing a case study, you'll often find that you naturally divide the analysis by years. This chronological approach makes intuitive sense; after all, the therapeutic relationship, like any relationship, unfolds over time. Yet this seemingly straightforward structure carries both opportunities and limitations. While it provides a clear framework, it might constrain your thinking into overly linear patterns.

In the best case studies you'll read, you'll notice that each phase contains both progress and regression, weaving together in complex patterns. Perfect linearity simply doesn't exist in therapeutic work.

You might find it helpful to think about your case study in the following distinct periods:

The initial phase invites you to explore how the therapeutic alliance formed, what brought your patient to therapy, and your early hypotheses about their psychological dynamics.

The middle phase often becomes your richest territory. Here, you'll document the core therapeutic work—the resistance, the unconscious conflicts emerging, and the gradual development of insight.

In the working-through phase, you'll track how your patient begins integrating their insights into daily life, often revisiting core issues with deeper understanding.

The termination phase asks you to consider how gains were consolidated and how both you and your patient processed the ending of your relationship.

To determine when one phase ends and another begins, look for what I call "central nodes"—critical turning points in the therapeutic relationship or your patient's life. These moments often illuminate the entire therapeutic journey.

Consider this example: your patient arrives furious because you didn't acknowledge them at a social event. This seemingly small incident unlocks a flood of material about their childhood as an unwanted pregnancy, their mother's preference for a sibling, and their deep hunger for recognition. The apparent slight becomes a window into their core wounds.

Or imagine documenting this scenario: after significant therapeutic progress, your patient falls in love and plans to move in with their partner. But instead of pure joy, they're overwhelmed with anxiety. Each discussion about the move intensifies their distress, revealing how profound life changes reverberate through their inner world.

These pivotal moments become your anchors in writing the case study. They help you structure the narrative while honoring the complexity of the therapeutic journey. Here are several guidelines to help clinicians divide their case studies into phases:

Five principles for phase division in long-term psychodynamic therapy

Dialectic of proximity-distance and trust crises

Psychodynamic therapists mark transitions between phases through fluctuations and crises in the therapeutic relationship:

Beginning phase: initial fragile therapeutic alliance, often characterized by a "honeymoon period" typically followed by a first trust crisis.

Middle phase: significant trust crises that challenge the therapeutic alliance and expose early abandonment patterns and relationship anxieties; processing of narcissistic injuries caused by "disappointment" with the therapist.

Advanced middle phase: ability to endure deeper relationship crises, restoration of trust after provocative interpretations, and dealing with idealization and de-idealization of the therapist.

Termination phase: tendency to provoke trust crises as resistance to ending, or alternatively, excessive idealization as a defense against feelings of disappointment and abandonment.

Cycles of resistance, progress and regression

Therapists identify the spiral movement of progress-regression, where each breakthrough is sometimes accompanied by resistance or regression:

Beginning phase: primitive resistances (lateness, cancellations, silences, avoidance of payment), which often mask fear of intimacy or exposure.

Middle phase: more sophisticated resistances—intellectualization, shifting focus from self to others, acting out outside the therapy room, and activating the therapist through transference.

Advanced middle phase: resistances related to fear of change and success, concern about losing the "sick identity," and significant regression following therapeutic breakthroughs.

Termination phase: resistance to ending through regression to earlier symptoms, creating new crises, or discounting the progress achieved.

Dialectic of dependence-independence and transference

Therapists track the development of transference relationships while dealing with the dynamics of dependence-independence:

Beginning phase: denial of dependence or, alternatively, regression to childlike dependence, primitive abandonment anxieties, and conflicts around the therapeutic frame.

Middle phase: struggle between the need for dependence and fear of engulfment, outbursts of rage when the therapist "doesn't provide enough," and alternating idealization and demonization of the therapist.

Advanced middle phase: confronting the fantasy that the therapist will solve everything, while expressing shame about dependence on the therapist; deepening of transference relationships to core and Oedipal issues.

Termination phase: deep ambivalence—fear of abandonment alongside the desire for independence, internalization of the therapist as an internal object, and processing dependence/independence as part of the separation process.

Emergence of traumatic material and its nonlinear processing

Therapists identify phases based on how traumatic material appears, recedes, and returns for processing:

Beginning phase: indirect hints of traumatic material, active avoidance of painful topics, while developing sufficient trust for their disclosure.

Middle phase: disclosure of traumatic materials often followed by withdrawal and "closing up," movement between flooding and avoidance, somatic phenomena following trauma disclosure.

Advanced middle phase: return to traumatic materials with a deeper processing capability, partial integration of dissociative content, and understanding the impact of trauma on current relationships.

Termination phase: dealing with traumatic residues that cannot be fully processed, accepting the limitations of healing, and recognizing parts that remain vulnerable.

Transformation of defense mechanisms and emergence of the authentic self

Therapists track changes in defense mechanisms and the emergence of the authentic self, recognizing the complex movement back and forth:

Beginning phase: rigid and primitive defenses (denial, projection, splitting), dominant "false self" in the therapy room, with rare glimpses of the authentic self.

Middle phase: collapse of certain defenses leads to anxiety and the establishment of new defenses, emergence of the authentic self in certain sessions and withdrawal from it in others, internal struggle over true exposure.

Advanced middle phase: more flexible movement between defense and exposure, anxiety attacks when the authentic self is more exposed, and growing ability to recognize defenses in real-time.

Termination phase: partial integration of the authentic self, recognition of the ongoing need for certain defenses, and ability to identify and accept "different parts of the self" even when they are in conflict.

Writing about the silences: A note on "dead" periods

Have you ever sat with a patient when it feels like you've both run dry, the well of words and insights suddenly empty? You both stare at the wall, session after session, and nothing emerges. Your notes become shorter and shorter until they almost disappear. "Patient reports nothing new," you write, feeling guilty about your lack of insight, wondering if other therapists handle these periods better, if they've discovered some secret technique for keeping the therapeutic waters flowing.

These dead periods haunt our case studies like unwanted ghosts. We tend to skip over them, rushing to document the next breakthrough, the next interpretation that worked. After all, who wants to write about nothing?

Yet I've noticed something curious about these seemingly empty spaces. Like an artist staring at a blank canvas too long, we begin to see things in the emptiness—subtle shifts in the quality of silence, barely perceptible changes in how our patient holds their body, microscopic variations in the way they say "nothing comes to mind." The emptiness itself becomes a kind of presence.

When writing about these periods, try treating them not as failures to be hidden but as negative spaces that define the shape of the therapy. Document your boredom, your frustration, your certainty that you're doing everything wrong. Write about how the silence feels different on different days—sometimes dead like a stagnant pond, sometimes alive like the pause between lightning and thunder. Along with this goes an unconscious assumption (which can become a conscious hope) that opportunity will occur at a later date for a renewed experience, in which the failure situation will be able to be unfrozen and re-experienced, with the individual in a regressed state, in an environment that is making adequate adaptation (Winnicott, 1954, p. 281). In several case studies, these periods occupy a central place in treatment.

Ofra Eshel (2019) writes in one of her case studies: "I was caught, silenced, and paralyzed by that black hole of deadness, dying, and struggle to rescue, which completely dominated the analysis" (p. 60). Remember those moments when you catch yourself thinking "I should be doing something more"? Write about those too. They're part of the story, just as much as the brilliant interpretations and emotional breakthroughs. Sometimes the most important therapeutic work happens in these apparent voids, like seeds germinating underground in winter.

Rather than dismissing them as uneventful, consider exploring their potential significance:

1. **Incubation periods:** these seemingly inactive phases might be times of internal processing and integration for the patient. Significant changes could be occurring beneath the surface, laying groundwork for future breakthroughs.
2. **Resistance manifestation:** stagnation might indicate resistance to change or fear of the next therapeutic step. Analyzing this resistance can provide valuable insights into the patient's core conflicts.
3. **Relationship testing:** the patient might be testing the therapeutic relationship's ability to withstand boredom or lack of obvious progress. This could be a recapitulation of early relational patterns.
4. **Countertransference insights:** the therapist's feelings of boredom or frustration can be valuable data, potentially mirroring the patient's internal state or early life experiences.
5. The emptiness and silence in the therapy room can echo **traumatic experiences of emotional abandonment** or lack of regulation, when the infant's needs were not met and they experienced a kind of temporary "psychic death" —a state in which the self feels disconnected, empty, and meaningless. In the therapeutic process, the shared experience of silence and emptiness between therapist and patient provides an opportunity to revive these early traumatic moments, but this time in a beneficial presence capable of containing the experience and helping to process it, thereby enabling a process of healing and development.
6. **Shift in therapeutic focus:** sometimes, apparent stagnation indicates that the current therapeutic approach has reached its limits, signaling a need for a shift in focus or technique.

"Holding and Interpretation", Winnicott (1986, p.118)

Patient: Once again, I have nothing on my mind. There may be an hour when nothing comes to me. If I were to speak only trivialities, it would be the same as saying nothing.

Winnicott responds to the patient with a profound statement. He notes that he is aware of the patient's intense fear of being mocked and abruptly cut off, and that the patient protects himself from these dangers. Winnicott adds that he observes they are once more addressing the patient's direct relationship with his mother or with another person who might frustrate him. Finally, Winnicott raises the possibility that the patient is beginning to contemplate interference in his relationship with his mother by his father. In doing so, Winnicott attempts to connect the patient's current silence to deeper emotional and familial patterns. From Winnicott's clinical example, we learn three specific ways to discuss seemingly "dead" periods in therapy:

First, document the patient's exact words about having "nothing" in their mind—this apparently empty statement already reveals their belief that only significant content is worthy of expression ("If I were to talk nothing but trivialities, that would be the same as nothing").

Then, connect the current silence to the patient's core fears—in this case, Winnicott links it to the fear of being mocked and suddenly cut off.

Finally, situate the silence within the patient's early relationships—Winnicott traces it back to both the maternal relationship (fear of frustration) and the Oedipal triangle (father's interference).

This shows how a seemingly "empty" moment can be written about as a rich clinical text that reveals defensive patterns, developmental history, and unconscious dynamics.

Clinical example: Working with Silence

Sarah, a 34-year-old architect, entered her session and settled into her usual position on the couch. Five minutes passed. Then ten. The silence felt different from previous sessions—not hostile, not anxious, but peculiarly dense, as though something was being held rather than avoided.

I noticed my own impulse to intervene, to "rescue" us both from this void. Instead, I attended to the quality of her stillness. Her breathing had slowed; her hands, typically restless, lay motionless. Was she retreating or arriving somewhere?

After twenty minutes, I said quietly, "You're very still today."

"I'm trying to feel if I exist when no one is asking me for anything," she replied.

This began what I could only tentatively call a phase of treatment. Sarah had functioned as her mother's emotional regulator from early childhood. But whether these silent periods represented her first encounter with a self separate from utility, or a reproduction of the deadness she'd known as a child, I couldn't determine. Sometimes her stillness felt alive with possibility; other times closer to disappearance.

My interventions were sparse and often felt inadequate. When I spoke, I sometimes sensed I'd interrupted something essential. When I remained silent, I wondered if I was repeating her mother's emotional unavailability.

Months later, Sarah began accessing memories of lying awake as a child, listening for signs that she still existed. Whether our work healed or replicated this experience remain ambiguous—perhaps it did both.

Demonstrating the evolution of therapy through dreams

Another way to describe the progress of treatment is through a dream-centric approach. It allows us to case presentation allows us to track the patient's progress not through external events or session-by-session accounts but through the evolving landscape of their inner world, as expressed by dreams, providing a unique and profound insight into the therapeutic process. By analyzing the evolution of dreams throughout therapy, readers can trace the patient's progress, setbacks, and unresolved issues, creating a comprehensive narrative of their psychological journey. Dreams often communicate more precisely than biographical narratives. They crystallize emotional truths that might take months to emerge through conventional therapeutic dialogue. While this approach might seem limited by its exclusive focus on dreams, with minimal detail about the actual therapeutic process, this apparent limitation is precisely its strength. By tracking only the unconscious material through dreams, we gain access to a purer form of psychological development, uncontaminated by conscious narratives or rational explanations.

The absence of conventional therapeutic details allows us to witness the raw evolution of the unconscious mind, suggesting that other clinical information might actually obscure rather than illuminate the core psychological transformation. This method privileges the unconscious as the true narrator of therapeutic change, implying that conscious therapeutic discourse might sometimes serve as a defense against deeper psychological truth.

Clinical example: the evolving dreamscape

Dream 1: The blind man's crossing

> I dreamt I was a blind man trying to cross a busy street alone. Cars were whizzing by dangerously close. Suddenly, an old man appeared and offered to help guide me across. I felt a surge of relief and gratitude. But just as we started to cross, he vanished without a trace. I stood there frozen, realizing with horror that the drivers were blind too. A police officer was directing traffic, but he kept waving the cars into a dead end. Accidents were piling up all around me, metal crashing and people screaming. I knew I had to get across, but I was paralyzed, engulfed by the chaos and my own blindness.

This initial dream powerfully captures the patient's anxieties about beginning therapy. The blind man attempting to cross a dangerous street reflects his vulnerability and uncertainty in entering the therapeutic space. The elderly guide who appears and then vanishes mirrors early transferential dynamics—both the hope for a helping figure and the deep fear that this help will prove unreliable, just as his early attachment figures were. The sudden realization that other drivers are also blind suggests his dawning awareness that his therapist too may be "blind" or imperfect, generating anxiety about the therapeutic process. The police officer directing cars into a dead end evokes his fear that therapy itself might lead nowhere, perhaps even making things worse. The overwhelming chaos and accidents in the dream speak to his terror of emotional exposure and intimacy in the therapeutic relationship. This dream offered crucial insight into the patient's initial defensive structure and the complex transferential field we would need to navigate.

Dream 2: The burning thorn field
Months into therapy, the patient dreams the following dream:

I am in a vast field of thorns engulfed in flames. Firefighters struggle in vain to contain the blaze, which only spreads more fiercely with each attempt to extinguish it. A peculiar solution emerges: only if a thousand men urinate on the fire can it be doused. Despite frantic searches, it seems impossible to find so many men.

This dream marks a pivotal middle phase in therapy. The burning thorn field represents the patient's accumulated pain and defenses, now fully acknowledged and "on fire." The ineffectual firefighters symbolize the patient's realization that conventional coping mechanisms are inadequate. The unusual solution of collective urination suggests a growing understanding that healing requires vulnerability and the "release" of long-held emotions. The struggle to gather a thousand men reflects the patient's difficulty in fully embracing this vulnerability, as well as a dawning recognition of the need for community and shared human experience in the healing process.

Dream 3: The ambivalent shore
As therapy nears its conclusion, the patient dreams the following dream:

I am the owner of a serene beach. The water is deep blue and inviting, yet there are rumors of hidden riptides. Some brave swimmers venture in, beckoning those on shore to join them without fear. These swimmers appear to be enjoying themselves immensely.

This final dream captures the termination phase through the imagery of a peaceful beach. The ownership represents a new sense of control over one's thinking. The deep blue water symbolizes the unconscious, now viewed with acceptance despite known risks (riptides). Confident swimmers embody the patient's new capacity for emotional risk-taking and connection, while their visible enjoyment suggests the rewards of engaging more fully with life.

Through these dreams, we witness the patient's journey from helplessness and fear of abandonment through a phase of confronting pain and recognizing the need for vulnerability to a state of cautious optimism and readiness to engage more fully with life.

Plot axes

The pendulum of treatment: Navigating the tension between growth and resistance

Crafting a plot in a psychodynamic case study is one of the most challenging aspects of writing. Similar to a literary work, every successful case study revolves around a conflict or series of conflicts. Just like in a captivating novel or an exciting play, the conflict is the driving force of the plot, creating tension and interest and drawing the reader into the inner world of the main character—in this case, the patient.

In a psychodynamic case study, conflicts typically occur within the patient's psyche, between opposing parts of their personality and especially in transference relations. This can be a struggle between the desire for change and the resistance to letting go of familiar defenses, or between the need for connection and the fear of intimacy. Just as in literature, these internal conflicts reflect the complexity and paradoxes of human existence, creating a powerful psychological drama. Therefore, when writing a case study, we must seek out the points of tension, the internal struggles, and the moments of collision and overcoming. These moments will capture the reader's attention, captivate them, and transform our case study into an unforgettable experience—just like excellent literature.

In psychodynamic case studies, the conflict often manifests as fragmented or split parts of the patient's psyche working against those parts seeking mental growth. The tension arises from understanding these non-compliant aspects, their motivations, and why they seem to want the patient to fail in therapy. A crucial goal for the therapist is to understand these parts, give them a voice, and attempt to communicate with them. The case may swing between despair and hope, frozen moments and rapid dialogues, dissolution and integration, autistic and depressive positions, or stillness and playful interaction. This pendulum movement is often observed in the transference, where the patient alternates between a willingness to get close to the therapist and resistance to developing dependency.

Clinical example

The case of "S" in Margaret Rubin's (2025) "Calamities and Secrets, the Power of the Fetish" exemplifies the pendulum of treatment—a rhythmic oscillation between connection and withdrawal, progress and regression. This pattern becomes increasingly evident as the therapeutic relationship deepens. When S achieves a moment of real connection with a horse, experiencing "a moment of deep intimacy," he immediately retreats to talking about mechanical aspects of his life—"his love of reassembling objects" (p108). As S becomes more vulnerable while discussing his experience with the grandchildren, he immediately attacks the therapist's empathic response: "I teared up, which S noticed and did not appreciate. 'If you are trying to do "empathy," it's not working'" (p118).

The major pendular swing, perhaps the most dramatic illustration, occurs when S begins to feel deeply dependent on the therapist. After experiencing separation anxiety on weekends and finding comfort in "remembering the comfort he felt with me Monday through Thursday" (p117), he abruptly disappears for six weeks: "He didn't return until the second week of October—he was gone six weeks" (p115). This pendular movement appears to be driven by S's fear of dependency and vulnerability. When the therapeutic relationship threatens his "universe of one," he withdraws to his protective patterns. As Rubin observes: "my suggestion had pitted his will against mine, which he heard as a demand for submission rather than a surrender to the analytic process and held onto his reins even tighter" (p115). The case illustrates how progress in therapy often follows this pendular rhythm, where each step toward intimacy and vulnerability triggers a compensatory movement toward safety and control, particularly in patients with severe early trauma.

Crises

In contrast to the steady, gradual unfolding of change characteristic of psychodynamic treatment's pendulum approach, acute crises in therapy are marked by sudden, volatile disruptions.

They tend to center around one central episode. These crises can abruptly alter the course of therapy, marking a clear division between "before" and "after" phases. When resolved, they symbolize significant growth and progress, often relating to transference dynamics or pivotal life events. Crises may be dramatic enough to redefine the therapeutic journey, and sometimes multiple crises occur within a single treatment course.

Sudden breakthroughs in treatment can paradoxically trigger crises as patients experience anxiety about dependency and closeness. The therapist's countertransferential reactions, particularly when they mirror early traumatic relationships, can create ruptures in the therapeutic alliance. Major life changes for either participant (pregnancy, illness, relocation) can activate abandonment fears and destabilize the frame. Interpretations that threaten core defensive structures or touch on dissociated trauma may precipitate acute crises. The emergence of erotic transference or aggressive impulses often leads to intense shame and withdrawal, especially when they conflict with the patient's self-image.

Example of an acute crisis

Claire Winnicott's (1980) case of K, a musician experiencing severe depression, illustrates this. K was sent to boarding school at a young age and experienced profound despair during analysis, blaming the therapist for perceived abandonment. A breakthrough occurred through a dream, symbolizing the therapist's presence, dispelling the patient's depression and leading to significant changes in her life.

K described a dream in which she was lying in her bed at home in her flat. At the foot of the bed on the right side, a huge pile of coal gradually disappeared before her eyes. Simultaneously, she noticed a camel on the other side of the bed, opposite to where the coal had been. She was very pleased to see it because she recognized it as the therapist. Claire Winnicott realized and expressed that the patient attributed special powers to her, believing she could dispel her depression, represented by the pile of black coal. The coal had vanished when she recognized the therapist as the camel (symbol of the two breasts). It appeared that when Claire Winnicott was present, her depression disappeared, but in her absence, she was left with broken pieces of coal, symbolizing the fragmented parts of the therapist due to her anger at her absence.

The dream and its interpretation were a turning point. Following this dream, in which Miss K connected via her transitional object with the early mother figure from before the breakdown, there were changes in the patient's attitude not only towards the treatment but in her life generally. Claire Winnicott wrote that Miss K always refers to this episode as a landmark because, from then on, she knew she didn't want to die.

Distrust-Honeymoon-Crisis-Resolution: The most common plot structure in psychodynamic case studies

The distrust-honeymoon-crisis-resolution plot structure has become the cliché par excellence of psychodynamic case studies, a narrative arc so ubiquitous it borders on self-parody. The classic narrative structure of psychodynamic case studies has become something between a tragic comedy and a familiar dance: a play where everyone knows the plot, yet still watches with bated breath. I've read dozens upon dozens of these.

You know the format: a patient enters the therapy room like a hesitant heroine. She sits at the edge of the couch, glancing sideways, half wanting to escape. The therapist—patient as a Buddhist, but smiling inwardly—already knows the script by heart.

Stage one: Resistance. She arrives late. Speaks minimally. Refuses to shed her defenses. He—gentle, persistent, unperturbed—continues to try.

Stage two: The therapeutic honeymoon. Suddenly—the breakthrough! She opens up. Secrets pour out. She falls in love with the process. Discovers an entire world she never knew existed. Like a midwife of souls, the therapist accompanies her with an engaging attitude.

Stage three: The inevitable crisis. A small mistake. A touch of trauma. And suddenly—everything falls apart. She retreats. He's confused. The therapy is stuck like a truck in mud.

But don't worry! The therapist goes for supervision. Returns with an insight. They overcome the crisis. Move forward. And the story repeats itself—this time slightly differently.

This is the eternal rhythm of psychodynamic case studies, a familiar formula that keeps recurring, again and again.

And yet, for all its familiarity, this structure persists. It endures not merely as a convenient template, but as a reflection of the rhythms and ruptures inherent to the therapeutic process itself. To dismiss it entirely would be to ignore the very real patterns that emerge in the delicate interaction between analyst and analysand.

The distrust phase

The first stage, distrust, usually begins with the patient's difficulty in devoting himself to the therapist and trusting her.

The patient can bring false parts, please the therapist, hide important secrets related to his life from her, avoid talking about pain, or say that his head is empty and he has nothing to talk about. He can also be late, miss meetings, or come at a different time than scheduled.

Clinical example
Michael Parsons (1999):

> She claimed I hadn't said the things she insisted she needed me to say. Behind all this was real despair. She informed me that sometimes she cut herself and she showed me a scalpel that she carried with her. She gave it to me to take care of for a few days but insisted on having it again. Every moment of feeling understood by me had to be destroyed as soon as possible. (p. 872)

The honeymoon phase

Writing about the therapeutic honeymoon phase challenges you as a clinician-writer. You must find words to capture both its transformative power and its temporary nature. In your clinical narrative, this period emerges as a time of profound possibility, when you observe the therapeutic space expanding to accommodate new forms of relatedness. You've built trust gradually through your consistent presence—showing up at the same time, in the same place, with the same attentive stance—until something shifts in the relationship's fundamental tone.

As you write about this phase, you notice how material begins to flow more freely, as if some internal dam has been breached. Dreams feature in your sessions, carrying their precious cargo of unconscious meaning. Your patient's narrative becomes richer, more layered, threading between past and present with increasing fluidity. Together, you begin weaving a new understanding of their life story, discovering patterns that connect early wounds to present struggles.

In describing this phase, you must resist the temptation to paint it in purely golden hues. Yes, there is something magical about watching your patient unfold into new possibilities—finally allowing themselves to be held, to be fed, to be seen in all their complexity. Yes, there is something deeply moving about witnessing someone claim parts of themselves they've long disowned—their aggression, their sexuality, their deepest longings. But as a skilled clinical writer, you also acknowledge the fragility of this moment, its character as a stage rather than a destination.

Sometimes this honeymoon arrives only after you've weathered storms of criticism and resistance, demonstrating your capacity to endure your patient's destructive impulses. You track how the therapeutic relationship deepens through these challenges, how trust grows in the soil of survived attacks. Your narrative captures the gradual shift from guarded separation to something closer, more symbiotic—while maintaining awareness that this too shall pass, that this merger serves a developmental purpose but cannot be a permanent state.

Your art lies in conveying both the beauty and the transience of this phase, helping your readers understand its necessity while preparing them for its inevitable transformation. Like all honeymoons, this one serves its purpose precisely because it cannot last forever.

Example of honeymoon phase

As Raymond sat across from me in our first session, I could sense a palpable shift in his demeanor. For the first time in his life, he seemed to realize that someone was genuinely interested in him, that his thoughts and feelings mattered. Growing up with two physician parents consumed by their careers, Raymond had never experienced true attentiveness or curiosity about his inner world. He had internalized the belief that he was uninteresting, almost devoid of an internal life. The concept of being at the center of someone's undivided attention was entirely foreign to him. But as soon as that channel opened, everything came pouring out like a dam bursting.

Raymond craved more and more, drinking in every word I said with an insatiable thirst. He used to arrive half an hour early, waiting in the waiting room, as if this way he would absorb more of the treatment atmosphere. His behavior reminded me of a man who had wandered the desert for years, suddenly discovering an oasis he couldn't tear himself away from. What struck me most was not just that Raymond felt interesting to me, but that he was beginning to find himself interesting. It was as if he was excavating buried parts of his psyche, unearthing thoughts and emotions long suppressed. In that room, Raymond wasn't just being seen—he was truly seeing himself for perhaps the first time.

The crisis phase

When documenting the crisis phase, it is essential to describe a significant turning point that connects directly to the patient's core distress and past trauma.

In your case write-up, detail the nature of the crisis carefully. While you may describe external events that triggered the crisis, pay particular attention to documenting moments where the crisis emerged from the therapeutic relationship itself. Common examples include the patient's reaction to therapeutic breaks or changes in the therapeutic frame. Be sure to explain how the honeymoon phase's dependent position may have activated the crisis by reawakening original trauma patterns.

When writing about countertransference during the crisis, include specific examples of your emotional reactions and behavioral responses. For instance, you might describe feelings of resistance toward the patient, including concrete manifestations like delayed greetings or schedule adjustments. These details help illuminate the unconscious dynamics at play.

Clinical example

Ofra Eshel (2019) analyzes a crisis in her work. Adam, a doctor who had been in therapy with Eshel for several years, entered a new phase of his treatment when he began caring for an elderly woman with cancer. His deep identification with this patient dramatically changed the nature of his analysis. The struggle for the woman's life—and Adam's complete immersion in it—lasted over a year. During this time, the analysis seemed to lose its meaning, despite Adam's consistent attendance at each session (p. 52).

Eshel felt as though she could only be swept along by the unfolding events, merely present amidst the myriad details of cancer treatments. She sensed that nothing she could say would truly resonate. Eshel questioned whether she was embodying the desperate struggle and paralyzed helplessness of a child seeking comfort from a mother consumed by illness.

Her interpretations increasingly sounded trivial, worthless, and empty—words that failed to connect or resonate, falling into an emotional void. Establishing any meaningful connection, communication, or space for insight and reflection within this analysis seemed impossible. The all-encompassing battle against death left no room for anything else to penetrate or compete. Eventually, Eshel found herself silenced, at a loss for words amid this overwhelming situation.

The therapist's transformation stage

When documenting resolution following a crisis, focus on your own transformative process as a therapist. Describe periods of uncertainty and self-doubt regarding interventions, demonstrating clinical honesty. Detail how supervision helped identify blind spots and understand projective identification dynamics—specifically, which aspects of the patient you unconsciously identified with or avoided.

Show how your growing awareness of these dynamics and countertransference contributed to a therapeutic breakthrough. Include specific examples of how insights shifted your therapeutic stance and impacted treatment outcomes. The emphasis is not on mastery but on documenting how overcoming impasses through self-reflection facilitates patient change.

Clinical example

During my work with Brenda, a patient who had experienced a severe car accident a decade ago, I found myself developing an intense, irrational irritation toward her limp. I caught myself thinking she was exaggerating her disability, convinced she could walk better than she showed the world. These hostile thoughts troubled me deeply, as they contradicted both my professional ethics and the medical evidence of her injury.

In supervision, we explored my unexpected antagonism toward her physical limitation. It emerged that I had unconsciously identified with her mother's invalidating stance—a woman who had consistently minimized Brenda's suffering, telling her to "just walk normally" and "stop seeking attention." I had unwittingly stepped into this dismissive maternal role, internally questioning the authenticity of her disability just as her mother had done.

This realization was transformative. Understanding how deeply I had internalized the role of the invalidating mother figure allowed me to recognize and work through my counter-therapeutic reactions. My journey from hostility to understanding paralleled the acceptance and validation that Brenda had always needed but never received. This insight enabled me to shift from unconsciously perpetuating her trauma to providing the genuine recognition of her experience that was essential for her healing.

The cyclical nature of therapeutic change

The sequence of events is not always as described. Many stages overlap or occur at different points. For example, some begin with a honeymoon phase followed by a crisis, while others start with a crisis and experience the honeymoon phase afterward.

Some treatments lack a honeymoon phase entirely, instead featuring only a slow and gradual development in the patient's ability to integrate and understand through a contemporary object (the therapist).

This process is an ongoing movement that any case study should illustrate: moving closer and farther away, distancing and approaching, experiencing crises and resolutions, encountering stuckness and untangling, and experiencing lows and highs.

Ideally, in the best case studies, each phase continues from what preceded it, with earlier stages hidden within what appears to have replaced them. The challenge is to show that the inner attitudes of the patient and therapist toward each other do not magically disappear. Rather than simply replacing an unfavorable position with a positive one, it is necessary to demonstrate that the negative position remains, but the overall mix changes.

Case studies evolving through interpretations

In Kleinian and object relations case studies, the narrative focuses on the patient's gradual acceptance of their psychic reality through interpretation. Initially, patients often resist interpretations using various defenses such as intellectualization, denial, or attempts to control the therapeutic process. The treatment evolves through small shifts as patients slowly begin to tolerate more psychic pain and insight. The therapist consistently engages in interpretative work while observing how patients attempt to influence the analyst's thoughts and feelings. Progress typically emerges slowly after long periods of resistance.

When writing such cases, emphasize:

- Initial defensive responses to interpretations
- The persistence of resistance and cycles of progress and regression

- How therapeutic work continues despite minimal visible change
- The gradual nature of progress, which appears only after extended periods
- The importance of maintaining an interpretative stance through resistance.

The case should demonstrate how meaningful change emerges from prolonged periods of apparent stagnation, reflecting the demanding reality of interpretative work.

Clinical example of a case study evolving through interpretations

Betty Joseph's case of Mr. A (1992) offers a richly detailed illustration of how psychic change unfolds through sustained analytic work. This case highlights the slow, often difficult process of transformation in a patient with rigid defensive structures.

In the case, Mr. A, a rigid obsessional man in his mid-thirties, entered analysis following severe anxiety and depression triggered by rejection from a female colleague. He exhibited a narcissistic, omnipotent worldview, perceiving others, including the analyst, as inferior and limited. Despite professional success, his personal life was notably constricted, featuring few friends (mostly "lame ducks" dependent on him) and an impoverished marital relationship marked by unusual sexual dynamics. Significantly, Mr. A failed to recognize these limitations, viewing them merely as personal choices rather than symptoms of emotional difficulty.

The case material focuses on sessions that occurred several years into the analysis when changes were becoming apparent. During this period, two significant dreams emerged that revealed the shifting internal landscape of the patient. First, he dreamed of a crumbling, collapsing house, and in a subsequent session, he dreamed of carrying books down a spiral staircase, discovering that one valuable book (later revealed as "The Fatal Conceit") had gone missing. These dreams symbolized Mr. A's growing anxiety as his omnipotent defenses began to weaken. He experienced the analyst as "stealing" something precious—his defensive omnipotence—leaving him vulnerable to uncomfortable feelings he had long avoided.

The process of change for Mr. A was marked by several significant developments. He gradually began to recognize his oscillation between arrogance and anxiety, eventually stating that "now he could see that ordinarily he was either in an arrogant state or full of anxiety." As analysis progressed, his relationship with the analyst revealed competing feelings: appreciation for being understood, alongside rivalry and paranoia about being "outwitted" or controlled. When he remembered the title of the missing book as "The Fatal Conceit," it demonstrated his unconscious recognition of how his grandiosity was both protective and ultimately destructive to his well-being and relationships.

Joseph describes the theoretical movement as a shift from a paranoid-schizoid position toward a depressive position, with an emerging capacity for concern and recognition of whole objects. Mr. A began developing an observing part of himself that could collaborate with the analyst while another part remained in his habitual defensive position. This split enabled him to gradually integrate previously disowned aspects of his experience.

Perhaps most importantly, Joseph's presentation emphasizes the gradual nature of change, showcasing that significant transformation requires years of consistent work to shift entrenched defensive structures. Rather than summarizing outcomes, she focuses on the subtle shifts occurring within sessions, including atmosphere and emotional tone. This attention to the moment-to-moment process is characteristic of the Kleinian approach to case study.

The case illustrates that lasting psychic change isn't achieved through mere cognitive understanding but through experiencing anxieties within the transference relationship, where they can be gradually recognized and tolerated. For Mr. A, this meant the slow, painful realization of his dependence on omnipotence, the costs of this defense, and the gradual emergence of more authentic relatedness despite strong resistance to change. It demonstrates that even in extremely rigid personalities, persistent analytic work can foster meaningful transformation through consistent attention to the transference and countertransference experience.

THE TERMINATION PHASE

A case is like an hourglass. Its entire system is built on the anticipation of an ending. In an interview with "The Paris Review", Sam Shepard (1997) expressed the difficulty with endings: "I hate endings. Just detest them. Beginnings are definitely the most exciting, middles are perplexing and endings are a disaster."

Shepard's disdain for endings reflects a broader unease with the notion of definitive conclusions, particularly in creative and exploratory processes. This reluctance resonates deeply with the complexities of psychodynamic treatment, where progress is often subtle, nonlinear, and difficult to quantify.

In the next chapter, which details case studies across different psychoanalytic schools, I describe the termination phase according to each psychoanalytic school. Here, I describe the general challenges clinicians face when describing the end of psychotherapy beyond the various approaches.

Excerpts from endings of three canonical case studies

We should not be justified in expecting such severe obsessional ideas as were present in this case to be cleared up in any simpler manner or by any other means. When we reached the solution that has been described above, the patient's rat delirium disappeared.

Sigmund Freud, 1909, The Rat Man, p. 220.

This hopefulness, and his ability to maintain a good relation to the analyst as an internal and external object, in spite of resentment, feeling of loss, and great anxiety, confirm my view that as the result of his analysis the good internal object was much more securely established in Richard; and this greater inner security reflected the ascendancy of the life instinct. It is my impression that the changes produced by this incomplete analysis were to some extent lasting.

Melanie Klein, 1961, Narrative of a Child Analysis, p. 466.

Via another informant I have learned a good deal about the personality of the woman whom Mr Z married. She appears to be a well-balanced, warm-hearted, socially outgoing person, without a trace of the paranoid certainty and need to control that had characterized Mr Z's mother. Even though she works in Mr Z's field, she is more what one might call an out-of-doors type than an intellectual. I concluded that Mr Z had chosen a partner who possessed his father's best features embedded in a matrix of femininity. And I concluded that he had made a good choice.

Heinz Kohut, 1979, The Two Analyses of Mr Z, p. 25.

These case study conclusions by Freud, Klein, and Kohut illustrate different conceptions of therapeutic success and contribute to the myth that treatments must have a successful ending.

These conclusions reinforce the notion that psychoanalytic treatments should have positive outcomes, whether through symptom relief, internal psychological changes, or improved life circumstances. However, this emphasis on successful endings may create unrealistic expectations and overlook the complex, ongoing nature of psychological growth and change

Myths and realities of termination

The difficulty lies in confronting the myths that have evolved in psychoanalytic literature regarding the end of treatment. While professional literature often describes ideal termination scenarios, there is typically a gap between these descriptions and actual practice. Analysts frequently write about treatment in ways that do not mirror their real-life methods (Gabbard, 2015).

According to Kantrowitz (2015), some literature on termination, often simplified in teaching, has unintentionally fostered myths about how analyses conclude. These myths create expectations for how analyses should end, potentially setting unrealistic goals and encouraging fantasies of completion that can negatively impact the individual patient's process.

Authors must grapple with these expectations while resisting the temptation to conform to them artificially. They must have the courage to present terminations that don't fit the standard narrative—cases where, for example, the ending is straightforward, and patients feel relief rather than grief, or growth continues unimpeded throughout the termination phase.

Non-mutual endings

Psychotherapists rarely document treatments that ended non-mutually, despite their educational value. According to Kantrowitz (2015), this reluctance stems from viewing such endings as failures, challenging professional competence. The psychoanalytic emphasis on "complete" analysis and fears of professional scrutiny further discourage documenting these cases.

Non-mutual endings often evoke unresolved countertransference and raise confidentiality concerns. However, excluding these cases from literature limits professional learning about the complexities of therapeutic relationships and leaves new therapists underprepared for such challenges.

Thoughts on writing treatment endings

The termination phase of a psychodynamic case study presents unique challenges, particularly in conveying both the resolution of therapeutic work and the inevitable feelings of loss that accompany endings.

Consider these nuanced approaches to writing about termination:

- Write authentically about the reason for ending—whether it's practical (relocation, financial constraints), clinical (achievement of therapeutic goals, reaching a natural plateau), or relational (impasse, boundary issues). Each type of ending carries its own psychological weight and meaning that should be carefully articulated.
- When describing the emotional texture of endings, resist the temptation to impose the traditional grief-work model. Not all patients experience the classical stages of mourning—some feel relief, others maintain emotional distance, and many experience complex, ambivalent reactions that don't fit neat categories. Honor the patient's authentic response rather than forcing their experience into predetermined templates.
- Pay attention to the timing and pacing of the ending. Was it gradual or abrupt? Planned or unexpected? Mutual or unilateral? The temporal dimension of termination often reveals crucial dynamics about attachment, separation, and agency in the therapeutic relationship.
- Consider how institutional contexts shape endings. Terminations in training clinics, time-limited treatments, or insurance-constrained settings each present unique challenges that deserve careful discussion. These external factors often interact in complex ways with internal psychological processes.
- When writing about "successful" endings, beware of triumphalist narratives that overstate therapeutic achievements. Similarly, resist defensive self-justification and excessive self-criticism when describing premature or difficult endings. Instead, aim for a nuanced exploration of the complex interplay between patient and therapist and the circumstances that led to termination.
- Remember that endings often illuminate core dynamics that were present throughout the treatment. Use the termination narrative to highlight these patterns while remaining true to the actual clinical experience rather than conforming to theoretical expectations about how endings "should" unfold.

Presenting the treatment achievements in a nuanced way

In the introduction to Marion Milner's book "The Hands of the Living God," Adam Phillips (2010) describes a conversation with Milner about her treatment of a patient named Susan:

> Towards the end of her life I would sometimes go on a Saturday afternoon to talk with Marion Milner, and to drink whiskey . . . But once in these conversations I asked her about Susan, about whether she thought the analysis had worked. "Of course she never got better," she said briskly, and there was a pause. And then she said, "but we got somewhere, she got somewhere," and there was another pause, and she said, "better."

Phillips writes in "The Hands of the Living God" that Milner never takes for granted what it would be for Susan to be better. It is, that is to say, a work of (modern) literature, not of propaganda. There's something in Milner's response that I deeply love, that makes me return to these lines again and again. When she says "we got somewhere, she got somewhere," she captures something so honest about therapeutic work. The simplicity of her words masks their profound insight—she's not claiming dramatic transformation or complete resolution, just movement, just "somewhere." I find myself drawn to how she acknowledges both the shared journey ("we") and the patient's individual path ("she"), while avoiding any grandiose claims about arrival at a particular destination. The beauty lies in her recognition that therapeutic progress isn't about reaching predetermined goals, but about movement itself—sometimes subtle, sometimes significant, but always uniquely personal. Her words remind me that our work isn't about "fixing" or achieving specific outcomes, but about accompanying patients on their journey toward their own "somewhere."

Many cases in the literature reflect idealizing endings, and there is a need for not-so-perfect cases. On the other hand, I completely understand that if you're selecting a case to graduate and be certified, you'll probably choose one with a "successful ending" —and why shouldn't you? You naturally want to highlight your achievements and hope your work impresses the reader. However, writing the conclusion will present a considerable challenge for you. When presenting achievements in psychoanalysis, it's crucial to remember that different psychoanalytic approaches conceptualize success in varying ways. Not all approaches consider symptom reduction as a central goal of treatment. For instance, Klein and Bion believe that what's important is improvement in the thinking apparatus—that is, the ability to tolerate frustrations, hold unwanted parts of the self, and reduce projections of undesirable aspects, among other things. Sometimes this process may actually increase psychological distress rather than diminish it. Summer, Barber, and Zilcha-Mano (2024) think it's crucial to look beyond mere symptom reduction and focus on broader indicators of psychological growth and adaptation.

KEY CONSIDERATIONS FOR PRESENTING ACHIEVEMENTS

1. Evolution of defense mechanisms: has the patient developed healthier, more flexible, and more effective ways of coping with stress and conflict?
2. Sense of agency: does the patient experience a greater sense of inner freedom and autonomy in their decision-making and self-expression?
3. Adaptability: has the patient's ability to adapt to various life situations improved?
4. Specific therapeutic goals: for instance, has an obsessional patient developed more adaptive thought patterns? Has a trauma survivor gained a stronger sense of empowerment and self-assurance?
5. Overall mental health: has there been a holistic improvement in the patient's psychological wellbeing?
6. Can the patient feel free to explore and reflect upon what is going on in his mind?

Clinical example: A balanced description of therapeutic achievements

When Eliza, a 52-year-old tenured academic, first came to see me, she was struggling with persistent feelings of inadequacy and a clear pattern of self-sabotage, both in her career and personal life. Despite her many achievements, procrastination and workplace conflicts repeatedly undermined her success. In her private life, she had never married and described a string of intense but short-lived relationships, each ending when intimacy became too close for comfort.

Over the course of four years together, I helped Eliza explore the powerful but often punitive internal voices she carried from childhood. As the eldest child of ambitious immigrant parents, she had learned to pursue excellence, yet always felt she fell short. Her relationships with men echoed emotional dynamics with her critical, distant father, while her self-sabotage seemed to reflect unconscious loyalty to her mother, who had abandoned her own professional dreams for the family.

During therapy, Eliza became increasingly able to recognize how she re-enacted these childhood dynamics as patterns in her present-day relationships, both at work and in romance. Yet, despite these insights, she often found it difficult to feel genuine pride in her accomplishments. She habitually returned to self-criticism, retreating to the safety of old, familiar patterns.

A breakthrough arrived unexpectedly after she was passed over for a major research grant. Rather than succumbing to self-recrimination, as she had in the past, she surprised both of us with her resilience. This response seemed to embolden her: she began to take creative risks in her research and sought out new collaborations that previously would have felt threatening.

In her personal life, Eliza started a relationship with a supportive partner who challenged many of her entrenched expectations. While she still experienced urges to pull away when intimacy deepened, she was more aware of these tendencies and sometimes managed to resist them.

As therapy moved toward termination, my own feelings were mixed. I was proud of Eliza's growth but wondered if more time would help her further integrate these changes. We spoke openly about these feelings. Eliza said, "I'm not 'fixed,' but I feel more myself—like I'm finally steering the ship, even if I'm not sure where I'm headed."

When therapy ended, our parting was bittersweet, marked by gratitude and an acknowledgment that some struggles remained. Months later, Eliza emailed to share that she had presented at a conference and genuinely enjoyed the experience—free, for once, from paralyzing self-doubt. Her journey illustrates the nonlinear, realistic nature of change at the end of therapy: progress, alongside ongoing work.

The key is to present these dramatic successes with the same clinical rigor and honesty that applied to more modest outcomes and failures. Document the process, acknowledge the complexities, and let the depth of change speak for itself without apologetic disclaimers or defensive justifications.

THE DISCUSSION SECTION

In a psychodynamic case study, the discussion section plays a critical role in synthesizing and interpreting the findings presented in the earlier sections, such as background history, the psychodynamic formulation, and the course of treatment.

The discussion should contain several key elements:

1. Integration of findings: the discussion should integrate the various elements of the case study, drawing connections between the patient's history, symptoms, therapeutic process, and outcomes.
2. Interpretation of data: analyze patient's unconscious processes, defense mechanisms, and transference patterns, grounding interpretation in psychodynamic theory.

3. Evaluation of treatment: assess therapeutic interventions, their impact, successes and limitations.
4. Transference and countertransference analysis: examine the evolution of transferential patterns, resistance manifestations, and therapist's countertransference responses. Consider how these dynamics influenced treatment course and outcomes.
5. Comparison with literature: compare findings with existing literature to contextualize the case within psychodynamic theory and practice.

GUIDELINES FOR DISCUSSION SECTION

- Writing style:
    - Use clear, accessible language
    - Avoid jargon and complex sentences
    - Ensure logical flow between sections

Use effective transitions.

- Theory-case integration:
    - Demonstrate how case material illustrates theoretical concepts
    - Show how theory helps understand patient dynamics
    - Connect clinical observations to theoretical frameworks
    - Use case examples to challenge or expand theoretical understanding

Highlight where case diverges from theoretical expectations.

- Structure:
    - Build arguments progressively
    - Connect paragraphs logically
    - Balance theoretical discussion with clinical material

Integrate research findings with case observations.

Example of discussion section

The treatment of Debbie highlights the intricate interplay between early object relations and adult attachment patterns. Her presenting symptoms of chronic emptiness and volatile interpersonal relationships, initially conceptualized through a borderline personality organization framework, revealed a more nuanced etiology as therapy progressed. The emergence of a fragmented self-structure, rooted in early experiences of maternal inconsistency and paternal absence, manifested in therapy through a complex transference-countertransference matrix.

Debbie's tendency to oscillate between idealization and devaluation of the therapist mirrored her early attachment experiences, providing a live demonstration of her internal object relations. This dynamic became particularly evident in the third month of treatment when Debbie abruptly canceled several sessions following a period of perceived closeness. The subsequent exploration of this rupture yielded significant insights into her fear of intimacy and unconscious belief that emotional connection inevitably leads to abandonment.

A pivotal moment in therapy occurred when interpreting Debbie's projection of "badness" onto others, including the therapist. This intervention, grounded in Klein's concept of projective identification (1952), facilitated a gradual integration of split-off aspects of her self-representation. Debbie's growing capacity to tolerate ambivalence marked a shift from paranoid-schizoid functioning to a more depressive position, as evidenced by her increased ability to maintain object constancy during periods of separation.

The treatment's emphasis on containment and mentalization, drawing from Bion's theory of maternal reverie and Fonagy's work on reflective functioning, proved instrumental in fostering Debbie's capacity for affect regulation. As therapy progressed, her use of primitive defenses such as splitting and projective identification diminished, giving way to more mature mechanisms like sublimation and humor.

Countertransferentially, I found myself alternating between feelings of maternal protectiveness and frustrated helplessness, mirroring early relational experiences. Recognizing this parallel process enhanced my understanding of Debbie's internal world and informed my interventions, particularly in moments of enactment.

While the case supports the efficacy of long-term psychodynamic psychotherapy for personality disorders, it also highlights the need for flexibility in technique. The integration of supportive elements alongside classic interpretive work proved crucial in navigating periods of regression and fostering ego strength.

WRITING A PSYCHODYNAMIC CASE REPORT FOR CHILD PATIENTS

Although the book primarily addresses the writing of case reports for adult patients, I would like to highlight several key points particularly relevant to writing psychodynamic case reports for children. Writing psychodynamic case studies for child patients requires a unique sensibility. When documenting our therapeutic journey with a child, we must weave together multiple threads of observation, interpretation, and understanding to capture the child's inner world and distinctive modes of communication.

Unlike adult case reports, which rely heavily on the patient's verbal expressions and conscious reflections, child case studies must skillfully integrate observations of play, movement, non-verbal behavior, and the shifting qualities of the therapeutic relationship itself. The writer must maintain a nuanced interplay between detailed behavioral descriptions and psychodynamic understanding, always remembering that in child therapy, action often speaks louder than words.

The narrative should begin by painting a vivid picture of the child's initial presentation—not just their symptoms and history, but their way of being in the room, their manner of play, their use of space, and their early ways of relating to the therapist. This requires a kind of "double vision" where we describe both the manifest behavior and its potential symbolic meaning while remaining humble about our interpretations.

The writer must also capture the intricate movement between interpretation and response that characterizes child therapy. Unlike adult cases where interpretations often lead to verbal elaboration, children's responses may emerge through changes in play, new behavioral patterns, or subtle shifts in relating. This requires us to document what we said and how the child metabolized our interventions through their preferred modes of expression.

Additionally, the role of the body and movement is of special significance in child case reports. Careful attention must be paid to documenting patterns of physical activity, tension and release, approach and avoidance, and how the child uses their body to express what cannot yet be put into words. This somatic dimension often provides crucial clues to the child's internal state and defensive organization.

The case report should also address the parallel process of working with parents, as this forms an essential context for the child's treatment. However, this material should be integrated in a way that maintains the primary focus on the child's therapeutic process while acknowledging how parental dynamics influence the clinical picture.

Finally, remember that writing about child therapy requires us to maintain contact with our capacity for play and imagination. The case should convey both clinical rigor and a sense of genuine engagement with the child's unique way of being in the world. This often means finding creative ways to describe play sequences, symbolic communications, and the subtle shifts in the therapeutic relationship that mark progress in child treatment.

By maintaining these sensibilities while writing, we can create case reports that do justice to the complexity and richness of child psychotherapy while providing valuable clinical insights for our colleagues in the field.

Key elements in writing child case studies

Physical environment: document how children transform the therapeutic space through play, territorial marking, and symbolic use of materials. The therapeutic space is not merely a passive container but a dynamic arena that is dialectically shaped with the child. The way a child organizes, deconstructs, and alters the therapeutic space often reflects the internal architecture of their world, providing a concrete expression of psychic states that are not yet accessible to verbal symbolization.

Non-verbal communication: track patterns of movement, gestures, spatial relationships, and changes in vocal tone and bodily tension. The body, as a primary medium of communication, precedes words in human development and preserves the essence of pre-verbal experiences. Within child psychotherapy, the bodily narrative offers a rich and authentic channel for observing the movement between states of integration and fragmentation, and between somatic aspects of attachment, anxiety, and emotional regulation.

Play development: follow the evolution of symbolic themes, conflicts, and solutions in play narratives. The potential space of play allows the child to process and transform traumatic experiences into narratives that can be controlled and managed. It is important to document not only the content of the play but also its formal qualities—the degree of flexibility, richness of imagination, narrative coherence, and the ability to shift dialectically between contrasting experiences—as indicators of psychological growth.

Interpretations: document timing, impact, and responses, both immediate and delayed. Interpretation in working with children is not simply a cognitive act but an emotional-relational intervention that occurs in the intersubjective space. Sensitivity to the timing, depth, and formulation of the interpretation reflects clinical intuition regarding the balance point between containing anxiety and exposing unconscious content that the child is capable of integrating.

Countertransference: utilize emotional responses as diagnostic tools, noting resulting actions and response patterns. Countertransference with children is often characterized by unique emotional intensity, stemming from the force of primitive projections and split self-states that children activate. The therapist becomes a container that processes split or disavowed identities, and precise monitoring of their internal responses offers a map for understanding the child's intrapsychic and interpersonal dynamics.

Development: addressing developmental challenges relevant to the child's specific stage illuminates the interaction between universal psychic forces and the unique biography of the patient.

Working with parents: engaging with parents exists in dialectical tension between recognizing their critical role as shapers of the child's emotional environment and maintaining the private, autonomous space of therapy. Nuanced documentation of how parental dynamics reverberate in the therapy room, alongside the conceptualization of integrated parental interventions, reflects the complexity of working in a systemic context while preserving the therapeutic alliance with the child.

RECOMMENDED READING

Psychoanalytic diagnosis, by Nancy McWilliams. Guilford Press, 2011.

The book "Psychoanalytic Diagnosis" by Nancy McWilliams is an essential resource for clinicians, as it provides a comprehensive overview of the application of psychoanalytic findings to character formation, personality disorders, and their implications for treatment. The text is structured in two parts—the first outlining the theoretical assumptions and psychoanalytic concepts that inform the diagnostic process, and the second describing the key personality disorders, their features, and the therapeutic considerations.

Psychodynamic formulation, by Deborah L. Cabaniss, Sabrina Cherry, Carolyn J. Douglas, Ruth L. Graver, and Anna R. Schwartz. Wiley-Blackwell, 2013.

This book provides a much-needed resource for mental health professionals, as it offers a structured approach to developing psychodynamic formulations. By integrating psychodynamic theory with considerations of genetics, trauma, and cognitive-emotional difficulties, the book equips clinicians with a comprehensive framework for generating effective psychodynamic formulations.

Stations along the via dolorosa towards good-enough endings, by Alina Schellekes. *American Journal of Psychoanalysis, 84,* 94–110, 2024.

This article examines the complexity of therapeutic endings, exposing the illusion of the "good-enough termination" and identifying psychological obstacles that affect both the patient and the analyst. It offers valuable insights for clinicians writing psychodynamic case studies by highlighting how our myths about endings shape clinical narratives and influence the documentation of the therapeutic journey.

Psychodynamic therapy: A guide to evidence-based practice (2nd ed.), by Richard F. Summers, Jacques P. Barber and Sigal Zilcha-Mano. Guilford Press, 2024.

This book advocates for personalized psychodynamic therapy adapted to individual needs, incorporating new insights from research, telepsychotherapy, and the acknowledgment of social determinants of mental health. It is essential for case study writers, providing over 40 diverse clinical examples that detail various treatment stages and therapeutic goals, serving as a comprehensive guide to crafting nuanced and culturally sensitive psychodynamic case studies.

Clinical case studies in psychoanalytic and psychodynamic treatment, by Jochem Willemsen, Elena Della Rosa, and Sue Kegerreis. *Frontiers in Psychology, 8*, 108. doi: 10.3389/fpsyg.2017.00108 2017

This paper is essential reading for anyone looking to construct a case study while adhering to a more scientific approach. It provides valuable information on the key components of a case study from a scientific perspective.

Clinical psychoanalytic case studies with complex patients: Watching experience at work, edited by Anne Zachary. Routledge, 2024.

This book presents a collection of psychoanalytic case studies that focus on working with complex and disturbed patients in various clinical contexts. Through detailed case presentations and vignettes organized into six thematic sections, it explores challenging clinical situations, including autism, violence, perversion, psychosomatics, hysteria, dementia, psychosis, and gender dysphoria. Each case examines critical aspects of psychoanalytic treatment, such as risk assessment, setting boundaries, and preliminary clinical considerations.

Case studies in child and adolescent psychoanalysis: Treating trauma, anxiety and aggression, edited by Christel Airas, translated by Kristiina Jalas. Routledge, 2024.

This collection provides a unique, unhindered view into the therapeutic process, showcasing the diverse ways children express their experiences through play, drawings, and dialogue within the safe and supportive context of the analytic setting.

Clinician's thesaurus: The guide to conducting interviews and writing psychological reports (7th ed.), by Edward L. Zuckerman. Guilford Press, 2010.

While not specifically focused on psychodynamic case studies, it provides a comprehensive overview of how psychological reports should be structured and written.

REFERENCES

Airas, C. (Ed.). (2024). *Case studies in child and adolescent psychoanalysis: Treating trauma, anxiety and aggression* (K. Jalas, Trans.). Routledge.

Alvarez, A. (1992). *Live Company: Psychoanalytic psychotherapy with autistic, borderline, deprived and abused children*. Routledge.

Cabaniss, D. L., Cherry, S., Douglas, C. J., Graver, R. L., & Schwartz, A. R. (2013). *Psychodynamic Formulation*. Guilford Press.

Eshel, O. (2019*). The Emergence of Analytic Oneness: Into the Heart of Psychoanalysis*. Routledge.

Forrester, J. (2017). *Thinking in cases*. Polity Press.

Gabbard, G. O. (2015). Foreword. In J. L. Kantrowitz, *Myths of Termination: What patients can teach psychoanalysts about endings* (pp. xiii–xv). Routledge.

Joseph, B. (1959). An Aspect of the Repetition Compulsion. *International Journal of Psychoanalysis, 40*, 213–222.

Joseph, B. (1992). Psychic Change: Some Perspectives. *International Journal of Psychoanalysis, 73*, 237–243.

Kantrowitz, J. L. (2015). *Myths of Termination: What patients can teach psychoanalysts about endings*. Routledge.

Klein, M. (1952). The origins of transference. In *The Writings of Melanie Klein*, Vol. 3. Hogarth Press, 1975, pp. 48–56.

Klein, M. (1961). *Narrative of a Child Analysis: The Conduct of the Psycho-Analysis of Children as seen in the Treatment of a Ten year old Boy*. Hogarth Press.

Kohut, H. (1979). The Two Analyses of Mr Z. *International Journal of Psychoanalysis, 60*, 3–27.

Milner, M. (2010). *The hands of the living God: An account of a psycho-analytic treatment*. Routledge.

McWilliams, N. (2011*). Psychoanalytic diagnosis: Understanding personality structure in the clinical process (2nd ed.)*. Guilford Press.

Parsons, M. (1999). The logic of play in psychoanalysis. *International Journal of Psychoanalysis, 80*(5), 871–884.

Phillips, A. (2010). Introduction. In M. Milner, *The hands of the living god: An account of a psycho-analytic treatment* (pp. xviii–xxxv). Routledge.

Rubin, M. (2025). Calamities and secrets, the power of the fetish. *Psychoanalytic Dialogues, 35*(2), 106–120.

Schellekes A. (2024). Stations Along the Via Dolorosa Towards Good-Enough Endings. *American journal of psychoanalysis, 84*(1), 94–110. https://doi.org/10.1057/s11231-024-09432-2

Shepard, S. (1997). The art of theater no. 12 (J. Lahr, Interviewer). *The Paris Review*, (147), Fall.

Stoller, R. J. (1986). *Sexual Excitement: The dynamic of erotic life*. Karnac Books.

Summers, R. F., Barber, J. P., & Zilcha-Mano, S. (2024). *Psychodynamic Therapy: A Guide to Evidence-Based Practice (2nd ed.)*. Guilford Press.

Willemsen, J., Della Rosa, E., & Kegerreis, S. (2017). Clinical Case Studies in Psychoanalytic and Psychodynamic Treatment. *Frontiers in Psychology, 8*, 108.

Winnicott, D.W. (1954). Metapsychological and clinical aspects of regression within the psycho-analytical set-up. In *Through Pediatrics to Psycho-Analysis: Collected Papers* (pp. 278–294). Karnac Books, 1992.

Winnicott, C. (1980). Fear of Breakdown: A Clinical Example. *International Journal of Psychoanalysis, 61*, 351–357.

Winnicott, D. W. (1986). *Holding and interpretation: Fragment of an analysis*. Hogarth.

Wolf, E. S. (1994). Varieties of Disorders of the Self. *British Journal of Psychotherapy, 11*(2), 198–208.

Zachary, A. (Ed.). (2023). *Clinical Psychoanalytic Case Studies with Complex Patients: Watching Experience at Work (1st ed.)*. Routledge. https://doi.org/10.4324/9781003202790

Zuckerman, E. L. (2010). *Clinician's thesaurus: The guide to conducting interviews and writing psychological reports* (7th ed.). Guilford Press.

CHAPTER 4

The therapist as storyteller

Weaving clinical wisdom into narrative art

....

Through the exploration of various narrative techniques and stylistic approaches, this chapter provides practical guidance on bringing your clinical work to life on the page, helping clinicians develop their voices as writers while honoring the profound nature of the therapeutic relationships they are documenting.

NARRATION

Whether the analyst is an orthodox psychoanalyst who rarely emphasizes his or her subjectivity or a relational therapist who conveys his emotions, the therapist must use the first and third person singular, or, in rare cases, first person plural and second person plural. That is it—no more options. Which to choose? Which is more reliable? Which is more engaging?

As exemplified by Melanie Klein's work on Richard, traditional psychoanalytic case studies often lean heavily on third-person narration. Klein's approach, referring to herself as "Mrs. K," creates a sense of objectivity and detachment.

Consider this excerpt from her "Narrative of a Child Analysis" (1961):

> Richard appeared worried and did not seem to listen. He looked at Mrs K.'s clock. Mrs K. asked whether this meant that he wished to go. Richard agreed but said he would not go before his time was up. He went to urinate. (p. 41)

This style can create a sense of clinical objectivity, as if the therapist is a mere observer. However, it can also distance the reader from the immediacy of the therapeutic encounter, potentially reducing empathy and engagement with both the patient and the therapist's experiences. Even during Melanie Klein's era, few clinicians wrote this way.

DOI: 10.4324/9781003538578-6

In contrast, Winnicott's narration in "Holding and Interpretation" (1986) is primarily in the third person, referring to the patient as "he" throughout the case study. This creates a sense of clinical detachment and objectivity in the narrative. However, Winnicott occasionally shifts to first person when describing his thoughts or interpretations, using "I" to convey his direct involvement in the analytic process. This interplay between third- and first-person narration gives the reader a dual perspective—both an external view of the patient's behavior and an internal glimpse into the analyst's reasoning.

Most case studies, including Freud's cases, use first- and third-person narration. This approach can create a more intimate connection with the reader.

This first-person style allows the therapist to share personal observations and interpretations directly, drawing the reader into a confidant-like relationship. It often conveys a sense of the therapist as an omniscient narrator, privy to insights about the patient that even the patient may not possess.

Direct quotes or third-person narration?

Another decision you'll face is whether to include direct quotes from your patient. While not all therapists choose to do this—some, particularly those from the Kleinian tradition, still prefer to write about patients entirely in the third person—it's become increasingly common and can add immediacy and authenticity to your written case.

In the following example, consider the reader's experience when they read a description in the direct quote versus when they read a description in the third person.

Direct quote:

Tom slammed his fist on the armrest of the chair. "Why can't they just leave me alone?" he shouted. "I'm sick of their constant nagging. It's like they think I'm still a child!"

Third-person description:

Tom expressed his frustration physically by hitting the chair's armrest. He vocalized his anger towards unnamed individuals, complaining about their persistent interference in his life. Tom conveyed feeling infantilized by their behavior, suggesting ongoing conflicts related to his autonomy and maturity.

Direct quotes create an intimate connection between the reader and the patient. They bring immediacy and raw authenticity to the case, helping readers feel as if they are present in the therapy room.

Third-person narration offers more analytical distance and allows the therapist to integrate their clinical observations with the patient's experience. This approach provides space for professional interpretation and can help maintain appropriate boundaries between the clinical material and the reader.

In practice, many modern case studies effectively combine both approaches, using direct quotes to illustrate key moments while embedding them within broader third-person clinical observations and analysis.

Tenses

The use of tense in case studies is an important stylistic choice that affects how the clinical material is experienced by both the writer and the reader. The present tense creates immediacy and dramatic tension that draws the reader into the emotional reality of the therapeutic encounter. It can make the clinical material feel more alive and immediate, as if it is unfolding before our eyes. This can be particularly effective when describing pivotal moments or emotional breakthroughs.

The past tense provides a sense of perspective and reflection that can be valuable in clinical writing. It acknowledges that we are looking back at events that have already occurred and been processed, allowing for more analytical distance. This can be helpful when we want to emphasize our understanding of patterns that emerged over time or when discussing the long-term significance of particular interventions.

In practice, many contemporary case studies effectively combine both tenses—using the past tense for background information and context, while shifting to the present tense for key scenes or moments we want to highlight. This creates a dynamic narrative that can both engage readers emotionally and maintain analytical clarity.

Example: Past tense:

Sarah came to therapy following her mother's death. During our first sessions, she sat rigidly in the chair, her hands tightly clasped in her lap. When she spoke about her mother, her voice remained steady, but tears rolled silently down her cheeks.

Example: Present tense:

Sarah comes to therapy following her mother's death. During our first sessions, she sits rigidly in the chair, her hands tightly clasped in her lap. When she speaks about her mother, her voice remains steady, but tears roll silently down her cheeks.

Example: Mixed tenses:

Sarah came to therapy following her mother's death. I remember being struck by her composure during those first sessions—even now, as I write about our work together, I can see her sitting rigidly in the chair. In our fourth session, she tells me about cleaning out her mother's closet, and as she speaks, the controlled facade begins to crack.

The present tense makes us feel like witnesses to a live event, while the past tense positions us more as thoughtful observers of something that has already occurred and can be analyzed.

Mixed tenses allow for layered storytelling that captures both the immediacy of therapeutic moments and the reflective distance of clinical understanding.

Profanity, dirty talk

Freud's recommendation for patients to speak freely through free association inevitably leads to content that isn't always "polite" or "clean": vulgarities, explicit sexual fantasies, uncensored erotic dreams, and other provocative material. Over psychoanalysis' century-long history, therapy sessions have undoubtedly included plenty of such raw, unfiltered content.

Yet, when reading psychodynamic case studies, we typically encounter a very different language: professional, dignified, and relatively sanitized, stripped of the vulgarities and bluntness heard in the therapy room. This reflects a deliberate choice by therapist-authors to prioritize literary sensitivity and reader comfort over absolute fidelity to the original therapeutic material.

While therapists' clinical ears can tolerate hearing anything, exposing the text to the public proves far more sensitive. Therapists often hesitate to document patients' exact vulgar language, even when it holds clinical significance. I once worked with a patient who repeatedly said, "I want to fuck you" during free association. While I discussed this openly in supervision, I avoided writing about it for years due to deep discomfort.

This avoidance isn't just about protecting patients; it's about protecting ourselves. Therapists often feel shame when exposing the excess parts of their own psyche stirred by patients' material. Writing about violent sexual fantasies or crude language risks inviting judgment about how we contain such content without judgment. There's also fear that readers might misinterpret explicit language as evidence of therapeutic failure ("If the patient speaks this way, did the therapist encourage it?").

NAVIGATING THE TENSION

1. **Acknowledge the discomfort**: authenticity in clinical work requires sitting with all parts of the self—including the "dirty" ones. Rather than hiding shame, name it. For example: *"I've chosen to quote the patient's harsh words verbatim because their raw lack of restraint revealed the emotional barriers at play."*

2. **Contextualize, don't sensationalize**: follow Winnicott's model: when describing erotic material, link it to attachment patterns or relational dynamics, not just shock value.

3. **Relational transparency**: adopt a *relational approach*: include explicit content only when it serves clinical insight. Explaining *why* certain language matters. For instance: *"The patient's repeated use of 'fuck' mirrored their need to articulate longing—a linguistic sign that became central to our work."*

Omniscience

Patrick Casement (2019) wrote: "In no other relationship can it be said that it is healthy to have one person intruding into the mind of another" (p. 120). He cites a patient who told him about her experience with her analyst:

> I felt violated by that woman. She seemed to think that she had the right to walk into my mind, without permission or invitation, *and she did not even remove her shoes*. (p. 120)

Casement wrote this to caution therapists against imposing an all-knowing stance on the patient that would leave no room for critical thinking and resistance. However, one could argue that every written case does precisely this: the therapist adopts, at least in significant portions of the case, an omniscient position. There is no written case where the therapist does not allow themselves to enter the patient's mind and treat it as their own domain. They report on how the patient responded to the therapist's subjectivity as if they fully know and understand it. While therapy may involve two-person psychology, only one person writes the case.

This omniscient stance, while potentially problematic, is necessary for writing cases.

In fact, this is also the contract between the author and the reader. The reader asks the writer: what do you know about the patient's mind? The clinician-writer willingly and gladly answers this question: I know a great deal.

Creating coherent narratives of the therapeutic process would be virtually impossible without an omniscient stance.

The paradox lies in how we consume these clinical narratives. The art of case writing attempts to establish that the therapist is at once an interpreter of minds and a mere witness. An interpreter because they perceive so much, so deeply; a witness because they present their insights as natural observations that any skilled clinician would make.

Yet this literary sleight of hand, while necessary for the genre, demands awareness. Like the novelist who shapes their characters' thoughts while pretending merely to observe them, the case writer must acknowledge their role as both witness and creator. The solution lies not in abandoning the omniscient stance—for without it, how could we construct meaningful narratives of therapeutic change?—but in wielding it with conscious artifice, allowing readers to see both the scaffolding of our interpretations and the limitations of our sight.

Here's an example of problematic positioning in clinical writing:

> Sarah's depression seemed connected to early maternal relationships. In our third session, I understood her mixed feelings about her mother through her tearful response to my interpretation about maternal ambivalence. Her tears confirmed my understanding of her unconscious dynamics regarding separation and loss. This reaction validated my theoretical framework about the origins of her depression.

This writing fails because it positions the clinician-writer at an impossible distance—claiming both absolute closeness and omniscient distance (speaking with complete certainty about the patient's unconscious). The narrator adopts a stance of total knowledge, leaving no room for ambiguity or complexity. The writing feels claustrophobic, as if there's no space between the clinician's interpretations and the patient's reality.

This kind of writing turns the patient into a mere illustration of theory rather than a complex human being. It collapses the necessary tension between empathic understanding and analytical distance that makes good clinical writing possible. Instead of inviting readers to think alongside the writer, it presents a closed system of perfect knowledge.

STYLE

Just as each therapist has a unique way of saying "How are you feeling today?" in the consulting room—a personal cadence, tone, and manner that becomes instantly recognizable to their patients—their writing style in case studies carries this same unmistakable signature.

Even in a single brief "hello" on the phone, we can often recognize the author's distinct psychoanalytic voice.

Every psychodynamic therapist encounters similar clinical phenomena—patients' struggles, therapeutic breakthroughs, resistances, and moments of insight. Yet what distinguishes a memorable case study from a forgettable one isn't the clinical content but the writing style through which it's conveyed. Just as every painter works with the same basic colors, every analyst writes about similar therapeutic experiences—but it's their distinctive writing style that transforms these common elements into something unique and profound.

Consider how different analysts' writing styles approach clinical material. Freud's writing style unfolds like a detective novel, building suspense and carefully laying out clues before revealing their deeper meaning. Winnicott's writing style meanders and circles, sometimes unclear yet deeply authentic, reflecting the very holding environment he describes. Bion's later writing style deliberately challenges and disorients the reader, creating through his prose the very experience of uncertainty he valued in analytic work.

I believe the writing style of a case mirrors the clinician's sensibility—more so than the theoretical content of their work. Some writing styles are sparse and precise, others rich and metaphorical; some flow with literary grace, others proceed with scientific precision.

Yet, possessing a distinctive style can be a double-edged sword, potentially obscuring rather than illuminating psychological insight.

Choosing a writing style means that the clinical voice you use in your case study requires careful consideration—the way you process the case in supervision, while valuable, may not be suitable for writing. The uncertainties, self-doubts, and immediate emotional reactions that emerge in supervision, even if authentic to your experience, need refinement. The writing requires a controlled, thoughtful syntax that serves the clinical narrative.

The clinical voice in psychodynamic case studies emerges through style itself—through word choice, rhythm, metaphor, and the delicate balance between professional distance and emotional resonance.

Some clinicians adopt a style that mimics the discovery process, letting their sentences meander through uncertainty before arriving at insight. Their writing persona becomes that of the thoughtful explorer, inviting readers to join them in puzzling through clinical material. Others write with crystalline clarity and decisive interpretation, fashioning themselves as confident guides through the therapeutic landscape while others write in dense theoretical language, peppering their narrative with technical terms and theoretical constructs

Even the rhythm of sentences betrays the writer's clinical sensibility. Short, declarative sentences suggest a mind that distills complexity into essential truths. Long, winding sentences that circle back on themselves might reflect a more associative way of thinking, one that honors the complexity and ambiguity of therapeutic work.

Most importantly, you must find the right distance from your clinical material. Like a painter who steps back from the canvas to see the work in its entirety, the clinical writer needs the right distance from the therapeutic material. Too close, and one sees only individual brushstrokes—the emotions, words, and gestures that emerged in the therapy hour; too far, and the creation becomes an abstract blur without details.

Step back far enough from your patient and the events of therapy to find the perspective where the clinical story can breathe and reveal its deeper meanings. This distance allows for freer association and deeper insights into the therapeutic process.

The narrator you create in your case study must be both you and not entirely you—a clinical voice that emerges from your experience but has enough distance to tell the story effectively. This narrative position allows you to be both the therapist who experienced the work and the clinician who can reflect upon and convey its meaning.

Your task is to find that nuanced interplay point where you can maintain both clinical authenticity and narrative effectiveness. The voice that emerges should be controlled yet engaging, personal yet professional, intimate with the material yet able to reflect upon it with clarity.

Consider this example of overwrought writing to avoid:

The moment the patient entered the room, I immediately felt the weight of her depression. Her red eyes, drooping shoulders, and broken voice told me the entire story before she even spoke. When she began describing the difficult week she'd had, I found myself swept into her pain, feeling tears welling up in my eyes, and almost forgetting my role as a therapist. I identified with her suffering to such an extent that I felt her sense of helplessness as if it were my own.

Instead, strive for precise, purposeful writing that promotes clinical understanding. Restraint, caution, and responsibility should guide your writing style. Choose details that enhance therapeutic insights instead of overwhelming with descriptions. Allow the significance of the clinical material to emerge through careful curation and thoughtful analysis, not through rhetorical flourishes or emotional excess. Keep in mind that effective clinical writing requires both restraint and intention—each element should justify its inclusion to deepen therapeutic understanding.

Choosing the writing style

Style in clinical case writing is not merely a matter of personal preference. A clinician does not sit down to write and ask: what stylistic choices will illuminate the patient's experience beyond clinical jargon? Rather, style in case writing emerges as both a response to constraints and a seizing of opportunities. Often, the constraints of the case study format present opportunities for clarity and insight. Additionally, style reflects the therapeutic relationships and the rhythm of treatment.

Case writers face a unique challenge. We cannot write a case study in a style other than our own, foreign as it may be. However, through conscious effort, we can certainly try to expand the range of possibilities in case writing. Within this framework, we can create a multitude of prosaic and poetic experiences that have not existed before.

Your writing style emerges from your unique combination of experiences—as a clinician, supervisee, student, and person. While you can learn from reading other analysts' case studies, the goal isn't to imitate their writing style but to develop your own authentic voice. This means finding ways to convey clinical material that feels true to your way of thinking and working while maintaining professional standards.

When considering psychoanalytic writing styles, Robert Stoller (1988) and Wilfred Bion represent opposite ends of a spectrum. Regardless of your leaning, it's important to be familiar with both. Stoller advocates for a style that prioritizes clarity, accessibility, and directness. Just as reading is akin to listening, writing should be linked to speaking. He encourages writers to use plain language that can be understood by a broad audience, avoiding jargon and complex theoretical constructs. Stoller's approach aims to ground writing in the vivid reality of clinical encounters. His style resists intellectualization and abstraction, favoring a more immediate and engaging form of communication. Elaborating on Stoller, the author of a case must maintain word discipline, engaging in a kind of diet while avoiding unnecessary embellishments that case writers sometimes develop.

In contrast, Bion's writing style represents a more challenging and complex approach (Ogden, 2012). Bion seeks to create a new language for describing the human psyche, one that doesn't necessarily aim to clarify or simplify. Instead, his writing immerses the reader in an emotional experience that mirrors the analyst's own encounters in the clinical setting. A significant portion of Bion's works embraces obscurity and confusion as integral parts of the reading process, encouraging readers to tolerate uncertainty and engage actively with the text. His style is intended not just to convey information but to provoke thought and foster an experiential understanding. Bion's writing challenges readers to become co-authors of the text, generating their insights and understanding through the act of reading.

This reminds me of the book of conversations I had with Eigen in the early 2000s (Eigen & Govrin, 2007). Eigen, deeply influenced by Bion, would sometimes utter sentences that were obscure and incomprehensible. Each time, I would stop him to dissect the components of his sentences until I understood something important: Eigen's ideas are like butterflies flying in the air. I wanted to capture each butterfly and analyze its parts, but Eigen insisted, saying: let them fly. From that moment, I listened to him meditatively, allowing his words to take me to distant places, letting my imagination fill in gaps in understanding. This is also how one should read Bion.

Between these two extremes, many psychoanalytic writers exist, each characterized by their unique style. Freud's writing remains that of a wordsmith, a linguistic magician whose style is open and provocative, inviting the reader into labyrinthine pathways of thought. His prose weaves between scientific observation and literary seduction, casting spells that expand psychological imagination.

Klein's intense focus on primitive anxieties and defenses comes through in her dense, interpretation-heavy prose, while Bion stands out as a linguistic challenge—his style intentionally obscure, layered with multiple interpretations. His writing demands intellectual rigor, forcing readers to work intensely to excavate meaning from dense theoretical landscapes. Each paragraph becomes an intellectual puzzle, requiring sustained mental effort and creative interpretation. Where Bion obscures, Klein illuminates—demonstrating how style can either reveal or conceal psychological truth.

Here are more examples of different styles in clinical writing:

I experienced a moment of irritation and discouragement and immediately offered the interpretation I think is correct . . . She was kicking about on the floor, in the hope that I, as a mother, would understand her pain, and trying at the same time to disturb my equanimity so that I would really kick her. The interpretation reached her, and, of course, my countertransference resolved, I was calm.

Etchegoyen, 1999, p. 288.

A patient took up position on the couch and lay silent . . . After a while it seemed as though our bodies were responding to each other in a kind of slow dialogue. I had the thought: two men whose bodies are moving together in response to each other? It seemed something homosexual was happening between us. But it did not feel erotic.

Parsons, 2009, p. 228.

The patient comes to the door and looks away so as to avoid my eyes. He is dirty and unkempt; he wears gloves but they are not a pair.

Bion, 1994, Cogitations, p. 218.

Her face had an unappealing embryonic quality, as though she were a baby in a test tube, distorted by the glass through which she was seen.

Eigen, 1993, The Electrified Tighttrope, p. 29.

He elicited my sadism aside from projecting his own into me. I wanted to spew it back, to thrash him like his dominatrix at the club. My interventions turned strident, desperate. Finally, staring at me with jaundiced eyes, he asked: "You know I get the feeling that you just don't like me. Am I right?"

Sirote, 2015, p. 4.

What can be said about these different styles? Etchegoyen's style is technical and reflective, concentrating on the analyst's internal process and countertransference. He uses psychoanalytic jargon and describes his interpretations and emotional responses. For instance, he mentions "countertransference" and describes his interpretation of the patient's behavior: "She was kicking about on the floor, in the hope that I, as a mother, would understand her pain." Etchegoyen focuses on the correctness of his interpretation and is fully occupied with how the truth in the interpretation benefited both the patient and himself, leading to a more relaxed atmosphere.

Parsons' case about two men employs an observational and introspective style, describing physical sensations and thoughts in a direct, somewhat detached manner. The therapist truly engages in a meditation of silence alongside his patient, and thoughts arise that refine what is occurring with the patient.

Bion's style is terse and observational, providing a quick, vivid snapshot of the patient's appearance and behavior. He uses short, concise sentences to create a clear image in few words. For instance, "He is dirty and unkempt; he wears gloves but they are not a pair" efficiently conveys the patient's state. Bion's description captures this sharp simplicity. It's as if he's photographing a single moment where the patient turns away his gaze, due to the suffering caused by entering the treatment room.

For those seeking to develop a more creative clinical writing style, Michael Eigen introduces readers to the full range of creative case studies. Eigen has a flair for the metaphorical and musicality of words, and he offers a masterful example of how psychoanalytic writing can be theoretically sophisticated and stylistically bold. His unique voice, combining raw emotional intensity with deep theoretical insight, has revolutionized how we can write about clinical experience. Sirote's writing style is raw and visceral, unafraid to depict intense emotions and impulses in the therapeutic relationship. His language is direct and colloquial, using provocative terms that add immediacy and impact to the description. The narrative builds dramatic tension, culminating in the patient's confrontational question.

All the writing styles I've discussed were employed by analysts with considerable writing talent. However, it is important to emphasize that it's perfectly fine to write a direct and matter-of-fact case study, free from literary embellishments, without metaphorical or poetic language. Psychoanalytic journals are full of such examples. This approach allows for a focus on what matters most—describing the therapeutic process and meaningful clinical insights. This is not just a legitimate approach, but one that many consider the most appropriate way for clinicians to document therapeutic processes.

The main point is this: you shouldn't feel the need to adopt a writing style that isn't your own. You don't need to strain to be brilliant or transform into a writer showcasing your virtuosic abilities. Effective clinical writing stems from authenticity and clarity, not from attempts to impress with complex linguistic structures or sophisticated metaphors that might distract from truly important professional insights.

You can find excellent examples of practical and pragmatic writing styles, free from professional jargon, in the book "Psychodynamic Therapy: A Guide to Evidence-Based Practice" (Summers, Barber, and Zilcha-Mano, 2024). Smartly concise, the authors are not trying to overwhelm. They are simply attempting to inform readers about "personalized psychodynamic therapy built on general psychodynamic knowledge and technique, free of jargon, and tailored to the needs of specific individuals" (p. 3). In crafting case studies, authors should strive for authenticity rather than forced originality. True originality often emerges naturally from the unique aspects of each therapeutic encounter and the writer's genuine voice. It's beneficial to focus on breathing life into the narrative, allowing it to unfold in a natural, relatable manner.

The value of humor in psychodynamic case studies

As a reader, I would be delighted to find more joie de vivre and humor in psychodynamic case studies.

Indeed, the gravity of psychological struggles often overshadows the lighter moments in therapy. Yet, laughter and joy are integral parts of the human experience and the healing process. Incorporating humor and moments of levity in case studies could provide a more holistic view of the therapeutic journey.

Moreover, moments of humor often reveal profound truths and can be powerful catalysts for insight. By including these aspects, case studies could better capture the warmth, humanity, and sometimes absurdity of the psychotherapeutic process.

Here is a short and amusing excerpt by Michael Parsons (1999) about a patient who demanded that Parsons tell her about his personal life, especially about his wife. He managed to turn the conversation into a playful one:

> Another time she asked me, in her abrupt, apparently out of nowhere sort of way, "Are you married to a Jew?" She herself is Jewish, and her Jewishness is important to her. I was at a loss, in the middle of a hard session, for how to respond. Then words came to me and it felt possible to risk them. I said, looking straight back at her, "It does sometimes feel like it". She looked, for a moment, as though she did not believe I could have said it, then looked shocked, and then creased up with laughter, eventually being able to say, "That was very funny". This was unconventional psychoanalysis, to say the least, but I realised on reflection that her question and my answer had contained a richness of unconsciously condensed comment on the analytic relationship between us, which would have been killed by any attempt to spell it out. The elusive genuineness of such moments is hard to convey, but when playfulness is earned, as that had been on both sides, it can carry a lot of meaning. (p. 880)

Having explored the nuanced aspects of writing style, we now shift our focus to the essential elements that bring a case study to life: the opening paragraphs introducing the patient, the art of characterization, and the subtle details that transform a clinical description into a compelling narrative.

THE OPENING PARAGRAPHS

Chekhov famously advised writers to begin their stories in medias res—in the middle of things. He suggested cutting off the beginning and end of a story during revision, arguing that these are the places where writers are most prone to artifice and fabrication.

Why did Chekhov focus on beginnings and endings? Because these points are where writers feel the greatest pressure to impose meaning and coherence. At the beginning, we want to set up the story perfectly, creating an elegant framework that makes everything that follows seem inevitable. We strain to establish patterns before they've naturally emerged, foreshadowing developments we only recognized in hindsight.

This insight applies powerfully to clinical writing. When crafting case studies, therapists face the same temptation to create overly perfect beginnings. We might write about initial impressions colored by our later understanding, inadvertently erasing the confusion, uncertainty, and gradual discovery that characterized the real therapeutic process.

Chekhov's warning reminds us to resist this impulse—not by literally starting in the middle, but by staying true to the messy, uncertain nature of therapeutic beginnings, preserving the sense of gradual discovery that defines real clinical work.

While Chekhov cautions us about the artificial coherence we might impose on beginnings, there's an intriguing paradox in clinical writing: the first session often contains crucial elements that will unfold throughout the treatment. The challenge for the clinician-writer is to capture this prophetic quality of beginnings without falling into retrospective oversimplification. How can we write about these early intimations of themes to come while preserving the uncertainty and gradual discovery that characterized our actual experience? The art lies in crafting opening sentences that both acknowledge the seeds of what will develop and maintain the genuine not-knowing that accompanied our first encounters with the patient.

Ogden writes (2005):

> Deciding how and where to begin a case study is no small matter. When it works, the opening of a clinical account has all the feel of the inevitable. It makes the reader wonder, how else would one begin to tell this story? (p. 16)

Here are several spectacular openings. Each one tells a different story, is written in a distinct style, and has its own unique goals.

Sigmund Freud from "Studies in Hysteria," 1895

> In the summer vacation of the year 189- I made an excursion into the Hohe Tauern so that for a while I might forget medicine and more particularly the neuroses. I had almost succeeded in this when one day I turned aside from the main road to climb a mountain which lay somewhat apart and which was renowned for its views and for its well-run refuge hut. I reached the top after a strenuous climb and, feeling refreshed and rested, was sitting deep in contemplation of the charm of the distant prospect. I was so lost in thought that at first I did not connect it with myself when these words reached my ears: "Are you a doctor, sir?" But the question was addressed to me, and by the rather sulky-looking girl of perhaps eighteen who had served my meal and had been spoken to by the landlady as "Katharina". (p. 124)

According to Mahony (1982), Freud's introductory passage in this case study evokes a cinematic quality, transporting the reader to a vivid scene. We can almost visualize Freud perched on the cliffs of Hohe Tauern, one of Europe's most breathtaking mountain vistas, seeking respite from his numerous obligations. The narrative takes an unexpected turn as Freud's solitude is interrupted by a young girl seeking his counsel. Freud's case studies are like Fabergé eggs of clinical literature, structured with meticulous attention to detail and aglitter with the favorite devices of psychoanalytic narrative. Each case unfolds layer by layer, revealing intricate psychological mechanisms beneath a deceptively simple exterior. Like these precious objects, Freud's cases—from the Wolf Man to Dora—combine artistic presentation with technical mastery, each narrative thread carefully woven into an exquisite whole that continues to capti-vate scholars more than a century after their creation. By starting with his vacation and desire to escape medicine, Freud creates an ironic setup for the case that follows, making the clinical material more engaging and accessible to readers.

Sue Grand from "The Reproduction of Evil" (2002)

In the tradition of relational therapists, Sue Grand (2002) begins her case not by introducing the patient but by presenting the excessive repulsion she felt by her patient's presence:

> ALICE'S BODY STANK, AND WITH THIS STENCH SHE INFECTED ME. She lay on the couch, and its fabric absorbed her sweat. Reclusive and obese, she spoke of little else but food, of body holes, of consuming and excreting, of her mother's hostility and neglect, of an empty purse, of always being "dead broke." It was winter, but when she was present I felt stifled in her sweat. Each session she wore the same polyester clothes; each session they appeared ever more soiled. It was as if she ate, slept, urinated, and def-ecated in the same clothes, day after day, week after week. I hated her body, and I tried not to smell her (xiii). [caps in original]

Through Grand's skillful use of sensory detail and provocative imagery, the reader is trans-ported into the heart of the therapeutic encounter, experiencing firsthand the complexities of Alice's psychological distress and the challenges of engaging with her on a deeply human level. It is an experience that lingers long after the page is turned, leaving an indelible impression on the reader's psyche.

Christopher Bollas from "When the Sun Bursts: The Enigma of Schizophrenia," 2015

> Nigel did not look up when I entered the waiting room, and for a moment I was con-fused. Surely—please, God—this could not be my patient? I looked at the motionless figure in front of me and asked if he would be kind enough to follow me to my office. He stood up quickly and stiffly, as if called to attention, and I led the way. First impressions can, of course, prove to be mistaken. But my first impression of Nigel was a lasting one. I was terrified. (p. 41)

What an Opening! Bollas's opening employs literary techniques to immerse the reader in a clinical encounter tinged with dread. The internal plea "please, God" humanizes the therapist, collapsing the distance between professional and reader. Terse prose mimics the therapist's alert-ness and the patient's robotic movements, creating palpable tension.

Crafting the opening of a psychodynamic case study is a bit like setting the scene for a cap-tivating short story. It's about drawing your reader in, making them feel like they're about to embark on a journey so intriguing, they couldn't possibly look away. The opening of a psycho-dynamic case study should capture the essence of the patient's experience in a way that's both engaging and illuminating. Maybe it's a poignant anecdote that encapsulates the central themes of the case, or a thought-provoking observation that leaves the reader hungry for more.

But here's the thing: just like a short story, there's no one-size-fits-all formula for crafting the perfect opening to a case study. It's all about finding the right balance between intrigue and insight, drawing your reader in while also providing them with a meaningful glimpse into the patient's world. When crafting the opening of a psychodynamic case study, resist the siren call of melodrama. Instead, seek the telling detail that illuminates the whole—perhaps a hesitation in the patient's gait or the peculiar way they arrange the cushions on your couch.

Let the reader inhabit the moment of first encounter, feeling the air shift as the patient enters your space. Eschew the laundry list of symptoms in favor of the single, resonant observation that captures the essence of the patient's struggle. Allow your prose to breathe, to pause where the silence in the room becomes palpable. Embrace the messiness of human interaction—the misunderstandings, the moments when your countertransference threatens to overpower your clinical judgment. Dare to reveal your own humanity, your doubts, your missteps. It is in these moments of vulnerability that the true work of therapy often begins. Above all, trust in the power of understatement.

Here are some specific aspects to consider:

1. **First impressions:** reflect on your initial impressions of the patient during the first phone conversation and when you met them in person. What were your expectations, assumptions, or anticipations based on this initial contact?

2. **Imagery and sensory details:** describe the sensory experience of meeting the patient for the first time. What did you notice about their appearance, body language, and demeanor? Were there any distinctive smells, gestures, or mannerisms that stood out to you?

3. **Communication patterns:** consider the patient's communication style and the content of their first words. Did they express themselves openly, or did they seem guarded or hesitant? What topics or themes emerged during the conversation?

4. **Unusual experiences:** reflect on any unusual or unexpected occurrences during the initial meeting. Was there a moment of connection or dissonance that foreshadowed future dynamics in the therapeutic relationship?

5. **Transferential dynamics:** pay attention to any transferential or countertransference reactions that arose during the first encounter. For example, "after the session I tried to recall his appearance, but I couldn't do so. He remained an unknown." Explore your emotional responses to the patient during the first meeting. Did you feel drawn to them, repelled by them, or ambivalent? Did you experience a sense of care or concern for their wellbeing?

CHARACTERIZING THE PATIENT

Crafting a vivid and dynamic portrait of a patient in a psychodynamic case study poses one of the most formidable challenges for a clinician-writer. This is evident from the number of apprentice case studies I've reviewed that begin with descriptions of initial impressions.

You know the style:

> Joseph, 42, arrived at the first session dressed in a dark, pressed suit. He sat upright and answered my questions with clarity and organization. When I asked about his marriage, he precisely described the points of friction with his wife, the frequency of arguments, and the solutions they had already tried. He talked about his work as a senior manager in high-tech and mentioned his achievements and challenges he had faced. Towards the end of the session, he scheduled a time for our next meeting.

This example provides factual information but misses the human encounter that occurred in the room. It doesn't convey how the therapist felt sitting across from Joseph, what arose in them during the conversation, or what might be happening in the unconscious layer of their relationship. Missing here is Joseph's psychological movement—the way his voice trembled slightly when he first shared his sense of loneliness in his marriage; the moment when his gaze softened as he mentioned his young daughter; or how his organized speech pattern began to break down as they approached the end of the session.

In some case reports, writers attempt to decipher the character in its entirety, seeking to understand it down to its most hidden foundations. However, sometimes you risk cutting too deeply, as a surgeon does, to reach the innermost organs, potentially harming the patient. Understanding comes not only from what is explicitly observed or interpreted, but also from what is left unsaid or unexplored. Like in visual art, the spaces between the "sounds" (or explicit content) are crucial in forming the complete picture.

I always share the following wonderful passage with clinicians who struggle to provide a deep and complex characterization of their client's persona. Elisabeth Bishop (Bishop, 1994), in one of her letters, describes exactly what they should strive for.

> Have you ever noticed that you can often learn more about other people—more about how they feel, how it would feel to be them—by hearing them cough or make one of the innumerable inner noises, than by watching them for hours? Sometimes, if another person hiccups, particularly if you haven't been paying much attention to him, you get a sudden sensation as if you were inside him—you know how he feels in the little aspects he never mentions, aspects which are really indescribable to another person and must be realized by that kind of intuition. (p. 18)

The most revealing moments in therapy often come not from what clients deliberately show us, but from the small, unconscious expressions of their humanity—a sudden catch in the throat, a shift in breathing, and the way they clear their throat when touching on difficult topics. These involuntary physical expressions can provide deeper insight into a person's inner world than hours of careful self-presentation.

When writing about patients, consider documenting these subtle physical manifestations of their experience. The way someone's voice changes when discussing loss, their unconscious gestures when anxious, the rhythm of their silence—these details can capture something essential about their lived experience that might be overlooked in more formal clinical observations.

Think about how your client inhabits their body in session—their posture when feeling vulnerable, their physical presence when feeling strong. Notice the small sounds and movements they make without thinking; these often reveal more about their emotional state than their carefully chosen words.

This kind of deep noticing allows us to write about our clients as complete human beings, not just collections of symptoms or behaviors. It helps us capture the felt sense of being with them, the subtle ways they express their inner world before it's translated into language.

When describing clients in clinical writing, try to include these intimate details of human presence. They help create a fuller picture of the person and their experience, going beyond diagnostic categories to capture something of their essential humanity and unique way of being in the world.

Consider how a single moment can reveal volumes:

> She hesitates at the threshold, one hand still on the doorknob. Her gaze flicks between the therapist and the chair furthest from the desk. "Is this . . . where I should sit?" she asks, voice barely above a whisper.

In this brief exchange, we glimpse the patient's uncertainty, her need for guidance, and perhaps a history of navigating unclear social boundaries.

The clinician-writer might reflect:

> I wondered if her hesitation mirrored a broader pattern of indecision in her life, a fear of occupying space without explicit permission.

This approach allows us to merge the external with the internal, the observed with the inferred, creating a richer, more nuanced portrait of the patient. It invites the reader to experience the gradual unfolding of understanding that characterizes the therapeutic process itself.

Here are several considerations to keep in mind when describing the character of patients:

- Seek out telling details and idiosyncratic gestures that speak volumes. Consider this example of a patient's subtle critique:

  He treated the analyst with respectful courtesy, but not without casually referring to shortcomings in the practice—a water stain, or little grammatical imperfections (Hartung and Steinbrecher, 2018, p. 188).

- Embrace unexpected adjectives and allow your prose to mimic the patient's psychic state. Bion illustrates this approach in his vivid description:

  He is always thinking, thinking. Where? In his head? Or in his stomach? . . . It is possible to speak of someone having "his belly as his god" (Bion, 1987, p. 163).

- Use metaphor to bridge the gap between clinical observation and lived experience. Capture moments of transformation and subtle shifts that hint at deeper changes. The following excerpt demonstrates this technique:

> Lucie was hardly sleeping any more. She looked worn out. She was getting thinner and thinner, and she remarked during a session that her "thirst" for work was being satisfied less and less, even though she was working as much as ever (Pelladeau and Marchand, 2018, p. 633).

- Dive deeper into the unconscious dramas playing out in the patient's mind. This example illustrates the complex interplay of behaviors and mental states:

> At night, for instance, he would get on his bicycle and ride more than 200km along country roads. In such states he appeared to be "not altogether himself"; at the same time the accounts had a dangerously suicidal ring to them (Nissen, 2018, p. 127).

When characterizing your patient, resist the temptation to present a static portrait. Instead, track the subtle shifts in their presentation, behavior, and internal world across the therapeutic journey. Note how their speech patterns evolve, how their physical presence in the room changes, and how their relationship to their own narrative transforms. Remember: a compelling clinical character is one whose development we can witness over time.

Clinical example

When Ruth first entered my office, she radiated an effortless warmth that immediately put me at ease. In her mid-eighties, with twinkling eyes and a crown of silver waves framing her face elegantly, she carried herself with the quiet dignity of someone who had witnessed decades of history unfold. She instantly reminded me of my mother's most reliable friend—who always arrived with fresh chocolate pie and delicious gossip. Ruth's resting expression was one of genuine delight, and her quick wit filled our early sessions with unexpected laughter. I remember thinking to myself, "I hope I have that kind of energy when I'm her age," only to realize, with a twinge of self-awareness, that I don't even have it now.

Week after week, Ruth would arrive promptly, impeccably dressed and armed with charming anecdotes about her bridge club and volunteer work. Upon finding that a man her age was flirting with her, she said to me, "It's great to feel 70 again." She was never cranky, never complaining—a quality I initially attributed to an admirably positive disposition. Her sociability and humor defined her, creating an atmosphere where even difficult topics could be approached with a light touch.

It wasn't until our fourth month of therapy that the cracks in this cheerful facade began to show. During a session where we discussed her recent retirement, Ruth's animated gestures suddenly stilled mid-sentence. Her smile remained fixed, but something in her eyes shifted—a momentary window into a different emotional landscape.

"You know," she said after a long pause, her voice noticeably quieter, "no one has ever asked me how I really feel about anything that matters."

This simple statement opened a door to a Ruth I hadn't yet met—a woman who had spent decades performing contentment while burying profound loneliness. She unfolded her story slowly over the following months, revealing the painful marriage she had endured for thirty years, the dreams she had abandoned to care for difficult parents, and the deep fear that without her cheerful persona, she would disappear entirely.

What fascinates me about Ruth's therapeutic journey is not just the contrast between her social presentation and private suffering, but how her authentic self emerged in gentle waves rather than dramatic revelations. The Ruth who brings laughter and warmth is not a false creation—she is genuine in her kindness—but she is only one fragment of a much more complex, vulnerable, and resilient woman who is only now learning to acknowledge her full emotional range.

SELECTING A PSEUDONYM FOR THE PATIENT

Freud was the first to take the liberty of inventing pseudonyms for his patients. However, many clinicians, both during his time and afterward, preferred to use just the first initial of the patient's name. Many clinicians use generic names or first initials to maintain neutrality and clinical focus, avoiding the creation of fictional characteristics that might distract from the patient's authentic presentation. Other clinicians prefer to choose names that they find meaningful and appealing. Choosing a name can be difficult, but sometimes a name can create an image in your mind.

Consider the weight of this decision: in choosing a name, the therapist is, in a sense, rewriting the patient's origin story. It's a curious inversion of the Adamic task—rather than the patient naming their experiences, the therapist names the patient. This linguistic genesis carries echoes of adoption, rebirth, and a narrative reframing that begins with the most fundamental marker of identity.

There's an interesting irony here, too. In the very act of disguising the patient's identity, the therapist reveals something profound about their own perception. The act of naming contains a distinct projective element. The name becomes a kind of Rorschach test in reverse, with the therapist unwittingly revealing aspects of their psyche in characterizing the patient. It suggests that the case is a layered text where the unconscious of both the patient and therapist are inscribed, waiting to be deciphered by the attentive reader.

This act of naming serves not just as a clinical necessity, but also as a literary device, a psychological tell, and a philosophical conundrum all rolled into one.

The pseudonym should reflect the patient's identity while considering cultural, ethnic, and age-related factors, ensuring gender appropriateness as well. Choosing a name that fits these demographic considerations helps maintain authenticity and respect for the patient's background.

When selecting a name for your patient, you offer insight into your understanding of their character and dynamics.

For instance, Robert Stoller demonstrates this approach eloquently:

> Let us call her Belle, for that suggests how she felt she was when analysis began: old-fashioned femininity; a touch of exhibitionism; gentle masochism; a slightly addled yet refreshing innocence; soft, round, dreamy erotism; an unbounded focus on males, romance, silken garments, flowers and bees, bosoms, bare behinds, and babies. (p. 59)

When you choose a name for your patient, take a moment to reflect on your choice. What associations does the name evoke? How does it relate to the patient's presentation, history, or dynamics? By sharing these reflections with your reader, you add depth to your characterization and offer a glimpse into your own analytic process.

Remember, the goal is not to reduce the patient to a stereotype, but to use the name as a starting point for a nuanced exploration of their psyche. This approach turns the simple act of anonymization into an opportunity for deeper clinical insight and engagement with your readers.

Sometimes, the name itself becomes the center of the case study. In one of her case studies, Sue Grand (2013) deliberately chooses not to assign a pseudonym to her patient, whose name was always fused with his twin brother.

As an identical twin in a large family, the patient was always referred to as "the twins," remaining inseparable and indistinguishable even to his own parents. His mother never called him by his name, which reinforced his sense of namelessness.

Grand explains that she cannot give the patient a false name.

The absence of a name mirrors the patient's own experience of being unrecognized and unacknowledged, drawing the reader into a shared dilemma.

EXTERNAL APPEARANCE AND BEHAVIOR: ATTIRE, DEMEANOR, AND MOVEMENT

Focusing on a patient's physical appearance contributes significantly to character depth and reader engagement. It helps create a vivid mental image, allowing readers to visualize the person more clearly. This visual element adds realism and relatability to the character, making them more three-dimensional and memorable.

Consider Robert Grossmark's (2012) portrait of Ruben:

[A] large, handsome American man of Brazilian descent, his voice resonant and his manner exuding confidence. He strides into the waiting room, greeting others with a casual "Hey! How are you?" His clothing—enviable yet worn with "unobligatory lightness"—speaks volumes. A half-smoked cigar in hand, he quips with Freudian wit: "Doctor: Sometimes a cigar is just a cigar!" (p. 194)

In these few strokes, Grossmark conjures not just a patient but a presence.

When crafting physical appearance, consider the following guidelines:

1. **Humanize:** paint your patient as a person, not a case number. Describe their unique attributes—the curl of their hair, the set of their shoulders, the timbre of their voice. Let the reader see them as you do.
2. **Observe keenly:** note the details that speak volumes. Is their gait hesitant or confident? Do their eyes meet yours or dart away? Are their clothes pristine or disheveled? Each detail is a brushstroke in the portrait of their inner world.
3. **Evoke the senses:** don't just tell; make the reader feel. Describe the tremor in their hands, the catch in their voice, the faint scent of tobacco that clings to their coat. Let the reader inhabit the room with you.

4. **Connect the physical and psychological:** show how their exterior reflects their interior. Does their tense posture mirror their anxiety? Does their meticulously coordinated outfit hint at a need for control?

5. **Be comprehensive:** address their attire, grooming, body language, and personal effects. Each element contributes to the whole.

6. **Respect individuality:** note unique features—scars, tattoos, cherished jewelry. These are not mere adornments but parts of their personal narrative.

7. **Capture first impressions:** record your initial reactions. These instinctive responses often hold valuable clinical insights.

8. **Evolve the description:** your description should be a portal inviting readers to step into your consulting room, sit across from your patient, and feel the weight of their presence. For it is in this vivid, immediate encounter that true understanding—and healing—begins.

9. **Track changes:** as the treatment progresses, note any changes in appearance. Improved self-care can indicate progress, while neglect may suggest a decline in mental state.

THE SYMPHONY OF COMMUNICATION

As you paint the portrait of your patient, do not neglect the music of their speech. The way they communicate is as telling as the words they choose, a symphony of verbal and non-verbal cues that can illuminate the depths of their psyche.

Listen closely to the cadence of their voice. Do they speak in staccato bursts or languid, meandering sentences? Note the vocabulary they employ—is it a story thread of erudite expressions or a patchwork of colloquialisms? Perhaps it's a curious blend, hinting at a complex educational or social background.

Observe the music of their conversational style. Are they a babbling brook, words tumbling forth in an unstoppable torrent? Or a still pond, each word dropped deliberately, creating ripples of meaning? Do they pepper their speech with laughter, a tinkling stream or a thunderous roar, that belies a nervous energy or genuine mirth?

And what of their emotional expression? Does anger flare hot and quick, scorching the air between you? Or does it simmer beneath the surface, a dormant volcano waiting to erupt? When sadness comes, does it manifest in quiet, dignified tears or in heaving, cathartic sobs that seem to emanate from the very depths of their being?

Capture the timbre of their laughter—is it a reluctant chuckle, as if joy is a stranger cautiously invited in? Or a full-bodied guffaw that shakes their frame and fills the room?

As you attune yourself to the patient's verbal symphony, do not overlook the duet that unfolds between you and your patient, an amalgam of words and silences. This linguistic tango, with its subtle leads and follows, reveals as much about the therapeutic relationship as it does about either participant. Observe how your measured tempo might quicken in response to the patient's staccato outbursts, or how a patient's halting rhythm gradually synchronizes with your steady cadence. Notice who initiates each new movement in this verbal choreography— do you gently guide with open-ended questions, or does the patient boldly stride into unexplored emotional territory? There's a musicality to the turn-taking, sometimes harmonious, other times discordant. You might hold a prolonged rest, allowing space for the patient's solo performance, or interject with a carefully timed counterpoint.

Pay attention to moments of synchronicity, when you and your patient find yourselves completing each other's phrases, and to instances of disconnect, when your rhythms fall jarringly out of step. This dance of dialogue rises and falls with periods of intense, rapid-fire exchanges giving way to contemplative pauses. Sometimes, you become an echo chamber, reflecting back the patient's words with subtle modulations. Other times, you introduce a new melody, a fresh perspective that the patient may embrace or resist. A patient's strategic silence can be as commanding as your insightful interpretation.

Here are some points that you might like to consider when writing about communication:

1. The cadence and rhythm of their speech
2. Their vocabulary and linguistic choices
3. The flow of their conversation (talkative vs. reserved)
4. Their emotional expression through speech
5. The quality of their laughter and crying
6. The importance of silences and non-verbal communication.

Communication: First example

David's silence envelops our room like dense fog, rendering each word heavy and effortful, as if we're both wading through molasses. Most of our sessions unfold in a wasteland of monosyllabic responses and dead-end exchanges. "Fine," "Maybe," "I guess"—these verbal crumbs are all I receive, each extracted with the delicacy of a dental procedure. I find myself oscillating between aggressive probing and resigned acceptance, sometimes drowning in silence with him, other times frantically tossing out lifelines of questions that sink without a ripple. The therapeutic space often feels like a mausoleum, where my questions and interpretations echo unanswered against cold marble walls.

But mention his mother, and suddenly the fog lifts, replaced by a crackling electric current of rage. "She's probably sitting in her kitchen right now," he'll say, his voice vibrating with concentrated venom, "planning her next attack, counting her victories." In these moments, I feel myself coming alive too, drawn into his orbit of vitality through hatred. His words flow with savage intensity, each syllable sharp and precise, like a blade being methodically sharpened. I notice my responses becoming more animated, as if his hatred has jump-started our therapeutic engine. Yet I'm also aware of my discomfort with this dynamic—how easily we both slip into this mode of shared antipathy, how seductive it is to feel connected through mutual destruction, finally.

It's as if hatred is his only life force, the sole flame that can thaw his frozen emotional landscape. These bursts of animated spite feel like witnessing a corpse suddenly sit up and deliver a blistering soliloquy, only to fall back into its eternal rest once the subject changes, leaving me to grapple with the ethical implications of these moments when I find myself almost grateful for his hatred, simply because it brings him—brings us—to life.

Communication: Second example

Sara's speech unfolds like intricate origami—each sentence carefully folded and unfolded, creating complex patterns that reveal and conceal simultaneously. "I've been thinking," she might begin, "about how when I was young—though not too young, just young enough to know better, which made it worse, really—my mother would say . . . but perhaps that's not relevant to what I meant to discuss about last week's incident at work . . . " In our sessions, she builds elaborate verbal structures and then methodically deconstructs them, often ending exactly where she began, yet somehow transformed.

As the child of two literature professors who dissected every word at the dinner table, Sara learned early that simple statements were dangerous—they could be analyzed, criticized, and torn apart. Her verbal origami developed as a defense: if she folded her thoughts into complex patterns, perhaps they couldn't be unfolded by others. When she speaks about her recent divorce, the patterns become particularly intricate: "I'm not saying he was wrong, exactly—though 'wrong' might not be the right word here—but there was something about the way he would look at me when I was trying to explain . . . although 'explain' suggests I had clarity, which I didn't . . ."

In our sessions, I find myself alternating between wanting to help her unfold these elaborate structures and recognizing that the folding itself might be precisely what needs to be understood. When I attempt straightforward interpretations, she responds by creating even more complex verbal patterns, as if my directness threatens her carefully constructed protective architecture. I've learned to communicate with her through a kind of gentle mirroring of her style, adding small folds to my own speech: "I'm wondering if perhaps the very complexity of how you're describing this might tell us something about . . . " This seems to help her feel safer, understood in her need for linguistic complexity. My attempts to smooth out these linguistic pleats are met with ever more intricate folds, as if the very act of straightforward speech might cause her carefully constructed world to collapse. Gradually, we're learning to appreciate the artistry of her defenses while gently exploring what lies within all those careful folds, constantly interweaving and informing each other.

AVOIDING CLICHÉS

Consider the following vignette:

> The patient presented with deeply rooted issues stemming from her troubled childhood. Coming from a dysfunctional family, Jane exhibited classic signs of resistance as she struggled to address her abandonment issues. Her core conflicts manifested in her relationships, where she consistently acted out her unresolved Oedipal complex. During sessions, she frequently projected her negative feelings onto me, while her defense mechanisms kicked in whenever we approached her underlying trauma.
>
> As we delved deeper into her psychological material, it became evident that her presenting symptoms were merely the tip of the iceberg. Her pattern of self-sabotage revealed itself through various unconscious behaviors. The breakthrough came when she finally connected with her authentic self, allowing her inner child to emerge. Through the supportive environment of therapy, she gradually began to gain insight into her maladaptive patterns.

The transference was particularly intense during this period as she processed her repressed emotions. Her primitive defenses began to give way to more mature coping mechanisms. In the countertransference, I found myself containing her disowned parts while maintaining appropriate therapeutic boundaries.

There are no unexpected words or surprising phrases in this text. Every cliché used— "dysfunctional family," "resistance," "abandonment issues," "Oedipal complex," "defense mechanisms," "psychic material," "inner child," "holding environment," "primitive defenses" — is standard psychoanalytic jargon. The narrative follows a predictable arc from symptoms to breakthrough, lacking specific details or unique observations that would make this patient come alive as an individual.

Here are common clichéd phrases and sentences frequently found in psychodynamic case studies:

Self/Identity related: "Her true/authentic self emerged . . ." "The false self predominated . . ." "Her fragmented self began to integrate . . ." "Issues of self and object constancy . . ." "Her self-states fluctuated between . . ."

Defense mechanisms: "Primitive defenses were activated . . ." "She employed splitting as a defense . . ." "Her characteristic defense constellation included . . ." "Denial and projection were prominent . . ." "Her defensive structure began to soften . . ."

Object relations: "Her internal objects were predominantly persecutory . . ." "Her object relations revealed . . ." "Internalized bad objects dominated . . ." "Her object world was characterized by . . ." "The introjected maternal object . . ."

Development/regression: "Regressed to a more primitive level . . ." "Pre-oedipal themes emerged . . ." "Oedipal dynamics became apparent . . ." "Early developmental deficits . . ." "Arrested development at the oral stage . . ."

Unconscious processes: "Unconscious phantasies emerged . . ." "The unconscious meaning became clear . . ." "Her unconscious communication suggested . . ." "The underlying dynamic revealed . . ." "Unconscious conflicts surfaced . . ."

Container/contained: "The therapeutic frame contained . . ." "I functioned as a container for . . ." "The holding environment provided . . ." "A containing function was established . . ."

Transference/countertransference: "Intense transferential reactions . . ." "In the countertransference, I felt . . ." "The negative transference intensified . . ." "A maternal transference developed . . ." "Erotic transference emerged . . ."

Acting out: "Acting out behaviors increased . . ." "She enacted her conflicts through . . ." "The acting out represented . . ." "Her tendency to act out . . ."

Let me demonstrate how we can transform convoluted jargon into more vivid, specific clinical writing:

Jargon version: "The patient's authentic self began to emerge as her primitive defenses softened. Her internal objects were predominantly persecutory, and she exhibited intense transferential reactions. The holding environment of therapy allowed her to work through her pre-oedipal themes."

Specific version: "Sarah's voice changed when she spoke about her painting—it became lower, more resonant, and her usual vigilant scanning of my face ceased. She began bringing her artwork to sessions, at first hiding it behind her chair and later propping it against the wall where we could both see it. When I commented on a particularly dark piece, she no longer rushed to explain it away, as she had done for months. Instead, she sat with the discomfort, eventually telling me how the swirling blacks and reds captured her rage at her mother's constant invasions of her privacy."

Jargon version: "The patient employed splitting as a defense and demonstrated significant acting out behaviors. Her object relations revealed early developmental deficits, particularly around separation-individuation issues."

Specific version: "Monday sessions would begin with elaborate tales of her boyfriend's perfection—his intuitive understanding and limitless patience. By Thursday, the same man would be described as emotionally vacant and manipulative. When I noted this pattern, Helen stared at the ceiling light until her eyes watered. 'Like my mother,' she whispered, 'I keep trying to make him all good or all bad because the middle ground terrifies me.' She missed the next two sessions, then sent me a long email at 3 AM about feeling untethered."

These more specific versions convey the same clinical understanding but do so through concrete details, sensory observations, and actual dialogue. They show rather than tell, allowing readers to draw their own clinical conclusions from rich descriptive material. The theoretical understanding remains embedded in the texture of real human interaction rather than announced through technical terminology.

USING "AS IF," "AS THOUGH," AND "ONE MIGHT HAVE THOUGHT"

When writing psychodynamic case studies, using phrases such as "as if," "as though," and "one might have thought" can significantly enrich clinical analysis and deepen the understanding of the patient's inner world. These phrases are particularly useful for introducing alternative interpretations or hypotheses about the patient's behavior or mental state. They allow the therapist to present speculative insights without committing to a definitive conclusion.

Examples

"The patient spoke about his father **as if** he were still alive, despite having passed away years ago."

"She moved through the room **as though** she were walking on eggshells, revealing her deep-seated anxiety."

"**One might have thought** that his constant self-deprecation was a defense mechanism against deeper feelings of grandiosity."

USING METAPHORS

Metaphorical language is central to psychoanalytic work (Capsi, 2018). Metaphors in psychoanalytic writing bridge theoretical concepts and lived experience, making complex psychological processes accessible. Like poetry, they can hold multiple meanings simultaneously, capturing the subtle shifts in therapy and internal transformations that direct description might miss. Through carefully chosen metaphors—whether of gardening, artistic restoration, or architectural transformation—writers can convey the atmosphere and gradual nature of therapeutic change.

In written cases, metaphors serve multiple crucial functions. They help capture the emotional texture and unconscious dynamics of the therapeutic relationship in ways that clinical language often cannot. When therapists describe their patients through metaphor—such as comparing a withdrawn patient to a closed origami figure whose intricate folds conceal its inner pattern or describing the therapeutic process as tuning an instrument whose strings respond differently each time they're touched—they convey both clinical observations and their subjective experiences of being with the patient. These metaphors can illuminate transference-countertransference patterns and make abstract theoretical concepts tangible.

Well-crafted metaphors in written cases also help readers enter the therapeutic space and understand the gradual nature of psychological change. For instance, when a therapist describes working with a traumatized patient as "like trying to approach a wounded animal that alternates between freezing and fleeing," readers can viscerally grasp both the patient's fear and the delicate nature of the therapeutic alliance.

Here are some examples:

> I told the patient that I thought that our time together must feel to him like a joyless, obligatory exercise, something like a factory job where one punches in and out with a time card. I then said that I had the sense that he sometimes felt so hopelessly stifled in the hours with me that it must feel like being suffocated in something that appears to be air, but is actually a vacuum.
>
> *Ogden, 2005, p. 175.*

> The non-communicating central self, for ever immune from the reality principle, and for ever silent. Here communication is not non-verbal; it is, like the music of the spheres, absolutely personal. It belongs to being alive.
>
> *Winnicott, 1965, p. 192.*

> After being lost in thought, words bubbled out of my mouth like captions in a comic book, the kind in which tragic guts of characters smears the page.
>
> *Eigen, 2011, p. 87.*

These examples illustrate how metaphors function at various levels of psychoanalytic discourse, transitioning seamlessly between concrete everyday experiences (a factory job with time cards), existential states (suffocation in a vacuum), and artistic forms (comic book captions). Each writer transforms familiar images into something uncanny and precise, revealing how psychoanalytic metaphors can make the invisible realm of internal experience not only visible but also palpable. While it is enjoyable to engage the metaphoric imagination, it is important not to allow it to overshadow your judgment. When writing psychodynamic case studies, metaphors can effectively illuminate unconscious processes and relational dynamics, but they must stay grounded in clinical reality instead of evolving into theoretical abstractions detached from the actual therapeutic encounter.

FROM PUNCTUATION TO PRECISION

The pioneering psychoanalytic case writers—Freud, Klein, Bion, Winnicott, and Kernberg—provided us with an exceptional education in clinical writing: they rarely, if ever, resorted to exclamation points or ellipses. In contrast, less experienced writers often use multiple exclamation points as if they were emotional amplifiers or scatter ellipses to suggest unspoken depths, inadvertently revealing their own uncertainty rather than illuminating the patient's experience. Clinicians often fall into the trap of over-dramatizing emotional moments through excessive punctuation—multiple exclamation points (!!!) or trailing ellipses (. . .) that hint at an emotional depth they cannot fully articulate. These punctuational crutches reveal not intensity but a lack of confidence in one's linguistic precision. The masters taught us that true clinical writing requires confidence in language itself—a confidence that needs no typographical crutches. Where a less experienced writer might write "You got it all wrong!!!" or "After the patient left, I felt sad . . . " a more nuanced approach allows the emotional complexity to emerge through a carefully constructed narrative. The exclamation marks and simplistic emotional statements serve as clear examples of what to avoid in psychodynamic case writing. In writing a case, trust the power of direct, unembellished description.

READ YOUR TEXT OUT LOUD

In the delicate art of writing clinical case studies, there exists a transformative practice often overlooked: reading your text aloud. This is not merely a stylistic exercise but a profound diagnostic tool for your writing.

Reading aloud reveals the hidden flaws in your work: awkward phrasings that trip the reader, theoretical jargon that clogs the narrative flow, and sentences that collapse under their own weight. The inner ear becomes a discerning editor, detecting where your language loses its clinical grace and where it gains genuine communicative power.

This practice transforms writing from a solitary act of documentation into a performative art. Each sentence must now survive not only visual scrutiny but also the more demanding test of auditory comprehension. Can your description of a patient's psychological journey be spoken with the same clarity and empathy with which it was experienced?

So read your case study aloud. Let your inner ear become the ultimate arbiter of your clinical writing's effectiveness. In doing so, you'll discover that great clinical writing is as much about how it sounds as what it says.

RECOMMENDED READING

Freud as a writer, by Patrick J. Mahony. International Universities Press, 1982.

Mahony's "Freud as a Writer" analyzes Freud's literary style and rhetorical techniques, revealing how his writing skills were instrumental in developing and conveying psychoanalytic concepts. The book examines how Freud's masterful prose, use of metaphor, and narrative strategies helped shape both the content and reception of psychoanalytic theory.

Studium and punctum in psychoanalytic writing: Reading case studies through roland barthes, by Dana Amir. *Psychoanalytic Review 105*, 51–65, 2016.

"The case study, like the photograph, seeks to take hold of something nearly intangible. It attempts to capture in time, space, and language something whose dynamic presence remains elusive" (p. 51). This beautiful text describes writing a case study as a process of mourning and transition from superficial knowledge to essential insight.

Structure and spontaneity in clinical prose: A writer's guide for psychoanalysts and psychotherapists, by Suzi Naiburg. Routledge, 2015.

This guide explores five distinct modes of clinical writing: paradigmatic, narrative, lyric narrative, evocative, and enactive. Each mode offers unique tools for expressing clinical experiences, ranging from building theoretical concepts to creating immersive therapeutic narratives. The book includes practical exercises and serves as an essential resource for clinicians, students, and writers interested in enhancing their clinical writing skills.

The situation and the story: The art of personal narrative, by Vivian Gornick. Farrar, Straus and Giroux, 2001.

This is an excellent resource for clinicians who need to write psychodynamic case studies. The book provides guidance on the art of personal writing, teaching readers how to recognize truth in the writing of others and in their own work.

REFERENCES

Amir, D. (2016). Studium and punctum in psychoanalytic writing: Reading case studies through Roland Barthes. *Psychoanalytic Review, 103*(1), 51–65.

Bion, W. R. (1987). *Clinical seminars and four papers.* Fleetwood Press.

Bion, W. R. (1994). *Cogitations.* Karnac Books.

Bishop, E. (1994). *One art: Letters* (R. Giroux, Ed.). Farrar, Straus and Giroux.

Bollas, C. (2015). *When the sun bursts: The enigma of schizophrenia.* Yale University Press.

Capsi, A. (2018). Metaphor in psychoanalytic discourse. *International Journal of Psychoanalysis, 99*(3), 567–584.

Casement, P. (2019). *Further learning from the patient: The analytic space and process.* Routledge.

Eigen, M. (1993). *The electrified tightrope.* Jason Aronson.

Eigen, M. (2011). *Emotional storm.* Wesleyan University Press.

Eigen, M., & Govrin, A. (2007). *Conversations with Michael Eigen.* Karnac Books.

Etchegoyen, R. H. (1999). *The fundamentals of psychoanalytic technique.* Karnac Books.

Freud, S. (1895). *Studies on hysteria* (J. Strachey, Trans.). In *The standard edition of the complete psychological works of Sigmund Freud* (Vol. 2). Hogarth Press.

Gornick, V. (2001). *The situation and the story: The art of personal narrative.* Farrar, Straus and Giroux.

Grand, S. (2002). *The reproduction of evil: A clinical and cultural perspective.* Analytic Press.

Grand, S. (2013). The twin who had no name: Namelessness and the subject of twinship. *Psychoanalytic Dialogues, 23*(2), 157–174.

Grossmark, R. (2012). The analyst's reverie and the process of therapeutic enactment. *Psychoanalytic Psychology, 29*(2), 185–203.

Hartung, J., & Steinbrecher, M. (2018). Clinical vignettes in psychoanalytic practice. *International Journal of Psychoanalysis, 99*(1), 181–198.

Klein, M. (1961). *Narrative of a child analysis.* Hogarth Press.

Mahony, P. J. (1982). *Freud as a writer.* International Universities Press.

Naiburg, S. (2015). *Structure and spontaneity in clinical prose: A writer's guide for psychoanalysts and psychotherapists.* Routledge.

Nissen, B. (2018). The analyst's reverie in clinical practice. *Psychoanalytic Quarterly, 87*(1), 119–142.

Ogden, T. H. (2005). *This art of psychoanalysis: Dreaming undreamt dreams and interrupted cries.* Routledge.

Ogden, T. H. (2012). Creative readings of classic psychoanalytic works. *International Journal of Psychoanalysis, 93*(2), 299–318.

Parsons, M. (1999). The logic of play in psychoanalysis. *International Journal of Psychoanalysis, 80*(5), 871–884.

Parsons, M. (2009). *Living psychoanalysis: From theory to experience.* Routledge.

Pelladeau, N., & Marchand, C. (2018). Working through in psychoanalytic treatment. *Psychoanalytic Psychology, 35*(4), 628–639.

Sirote, A. (2015). The patient who had me committed: A mutually influential relationship between patient and analyst in the context of a broadening analytic frame. *Psychoanalytic Perspectives, 12,* 1–14.

Stoller, R. J. (1988). *Patients' responses to their own case reports.* Journal of the American Psychoanalytic Association, *36*(2), 371–391.

Summers, R. F., Barber, J. P., & Zilcha-Mano, S. (2024). *Psychodynamic therapy: A guide to evidence-based practice.* Guilford Press.

Winnicott, D. W. (1965). *The maturational processes and the facilitating environment.* Hogarth Press.

Winnicott, D. W. (1986). *Holding and interpretation.* Hogarth Press.

CHAPTER 5

Confidentiality strategies

···

The greatest nightmare for every therapist writing a case study is that the patient discussed in the case will recognize themselves in the text.

Consider the following example:

Years after completing her psychodynamic therapy, Emma, a former patient, stumbles upon a psychology journal online. A particular case study written by her former therapist captures her attention, describing a patient called "Anna," a creative professional with anxiety and self-esteem issues. As Emma reads, she is struck by the uncanny resemblance to her own therapeutic case.

The case recounts a background eerily similar to Emma's: a demanding family environment and feelings of inadequacy despite professional success. As she delves deeper, Emma recognizes unique metaphors she used in therapy, specific interventions her therapist employed, and even a dream she once shared—standing on stage, unable to perform.

Emma is overwhelmed by a profound sense of betrayal. The realization that her private experiences have been publicly documented, even under a pseudonym, leaves her feeling exposed and vulnerable. She worries about who else might recognize her story and feels a deep mistrust toward the therapeutic process she once valued.

Emma arranges a meeting with her therapist. As she sits across from the therapist once again, the familiar setting feels different, tinged with tension and mistrust. Emma voices her feelings of betrayal, questioning how her deeply personal experiences could be shared without her explicit consent.

The therapist, caught off guard, apologizes and explains the efforts made to disguise her identity, emphasizing the intention to contribute valuable insights to the field. However, Emma remains unsettled, struggling to reconcile this explanation with her sense of having been exposed.

The meeting ends with unresolved tension. Emma leaves feeling that the trust she once placed in the therapeutic relationship has been irrevocably altered. The conversation lingers in her mind, leaving her questioning the ethics of sharing clinical material and the boundaries of confidentiality, even years after therapy has concluded.

DOI: 10.4324/9781003538578-7

The therapist also feels terrible. He believes that the trust of a patient dear to him has been destroyed. He feels his reputation has been damaged. He returns to therapy to work on this difficult experience and to supervision to understand how he should deal with Emma and whether there is any point in continuing a dialogue with her.

This example is not uncommon. It has happened to many therapists and is well documented in the literature (Thomas-Anttila, 2015; Aron, 2016). It shows how complex the issue of confidentiality is.

There are no easy solutions to writing case studies while respecting confidentiality. Each case involves considerable effort to find a unique solution that fits the patient's nature and the quality of the therapeutic relationship.

The issue of confidentiality in psychoanalytic practice has become even more complex in the age of the internet and social media.

With the widespread availability of online academic journals, databases, and even social media platforms where professionals discuss cases, patients now have unprecedented access to information that was once largely confined to professional circles. They can easily search for and find case studies that might resemble their own experiences, potentially compromising the anonymity that analysts strive to maintain (Aron, 2016).

This new reality of easy access is indeed a central reason for clinicians' growing reluctance to write case studies. Many therapists are increasingly hesitant to publish detailed accounts of their work, fearing that the risk of patient identification has become too high in our interconnected digital world.

This trend poses a significant challenge to the field, as case studies have traditionally been a vital tool for advancing psychoanalytic theory and practice and training new professionals.

However, we need patients to write about them. Case studies are an essential tool for the development of psychoanalytic knowledge, for training new therapists, and for advancing clinical thinking. Without them, theory remains disconnected from the complex and living therapeutic field.

GLEN GABBARD'S STRATEGIES TO SECURE CONFIDENTIALITY

In a highly recommended paper that remains relevant today, Glen Gabbard (2000) proposed strategies to address the ethical dilemma of using clinical material in psychoanalytic case studies. Each strategy has its distinct advantages and disadvantages, and Gabbard argues against a uniform approach, suggesting that a combination of methods may often be the most effective.

Based on Gabbard's paper, here are descriptions of four methods for maintaining confidentiality in psychoanalytic case reports:

Disguise: involves altering identifying details while preserving the essence of clinical material. The challenge lies in balancing anonymity with scientific integrity while being mindful that patients might still recognize themselves.

Patient consent: requires obtaining explicit permission from patients to publish their case material. While transparent, this approach raises concerns about the impact of transference on consent and the effects of publication on treatment.

Composites: combines characteristics from multiple patients into a single case example, particularly useful for illustrating common themes or when confidentiality concerns are heightened. Readers should be informed when this method is employed.

Colleague as author: having a colleague write up the case material can be valuable when addressing sensitive countertransference issues, allowing the treating clinician to contribute while maintaining some distance from the written account.

I will expand on the first two more common methods and provide examples and suggestions.

Disguise

Thick disguise

This strategy involves altering identifiable details about the patient to protect their privacy while maintaining the essence of the clinical material. Thick disguise safeguards patient confidentiality and enables the analyst to share valuable clinical insights without revealing the patient's identity. However, the disguise may modify the material to such an extent that it loses its clinical relevance or accuracy, potentially misleading readers. The use of disguise in psychoanalytic case studies is a double-edged sword that both protects and may mislead. The analyst must change external identifying details while preserving the essential clinical material and internal dynamics that define the case. Yet this artful obfuscation carries with it the seeds of a deeper deception. Each alteration, each carefully considered change, represents a step away from the unvarnished truth. The analyst becomes not just an observer but an editor, reshaping reality with each stroke of the pen. The reader, unaware of these subtle manipulations, may find themselves led astray, with their understanding of the case built upon a foundation of well-intentioned inaccuracies. Consider Freud's case of Katharina (1893), where the "grievous disguise" of changing the abuser from father to uncle altered not just a detail, but the very heart of the case. This is not a mere change of scenery, like renaming a mountain, but a fundamental shift in the emotional and psychological terrain of the patient's experience.

SOME SUGGESTIONS FOR PROPER DISGUISE

When altering dream content, preserve the symbolic meaning while changing specific details. For instance, transform settings while maintaining themes and emotional undercurrents.

Avoid exaggerated disguise that distorts the clinical situation. Changing too many core elements, like gender or primary issues, compromises the scientific integrity of the case study.

Consider creating composite cases when dealing with particularly sensitive or potentially identifiable situations. This allows for the preservation of clinical insights while further obscuring individual identities.

Adapt the level of disguise to the digital age. Be mindful that information is more easily accessible and potentially able to be cross-referenced, requiring more thorough disguise techniques.

Show the disguised case study to trusted colleagues and ask them to evaluate it from the patient's viewpoint. Specifically, inquire whether they believe the patient would be able to identify themselves if they were to read the case study, and if so, whether they might feel hurt or exposed by the description.

Clinical example

The patient, whom we will call "Jackson," is a 42-year-old man who sought therapy due to persistent anxiety and difficulties in forming and maintaining intimate relationships. Jackson works in the legal profession, an occupation he finds demanding and isolating. He shared a history of childhood trauma, including emotional neglect from his parents, which he attributes as a central factor in his current relationship struggles. His father was frequently absent due to professional commitments, while his mother was emotionally distant, leaving him with a profound sense of lack of support and unworthiness of love.

The therapy began by creating a safe and reliable space where Jackson could explore his inner world. The therapist clarified the psychodynamic approach, emphasizing the exploration of unconscious processes and their influence on his current behavioral patterns. Jackson was encouraged to speak freely about his thoughts and feelings through a process of free association, aimed at uncovering subconscious conflicts.

During the sessions, the therapist focused on Jackson's relationships and attachment patterns. It became evident that Jackson's challenges in creating closeness were tied to a deep fear of abandonment, a theme echoing his childhood experiences. The therapist helped Jackson understand the connection between feelings of worthlessness and fear of rejection and his early interactions with his parents.

In one session, Jackson described a recurring dream in which he found himself in a large, empty house. As he wandered through the rooms, he felt an increasing sense of discomfort, as if someone were following him. Finally, he reached a locked door, behind which he sensed a threatening presence. Despite his fear, he felt a strong urge to open the door but always woke up before he could do so.

The recurring dream was examined as a symbolic expression of Jackson's internal struggles. The empty house was interpreted as a metaphor for feelings of emptiness and loneliness, while the locked door symbolized repressed memories and emotions. The therapist encouraged David to confront these fears, suggesting that the threatening presence behind the door might represent aspects of himself that he had disowned.

As therapy progressed, Jackson began to recognize that his fear of vulnerability had led him to sabotage potential relationships. He would emotionally withdraw when he felt someone getting too close, similar to the emotional distance he experienced in his relationship with his mother. Through dream analysis and the exploration of transference relationships, in which he projected feelings toward his parents onto the therapist, he gained insight into these patterns.

Jackson's progress was marked by his growing ability to express emotions and communicate his needs in relationships. He reported a deeper sense of connection with others and a decrease in anxiety about potential rejection. The therapy aimed to help Jackson integrate these insights into his daily life while fostering healthier relationships and a more positive self-perception.

Considerations for disguise

When presenting a case study such as Jackson's, therapists need to carefully consider how to disguise various elements to protect confidentiality while maintaining the integrity of the essential psychodynamic insights.

Historical background: alter the patient's name and profession. You can change "Jackson" to "Michael" and present him as a software engineer instead of a lawyer. Additionally, modify the family background—for instance, you might portray a father who was emotionally distant due to personal challenges instead of work-related absences, and a mother who was immersed in her career rather than being emotionally unavailable. These revisions will significantly protect the patient's true identity while maintaining the central themes critical to understanding the psychological dynamics—emotional neglect and challenges in forming close relationships.

Dream: creatively redesign the dream while ensuring its symbolic depth remains intact. For example, you can shift the setting from an empty private house to an abandoned office building, or even to a completely different venue like a library or museum, provided you retain the core themes of loneliness, searching, and confronting the repressed. The key is to uphold the emotional and dynamic essence of the dream, rather than its specific particulars.

Opening and session content: present the course of the sessions with adjustments to details that are not crucial for understanding the therapeutic process. You can rearrange events, blend incidents, or introduce fictional elements that do not change the therapeutic core. Highlight the psychodynamic mechanisms such as transference, resistance, and processing, which are fundamental to therapeutic work and carry significant professional weight.

Keep in mind that the goal is to strike a delicate balance between safeguarding the patient's privacy and preserving the clinical and educational value of the case study. Any adjustments you decide to make should ensure the patient remains anonymous while still conveying the vital professional insights gained from the therapy.

Thin disguise

A thin disguise might involve merely changing David's name while retaining specific details about his profession, the nature of his childhood trauma, and the exact content of his dream. This approach is unethical since it risks David recognizing himself or being identified by others, thus breaching confidentiality. Such minimal alteration does not adequately protect the patient's identity, potentially causing distress or harm.

Exaggerated disguise-not advisable

An exaggerated disguise might entail changing David's gender, describing him as a 60-year-old woman working as a nurse, and focusing on issues unrelated to his actual therapy, such as substance abuse. This is unethical as it distorts the case, misrepresenting the clinical situation and therapeutic process. Not adhering to the facts compromises the scientific integrity of the case study and can lead to misleading conclusions about the therapeutic approach and outcomes.

As you engage in this process of creative concealment, pay attention to the choices you make. What aspects of the case do you choose to emphasize or downplay? How do your disguises reflect your own understanding of the core dynamics at play? The act of obscuring can often reveal more than it hides, offering new perspectives on the therapeutic work.

Consent

Many clinicians believe that obtaining a patient's consent for publication is an ethical obligation, the neglect of which takes a toll on both the therapist and the patient. The duty of confidentiality is based on ethical and clinical principles, and its breach introduces elements of concealment, denial, guilt, and dishonesty into the therapeutic relationship. However, others argue that "asking the patient for permission to publish may shatter the setting." The patient may consent, "but their evolution will be negative." (Micu, 2019, p. 1022)

Written consent serves as a tangible testament to the patient's autonomy, a contract that binds analysts and analysands in a shared commitment to ethical practice.

Crastnopol (1999) notes that many patients agree to be subjects in case studies because they seek a deeper connection with their therapists. Being featured in a professional article allows patients to engage with the therapist's professional world, offering them a broader community that serves as both a source of reflection and a supportive environment. This can enhance the analytic work and provide benefits to the patient.

However, involving patients in the writing and publication process can complicate treatment, sometimes beneficially and sometimes harmfully. As a result, many clinicians feel anxious or intimidated by these complexities and may choose not to write about their patients.

Stimmel (2013) states: "Patient consent is a slippery concept. The basic reality is that neither a patient nor his analyst can possibly anticipate the fate of the myriad meanings that being written about will evoke; that they will transmute over the course of an analysis is certain." (p. 96)

The one lesson anyone who engages in writing clinical material learns is that what you intend as a therapeutic embrace can be perceived as a violation of trust, while what you worry might be a violation can instead be experienced as a profound validation of the patient's experience. There's simply no way to predict with certainty how the written portrayal will be received.

Aron (2016) supports agreement and prefers it over disguise. However, when he consulted with a lawyer on this matter, the lawyer advised him that from a legal standpoint, it is preferable for the therapist not to involve the patient in their personal affairs, that is, in their writing projects.

Using the case study to advance the treatment

Judy Kantrowitz's (2006) research reveals an intriguing trend among psychoanalysts regarding the use of clinical material in professional writing. Her findings indicate that the number of analysts who exclusively use disguised material is more than double that of those who consistently seek their patients' permission to write about them.

Kantrowitz notes an interesting geographical distinction: analysts outside the United States tend to rely more on disguise alone compared to their American counterparts. However, she emphasizes that globally, analysts are increasingly concerned about the accessibility of published material.

Kantrowitz identifies a worldwide trend where more and more analysts are concluding that seeking permission before publishing clinical material is necessary. Furthermore, she points out that some analysts see therapeutic value in the permission-seeking process itself. In their view, when patients read written material about themselves, it can illuminate central issues in their character and conflicts, which can then be explored and processed within the analytic treatment. I would add that obtaining patient consent for case study publication is particularly important when there is a history of intrusiveness, coercion, or neglect of the patient's needs.

Kantrowitz (2006) highlights various ways patients benefit from reading about themselves: (1) as a means of gaining validation; (2) to resolve misunderstandings from both perspectives; (3) to enhance understanding of transference-countertransference dynamics and to bring past experiences to life emotionally in the present; (4) to uncover and explore the therapist's perceptions and emotions regarding the patient; and (5) to aid in the process of de-idealizing the therapist. Kantrowitz writes about such examples.

However, this recommendation should also be carefully considered. Asking the patient for permission to publish a case study also has many drawbacks.

According to Kantrowitz (2006), there are several disadvantages to seeking patient consent for writing a case study:

- **Therapeutic disruption:** introducing the idea of publishing a case study can interfere with the therapeutic process. Patients might perceive the request as prioritizing the therapist's interests over their own, potentially weakening the therapeutic alliance and hindering progress.
- **Emotional reactions:** patients may experience strong emotions, such as anger or betrayal, upon learning about the publication, complicating their relationship with the therapist and possibly leading to premature termination of therapy.
- **Evolving perceptions:** a patient's feelings about consenting to publication can change over time. They might initially agree but later feel uncomfortable or regretful, especially if they feel exposed or misunderstood by the written account.
- **Altered perception of the therapist:** reading about themselves in a case study might change how patients view their therapist. They could become more aware of the therapist's thoughts and feelings about them, which could affect the therapeutic dynamics.
- **De-idealization:** the process of reading the therapist's account can lead to a de-idealization of the therapist. Patients might realize that their therapist is not as perfect as they imagined, which can be both beneficial and challenging within the therapeutic context.

Levine (as cited by Kantrowitz, 1999) adds another layer of complexity by arguing that involving patients in the publication process could lead readers to believe that case studies are censored by patients' needs, thus compromising the perceived authenticity of the literature. He suggests that if patient approval becomes a standard practice, it might limit the topics covered in psychoanalytic literature due to concerns about patient sensitivities, ultimately affecting the field's depth and breadth.

FURTHER SUGGESTIONS CONCERNING CONSENT

1. When a clinician uses clinical material from a patient who is either a public figure, or works in the mental health field, obtaining consent becomes not just advisable but imperative. The stakes are higher, the risks of recognition more acute.

2. Recognize that obtaining patient consent means relinquishing sole authorship. Be prepared for significant compromises and revisions to your work as a writer.

3. Don't assume that obtaining consent is the end of the process. Patients may agree to avoid disappointing their therapist.

   a. Engage in in-depth discussions with the patient about their decision:

      i. Explore their motivations for agreeing

      ii. Discuss any reservations or concerns they might have

      iii. Analyze the impact of the publication on the therapeutic relationship.

4. Consider having the patient write their own case. Compare the two accounts as a therapeutic exercise, potentially advancing the treatment process.

5. Provide the patient with the chance to review and comment on drafts at different stages, not solely the final version.

6. Talk to the patient about how potential public recognition may impact them both personally and professionally, and create a plan to address any concerns about consequences.

RECOMMENDED READING

Disguise or consent: Problems and recommendations concerning the publication and presentation of clinical material, by Glen Gabbard. *International Journal of Psychoanalysis 81*, 1071–1086, 2000.

   An essential read for anyone grappling with confidentiality issues in writing psychodynamic case studies.

Writing about patients: Responsibilities, risks, and ramifications, by Judy L. Kantrowitz. Other Press, 2006.

   Judy Leopold Kantrowitz conducted a comprehensive study that explored the ethical and clinical implications of writing about patients in psychoanalytic literature. Her research involved interviews with 141 analysts, focusing on their approaches to patient confidentiality and the potential consequences of patients encountering written materials about themselves. The study examined analysts' decision-making processes regarding patient disguise versus obtaining consent for publication. It also investigated their perspectives on the clinical ramifications of patients reading about themselves, whether intentionally or by chance.

Confidentiality and consent issues in psychotherapy case reports: The wolf man, Gloria and Jeremy, by Kerry Thomas-Anttila. *British Journal of Psychotherapy 31*, 360–375, 2015.

To illustrate the challenges inherent in documenting therapeutic work, the author presents examples from three cases: Freud's patient Sergei Pankejeff (known as the "Wolf Man"), Gloria (the subject of the "Gloria Films"), and a contemporary patient, "Jeremy", whose therapist published an account of their work together. These cases highlight the complexities and potential pitfalls of translating the therapeutic experience into written form.

Ethical considerations in psychoanalytic writing revisited, by Lewis Aron. *Psychoanalytic Perspectives 13*(3), 267–290, 2016.

The article is groundbreaking in treating case writing as a form of clinical enactment that requires careful consideration and consultation. Aron argues that the decision to write about patients, and how to do so ethically, should be viewed as part of the therapeutic process itself rather than a mere technical or legal matter. His emphasis on the need to consider each case individually while being mindful of broader ethical principles provides a sophisticated framework for clinical writing.

REFERENCES

Aron, L. (2016). Ethical considerations in psychoanalytic writing revisited. *Psychoanalytic Perspectives*, *13*(3), 267–290.

Crastnopol, M. (1999). The analyst's professional self as a "third" influence on the dyad: When the analyst writes about the treatment. *Psychoanalytic Dialogues*, *9*(4), 445–470.

Freud, S. (1893). Case histories from *Studies on hysteria*: Katharina. In J. Strachey (Ed. & Trans.), *The standard edition of the complete psychological works of Sigmund Freud* (Vol. 2, pp. 125–134). Hogarth Press.

Gabbard, G. O. (2000). Disguise or consent: Problems and recommendations concerning the publication and presentation of clinical material. *International Journal of Psychoanalysis*, *81*(6), 1071–1086.

Kantrowitz, J. L. (1999). The role of the preconscious in psychoanalytic work. *Journal of the American Psychoanalytic Association*, *47*(3), 739–764.

Kantrowitz, J. L. (2006). *Writing about patients: Responsibilities, risks, and ramifications.* Other Press.

Micu, M. (2019). Confidentiality and consent in psychoanalytic case writing: Contemporary perspectives. *International Journal of Psychoanalysis*, *100*(5), 1015–1035.

Stimmel, B. (2013). Patient consent and the ethics of case study publication. *Psychoanalytic Review*, *100*(1), 85–105.

Thomas-Anttila, K. (2015). Confidentiality and consent issues in psychotherapy case reports: The Wolf Man, Gloria and Jeremy. *British Journal of Psychotherapy*, *31*(3), 360–375.

PART 2

The specifics

....

FROM KLEIN TO RELATIONAL: A JOURNEY THROUGH
FIVE PSYCHOANALYTIC LANDSCAPES

The following chapters outline the main characteristics of case studies across five approaches: Klein, Bion, Winnicott, Kohut, and the relational approach. Each approach has a distinct dominant focus regarding the greatest challenges, related concepts, therapeutic atmosphere, therapy goal, and transformation. Each aspect shapes how we understand therapeutic work and write about it in our clinical narratives.

For each approach, I will use clinical vignettes to demonstrate how different clinical phenomena are described in psychoanalytic writing. These vignettes help clinicians understand how abstract theoretical concepts like projective identification, alpha function, or transmuting internalization are brought to life through clinical writing, demonstrating how different theoretical frameworks shape the way we observe and describe similar clinical phenomena.

I acknowledge that these chapters may provoke criticism, as few case studies today are written with strict adherence to a single approach. Many prefer theoretical pluralism over confinement to one specific method.

I certainly accept this view, and I do not intend to return the field to a monolithic world nor do I encourage clinicians to be purists. However, it's important not to delude ourselves into believing that the psychoanalytic world functions like a department store where each therapist freely takes whatever they want from any approach depending on the patient and the content emerging in therapy. While most of you indeed work with more than one approach, you typically combine approaches that share deep internal connections, rather than implementing a seamless pluralistic synthesis. For example, therapists tend to integrate theories with conceptual proximity, such as Winnicott and Kohut, or Klein and Bion.

DOI: 10.4324/9781003538578-8

Each approach carries its own worldview regarding the deepest questions about the human psyche. They differ fundamentally in their techniques, treatment goals, understanding of transference, and views on human suffering.

Understanding these distinctions is crucial for developing a nuanced and effective clinical practice, even within a broadly pluralistic framework.

One cannot engage in writing case studies in the twenty-first century without being intimately familiar with the tradition of case studies that preceded it.

I believe that therapists in training should learn pure, monolithic approaches before becoming integrative, as integration should be based on extensive knowledge of different approaches (see Govrin, 2014).

In the next five chapters, we shall breathe the rarefied air of the therapeutic atmosphere, chart the cartography of treatment goals, and examine the flora and fauna of clinical phenomena that characterize each approach.

This is not a prescription, but an invitation—an invitation to explore, to feel, to understand the rich diversity of our field, and ultimately, to find one's own unique voice in the grand symphony of psychoanalytic discourse.

REFERENCES

Govrin, A. (2014). The vices and virtues of monolithic thought in the evolution of psychotherapy. *Journal of Psychotherapy Integration, 24*(2), 79–90. https://doi.org/10.1037/a0035972

CHAPTER 6

A case study in the spirit of Melanie Klein

THE GREATEST CHALLENGES

> Psychical truth is the hallmark of the Kleinian approach. Always bear in mind the lines of Samuel Johnson cited by Bion, Rosenfeld, and Segal (1961) in their joint obituary to Klein: "Whether to see life as it is will offer us much consolation I know not; but the consolation which is gained from truth, if any there be, is solid and durable; that which may be derived from error must be, like its original, fallacious and fugitive." (p. 7).

In Kleinian case studies, it is rare to witness extreme dramas or dramatic enactments. Instead, the emphasis lies on interpretations and the unconscious gradually unfolding over time, like a slow-opening fan. These cases reveal subtle shifts in internal object relations, primitive anxieties, and defensive constellations that emerge through the analyst's patient attention to transference developments. While lacking the theatrical moments that might characterize other therapeutic approaches, the Kleinian case illuminates the delicate work of making contact with split-off parts of the self through consistent interpretive work. It is a case study of patience for an increasingly impatient time.

When writing Kleinian case studies, it is essential to capture how the analyst directly engages with the patient's infantile and psychotic parts. Unlike case studies from other orientations that may focus primarily on rational discourse or conscious material, a Kleinian case study should vividly portray the primitive anxieties, fantasies, and defenses as they emerge in the room. The writing should demonstrate how the analyst's interventions flow from these archaic experiences rather than addressing them from the outside. Kleinian case studies often possess a raw, immediate quality that might feel unsettling, as they aim to capture the direct engagement with the psychotic core of the personality. The writing itself

DOI: 10.4324/9781003538578-9

becomes a vehicle for conveying the depth and intensity of these primitive experiences in the therapeutic encounter.

Another significant challenge in writing Kleinian case studies stems from Klein's (1952) revolutionary concept of transference as a "total situation". This approach, originating from her work with children, where every toy and figure in play represented aspects of the self or internal objects, extends to adult analysis. In adult work, this means understanding every character the patient mentions as potentially representing a part of the self or an internal object. Betty Joseph (1985) further developed this concept, emphasizing that everything the patient brings to analysis—every story, relationship, or current situation—is part of the transference situation. This presents a unique writing challenge: how to capture this multilayered understanding where nothing is "just" a story, but rather everything represents aspects of the patient's internal world unfolding in the therapeutic relationship.

Let me demonstrate how everyday statements from a patient can be interpreted in the Kleinian approach as expressions of transference and internal material:

In the Kleinian approach, everyday conversational routines take on deeper meaning within the therapeutic relationship. When a patient mentions that it's raining heavily outside, the traditional Kleinian therapist might hear this as an expression of a desire to flood the therapeutic space with emotions, like tears that cannot be contained, or as a description of the patient feeling "overwhelmed" by threatening emotional content. The rain might symbolize aggressive or libidinal impulses that the patient feels are "leaking" or "pouring" into the therapeutic space and cannot be controlled or contained.

When a patient reports seeing a car accident on the way to the therapy session, the therapist might hear this as an expression of anxiety about a collision between opposing internal parts, or anxiety regarding harm to the self or the therapist within the context of the transference relationship.

Even when the patient complains about the quality of food at a restaurant, noting they couldn't finish their meal, the Kleinian therapist might see this as an expression of concern that the "emotional nourishment" she offers isn't good or nourishing enough, or that the patient feels unable to "digest" the interpretations in therapy.

In a Kleinian case study, the therapist not only documents these everyday statements but describes how she interpreted their unconscious meaning within the transference relationship and the patient's response to these interpretations—a response that itself forms part of the ongoing dynamics of transference and countertransference. This creates a rich, multilayered case study, demonstrating how "nothing is just a story" in the Kleinian approach to therapy.

RELATED CONCEPTS

Death instinct, fantasy, schizoid-paranoid position, depressive position, envy, greed, manic defense mechanisms, schizoid-paranoid defense mechanisms, introjection, projection, projective identification, reparation, psychotic patients, and patients who are difficult to reach.

THERAPEUTIC ATMOSPHERE

The Kleinian approach includes a variety of therapeutic styles:

1. Klein and Segal's precise, formal style focuses on fantasy interpretations.
2. Betty Joseph's style is similar, but emphasizes interpretations centered on the immediate dynamics of transference relationships.
3. Irma Brenman Pick promotes a warmer, more compassionate approach that prioritizes authentic therapeutic responses.

In all Kleinian treatments, certain principles should guide your narrative approach. The writing should maintain a direct focus on interpreting unconscious material without softening the emotional impact. I'd suggest focusing on how interpretive work strengthens the patient's capacity for insight and understanding. In case presentations, emphasize how deep interpretations foster the patient's curiosity about their inner world. Rather than highlighting moments of support and reassurance, document how consistent interpretive work cultivates the therapeutic space and enables patients to explore their psychological experiences.

From the outside, Kleinian therapy sometimes looks like a chess game with moves and countermoves between patient and therapist[1]. Actually, it is a sophisticated process of containing and processing projected elements of the patient's psyche.

THERAPY GOAL

When writing about therapeutic goals in a Kleinian case study, it's essential to focus on the central aim: the pursuit of psychic truth through the therapeutic relationship. This pursuit involves a dynamic between both the therapist's and patient's relationship to truth—the therapist's commitment to uncovering it and the patient's simultaneous desire for and resistance to knowing it.

The main therapeutic goal in Kleinian work is to help patients reclaim split-off and projected parts of themselves. Unlike traditional perspectives that emphasize repression, Kleinian theory focuses on how patients actively split off and project unwanted aspects of themselves. This process occurs within the therapeutic relationship, where the therapist serves as both container and interpreter of these projected elements.

The therapeutic relationship operates through a complex interplay where the therapist functions as an active and attentive interpreter.

As Joan Riviere (1927) stated, psychoanalysis "is not concerned with the real world, nor with the child's or the adult's adaptation to the real world, nor with sickness or health, nor virtue or vice. It is concerned simply and solely with the imaginings of the childish mind, the phantasied pleasures and dreaded retributions." (p. 87)

Progress in Kleinian therapy is evidenced by the patient's increased ability to tolerate psychological truth and their growing capacity to integrate split-off parts of themselves. This development manifests in enhanced emotional processing and more authentic relationships. Such change occurs not through supportive interventions but through the consistent offering of truth and the strengthening of the patient's capacity to know and integrate reality. The case should illustrate how truth emerges within the therapeutic relationship, demonstrating the subtle shifts in the patient's ability to recognize, own, and integrate previously disowned aspects of themselves. This process of working through the depressive position becomes the central focus of the therapeutic work, as the patient develops the ability to integrate both good and bad aspects of self and object; consequently, this integration process forms the core of the case study itself.

CAPTURING TRANSFORMATION: WRITING ABOUT CHANGE IN KLEIN'S FRAMEWORK

When writing a psychodynamic case study, search for and document changes in the quality of the patient's unconscious fantasies and the ways they are expressed in treatment. Focus on documenting projective processes and changes in these processes—particularly how the patient attempts to rid themselves of parts of their selves by projecting them outward and the consequences this has on their ability to think and function. Explain how excessive projection of aggressive parts significantly weakens the ego, as the aggressive components of emotions and personality are closely linked in the psyche to strength, power, vigor, knowledge, and other desirable traits.

When the patient projects these parts outward, they become depleted of vital resources for functioning. Similarly, document how excessive projection of positive traits results in a comparable outcome: a loss of essential parts of the self, including the ability to think, which distorts reality. Characterize this not merely as a functional disturbance but as a significant injury to the psychic structure itself.

Focus specifically on how the loss of distance involved in projection removes thinking from the realm of possibility. When the patient cannot distinguish between self and other, or inside and outside, the ability to objectively think about reality vanishes. Thinking requires a certain distance from the subject being evaluated, and without this distance, the mental process collapses. Describe therapeutic change as a gradual process in which the patient begins to reclaim parts of themselves that were projected outward. Document how the patient develops the capacity to tolerate mixed and complex feelings instead of projecting them, and how this restoration enhances their psychic strength and ability to think.

Illustrate how extreme splits between good and bad gradually moderate, leading to the patient's development of synthetic capacity—the ability to integrate contradictory aspects of themselves and others. Describe the change as a restoration of psychic integration, where the split and projected parts of the personality reunite, and with this reunification, the full capacity to think, experience, and recognize reality returns.

Clinical example

During a session, Sarah suddenly fell silent and shifted uncomfortably in her chair. When I commented on this change, she responded with unusual hostility: "You're always watching me, analyzing everything. It's suffocating." Instead of defending against this accusation, I interpreted her experience of me as a persecutory object: "Perhaps right now I feel like a dangerous, intrusive presence who might see parts of you that feel frightening or shameful."

Sarah's eyes welled with tears. "Like my mother," she whispered, "always pointing out my flaws." But then her tone hardened: "At least I'm not cruel like her." I noted how quickly she moved to split off and project the "cruel" part onto her mother, protecting herself from acknowledging her own aggressive impulses.

I offered: "It seems that right now, any observation feels like an attack, and you need to quickly locate all the cruelty in your mother to feel safe. Perhaps there's a part of you that feels both terrified of being seen and desperately wanting to be understood."

This interpretation led to a significant shift. Sarah's posture softened, and she spoke about her fear that if she acknowledged her own aggressive feelings, she would become "exactly like her." This moment illustrated the movement from paranoid-schizoid positioning toward a more depressive position, where she could begin to integrate previously split-off aspects of herself.

This vignette captures key Kleinian elements: attention to primitive anxieties, interpretation of splits and projections, and the gradual movement toward integration through the therapeutic relationship.

BETTY JOSEPH: HERE AND NOW, INSTEAD OF BREAST AND PENIS

The art of writing psychoanalytic case studies in Betty Joseph's tradition requires a distinct focus on capturing the immediate therapeutic encounter rather than exploring historical reconstructions or unconscious phantasies (Aguayo, 2011). Betty Joseph's approach evolved significantly over her career, reflecting both her clinical experience and the changing nature of psychoanalytic patients. This evolution was driven by her growing dissatisfaction with interpretations that, while technically accurate, failed to "get through" to patients.

Joseph writes:

> Much of our understanding of the transference comes through *our understanding of how our patients act on us to feel things* for many varied reasons; how they try to draw us into their defensive systems; how they unconsciously act out with us in the transference, trying to get us to act out with them; how they convey aspects of their inner world built up from infancy—elaborated in childhood and adulthood, experiences often beyond the use of words, which we can often only capture through the feelings aroused in us, through our countertransference, used in the broad sense of the word.
>
> *Joseph, 1985, p447.*

In writing a case study in the spirit of Joseph's approach, it is important to focus on how the patient utilizes their own mind. The clinician should document how the patient engages with their own understandings and insights, and carefully track what occurs with those parts of the personality that gained insight, even if only momentarily. The emphasis in the description should be on how the patient experienced the interpretations provided to them and how they responded to these interpretations.

The case should include thorough documentation of the therapeutic interaction, focusing on the specific way the patient employs the therapist in real time. It should describe how the patient tends to utilize the interpretations offered to them, and how they engage their own mind during the therapeutic hour. These descriptions should be concrete and anchored in precise examples from the sessions.

It is crucial to avoid interpretations that are not immediately accessible to the patient. According to Joseph, one should refrain from attaching explanatory or causal formulations to interpretations until the patient can identify what is being discussed. The case study should demonstrate how efforts were made to describe the experience that is directly available to the patient—an experience they can identify and acknowledge—before any explanations are provided.

The written case should pay special attention to how the therapist monitors minute changes and subtle transitions in therapy, including shifts in atmosphere, actions, and pressures experienced during the therapeutic hour. The therapist should outline their attention to these details, emphasizing that this is a selective and specific focus aimed at not missing the essential message of the patient's communication (Blass, 2011).

In summary, a written case in the spirit of Betty Joseph's approach should emphasize tracking how the patient uses their mind, the therapist's interpretations, and the therapeutic relationship, while focusing on the immediately available experience. This contrasts with prioritizing causal or historical aspects, or interpretations that are not directly accessible to the patient. The emphasis is on the process of internalizing the therapist's thinking and containment through ongoing clarification of the experience available to the patient in real time.

When writing a case study using Joseph's technique method, several key elements should be emphasized:

1. Immediate experience over historical material—unlike her earlier work, which followed the traditional Kleinian emphasis on linking past and present, Joseph's mature technique focuses on documenting the patient's immediate experience in the consulting room. While historical material isn't ignored, it should remain in the background, informing understanding without becoming the primary focus.

2. Natural language over technical terms—Joseph moved away from Kleinian part-object anatomical language (like "breast and mouth"), preferring instead the natural language of "you and I" (Aguayo, 2011). Case studies should reflect this shift, using the patient's own language rather than imposed theoretical terminology.

3. Countertransference as a diagnostic tool—document how the analyst differentiates between their subjective reactions and the distortions induced by the patient. This includes careful attention to how patients attempt to manipulate the analyst into making particular kinds of interpretations.

4. Working with narcissistic pathology—Joseph's technique evolved partly in response to treating more narcissistic and borderline patients. Case studies should detail how these patients create pathological organizations, including:

   a. Their attempts to strip objects of desirable qualities
   b. Their difficulties with dependency
   c. Their creation of "near-death" psychic states
   d. Their ways of organizing the analyst according to their defensive needs.

5. Present moment—focus on describing:

   a. The patient's actual behavior in sessions
   b. How they attempt to maintain psychic equilibrium
   c. Their ways of deadening or enlivening analytical work

    d.   The analyst's efforts to maintain authentic contact
    e.   The immediate impact of projective and introjective identification.

This approach represents a significant evolution from traditional Kleinian case writing. While maintaining theoretical sophistication, it prioritizes immediate clinical experience over historical reconstruction, authentic engagement over technical language, and present-moment understanding over past-to-present interpretation. For example, rather than interpreting a patient's "twisted carrots" dream through part-object symbolism (as "twisted nipples"), Joseph's approach would focus on how the patient uses such material in the immediate therapeutic relationship, including attempts to manipulate the analyst into making particular kinds of interpretations. The case should capture how unconscious dynamics are lived out in the therapeutic relationship rather than simply interpreted, demonstrating how meaning emerges through the present therapeutic encounter while being aware of historical material in the background.

What causes change?

In Joseph's technique, change is achieved when the patient internalizes the analyst's thinking (Blass, 2011). When writing case studies following Betty Joseph's approach, it is essential to document how therapeutic change occurs through the patient's gradual internalization of the analyst's thinking capacity. The case should trace how a part of the patient's self begins to form an alliance with the analytical process, revealing the subtle shifts as patients start recognizing their defenses and gaining genuine insight. In documenting this process, focus on how patients gradually relinquish their defenses and integrate previously projected or repressed aspects of themselves.

These moments of integration often arise through complex interactions in the therapeutic relationship, which should be carefully detailed in your writing. Another challenge is describing the patient's behaviors and communications in clear, experience-near language without resorting to interpretations about underlying fantasies or explanations connecting current behavior to past experiences. Finally, the therapist must be able to recognize and articulate their own responses to the patient's projections and pressures to behave in certain ways without becoming overtly involved in acting out.

These subtle dynamics between patient and therapist are crucial to Joseph's method and must be observed, documented, and analyzed meticulously in the case study. The therapist must navigate a delicate tension between experiencing the patient's projections and maintaining enough distance to process and understand them. This demands a high degree of self-awareness and the ability to reflect on and articulate the complex interplay between patient and therapist in the therapeutic relationship.

Clinical example

Jeremy, a young lawyer, arrived late for his therapy session, visibly flustered and embarrassed. As he settled into the chair, he immediately began to express frustration about the strictness of psychoanalysts regarding time, accusing me of being overly rigid and controlled by the clock. He launched into a lecture about how therapists are always bound by time, implying that this rigidity was unreasonable and impersonal. I listened attentively to how Jeremy's unconscious fantasies manifested directly in the here-and-now of the session. His lateness and subsequent attack on analytic boundaries might signify multiple layers of unconscious dynamics. One possibility is a greedy fantasy of wanting unlimited time and attention (the breast/time all to himself), followed by guilt about this desire, which leads to self-punishment through lateness, resulting in actual deprivation that he then projects onto the analyst. The dynamic might reflect an Oedipal situation where Jeremy tests the analyst's loyalties—questioning whether the analyst is more committed to psychoanalysis than to him, akin to a child wondering about parental loyalties. Through his late arrival, complaints, and grumbling, Jeremy enacts the child who bursts in on his parents, demanding to know why one parent (the analyst) prefers the other (psychoanalysis) over him. His guilt about intruding into the primal scene might then be projected onto the analyst through accusations about rigid boundaries.

Jeremy's anger about time boundaries becomes a way of creating an immediate experience of his internal object relationships within the therapeutic encounter. I said to him: "I wonder if right now, by coming late and then attacking me about time boundaries, you're showing me something about your struggle with wanting all our time for yourself. Perhaps you feel a longing for more time with me, and as a result, you punish yourself by arriving late—but then you immediately try to rid yourself of the resulting guilt by turning me into someone rigid and withholding. It seems that rather than face your own desires for unlimited time with me, you ensure you get less time and then make me feel responsible for your deprivation." Jeremy fell silent for a long time, his previous agitation visibly subsiding. Then he spoke more quietly, "You know, I actually rushed here today, racing through traffic, knowing I was late . . . and the whole time I was thinking about how angry you'd be, how you'd scold me."

He paused, then added thoughtfully, "But I guess I was the one who ended up being angry and scolding you." His ability to receive this interpretation seemed to stem from how it captured precisely what he was experiencing and enacting in the moment, rather than explaining or analyzing it from the outside.

The interpretation acknowledged both his demanding wishes and his guilt about them, while showing how he was actively managing these feelings through his behavior in the session. By articulating this dynamic as it was happening, the interpretation helped transform an unconscious enactment into something that could be thought about and understood, reducing his need to continue acting it out through anger and accusations.

The vignette demonstrates how every aspect of Jeremy's behavior—his lateness, his accusations, his anger—is part of a unified unconscious fantasy being enacted in the therapeutic relationship. Each element contributes to understanding how he handles his greedy wishes and subsequent guilt. Instead of explaining Jeremy's behavior, the interpretation captures exactly what he is doing in the moment—showing him how he's actively creating a situation where he both punishes himself and makes the analyst feel guilty.

CONTEMPORARY KLEINIAN THERAPISTS: IRMA BRENMAN PICK

If you haven't found your place yet, you might draw inspiration from another group of contemporary Kleinian therapists. Irma Brenman Pick represents a significant evolution in Kleinian thinking, offering a theoretical framework that maintains Klein's fundamental concepts while emphasizing the therapist's authentic emotional engagement. Her approach, which initially faced resistance within the Kleinian community, has become influential for a new generation of therapists seeking to combine technical precision with genuine emotional availability (Brenman Pick, Davids, and Shavit, 2018). Central to her framework is the concept of authenticity—the idea that to genuinely investigate patients' internal objects and identifications, therapists must simultaneously own and examine their own. This framework allows therapists to remain faithful to Kleinian theory while acknowledging and working with their emotional responses in the therapeutic process. Brenman Pick writes case studies that appear both traditional and lively at once. When writing case studies in Brenman Pick's spirit therapists should document both the patient's material and their own authentic internal experiences. The case narrative needs to capture the therapist's process of working through alongside the patient, including moments of regression necessary for attuning to the patient's communications and processing projections. To be authentically creative in this work, therapists must remain self-reflective, owning their reactions, feelings, and inclinations to act, while analyzing their projections. This involves describing how the therapist maintains their capacity for understanding while enduring intense emotional states, particularly when feeling overwhelmed by the patient's material.

As Brenman Pick herself notes:

> If we feel at the mercy of an analytic superego that does not support us in knowing about our internal buffetings, we are, like the patient, in danger of wrapping it all up competently. We may act out by becoming excessively sympathetic to our patients, or taking the others to court in a superior or angry way, or becoming excessively sympathetic to the others, taking the patient to court in a superior or angry way.
>
> *Brenman Pick, Davids and Shavit, 2018, p20.*

The case study should therefore include careful documentation of the therapist's struggles with their own analytic superego and how these are managed in service of the therapeutic process.

Your writing should demonstrate how you navigate between incisive interpretation and emotional containment. Merav Roth (2021) called this "two-armed therapy," highlighting the need to balance gentle confrontation with pain while maintaining compassion. Working only with vulnerability through indirect approaches perpetuates avoidance, while focusing solely on confrontation without understanding the patient's defensive choices risks aligning with their punitive superego. The therapist must recognize psychological defenses while carefully guiding toward engagement with underlying pain.

This style of case writing requires candor about your emotional processes while maintaining technical sophistication in describing the therapeutic work. The goal is to create a narrative that captures both the technical aspects of Kleinian work and the human experience of engaging deeply with another person's psychological pain.

Clinical example

A patient, Ms. R, came to analysis following a traumatic miscarriage. In our early sessions, she spoke in a detached manner about her medical procedures while meticulously arranging and rearranging items in my office. I noticed that I was becoming increasingly frustrated with what I perceived as her "obsessive" avoidance, feeling an urge to confront her defenses and push for emotional contact. However, when I allowed myself to sit with these reactions, I recognized my own fear of the raw grief she carried—a grief that threatened to overwhelm us both. Like the medical staff who had treated her with clinical detachment, I was tempted to hide behind technique rather than meet her in that painful space. During one session, Ms. R was describing organizing her closet when she suddenly paused, holding a small stuffed animal. "I bought this for . . . " she trailed off, her hands trembling slightly. In that moment, I felt tears well up in my own eyes—not from pity, but from finally allowing myself to feel with her the magnitude of her loss. Rather than interpreting her "resistance," I quietly suggested that perhaps we both needed time to build the strength to look at what had been lost. She began to cry softly, continuing to hold the stuffed animal. For the first time, her grief could exist between us without either of us needing to push it away or take control of it. This marked a turning point. As I worked through my own fear of being overwhelmed by painful emotions—my reflexive retreat into either confrontation or false reassurance—I could better help Ms. R gradually face her trauma. The "obsessive" behaviors diminished not through interpretation but through my willingness to join her in bearing what had felt unbearable alone. This required allowing myself to be genuinely affected while maintaining enough psychological space to think about and metabolize the experience. Only by working through my own defenses against knowing could I help the patient begin to know her own truth.

This vignette, like the original text, demonstrates how authentic clinical thinking involves noticing not just the content of what is said, but the living process of how therapist and patient co-create both deadness and aliveness in their encounter. The key intervention emerged from staying with my own countertransference experience of constraint rather than rushing to make sense of it intellectually.

DEMONSTRATIONS OF CLINICAL PHENOMENA

Negative therapeutic reaction and envy

According to Spillius (2007) "Negative therapeutic reaction is a sequence of behavior in which a tacit or explicit recognition of progress by the patient is followed by a worsening of his condition and by an open or disguised attack on the analysis." (p. 129)

In writing clinical material, clinicians need to pay special attention to how patients who are clearly benefiting from therapy nevertheless dismiss and attack the therapist or the therapeutic work. Klein specifically identified this devaluation as an expression of envy. The case writer should aim to capture both the manifest content of these attacks and their unconscious envious underpinnings, demonstrating how this dynamic plays out in the therapeutic relationship and impacts the treatment process.

Clinical example

Emily, a 35-year-old patient, has been in analysis for two years struggling with chronic depression and difficulties in relationships. In recent sessions she has made some progress in understanding the roots of her self-sabotaging behaviors. However, after a particularly insightful interpretation about her tendency to push away those closest to her, Emily arrives at the next session in a markedly worse state. She reports a disturbing dream:

"I was in a dark kitchen. You were there stirring a large pot of soup. I was hungry and approached to get some, but as I got closer I saw the soup was filled with writhing worms and maggots. You smiled and offered me a bowl. I felt disgusted and furious. I grabbed the pot and poured it over your head."

Upon exploring the dream, Emily becomes agitated and accuses me of being smug and self-satisfied with her progress. She insists that the treatment is making her worse and threatens to quit therapy. I recognize this as a negative therapeutic reaction stemming from Emily's unconscious envy. Rather than becoming defensive, I gently interpret Emily's anger as potentially arising from her feeling that I possess something valuable (insight, nourishment) that she both desperately wants and resents needing. I also point out how Emily's attempt to pour the "contaminated" soup over my head in the dream might represent her unconscious desire to spoil and devalue what I have to offer, perhaps to alleviate her own painful feelings of envy and inadequacy.

Manic defenses

Manic defenses are characterized by a sense of omnipotence, denial, and disparagement of the object. These defenses protect the ego from the pain and anxiety associated with dependence on loved objects. Klein states that the ego argues, "Surely it is not a matter of such great importance if this particular object is destroyed. There are so many others to be incorporated" (Klein, 1975, p. 163). This disparagement of the object's importance is a key feature of manic defenses.

Clinical example

The patient dates numerous men but invariably finds a flaw in each one to avoid becoming attached. Typically, she criticizes her partners' genitals, deeming them too small or unsatisfying. This allows her to maintain a sense of contempt toward potential partners, protecting her from the vulnerability of emotional attachment.

In our sessions, I notice that while she appears polite and attentive, accepting my interpretations without resistance, there is a lack of genuine curiosity or engagement. This behavior suggests to me a reluctance to form a meaningful connection or to internalize the nourishing interpretations I offer.

Recently, she shared a dream that I believe perfectly illustrates her manic defenses:

"I'm at a buffet with an endless array of dishes. As I sample each one, I find them all lacking in flavor. I keep moving from plate to plate, tasting and discarding, feeling increasingly superior to the chefs who prepared such mediocre food. Eventually, I leave the buffet, feeling hungry but triumphant."

In interpreting this dream, I emphasized how her manic defenses manifest in her tendency to devalue and discard potential sources of nourishment, whether they be relationships or therapeutic insights. I understood the endless buffet as representing the abundance of potential connections, while her dissatisfaction and sense of superiority reflect her manic denial of dependency needs. Her leaving hungry yet triumphant symbolizes how these defenses protect her from vulnerability but ultimately leave her emotionally unfulfilled.

Splitting

According to Melanie Klein, splitting is a fundamental defensive mechanism in which the ego divides both itself and its objects into "good" and "bad" parts. This binary splitting is seen as essential for early development, enabling the infant to protect and introject a "good" object around which the ego can cohere. Klein views splitting as interconnected with projection and introjection, forming a cycle where split parts are projected into objects and then reintrojected, influencing the structure of the ego and superego. While some splitting is necessary for integration, excessive or rigid splitting can impair later integration and weaken the ego (Spillius et al., 2011). When writing clinical notes about splitting, clinicians should focus on describing specific instances where the patient demonstrates all-good or all-bad representations of significant others, themselves, or the therapist, while noting how these split representations may shift over time and impact the therapeutic relationship.

Clinical example

Natali, a 33-year-old painter, began the session by remarking began by remarking on my new hairstyle, noting it made me appear more approachable yet less professional. This observation hinted at the complex splitting process occurring in her mind. In the dream Natali shared from the previous night, she was preparing for an art exhibition when the gallery suddenly filled with faceless critics defacing her artwork with harsh critiques in red paint. Amidst the chaos, she noticed a single critic with a trendy haircut who was particularly vocal in her criticism, even throwing mud at Natali's paintings. Paralyzed, Natali could only watch as the destruction unfolded. However, she also observed a solitary figure apart from the crowd—a figure with my face, carefully restoring one of her paintings with vibrant colors. As we explored her associations, Natali expressed feeling overwhelmed by self-doubt and fear of judgment regarding her upcoming exhibition. She noted that the faceless critics reminded her of her highly critical mother, who never supported her artistic pursuits. I suggested that the dream figures might represent split aspects of herself that she was projecting onto me—the harsh inner critic who devalues her work (represented by the trendy-haired critic) and the nurturing, creative part that believes in her artistic abilities (represented by the restoring figure). By splitting and projecting these conflicting self-representations onto me, she could maintain some distance from her internal conflict about her artistic worth. When I shared this interpretation, suggesting that she may experience me as both the harsh critic and the supportive figure, Natali became visibly uncomfortable. She firmly denied seeing me as critical or judgmental in any way, insisting that I had always been completely supportive. Her strong resistance to acknowledging any negative feelings toward me seemed to confirm the intensity of the splitting and the difficulty she had in integrating these opposing experiences of both herself and me in the therapeutic relationship.

Harsh superego: Clinical example

In presenting this clinical material of a schizophrenic patient, Ms. A, I aim to demonstrate how a primitive and persecutory superego manifests through bizarre fragmentation, projection, and confusion between internal and external reality.

Ms. A's communications were often fragmented, typically consisting of whispered phrases and unfinished sentences. She frequently trailed off mid-thought, expecting me to grasp her meaning. When my interpretations resonated with her internal experience, she would show this through subtle changes in her posture or a momentary softening of her typically rigid facial expression. At times, she would nod vigorously while simultaneously covering her ears, displaying both acceptance and fear of understanding.

During our early sessions, Ms. A often stared at the walls, claiming they were "pulsing with accumulated screams" of her past misdeeds. She described feeling colonized by "swarms of wasps" that had nested in her brain, stinging her whenever she had a thought or feeling of her own. These wasps, she explained, came from a "hive mother" who could broadcast her disapproval through radio waves that penetrated Ms. A's skull.

Her ability to verbalize varied dramatically. During periods of relative integration, she could speak with surprising lucidity about her internal experiences. However, when overwhelmed by anxiety, particularly when feeling "colonized by foreign substances," she would become almost entirely mute, communicating primarily through gestures and written notes. These periods of muteness often improved when I could accurately interpret the specific nature of her anxieties.

The relationship between her aggression and anxiety was particularly striking. After episodes where she acted out physically—throwing objects at hospital staff or trying to "extract the surveillance devices" from her own body—she would fall into states of profound terror and self-persecution. In one instance, after throwing her water glass against the wall, she spent the next three sessions curled in a corner, convinced that shards of glass were circulating through her bloodstream, cutting her from within. It became increasingly clear that when her aggression was directed outward rather than against herself, it triggered overwhelming guilt that manifested in somatic delusions and intensified her persecutory anxieties.

The transference relationship revealed complex layers of projection and introjection. In one significant session, she arrived convinced that her organs were gradually dissolving because they had "failed their inspection." When I interpreted that perhaps she felt her internal parts were being subjected to harsh scrutiny and punishment, she looked at me with sudden clarity and said, "The inspection happens through your eyes—they contain microscopes that see all my rotten parts."

Yet alongside these intense projections, Ms. A showed moments of insight. After one particularly difficult session where she was certain I had installed surveillance equipment in her teeth, she returned the next day saying, "Sometimes I wonder if these thoughts about you are really my own thoughts about myself, but that feels even more frightening." This capacity for momentary reflection, however, often triggered intense anxiety, leading her to feel that her words had become "poisonous gas" filling the room.

As treatment progressed, she developed her own unique way of communicating her internal world by creating intricate drawings of what she called her "inner architecture"—bizarre blueprints of her internal landscape that she would annotate with cryptic yet meaningful symbols. These drawings became a valuable medium for understanding her internal object relations and the workings of her primitive superego.

This material illustrates how a primitive and harsh superego can manifest through bizarre somatic delusions, a profound confusion between self and object, and intense projective identification. The therapeutic work involves carefully containing and interpreting these processes as they emerge in the transference relationship, allowing for brief moments of integration while respecting the patient's need to maintain certain defensive organizations.

Symbolic equation

According to Hanna, symbolic equation is a phenomenon where there is no distinction between the symbol and the thing symbolized. In this state, the symbol is not merely a representation but is experienced as if it were the actual object itself. This is in contrast to proper symbol formation, where the symbol is recognized as having its own characteristics separate from what it symbolizes (Segal, 1957).

When documenting symbolic equation in clinical notes, particularly in severely disturbed or psychotic patients, clinicians should focus on describing specific instances where the patient experiences symbols as literally equivalent to what they represent, rather than as representations that stand for something else.

Clinical example

John, a 28-year-old former law student, had been diagnosed with paranoid schizophrenia. His condition manifested shortly after he started his first internship at a prestigious law firm. John's psychotic symptoms included persistent delusions that he was being monitored and controlled by a secret government agency. He believed that time itself was a construct used to manipulate the masses.

During a therapy session, John was asked by his therapist why he refused to wear a watch. John replied angrily, "Are you expecting me to chain myself up like a prisoner?" In this case, John equated the watch (the symbol) with actual chains or bondage (the thing symbolized).

John's refusal to wear a watch was not merely a quirk, but a symptom of his psychotic thought process. His symbolic equation of watches with imprisonment stemmed from his paranoid delusions. In his mind, the watch wasn't just a timepiece; it was a literal instrument of control and surveillance. This inability to distinguish between the symbol and the symbolized object is characteristic of psychotic thinking, where the boundaries between internal and external reality become blurred.

Furthermore, John's psychosis was evident in his inability to grasp the metaphorical nature of language. He took figurative expressions literally, often leading to misunderstandings and social isolation. His rigid, concrete thinking extended beyond watches to other aspects of his life, severely impacting his ability to function in society and maintain relationships.

Reparation

Reparation, as conceptualized by Melanie Klein (1975), is a psychological process central to her theory of the depressive position. It involves the individual's recognition of the harm caused to their internal and external objects (representations of loved ones) through aggressive impulses or fantasies and the subsequent desire to repair and restore these objects. This process is deeply rooted in feelings of love, guilt, and concern for the wellbeing of the object.

Reparation emerges when the individual moves beyond the paranoid-schizoid position—characterized by splitting objects into wholly good or bad—and begins to integrate these aspects, recognizing that the loved object is both good and bad. This realization evokes guilt for past destructive fantasies or actions, motivating efforts to mend the damage and preserve the relationship with the object.

For clinicians exploring reparation in their writing or practice, it is essential to emphasize its role in facilitating psychological integration and growth. Reparation reflects a shift from defensive mechanisms like splitting or denial towards a mature capacity for concern and responsibility. In therapeutic settings, this process can be observed in patients' attempts to repair damaged relationships or inner conflicts, often mirrored in their interactions with the analyst. Highlighting reparation's connection to creativity and its potential to transform destructive impulses into constructive actions can enrich clinical understanding and application.

Clinical example

A 7-year-old girl in analysis presented a dream in which she was in a garden filled with wilted flowers. In the dream, she felt deeply sad and guilty, believing she had caused the flowers to die by forgetting to water them. As she stood there, filled with remorse, she noticed a watering can nearby. With determination, she began carefully watering each flower, watching with relief and joy as they slowly came back to life, their vibrant colors returning. The girl's associations revealed that the wilted flowers represented her mother, whom she felt she had "damaged" through her angry outbursts and disobedience. The act of watering and reviving the flowers symbolized her unconscious wish to make reparation—to heal and restore her relationship with her mother. This dream illustrates Klein's concept of reparation, where the child, having experienced guilt over fantasized attacks on the loved object, attempts to repair the damage and restore the object to its previous good state. The dream shows the movement from the paranoid-schizoid position, where the child feels she has destructively damaged the object, to the depressive position, where she recognizes her love for the object and wishes to make amends. The analysis of this dream helped the girl work through her ambivalent feelings toward her mother and develop a more integrated view of their relationship. It marked an important step in her emotional development, fostering her capacity for concern, empathy, and the ability to take responsibility for her actions.

Manic reparation

In manic reparation (Klein, 1940), the individual attempts to undo damage done to the object in phantasy, but does so in an omnipotent, unrealistic way that denies the true extent of the damage and the genuine feelings of guilt and concern. Rather than truly acknowledging and working through depressive anxieties, manic reparation involves magical thinking and a sense of triumph over the object. The person may engage in frantic attempts to "fix" things, but these efforts are not grounded in reality or genuine remorse. Instead, they serve to deny the person's dependence on the object and their true feelings of loss or guilt. Manic reparation often involves a reversal of roles, where the person fantasizes about restoring or even improving the object, as if they had the power to create or control it. This allows them to avoid facing their own destructive impulses and the real consequences of their actions.

To effectively describe manic behavior, it's important to highlight how manic reparation serves as a defense against experiencing the full weight of guilt and concern for the object. Note any instances where the patient seems to reverse roles with the object, fantasizing about being the one to create or control it. This reversal can be a way for patients to deny their dependence on the object and avoid facing their own destructive impulses. In the case study, look for patterns where the patient's attempts at reparation provide temporary relief from anxiety but ultimately prevent them from working through their depressive position meaningfully.

Clinical example

Tommy, a 5-year-old boy, was initially referred to me due to aggressive outbursts at school. In our early sessions, I observed a pattern in his play that was quite revealing. Tommy would build elaborate block towers with frantic energy, only to knock them down violently moments later. What struck me was his insistence on immediately rebuilding them, often bigger and what he called "better" than before. When I would comment on the destruction, Tommy would adamantly claim he was "fixing" things and making them "perfect." As our therapy progressed, I noticed subtle changes in Tommy's behavior. He began to slow down a bit and seemed more willing to acknowledge feelings of sadness when his creations fell. One session stands out in my mind as particularly significant. On this day, Tommy carefully constructed a small house with blocks. When it accidentally toppled over, instead of his usual frantic rebuilding, he paused. After a moment of silence, he turned to me with tears in his eyes and said, "I broke our home." I gently acknowledged his feelings, and we worked together to rebuild the house. I noticed Tommy taking extra care to make it sturdy this time. He even added small details like windows and a door. When we finished, Tommy stepped back and remarked, "If it falls again, we can fix it together."

While it's important not to overstate the progress, this moment seemed to indicate some positive shifts in Tommy's behavior. He appeared more able to sit with difficult feelings like loss and guilt, and showed a willingness to take responsibility for his actions. His approach to rebuilding the house was more measured and collaborative, suggesting some improvement in his problem-solving skills and ability to work with others.

UNDERSTANDING THE OEDIPAL TRIANGLE IN CLINICAL WRITING: BRITTON'S CONTEMPORARY VIEW

When writing case studies from a Kleinian perspective, particularly following Britton's contemporary interpretation (1988, 1989), it's essential to capture how the Oedipal triangle manifests as a universal human experience of exclusion and thirdness. Unlike Freud's classical Oedipal complex, which is firmly rooted in traditional family structures and gender roles, Britton's conceptualization offers a more flexible framework that applies to various family configurations and therapeutic situations.

In clinical writing, emphasis should be placed on describing the emotional experience of being outside a couple, the feelings of rejection, and the painful transition from being the center of attention to recognizing the autonomous relationship between others. These experiences echo the infant's first discovery that their parents have a relationship from which they are excluded. Britton's concept of the "other room" (Britton, 1998) represents not just the parents' bedroom but any space—physical, emotional, or mental—that the subject cannot access. When writing case material, it's crucial to observe how patients handle these experiences of exclusion and document their defensive patterns, such as splitting the good object from the threatening third or denying the reality of triangular relationships.

It's important to note in clinical writing how patients may transform triangular situations into purely dyadic ones and react to interpretations as threatening intrusions. The evolution of the patient's capacity to tolerate triangular relationships throughout treatment should be carefully documented. Britton's framework allows us to understand these dynamics in non-traditional family structures, emphasizing the emotional experience rather than requiring a specific family configuration. This makes his theory particularly relevant for contemporary clinical work and case writing, as it can be applied to various family structures and therapeutic situations.

Here is an example of manic reparation that transformed into genuine reparation:

Rita, a 35-year-old woman, entered analysis primarily due to persistent difficulties in romantic relationships and a pervasive sense of isolation. As our work progressed, it became evident that her struggles centered around managing triangular situations and the psychic pain of exclusion, particularly manifesting in her inability to tolerate relationships from which she feels excluded.

Rita's early experiences significantly shaped her relationship to triangular situations. Growing up with an alcoholic father and depressed mother, she developed a defensive strategy of trying to control and monitor the parental relationship. Rather than face the pain of not being part of the couple, she positioned herself as a manager of the parental couple's relationship, effectively attempting to insert herself between her parents.

A recent dream powerfully illustrated her unconscious handling of triangular relationships: she was performing alone in a circus, responsible for controlling various wild animals. In the audience sat an old man, leering at young women, with open pants and drool dripping from his mouth. Sarah felt both disgusted by him and responsible for controlling his behavior.

This dream reveals Rita's defensive organization against triangular reality. The circus ring represents her attempt to control and manage coupling (the wild animals that might mate), reflecting her fantasy of maintaining purely dyadic relationships where no third can enter. The old man in the audience embodies multiple layers of meaning: he represents both the threatening aspect of the Oedipal triangle and, significantly, Rita's own split-off sexual desires. Her expressed disgust towards him serves as a defense against recognizing these disavowed aspects of herself—her own sexual yearnings and desire for intimate connection that she finds shameful and threatening.

When Rita associated the old man with me, it revealed not only her experience of analytic thinking as a threatening couple (me and my thoughts) from which she feels excluded but also the projection of her own "dangerous" sexual desires onto the analytic relationship. Her attempt to control both the wild animals and the older man's behavior reflects her broader struggle with managing both external triangular relationships and her internal sexual impulses.

In the transference, Rita's inability to tolerate my separate thoughts and perspectives manifests in her inability to contain disharmony. Any interpretation that suggests a different understanding is experienced as a catastrophic reminder of exclusion. She seeks not understanding but rather complicity in denying both the reality of triangular relationships and her own sexual desires.

Our ongoing work focuses on helping Rita gradually develop the capacity to tolerate triangular situations and reintegrate her split-off desires. This involves working through her defensive need to control relationships and helping her acknowledge and accept her own sexuality as part of her adult self.

TERMINATION PHASE IN A KLEINIAN ORIENTATION

The Kleinian approach to termination emphasizes addressing depressive anxieties and mourning. The process involves integrating split-off aspects of the self and objects, facilitating a transition from the paranoid-schizoid position to the depressive position. The patient is encouraged to confront feelings of loss, guilt, and a need for reparation. Additionally, the therapist may address anxieties stemming from the paranoid-schizoid position, assisting patients in grappling with envy, greed, destructive wishes, and aggression. The termination process entails working through these primitive emotions and defenses to achieve a more integrated and mature psychological state.

How do we summarize the achievements of the Kleinian treatment?

Well, in reporting Kleinian therapeutic gains, less is definitely more—we're truth-tellers first, cheerleaders second (if at all).

In this regard, as Betty Joseph (2018) noted in her paper "Ending Analysis", the end of treatment is prone to obscuring the truth due to both parties' desire to alleviate their anxieties.

Here is how Joseph chose to describe the conclusion of treatment with one of her patients:

> I do not think with this patient that she is protected against future panics, mini-breakdowns, against turning against me or the analysis, but I do think that now her relationship with analysis, with her good internal objects, is strong enough for her to face her ambivalence and to regain contact with her warmth and insight and recover her equilibrium. (p. 1434)

What a moderate, wonderful, modest tone that remains faithful to the truth while emphasizing the treatment's achievements without a hint of exaggeration or sentimentality. From Joseph's humble tone, we can learn how to be precise about the occurring and reticent about feelings.

Clinical example

As we approached the termination phase with Keri, the complex interplay of her internal object relations came into sharp focus. Her polite demeanor and intellectual engagement had long masked a deep-seated narcissistic organization, which became increasingly apparent as we neared the end of our sessions.

Keri's approach to our work was marked by a peculiar blend of consistency and emotional detachment. She arrived punctually, shared her thoughts, and listened attentively; yet, her responses often took the form of academic dissertations, effectively diluting the emotional impact of our exchanges.

As the end drew near, Keri's defenses intensified. She became more verbal, often speaking in abstract terms about psychoanalytic theories, as if to assert her intellectual equality and deny her need for me. However, this coincided with an increase in reported somatic symptoms—headaches, insomnia, and digestive issues—revealing the psychic cost of maintaining her defenses.

A pivotal moment came when Keri shared a significant dream:

"I'm at a large dining table laden with food. My hands are gloved; I can't remove them. A shadowy figure at the other end eats with relish. The gloves turn into infant hands. The figure approaches with a milk-filled goblet, revealing itself as an older, confident version of me. As it tries to feed me, I shrink into an infant. The room spins, and I wake up dizzy."

This dream encapsulated many of our core themes. The feast represented the nourishment of our work, but also the good breast that Keri both craved and envied. The gloves symbolized her emotional defenses, while their transformation into infant hands revealed her disavowed vulnerability. The shadowy figure becoming her idealized self portrayed both her potential for growth and her ambivalence about dependency.

As we worked through this dream, Keri connected more deeply with her conflicting feelings about our impending separation. She acknowledged her fear of losing the nourishment of our sessions, but also her terror of fully accepting her need for this nourishment.

In our final sessions, Keri's work centered on mourning and consolidation rather than new therapeutic gains. She reflected on our three years together, noticing both her increased capacity for emotional awareness and her lingering tendency to intellectualize when feeling vulnerable. While she could now better recognize her split internal objects, full integration remained a work in progress. She acknowledged this with a mix of sadness and acceptance, noting that endings often stirred up familiar fears of abandonment; yet, she could now hold these feelings without complete retreat into defensive intellectualization. These final hours reflected the modest yet meaningful shifts in her internal world—not a dramatic transformation but rather a quiet strengthening of her capacity to bear psychic pain and ambivalence.

Despite the ongoing challenges, I believe that Keri's good internal object has become more stable and well-established than it was at the beginning of our work. While she may continue to face internal conflicts, the strengthened good object provides a more reliable foundation for her to draw upon during future crises. Our work has helped anchor this good object more firmly within her psychic structure, providing a source of inner strength that she can increasingly access and rely upon as she continues her journey of growth and self-discovery.

SUGGESTIONS FOR WRITING A CASE STUDY BASED ON KLEIN'S THEORY

The purpose of these recommendations, written at the end of each approach, is to help clinicians effectively document and present their psychoanalytic work from a specific psychoanalytic perspective. These guidelines aim to inspire thought and creativity rather than serve as rigid rules. They should be approached flexibly and creatively, used in ways that align with the writer's integrity, originality, and freedom of expression. Each clinician brings their unique perspective and style to case documentation while maintaining the essential elements of Kleinian understanding.

Exploration of "general childhood situations"

In your analysis and case write-up, it's essential to keep in mind and explore what Elizabeth Spillius called Klein's key "general childhood situations":

> [L]ove and hate of the breast; an epistemophilic instinct directed at mother's body and its contents; reparative attempts for having attacked the mother and father; the primal scene; the Oedipus complex; and the fragmenting splits of paranoid/schizoid as well as the development of the depressive position.
>
> *Spillius, 2007, p. 76.*

Focus on what is most important to your patient and provide examples from the patient's narrative or behavior in therapy that suggest these dynamics at play.

For instance, when discussing love and hate towards the breast, you might describe the patient's ambivalent feelings towards nurturing figures in their life. When exploring the epistemophilic instinct, you could discuss the patient's curiosity or anxiety about hidden aspects of others. For reparative attempts, describe any patterns of guilt and attempts to make amends in the patient's relationships.

Outline any patterns you've noticed in the patient's relationships, work life, or daily functioning. This could include recurring conflicts in personal relationships, difficulties in professional settings, or struggles with daily tasks and self-care. Look for themes that appear across different areas of the patient's life.

As you describe these current issues, begin drawing tentative connections to possible early experiences, keeping in mind specific themes from early childhood. For instance:

1. **Dependency:** note any excessive neediness or, conversely, rigid self-reliance in current relationships. These may link to early experiences of unreliable caregiving or premature responsibilities.

2. **The two positions:** when writing case studies in the Kleinian tradition, pay careful attention to including both the paranoid-schizoid and depressive positions in the assessment of the patient. Evaluate the patient's level of integration, ability to tolerate ambivalence, and capacity for concern and reparation. The case study should note any splitting, projection, and persecutory anxiety characteristic of the paranoid-schizoid position, as well as signs of mourning, guilt, and attempts at reparation indicative of the depressive position.

3. **Oedipus complex:** when documenting triangular space capacity, assess the patient's ability to recognize and tolerate that their love objects have independent lives and relationships beyond the dyadic bond. Note their reactions to situations where they are not included—do they respond with catastrophic pain and protest, or can they acknowledge the legitimate separateness of others? In the therapeutic relationship, observe whether they can accept that you have other patients while maintaining a fantasy of being uniquely special to you—an Oedipal illusion that deserves careful attention. Watch for their capacity to think about relationships from multiple positions: as participant, as observer, and as the one temporarily excluded. Document specific instances where they either demonstrate flexibility in moving between these positions or reveal rigid insistence on exclusive dyadic relating.

4. **Envy:** pay attention to intense feelings of hostility or contempt toward figures perceived as nurturing and successful, potentially rooted in early experiences of deprivation or sibling comparison.

5. Documenting the strength and presence of the good internal object, observe these key aspects:

   a. Describe the patient's capacity to maintain emotional equilibrium between sessions, especially during breaks and separations. Note their ability to hold onto positive therapeutic experiences rather than immediately attacking or devaluing them.

   b. Document instances where the patient demonstrates the ability to tolerate frustration and anxiety without complete psychological collapse. Pay attention to their capacity to maintain reflective functioning even when experiencing difficult emotions.

   c. Assess their ability to acknowledge both positive and negative feelings toward the same object without excessive splitting. Look for moments when they can integrate loving and aggressive impulses.

   d. Consider the patient's relationship with interpretation—do they use it for genuine understanding or primarily as an intellectual defense? Note their ability to metabolize interpretations over time.

   e. Observe their capacity for genuine concern about others, distinct from manic reparation or obsessional worry. Watch for evidence of authentic guilt and the ability to make reparation.

   f. Document their ability to maintain object constancy during periods of strong negative affect. Pay special attention to how they handle endings and transitions.

   g. Remember to ground these observations in specific clinical examples rather than general statements. Choose vignettes that clearly demonstrate the quality of object relations being described.

When drawing these connections, present them as hypotheses rather than definitive interpretations. You might use phrases like "These difficulties in maintaining close relationships may potentially echo early experiences of unreliable caregiving" or "The patient's intense self-criticism could possibly be linked to early experiences of feeling responsible for parental conflicts."

Transference and interpretation

When documenting Kleinian therapeutic work, clinicians can take three main approaches to analyzing the relationship between past and present:

1. The classical approach (Klein-Segal, uncommon today): interpret both conscious memories and unconscious material from early life, directly linking past to present in transference interpretations.

2. The here-and-now focus (Betty Joseph): prioritize immediate therapeutic interactions and present moment experiences, with less emphasis on historical interpretation. Document real-time manifestations of transference, defense mechanisms, and relational patterns.

3. The two-step method (combined): in the integrated approach, the therapist begins by focusing on the living dynamics occurring in the current therapeutic space—namely, the

transferences, resistances, and relationship patterns that emerge between therapist and patient in the present moment. After these dynamics are recognized and deeply interpreted, the therapist expands the view toward past experiences, connecting the patterns identified in the treatment room to formative early experiences. This approach combines Betty Joseph's focus on the therapeutic "here and now" with the original Kleinian emphasis on unconscious fantasies and early object relations. Thus, show how the patient's behavior in the therapeutic encounter receives an initial interpretation that illuminates what is happening in the present moment and is subsequently enriched by understanding the deep roots of these patterns in the patient's psychological history.

Whichever approach is chosen, provide specific examples of interactions, interpretations, and patient responses. Detail how early relational patterns manifest in the therapeutic relationship, supporting observations with concrete clinical material rather than theoretical abstractions.

Patient's response

Provide a detailed account of how the patient responded to your interpretations and explicit links between past and present. Describe both immediate reactions and any changes observed over time. Note that Joseph (1975) advised to pay attention to "the actual way he speaks and the way he reacts to the analyst's interpretations rather than to concentrate primarily on the content of what he says." (p76)

Pay attention to verbal and non-verbal responses. Did the patient show signs of insight, resistance, or emotional breakthrough? How did their narrative about themselves and their past evolve?

Observe where, on the surface, the therapy appears to be progressing well. There are signs of understanding, seemingly good rapport, expressions of gratefulness from the patient, and even reports of positive changes. However, beneath this facade, you—the therapist—experience no genuine contact, and your interpretations remain insignificant (see Joseph, 2000).

Countertransference

When writing a Kleinian case study, you should describe your countertransference not as personal reactions but as valuable information about the patient's internal world and primitive anxieties being projected onto you. Frame your experiences as windows into understanding your patient's psychic reality and defensive organizations.

In writing a case study according to Betty Joseph's approach, document the countertransference in a specific and structured way that focuses on several key aspects:

Document the patient's unconscious seduction: describe how you identified that the patient is trying to get you to think, believe, feel, and interpret in a particular way. Record the moments when you found yourself inclined to understand or interpret in a certain manner and how you recognized this as a countertransference response.

Analyze the identification process: write about the identification process itself—how you noticed that you were being led in a certain direction, how you recognized this as a countertransference reaction, and how you tried to understand how and why the patient was leading you to do this.

Document attempts at "imprisonment" in the patient's internal world: describe the sensitivity you developed to the patient's (unconscious) attempts to seduce you into thinking in a particular way, or to keep you "trapped" in a certain line of thought or way of feeling (such as inferiority or superiority).

Document the use of "you want me to . . ." interpretations: describe how you arrived at interpretations along the lines of "you want me to think" or "you want me to feel,"

Write about the use of interpretation: document the way the patient uses interpretation—whether it encourages acting out rather than genuine insight, and how the patient responds (agreement, apparent insight, omnipotence, mania, or stupidity).

Most importantly, present your countertransference as a tool for understanding your patient's unique way of maintaining psychic equilibrium rather than as evidence of progress or regression. Your case should show how you used your countertransferential experience to stay close to the patient's reality while avoiding moral judgments or pressure for specific kinds of change.

NOTES

1 There was indeed such a quality to some psychodynamic treatments in the past. As Fred Busch (2016) writes:

"In my early training as an analyst, as was typical at the time, there was a quality of 'gotcha' to the kind of interpretations that were recommended—i.e., the analyst not only found something the patient was trying to hide, but it was often something not pleasant about the patient." (p. 349)

This quote reflects a historical approach in psychoanalytic practice where interpretations were often aimed at uncovering hidden, often unflattering aspects of the patient's psyche. The 'gotcha' quality suggests a somewhat confrontational or triumphant attitude on the part of the analyst in revealing these hidden truths, which was considered a standard approach to interpretation at that time in psychoanalytic training and practice.

RECOMMENDED READING

Authenticity in the psychoanalytic encounter: The work of Irma Brenman Pick, by Irma Brenman Pick, M. Fakhry Davids, & Naomi Shavit. Routledge, 2018.

This volume serves as an essential resource for understanding the work of Irma Brenman Pick and how contemporary Kleinian theory can blend technical sophistication with authentic human connection.

Introduction to the work of Melanie Klein, by Hanna Segal. Heinemann Medical Books, 1964.

In this concise and accessible volume, Segal offers a thorough overview of Klein's essential theoretical concepts. What makes this book especially valuable is Segal's skillful use of detailed clinical examples to illustrate key Kleinian phenomena such as phantasy, defense mechanisms, and psychic positions. These vivid clinical vignettes enhance readers' understanding of how Klein's abstract theoretical concepts play out in actual clinical practice. The book has become a foundational text in Kleinian literature, with most clinicians starting their exploration of Kleinian theory through this work.

Five exemplary case studies of Kleinian theory

Notes on the psycho-analysis of the super-ego conflict of an acute schizophrenic, by Herbert Rosenfeld. *International Journal of Psychoanalysis 33*, 111–131, 1952.

In this case, Rosenfeld illustrates how a psychotic patient's seemingly incomprehensible behaviors and communications can be understood through careful attention to unconscious phantasies and early object relations. The case demonstrates how to track and describe changes in the patient's functioning by analyzing shifts between paranoid-schizoid and depressive positions.

A clinical contribution to the analysis of a perversion, by Betty Joseph. *International Journal of Psychoanalysis 52*, 441–449, 1971.

The case discusses a rubber fetishist whose perverse activities involved three main scenarios: sexual intercourse with a woman while both wore rubber (usually black), being attacked by figures in rubber while he wore rubber, and wearing rubber from head to toe, which would excite his whole skin to the point of ejaculation. What makes this case particularly valuable is Joseph's careful attention to how the perversion manifests in the therapeutic relationship itself, rather than simply interpreting its symbolic meaning. Her writing demonstrates how to move beyond simply cataloging symptoms or behaviors to illuminate the deeper character structure through close observation of the therapeutic process.

The riddle of anxiety: Between the familiar and the unfamiliar, by Rosine Perelberg. *International Journal of Psychoanalysis 99*, 810–827, 2018.

The paper follows Khalish, a man grappling with vertigo, physical injuries, and intricate sexual dynamics, including encounters with transsexuals. Perelberg illustrates the gradual emergence of meaning through the patient's symptoms, dreams, and acting out—from his initial bodily fragmentation to the revelation of early trauma and archaic phantasies about the maternal body and combined parental object.

"Making a person": Clinical considerations regarding the interpretation of anxieties in the analyses of children on the autisto-psychotic spectrum, by Joshua Durban. *International Journal of Psychoanalysis 100*, 921–939, 2019.

"Rafael would touch my nose and then his, my mouth and then his, my ears, hands and legs and then touch his own. I was initially taken aback by this physical contact and tried to stop it, as I would have done with any patient's attempt to touch me. Rafael kept on insistently trying to initiate this ritual, which he called "making a person." He did this, as was not his custom, in a very gentle and non-eroticized way, while maintaining an unusually long eye contact." (p. 933)

The case powerfully illustrates how psychoanalytic technique must be modified and expanded when working with children on what Durban calls the "autisto-psychotic spectrum." Rather than relying solely on verbal interpretation, the analyst must be willing to engage in concrete physical interactions and interpretations-in-action while maintaining analytic discipline.

The process with adult patients, by Donald Meltzer. In *The Psycho-analytical Process* (pp. 53–65). Heinemann Medical Books, 1967.

In this case study, Meltzer presents a four-year analysis of an 11-year-old child who initially sought treatment for learning difficulties, accident proneness, screaming fits, and intense sibling jealousy.

Through this case, Meltzer demonstrates how genuine analytic cooperation and responsibility develop gradually, moving from spontaneous play to representation in play and drawing, then to dream analysis, and finally to full analytic cooperation. He emphasizes that true analytic responsibility goes beyond external behavioral improvement and involves the patient's ability to take ownership of their psychic reality and internal object relations. The case illustrates how this responsibility, initially shared by parents and the analyst, must ultimately be taken on by the patient's ego. Meltzer shows that this process includes not just practical responsibilities like attending sessions, but more fundamentally, the willingness to endure the pain of the depressive position and engage in genuine analytic work.

REFERENCES

Aguayo, J. (2011). The evolution of psychoanalytic technique: Betty Joseph's contribution to contemporary Kleinian practice. *International Journal of Psychoanalysis, 92*(5), 1137–1156.

Bion, W. R., Rosenfeld, H., & Segal, H. (1961). Melanie Klein. *International Journal of Psychoanalysis, 42*(1), 4–8.

Blass, R. B. (2011). On the clinical value of Betty Joseph's approach to psychoanalytic technique. *International Journal of Psychoanalysis, 92*(4), 827–848.

Brenman Pick, I., Davids, M. F., & Shavit, N. (Eds.) (2018). *Authenticity in the psychoanalytic encounter: The work of Irma Brenman Pick*. Routledge.

Britton, R. (1988). The missing link: Parental sexuality in the Oedipus complex. *International Journal of Psychoanalysis, 69*(3), 329–340.

Britton, R. (1989). The Oedipus complex today: Clinical implications. *International Journal of Psychoanalysis, 70*(3), 435–450.

Britton, R. (1998). *Belief and imagination: Explorations in psychoanalysis*. Routledge.

Busch, F. (2016). Creating a psychoanalytic mind: A psychoanalytic method and theory. *International Journal of Psychoanalysis, 97*(2), 345–366.

Durban, J. (2019). "Making a person": Clinical considerations regarding the interpretation of anxieties in the analyses of children on the autistic-psychotic spectrum. *International Journal of Psychoanalysis, 100*(4), 921–939.

Joseph, B. (1971). A clinical contribution to the analysis of a perversion. *International Journal of Psychoanalysis, 52*(4), 441–449.

Joseph, B. (1975). The patient who is difficult to reach. In P. Giovacchini (Ed.), *Tactics and techniques in psychoanalytic therapy* (Vol. 2, pp. 205–216). Jason Aronson.

Joseph, B. (1985). Transference: The total situation. *International Journal of Psychoanalysis, 66*(4), 447–454.

Joseph, B. (2000). *Psychic equilibrium and psychic change: Selected papers of Betty Joseph*. Routledge.

Joseph, B. (2018). Ending analysis. *International Journal of Psychoanalysis, 99*(6), 1421–1440.

Klein, M (1940). Mourning and its relation to manic-depressive states. In *The Writings of Melanie Klein* (Vol. 1, pp. 344-369). Hogarth Press.

Klein, M. (1952). The origins of transference. *International Journal of Psychoanalysis, 33*(4), 433–438.

Klein, M. (1975). Love, guilt and reparation. In *Love, guilt and reparation and other works 1921-1945* (Vol. 1, pp. 306-343). Hogarth Press.

Meltzer, D. (1967). The process with adult patients. In *The psycho-analytical process* (pp. 53–65). Heinemann Medical Books.

Perelberg, R. (2018). The riddle of anxiety: Between the familiar and the unfamiliar. *International Journal of Psychoanalysis, 99*(4), 810–827.

Riviere, J. (1927). A contribution to the analysis of the negative therapeutic reaction. *International Journal of Psychoanalysis, 8*(3), 304–318.

Rosenfeld, H. (1952). Notes on the psycho-analysis of the super-ego conflict of an acute schizophrenic. *International Journal of Psychoanalysis, 33*(2), 111–131.

Roth, M. (2021). Two-armed therapy: Balancing confrontation and compassion in psychoanalytic work. *Contemporary Psychoanalysis, 57*(2), 185–205.

Segal, H. (1957). Notes on symbol formation. *International Journal of Psychoanalysis, 38*(6), 391–397.

Segal, H. (1964). *Introduction to the work of Melanie Klein.* Heinemann Medical Books.

Spillius, E. B. (2007). *Encounters with Melanie Klein: Selected papers of Elizabeth Spillius.* Routledge.

Spillius, E. B., Milton, J., Garvey, P., Couve, C., & Steiner, D. (2011). *The new dictionary of Kleinian thought.* Routledge.

CHAPTER 7

A case study in the spirit of Wilfred Bion

....

THE GREATEST CHALLENGES

Bion's theory has been subjected to so many creative interpretations that it is challenging to ascertain a single mode of psychodynamic case. According to Ogden (2012, p. 97), Bion's aim was not to be grasped but rather to serve as a catalyst for the reader's own thinking. While Bion's unique writing style was distinctly his own, his emphasis on capturing the immediacy of the analytic moment offers valuable insights for contemporary case writing. The challenge—and opportunity—in writing a case study influenced by Bionian thinking is to convey the aliveness of the therapeutic encounter while remaining attuned to the experiential truth of what transpires between patient and analyst. As Bion notes, "Psychoanalytic observation isn't concerned with what has happened or what will happen, but with what is happening" (Bion, 1967a, p. 273). The goal is to use theory in service of understanding rather than to constrain our observations. Moreover, many of Bion's concepts invite multiple interpretations and meanings. This multiplicity encourages creative engagement from both writer and reader, allowing the case study to become a living document that stimulates thinking and dialogue. Understanding emerges through active engagement with the text, as readers bring their own clinical experience and theoretical perspectives to bear. This approach to case writing aims to balance immediate experience with thoughtful reflection, theoretical understanding with openness to uncertainty, and clinical description with creative expression. An excellent way to grasp Bion's clinical work is through his seminars, particularly the Los Angeles Seminars (1967) and the Brazil Seminars (1978). For example, consider the following selection of his texts, the inspirational sentences he wrote, and observe what associations arise in relation to this or that patient.

DOI: 10.4324/9781003538578-10

Consider the following inspirational text written by Bion and observe what associations arise in relation to your patients:

> When you have a particularly dark spot, turn onto it a shaft of piercing darkness. Rid yourself of your analytic theories. Rid yourself of what you picked up about the patient; get rid of it.
>
> *Bion, 2013, p. 8.*

> Allow your desires to play as small a part as possible in the analysis. *Suppress desire.*
>
> *Bion, 2013, p. 5.*

> There are millions of interpretations, but there is only one experience, and that is the experience which the analyst here had with this patient—while none of us had it.
>
> *Bion, 1987, p. 7.*

> You should be concerned with what does *not* make a pattern, because if it has made a pattern, then you should have given that interpretation. You should have told the patient what the pattern is that is made because while you're busy remembering it, the patient is talking, and something is happening.
>
> *Bion, 2013, p. 25.*

While Bion's ideal of approaching case writing with a complete suspension of purpose and the adoption of radical not-knowing is philosophically compelling, it is practically impossible to implement fully. Such a pure approach would likely result in poetry or stream of consciousness rather than in a coherent case study.

No writer can fully meet these demands, as the case study genre requires a certain degree of organization and order that doesn't exist in free associative writing. Instead should strive for a delicate balance—preserving openness to emerging material while creating a sufficient framework for clinical understanding.

Thus, every Bion-inspired case study contains an inherent tension between the structural requirements of the format and the intuitive, open way of thinking that Bion encouraged. The meeting of these contrasting elements creates a fertile and challenging dialectic, making Bionian case writing one of the most complex and rewarding tasks in the psychoanalytic field.

Addressing the challenge of structured guidance on how to transform Bion's poetic, ambiguous, and interpretatively rich approach to a written case requires a subtle tension. My approach acknowledges the tension between structure and openness, using the current guide as a container for exploring Bion's ideas while constantly reminding readers of the importance of remaining flexible, intuitive, and receptive to the unique aspects of each clinical encounter.

But consider this: from Bion's perspective, the very notion of a "case study" has become too comfortable in its own skin—it knows too well what it means to be a case study. This self-awareness, this settled identity as a case study, paradoxically undermines its essential function. A true case study should disturb our existing knowledge and should make us uncomfortable with what we thought we knew.

RELATED CONCEPTS

Reverie, container-contained, P-$S \leftrightarrow D$, dream work alpha, the non-psychotic, and the psychotic part of the personality, selected fact, reversible perspective, alpha and beta elements, alpha function and beta particles, the grid, emotional experience, pre-conception, attacks on linking, projective identification, capacity to tolerate frustration, ultra-sensuous, bizarre elements, thoughts without a thinker, transformations in "O".

THERAPEUTIC ATMOSPHERE

Grotstein wrote once (2000, p. 69) that in a Bionian therapy, the therapist is like a driver in a racing car video game. As they observe the road on the screen, a multitude of obstacles and unexpected surprises descend upon them at a stunning speed. This metaphor vividly illustrates the dynamic and unpredictable nature of the therapeutic process, where the therapist must navigate rapidly changing emotional landscapes and unforeseen challenges in real time.

THERAPY GOAL

According to Bion, the primary goal of psychoanalysis is to uncover and engage with inner emotional truth. This ultimate, often unknowable truth is symbolized as "O" (Bion, 1970). The therapist's aim is to create a space where "O" can emerge and evolve, facilitating the patient's growth and transformation. This process involves moving beyond surface-level understanding and instead focusing on the immediate, lived emotional experience within the therapeutic relationship. The fundamental human problem lies in the experience of catastrophic beta elements—raw, unprocessed psychic materials that overwhelm the individual. Through therapy, these beta elements can be transformed into more manageable, thinkable alpha elements through what Bion calls alpha function (Bion, 1970). This process requires the therapist to cultivate a state of openness and receptivity, suspending memory, desire, and understanding, to allow for genuine engagement with the patient's psychic reality. The ultimate goal is to help the individual become more at one with their emotional truth, developing a deeper, more authentic sense of self that can tolerate the inherent catastrophe of existence while maintaining the ability to think and grow.

When describing therapeutic goals in a Bionian case study, focus on capturing the transformational nature of the therapeutic process rather than listing achievements or changes. The writing should convey:

1. The emergence of emotional truth ("O") through the therapeutic relationship, showing how moments of contact with unconscious reality manifested in sessions.
2. The transformation process—how raw emotional experiences (beta elements) evolved into thinkable elements (alpha elements). Document this without imposing theoretical language that might obscure the immediate experience.
3. The development of the patient's capacity to contain and process previously overwhelming experiences. Rather than describing this theoretically, illustrate it through specific clinical moments.

4. The therapist's internal work of suspending memory, desire, and understanding. Show how this facilitated (or sometimes hindered) authentic engagement with the patient's psychic reality. Your case should maintain tension between the need to communicate clinical understanding and Bion's emphasis on approaching each session without preconceptions. While complete adherence to Bionian ideals might make writing impossible, strive to preserve the aliveness and uncertainty of the therapeutic encounter within the necessary structure of a case report. For example, the writing itself should demonstrate how interpretation emerges naturally from deep engagement with the patient's experience rather than being imposed from outside. This perspective transforms case writing into a narrative that captures the alive, evolving nature of the therapeutic process. It aligns with Bion's emphasis on emotional truth and the importance of staying with uncertainty rather than rushing to premature understanding.

CAPTURING TRANSFORMATION: WRITING ABOUT CHANGE IN BION'S FRAMEWORK

From Bion's perspective, change in therapy arises from the analyst's ability to enter a state "without memory or desire," creating space for new emotional truths to surface. Through the analyst's reverie and containment of the patient's projective identifications, previously unthinkable experiences become gradually metabolized and integrated. This process is not linear but involves a complex interplay of progress and regression as the patient develops their own capacity for emotional processing.

Remember that Bionian change is not linear or easily categorized. Your case studies should reflect this complexity by highlighting moments of transformation without imposing an artificial narrative structure or premature conclusions. Allow the case material to breathe and maintain some uncertainty and aliveness that characterize the therapeutic process.

DEMONSTRATIONS OF CLINICAL PHENOMENA

Container/contained

Bion's concept of container/contained (Bion, 1962) is a fundamental theory in psychoanalysis that describes the dynamic relationship between two entities, where one (the container) receives, holds, and processes the raw experiences, emotions, and thoughts of the other (the contained). Originally with characteristics of the mother-infant relationship, this concept extends to various aspects of psychological development and therapeutic interactions.

Clinicians face several challenges when writing a case that focuses on Bion's container/contained notion. First, they must bridge the gap between the abstract nature of the theory and its concrete manifestations in therapy. This requires skillfully illustrating how the conceptual framework of container/contained plays out in real therapeutic encounters, providing vivid examples that bring the theory to life.

The clinician must also emphasize the reciprocal nature of the container/contained relationship. It's not merely about the patient projecting and the therapist containing; there is a dynamic interplay that must be conveyed. This includes describing instances where containment fails or is challenged, as these moments often provide rich insights into the therapeutic process.

In light of the distinctions between Bion's containing and Klein's projective identification, clinicians face additional challenges. They must navigate the complex theoretical landscape that differentiates these concepts, requiring a nuanced understanding of both theories and the ability to clearly articulate their distinctions in the clinical material.

The clinician must also grapple with the concrete nature of Bion's containing process as opposed to a purely phantasy-based understanding of Klein's theory. The clinician must address the concept of "third-stage projective identification" as described by Sandler (1988, p. 18). This involves showing how parts of the self or internal objects are externalized directly into the external object (therapist), distinguishing this from Klein's "first-stage projective identification." Container/contained is not a phantasy as in Klein's theory. It is a concrete "putting into the object" unwanted parts (Sandler, 1988). This involves describing how the patient's unbearable parts are actually put into the therapist and how the therapist experiences, modifies, and contains these projections in a real, tangible way.

Clinical example

After a two-week break in treatment due to my vacation, the patient entered the session agitated and out of breath. He spoke in a confused whisper, and it was difficult to understand his words. He discussed various recent events: an argument with his mother over a trivial matter, a phone call from his employer reprimanding him for a task he was dissatisfied with, and frustration over having to pay a hefty fine for being caught speeding on the highway.

Quickly and intuitively, the following interpretation arose: "You're telling me about all these stressful situations that you can't bear, so that I can listen to them and then give them back to you so you can think about them."

There was no point in delving into the various contents of his complaints before the patient became aware of what had just transpired between us.

Immediately after this interpretation, the patient shared the following dream from the previous morning: "I intend to swim in my private swimming pool, but it turns out to be dirty with garbage and waste floating on it. Time passes, and I start to despair that the person responsible for cleaning the pool won't arrive, and then I won't be able to swim in it".

"Maybe," he said thoughtfully, "the dirty pool isn't just about needing someone to clean up my mess. It's about my fear of diving into the messiness of life itself." This led to a rich dialogue about how his need for everything to be "clean" and perfect had prevented him from fully engaging in relationships and work.

The dream confirmed that he uses analysis as a tool to contain unwanted components that he cannot manage himself. The sense of immediacy and urgency in the situation was related not to the specific contents of the events troubling him, but to the containment function he was seeking. The dream's symbolism was particularly telling—the absent pool cleaner represented me, his therapist, who wasn't there during the break to help "clean up" his psychological waste. Through our mutual exploration, a new understanding was born—one that neither of us could have reached alone. The patient wasn't just depositing his anxieties; we were together creating a new way of thinking about his experience.

Alpha function

This is a mental process that transforms raw experiences (beta elements) into meaningful psychological content that can be used for thinking, dreaming, and memory formation (Symington, 1996, p. 62). Beta elements represent raw, unprocessed mental experiences that the mind struggles to comprehend or integrate. These elements exist as sensory impressions devoid of meaning or as nameless sensations that generate frustration. As undigested mental content, beta elements feel like foreign objects within the psyche and are perceived by the mind as suitable only for evacuation because they cannot be thought about or processed internally. Following the pleasure principle, the mind attempts to expel these uncomfortable elements, typically through projective identification. Alpha function serves as the crucial transformative process, acting as a bridge between immediate sensory perceptions and higher-order cognitive processes. It allows you and your patients to make sense of experiences, integrate them into existing mental frameworks, and use them for psychological growth and adaptation.

When writing case studies using Bion's theoretical framework, you need to be mindful of how alpha function manifests in your clinical work. The primary challenge you face is that alpha function operates at a level that isn't directly observable. This requires you to develop a keen ability to recognize and articulate the transformation of raw sensory data into meaningful psychological content in your patients' material. In your case writing, focus on depicting the intersubjective nature of alpha function within the therapeutic relationship. Describe how you use your own alpha function to process your patient's beta elements and how this impacts their developing capacity for alpha function. This involves illustrating the connection between the alpha function and key Bionian concepts such as containment, reverie, and projective identification. Your case study should demonstrate the link between alpha function and higher-order mental processes. Track your patient's psychological growth by showing how improvements in alpha function manifest in their thinking, dreaming, and memory formation. Pay particular attention to instances where alpha function fails or is impaired, as these moments often reveal crucial information about your patient's psychological functioning. When describing these situations, focus on articulating experiences of "nameless dread" or psychotic states in a way that captures their complexity while maintaining clinical clarity.

Clinical example: Alpha function in mother-toddler relationship

A 5-year-old boy needs to undergo a chest X-ray at the hospital. In the past, he had two surgeries, one on his mouth and another on his leg. The mother, who is empathetic and caring, prepares the boy for his encounter with the hospital and the treating doctor. Everything seemed fine until examination time arrived, when the boy needed to remove his clothes. He started screaming, refused to cooperate, and wouldn't undress. All the mother's efforts to calm him were in vain. The mother called for the father, and with no other choice, while the boy screamed and cried, they were forced to undress him so he could undergo the examination by force. After the examination, the boy calmed down, played, and seemed to return to himself.

In the evening, the mother talked with her toddler about what had happened. He asked her to tell him about the day's events. The mother recounted and described how they arrived at the hospital, how they entered the room that was initially dark and scared him, and how he played with the toys in the doctor's room before the examination, "and then you were courageous and willing to undergo the examination," she said, hoping to "bypass" the emotional occurrence that was very difficult for her. "But, Mom, I didn't agree," he told her. The mother remained silent. Then she said, "You're right, you didn't agree, and Dad and I had to force you," she replied. The boy appeared calmer and fell asleep shortly after. In this case, the boy asked for his mother's help to use her alpha function to transform unbearable beta elements (his parents forcibly undressing him and holding him tightly during the examination) into emotional material that he could bear and digest. The request is likely related to the boy's good experience with his mother activating her alpha function. The most interesting thing is that the boy demands that his mother process a painful emotional truth. For the alpha function to work, it must be faithful to the experiential, emotional truth, even if it's painful. A distorted and soothing story cannot be beneficial in processing and calming. The boy's calming down is related to the fact that the mother was ultimately able to express the emotional truth.

Clinical example: Parental failure of alpha function

The patient, a mother of three young children in her thirties, suffers from anxieties related to disaster. She visualizes terrible scenes happening to her children: they run into the street and get run over, her infant falls into a crocodile enclosure at the safari, her 4-year-old son is murdered by a man with a rifle, and the family car accidentally enters an Arab village, where locals lynch them. The patient describes her parents as "impenetrable" to their children and closed off to any emotional communication. The mother was a passive and submissive figure who did not express her opinions without her husband's approval. The father is a dominant and authoritarian figure, fundamentally insecure and frustrated by feeling stuck in a junior position at work. In her childhood, she didn't share many fears with her parents, particularly her fear that they would die. One day, she fell and jumped into a pit to see what was in it, perhaps out of curiosity or to discover what would happen to her. She was injured and miraculously managed to find her way out but didn't tell her parents. Despite arriving home hurt, her parents didn't notice. Thus, a double life developed within her: one part bright and visible, where she was a good, pleasing child who excelled in her studies, and another darker side filled with frightening horror scenarios and aggressive fantasies towards herself and her parents. None of this was communicated to her environment or processed with a significant other. A child who can share her severe fears with nurturing parents will benefit from an important alpha function: the parents will soothe, selectively share their own fears, understand, and embrace, thus processing the raw material and returning it to the child in a different form. In this way, the fears transform and return to the child in a more softened form, allowing for symbolization and space to think about them. This patient "imprisoned" her fears within herself, and when she became a mother, they were displaced onto her children and family.

The therapist's transformative dream

The analytic field serves as a shared space for dreaming between the analyst and the patient, where the analyst's ability to dream is essential when working with both psychotic and non-psychotic states. Let me explain how to incorporate this understanding into your written case.

When writing about non-psychotic functioning, describe how your patient brings their dream into the analytic field, activating your own dreaming capacity. Through analytic intuition (Sapienza, 2001), you detect aspects of the patient's dream that, while part of symbolic thinking, may be distorted or blocked by defenses. Your task is to re-dream the dream, modifying its circumstances to facilitate new symbolic connections and enriched meanings. This process creates what we call "dreaming a dream for two."

In contrast, when writing about situations where the alpha function is unavailable, focus on describing how the patient struggles to think about their world. Explain how stimuli appear as beta elements, lacking mental quality and meaning. Since these cannot be transformed into symbols, they manifest as what Bion termed "nameless dread" (Bion, 1962b). Detail how the patient attempts to expel these through massive projective identification, sometimes involving parts of their thinking mechanism and mental functions, leading to bizarre objects (Bion, 1956).

Pay attention to instances where dreaming becomes impossible—the domain of the psychotic aspect of the personality. You might observe pictograms appearing in non-dreams, which resist organization and expression. When describing these phenomena, note how any sketches of scenes or plots appear inert, lacking meaning, associations, or emotional resonance for new connections. These are better understood as non-scenes and non-plots, sometimes manifesting as efforts to find someone who can provide meaning (Cassorla, 2003).

Meltzer (1983) beautifully captures this process in clinical work:

> What seems to happen is that the analyst listens to the patient and watches the image that appears in his imagination. It might cogently be asserted that he allows the patient to evoke a dream in himself. Of course that is his dream and will be formed by the vicissitudes of his own personality [. . .] From this point of view one might imagine that every attempt to formulate an interpretation of a patient's dream could imply the tacit preamble, "While listening to your dream I had a dream which in my emotional life would mean the following, which I impart to you in the hope that it will throw some light on the meaning that your dream has for you'." (p. 90)

Clinical example

In his third year of therapy, David arrives for a session after a three-week break due to the COVID-19 lockdown (he refused to meet via Zoom). David recounts that on his way to me, he drove along the river and noticed its polluted waters, marked by oil stains, dead fish, and a foul smell. I interpret this as a sign of the "stagnant and stinking waters" that exist in his mind without the possibility of proper drainage and flow. Without a mental function of another capable of draining the pollution and introducing fresh water, the mind becomes blocked and cannot continue its flow to clear the stale water. During the session itself, David often "gets stuck" and complains that he cannot find the words to express his thoughts.

That night, I had three dreams.

In the first dream, my grandmother appears, stumbling into a stream as she tries to jump from the pier to an old rowing boat. My father quickly rushes to extend his hand and pulls her back onto the boat.

In the second dream, an earthquake occurs in the depths of the sea, and huge waves threaten to cover the city. I am on the shoreline and feel an overwhelming sense of danger.

In the third dream, of which I only remember part, I am on a huge ship carrying tourists in the Atlantic Ocean. The sea appears calm and peaceful, but everyone knows that a giant, hungry shark is lurking in the depths, and no one knows when it will strike the ship and its passengers.

I believe the dreams are connected to David, and I identify the danger, the rescue, and the terrible persecution experienced during the lockdown, which was intensified by the forced break in the absence of a transformative function that could manage the projections and process them.

When David arrives the next day, he senses a change in me. I am surprised to see that he speaks fluently and no longer gets stuck. The channel of projective identification—reverie—has reopened, allowing David to be freed from the blockage that had forced him to remain alone with difficult content.

Development of the container within the analytic field (Antonino Ferro; 2018, Civitarese, 2022)

Antonino Ferro and Giuseppe Civitarese developed Bion's model and the field theory. Ferro expanded on Bion's model and field theory with a key insight: the goal of analysis is to develop mental tools. Instead, it is to develop mental tools to contain and process emotions and thoughts. The container is developed collaboratively by the analyst and patient. As they work together, the patient gradually internalizes this capacity, especially when their connection is tested and they must reconstruct it together. This represents a fundamental shift in psychoanalysis, moving from exploring conscious content to developing tools for thinking, feeling, and dreaming.

Ferro suggests various exercises for developing creative talent, where the analyst fosters the patient's ability to feel and experience frustration through the therapist's creative alpha function (2018, p. 125). The basic dream function involves turning beta elements into alpha elements. Projective identification eases the mental mechanism by projecting unwanted elements into another person's psyche. If this consciousness is open, it will not only be permeable to the influence of mental material from outside, but it will also create a sense of depth, as well as a sense of movement and flow due to expected mutual exchanges between psyches. The projected material will return in a different form, which will be easier to bear.

According to Civitarese (2022), raw thoughts and emotions initially exist in our minds like smooth blocks—they float separately without connection or structure. To grow mentally, we need to transform these primitive experiences into elements that can be linked together, similar to how LEGO bricks require connectors to build something meaningful. When our raw sensations and feelings remain unprocessed, they resemble building blocks without connections, making it impossible to construct new understandings or create stable mental frameworks. The ability to connect and organize these elements allows us to develop more complex and meaningful psychological structures.

The field theory in psychoanalysis, drawing from physics, emphasizes that psychological phenomena emerge from an interactive system where every element influences and is influenced by every other element—just as in electromagnetic or gravitational fields. In this perspective, psychological experience is not located solely within individuals but exists in the dynamic interplay between people and their environment.

When applied to case writing, this understanding transforms our approach to clinical description. Instead of focusing solely on the patient as an isolated entity or just on the patient-therapist dyad, we need to capture the entire field of interactions and influences.

When documenting clinical work, approach the case study as a storyteller.

Present the evolving narratives in the analytic field, showing how meanings develop and transform through the therapeutic dialogue. When describing transformations in therapy, track how raw emotional experiences (beta elements) become thinkable (alpha elements) through the therapeutic process. Show how projected material returns in modified form through your interventions.

Remember that each case study should tell a story of developing containment and meaning-making capacity (Ferro, 2018, p. 121). Your writing should capture both the content of sessions and the gradual expansion of the therapeutic field.

Your case studies should demonstrate different levels of attunement through concrete examples. For instance, when presenting an intervention, show how it matched the patient's capacity to tolerate emotional complexity. Consider including multiple responses to the same clinical moment, demonstrating the gradual expansion of understanding.

As Ferro illustrates (2018, p. 121): "Yesterday, a dog bit me."

Basic: "What a terrible experience."

Moderate: "What a terrible experience, especially if it's a dog you trusted."

Full: "What a terrible experience, especially if it's a dog you trusted, and maybe something I said to you yesterday made you bleed."

Your case should capture how raw emotional experiences become thinkable through the therapeutic process. Show the gradual development of containment and meaning-making capacity in both the content you present and your writing style itself.

Attacks on linking

When we forcefully push away parts of ourselves that we can't stand or accept into someone else—a process that Klein saw as creating a threatening, persecutory version of that other person—something more complex can happen. If this rejection includes an attack on our own capacity to think and make sense of things, it creates what Bion called "bizarre objects." (Bion, 1954). These are deeply confusing experiences that neither the patient nor the therapist can easily understand or work with.

These bizarre objects emerge when the mind not only rejects unwanted aspects of the self but also damages its own ability to process and understand experience. The result is more than just seeing others as threatening—it creates a state where reality itself becomes twisted and incomprehensible. It's as if the person has not only discarded parts of themselves but has also broken the mental tools needed to make sense of their experience (Aguayo, 2023).

When writing clinical material about attacks on linking, clinicians should focus on documenting not just the content of what was attacked, but the precise way the patient dismantles emerging connections, paying special attention to moments when understanding itself becomes threatening and how this manifests in the therapeutic relationship.

Clinical example

During a particularly significant session, Mr. D was discussing his promotion at work. As he began to make connections between his current success and his childhood feelings of inadequacy compared to his sister, he suddenly became agitated. His speech became fragmented, and he shifted to complaining about the room's temperature. When I interpreted the emerging link between his present achievement and past pain, he experienced a violent headache and claimed he couldn't think anymore. The session devolved into concrete discussions about physical discomfort, with Mr. D insisting we focus only on his immediate bodily sensations. This pattern—where emerging understanding led to physical symptoms and cognitive disruption—illustrated how he attacked the linking function of his mind when emotional connections became too threatening. In subsequent sessions, we worked to help him gradually tolerate these connections, though the process remained challenging and nonlinear.

The state of NO-THING

When an infant experiences separation from its mother (Bion, 1962a, 1970), it faces overwhelming anxiety. At this early stage, the infant cannot comprehend or tolerate the notion of being separate from the mother, who provides life and nourishment. This unbearable experience is what Bion calls "No-mother" or "No-breast." Unable to process this absence, the infant might resort to creating substitutes, like thumb-sucking, which serve as a kind of hallucination of the missing breast. Through these actions, the infant attempts to recreate what's missing and maintain an illusion of control over it. The mother plays a crucial role here. When she can emotionally "contain" the infant's anxieties—taking them in and processing them through her mind—she helps reduce their intensity. This containment gradually enables the infant to develop a different relationship with absence. As this process unfolds, something remarkable happens: the unbearable "no breast/no mother" slowly transforms into what might be called a "presence of absence." Instead of experiencing absence as an overwhelming void, the infant begins to develop the capacity to hold the idea of absence in mind. This creates a psychological space where the thought "mother is not here" can exist without being overwhelming. This development is crucial: the mother's emotional presence and containment help the infant tolerate her physical absence. The infant learns that separation doesn't equate to catastrophe. This capacity to tolerate absence—what Bion calls bearing the "NO-THING"—becomes the foundation for thinking itself. Within this newly developed mental space, the physical absence of the mother can be transformed into a symbolic presence. The absent mother can be held in mind through images and, later, through words. This ability to represent absence through symbols marks a fundamental achievement in psychological development—the capacity for symbolic thought (Reiner, 2022). Bion (1970) adds that if a person can suffer pain, they can also "suffer" pleasure, so the real problem is not pleasure or pain, but the ability of the psyche to bear emotional reality. If reality cannot be suffered, then it will be difficult to experience pleasure because pleasure is also an unbearable reminder of absence (see Reiner, 2022). The task of writing on NO-THING requires navigating pre-verbal or difficult-to-articulate experiences. This demands a high degree of empathy and interpretive acumen to accurately represent the patient's subjective experience of absence and presence while differentiating between healthy symbol formation and pathological hallucinatory gratification. The written case should also elucidate how the patient's relationship to NO-THING influences their broader psychological functioning, including their capacity for relationships, frustration tolerance, and creative thinking. Moreover, the clinician must demonstrate how the concept of NO-THING manifests within the therapeutic process itself, perhaps through exploring the patient's experiences of the therapist's absences between sessions or during breaks. This exploration can provide valuable insights into the patient's evolving capacity to tolerate separation and create mental space for absent objects.

Clinical example

Veronica experienced early separation from her mother at three months when her mother was hospitalized for a month. She was cared for by her emotionally distant grandmother, who provided for her physical needs but offered little emotional warmth. Throughout her childhood, her parents maintained this pattern—meeting practical needs while remaining emotionally uninvolved.

In therapy, Veronica presented with a frozen, unchanging smile that felt empty rather than genuine. She described a heaviness in her heart that she couldn't understand or locate physically. She lived a confined life between home and work, displaying significant difficulty in accessing or expressing her emotional world. Her responses to questions about feelings were minimal and uncertain, suggesting a profound disconnection from her inner experience.

I felt I could not work with her to create a deeper connection. One day, after a year of frustrating and unproductive sessions, she shared a dream for the first time in therapy. In the dream, she is next to a balloon seller with balloons shaped like colorful animals. She asks to buy a balloon, but every time the seller inflates one, the air escapes from some hidden hole, leaving no animal-balloon created—balloon after balloon. Veronica didn't know how to associate any meaning with the dream and couldn't articulate anything about it. I suggested that she dreamed about therapy: the balloon seller (the therapist) offers to breathe spirit (life) into her frozen and motionless inner world and create animals there, representing instincts. But in her experience, her world is perforated and fails to produce movement and life.

According to Bion (1962a, 1970), nothing can be located in the psyche without its absence also being able to exist. This explains Veronica's limited life and her emotional poverty. According to Bion, one cannot feel or remember the loss, but the loss "remembers" the patient through a sense of emptiness that cannot be filled.

Catastrophic change

Catastrophic change in Bion's theory signifies a distinct mental configuration that is fundamentally different from trauma or ordinary life disruptions. While it's tempting to use this term in its everyday sense to describe severe disruptions or traumas, Bion's concept points to something more specific and profound in psychic life (Sandler, 2005, pp. 101–112). It describes an internal upheaval that occurs when established psychological patterns confront profound disruption, particularly when faced with emotional truths that threaten existing defensive structures. This resistance to growth is marked by an intolerance of meaninglessness and an inability to face the unknown aspects of emotional reality.

The concept encompasses a complex emotional experience triggered by the violent emergence of feared inner truths. Unlike trauma, which implies a causal relationship between external events and psychological response, catastrophic change describes a mental configuration that arises from within. It manifests in patients' desperate attempts to maintain meaning and control, often through floods of words or somatic complaints. The patient's inability to tolerate uncertainty and meaninglessness creates a paradoxical situation where their very resistance to change becomes the catalyst for a catastrophic response. This response isn't necessarily proportional to external events but reflects the intensity of internal resistance to psychic growth.

> The key distinction from trauma or common usage lies in understanding catastrophic change as a mental state rather than an event or its impact. It describes the mind's encounter with its transformative possibilities and the terror this encounter can evoke, independent of external causality.

When documenting catastrophic change in clinical writing, clinicians should resist the temptation to use the term in its everyday sense to describe dramatic external changes or psychological traumas. Instead, case studies should capture the specific mental configuration at play, detailing how the patient's encounter with emotional truth creates an internal upheaval that threatens their entire system of meaning-making. The writing should demonstrate how this state emerges not from external events but from the patient's fundamental resistance to psychic transformation.

Clinical example

A patient in his forties, highly successful in the tech industry, entered therapy presenting with what he termed "minor efficiency issues." His initial sessions were marked by intellectual discussions about productivity and optimization. He approached therapy as he did his work—as a system to be analyzed and improved.

The catastrophic change occurred during a session in which he was describing his latest project—an AI system designed to predict and optimize user behavior. As he enthusiastically explained how the system could eliminate uncertainty in human decision-making, I suggested that perhaps his fascination with predictive systems reflected a deeper need to control the unpredictable aspects of human relationships and emotions. I noted how his own relationships, particularly with his recently departed college-age daughter, seemed to be managed through technological systems—scheduled video calls, shared digital calendars, and tracking apps—as if trying to transform the messy reality of human connection into controllable data points.

I am not sure what happened but this interpretation seemed to strike at the core of his defensive structure. He later described this moment: "It was like all my code was suddenly deleted. I had no operating system left. I couldn't even understand who I was anymore." His usual articulate demeanor collapsed; he sat in silence, then began speaking in fragmented sentences, reporting feeling "completely alien" to himself.

In subsequent sessions, he remained in this state of profound disorientation. His entire framework for understanding himself and his relationships had been dismantled. Without his systems of control and optimization, he felt "naked" and "exposed to raw existence." What made this a true catastrophic change was not just the emotional pain, but the complete loss of his organizing principles for making sense of experiences. He described feeling like "an astronaut whose tether has broken—floating in space without any coordinates." This state revealed how his technical, systematic approach to life had served as a defense against the fundamental uncertainty of emotional experience, particularly around loss and separation.

Selected fact

According to Bion, a "selected fact" is a crucial element in the process of understanding and creating coherence in seemingly disparate information or experiences (Bion, 1967a). This concept, which Bion borrowed from the mathematician and philosopher Jules-Henri Poincaré, is particularly relevant in psychoanalytic work and scientific thinking. Biran and Pud (2023) note that "the selected fact is revealed through movement between the paranoid-schizoid position, which breaks down and splits components, and the depressive position, which seeks the whole and connects components" (p. 93). Bion believes that the analyst must experience the selected fact as part of the synthesis that occurs in treatment. It can be said that the selected fact is an intuition-based interpretation that has been creatively conceived (Sandler, 2005).

In "Second Thoughts," (1967a) Bion writes:

[A]n "evolution", namely, the coming together, by a sudden precipitating intuition, of a mass of apparently unrelated incoherent phenomena which are thereby given coherence and meaning not previously possessed . . .

From the material the patient produces, there emerges a configuration that resembles the pattern of a kaleidoscope, which appears to belong not only to the situation unfolding but also to several others that were not previously seen as connected and that it has not been designed to connect. (p. 127)

Key aspects of the selected fact:

1. **Emotional experience**: Bion emphasizes that a selected fact is not merely an intellectual construct; it is an emotional experience. It's the feeling of discovery, of suddenly perceiving a coherent whole where there was once only disorder.
2. **Timelessness**: in Bion's view, the experience of a selected fact occurs in a state where time is excluded. This suggests a moment of insight that transcends linear thinking.
3. **Unifying disparate elements**: the selected fact brings together previously unconnected or seemingly unrelated elements. It creates a new understanding by revealing relationships that were not apparent before.
4. **Epistemological significance**: the concept fundamentally explores how we come to know or understand something. It marks a pivotal moment in the creation of knowledge or insight.
5. **Beyond logic**: Bion stresses that the relationships revealed by a selected fact are not necessarily logical. They are based on emotional experience and intuitive understanding rather than formal logic.

6. **Naming and particularizing**: often, one element names the selected fact, becoming the focal point that illuminates the connections between other elements.

7. **Sudden ordering**: the selected fact introduces order where previously there appeared to be disorder, allowing for a new, comprehensive view of the whole.

Capturing the sudden, intuitive nature of the emergence of the selected fact in a written case can be challenging, as it often occurs in a moment of timelessness that transcends linear narrative. The clinician must find a way to convey this sudden insight without losing its spontaneity and emotional impact.

Describing the emotional experience associated with the selected fact presents another challenge. The clinician needs to articulate not just the intellectual content of the insight but also the visceral, felt sense of discovery and coherence. This requires a nuanced interplay between clinical objectivity and subjective experience.

The clinician must also illustrate how previously disparate elements suddenly coalesce into a meaningful whole. This involves tracing the connections between seemingly unrelated aspects of the patient's material, which may not be immediately apparent to the reader. The challenge lies in making these connections clear without oversimplifying the complex insight process.

The clinician faces the task of situating the selected fact within the broader context of the psychoanalytic process. This involves showing how the selected fact emerges from and contributes to the ongoing therapeutic work, without reducing it to just another clinical observation.

Clinicians employing the concept of selected fact face a significant challenge in distinguishing between a genuine selected fact and an overvalued interpretation (Britton & Steiner, 1994). What may initially seem like a compelling observation or interpretation can sometimes be inaccurate or mistaken. These errors may stem from the analyst's own defensive needs, leading to what Britton and Steiner (1994) term an "overvalued idea." The task for the clinician in writing the case is to convey not only the moments of insight but also the process of critically examining these insights.

The case should convey the transformative power of the selected fact in the psychoanalytic process. This requires a sophisticated integration of Bionian theory with detailed clinical observation, resulting in a narrative that captures both the intellectual and emotional dimensions of this crucial psychoanalytic phenomenon.

Clinical example

The patient, 45, married a woman in her thirties on the condition that they would not have children. After eight months, his partner announced her pregnancy, causing him significant distress. This was the first time in two years of analysis that I could discern his genuine distress. Typically, he arrived calm and in a good mood, eager to please, warmly accepting any interpretation I gave and even building on it. I found it difficult to reach him; something in him remained blocked and opaque, and the quality of our contact felt flat. At times, I questioned whether analysis was the right treatment method for him.

The patient's mother idolized her son, intent on preventing him from experiencing any mental pain or frustration. When he expressed distress, she reassured him that "everything will be fine" and tried to convince him logically that he had no reason to feel as he did, focusing on his perfection and success. It seemed that she treated him like a rare and valuable possession she had acquired, and the difficulties he reported seemed to tarnish him.

The session took place during this period. Due to circumstances related to me, the session was moved to a different time than our usual hour, and it slipped my mind. When there was a knock on the door, I expected another patient. He noticed my surprise when I opened the door and immediately understood what had happened. He repeatedly offered to reschedule, insisting he had no problem giving up the session. His eyes yearned for me to accept his generous offer, which included forgiveness from his side. It seemed to me that my mistake actually pleased him, as if it were an opportunity not to be missed. When I brought this up to him, he said he felt relief because my mistake made him feel less guilty about all the times he was late. He recognized that the situation was uncomfortable for me and wanted to ease it.

Then he shared a dream: the house was filled with dirty baby clothes thrown everywhere, and the housekeeper was about to arrive. In the dream, a terrible argument broke out between him and the housekeeper. The housekeeper insisted on washing each garment separately at high heat, while he just wanted to get rid of the mess and have the clothes put in the closet. He shouted and almost raised a hand to her.

We can analyze the "selected fact" of the case as follows. The dream of dirty baby clothes and the conflict with the housekeeper revealed the selected fact: the patient's struggle with the "dirty" aspects of himself and his tendency to hide rather than confront them. I am the housekeeper insisting on cleaning each garment at high heat and causing pain instead of eliminating the disorder once and for all and pushing the clothes into the closets. This also explains why the impending baby threatens to ruin his life: his mother expected him to always be happy, successful, and in a good mood, without seeing himself as someone who could get dirty with pain, failure, or shame. He will confront a screaming, dependent, helpless, messy, excreting baby who requires constant attention.

This also explains why our session was skipped. It was an enactment: I wanted to forget it because, apparently, something in me resisted the perfect match that characterized his relationship with his mother and then with the world. Something in me sought to resist this, creating dissonance in the setting by forgetting the session. But as soon as he understood that I had "dirtied," he wanted my dirt to erase his stains from his many delays, and then rushed enthusiastically to clean and restore the perfect match through his generous offer to come another day. We note that the adaptive context of abandonment continues in elaborations on different levels and thus constitutes the selected fact of the session—or what I would term, the "selecting fact."

In this clinical example, what distinguishes understanding as a "selected fact" rather than a routine psychoanalytic interpretation is how it suddenly unites multiple, seemingly unrelated elements into a coherent whole. The patient's eagerness to forgive the analyst's forgotten session, his reaction to the pregnancy news, his dream about dirty baby clothes, and his historical relationship with his mother—all these disparate elements suddenly crystallize around the theme of avoiding "dirty" aspects of experience. This insight emerges not through logical deduction but through an intuitive leap that creates new meaning, characteristic of Bion's concept of selected fact.

What distinguishes this as a selected fact is also its transformative power in understanding the entire treatment. It reveals not just a pattern but illuminates why previous therapeutic work felt "flat" and why the patient struggled with genuine emotional contact. The selected fact isn't merely about connecting dots; it fundamentally reshapes the analyst's understanding of the whole treatment. The moment carries what Bion describes as emotional truth—it's not merely an intellectual observation but an emotionally felt experience that brings previously disconnected elements into a new configuration, allowing both analyst and patient to see their relationship and the patient's life patterns in a completely new light.

Bion's concept of psychic growth

Bion wrote that ". . . healthy mental growth seems to depend on truth as the living organism depends on food." (1965, p. 38)

According to Bion, psychic growth is a transformative process that entails a shift from psychosis to neurosis, drawing on Freud's classical definitions of these terms. This journey signifies a fundamental change in an individual's mental functioning and their relationship with reality.

In essence, Bion conceptualizes psychic growth as a progression from a state of near-total intolerance of frustration to one where frustration can be more easily endured. Growth is seen as a process of dreaming and re-dreaming, allowing patients to think what was previously could not be apprehended.

However, Bion acknowledges that this journey of psychic growth has its limits. He posits that primary narcissism and primary envy act as fundamental constraints on this developmental process. These primal psychological states, rooted in the earliest experiences of the infant, set the outer boundaries of how far an individual can progress in their ability to tolerate frustration and delay gratification.

The clinician must trace the patient's journey of psychic growth over time, highlighting key moments of transformation and development. This requires identifying shifts in the patient's ability to tolerate frustration, changes in their thought processes, and improvements in their capacity to grasp reality. The challenge lies in articulating these often subtle and gradual changes in a clear and meaningful way while also recognizing the ongoing influence of primary narcissism and primary envy.

Psychic growth: First clinical example

Dan has been in therapy for three months. Towards the end of the session, he becomes anxious and wants to know how much time he has left. He mentions that he doesn't want me to interrupt him, so he remains silent for 5 minutes to avoid starting a new topic. In the next session:

Patient: "The bitch teacher refuses to give me extra time, even though she knows I suffer from ADHD and deserve it. She pounced on me when I asked her to consider it, as if I were asking for special privileges."

Therapist: "Just like Oliver Twist asking for one more spoonful of soup (one of the patient's favorite books)."

Dan: "Exactly. What does she think? Of course, I didn't dare say anything to her; I just smiled and said, 'Of course, of course, sorry I asked.' But in my heart, I thought, 'What a bitch.'"

Therapist: "Oliver eventually ran away from that terrible place where children wandered hungry and afraid to make a sound."

Dan: "True, but then he got involved with criminals who forced him to steal."

Therapist: "At least the thieves gave him food, and he didn't have to study or be around adults."

Dan: "But they thought he was a criminal and wanted to put him on trial."

Therapist: "All the options in his life were bad."

In this session, the patient didn't check his watch. The transformation brought about through the alpha function to his hunger for more time and control seemed to ease him. The story of Oliver Twist illustrated that the therapist understands the experience of being a child longing for more and the anger that his demands provoke, as well as how dependent he is on adults and the complicated choices he faces if he decides to leave. His ability to tolerate frustration grew slightly.

Psychic growth: Second clinical example

During the termination phase with Ms. B, a 35-year-old writer struggling with creative blocks, she shared a significant dream: "I'm in a laboratory filled with bubbling beakers. I'm trying to mix chemicals, but they keep exploding or evaporating. In frustration, I knock over a vial. To my surprise, the spilled liquid forms intricate patterns on the floor. As I study these patterns, they begin to move and transform, sometimes into recognizable shapes, other times into abstract swirls." The dream revealed her growing capacity to transform overwhelming experiences (exploding chemicals) into meaningful patterns—a nascent alpha function at work.

After a heated argument with her partner, Ms. B arrived at the session claiming all progress was lost, unable to think or write. However, when invited to sit with this experience without immediately trying to understand it, she shifted from feeling overwhelmed to observing her state: "It's like I'm back in that lab from my dream. Everything's exploding, but I'm not knocking anything over this time. I'm just watching." This transition from being consumed by emotional turmoil to developing a capacity for reverie demonstrated emerging psychic growth. While her ability to contain and transform beta elements remained inconsistent, these moments indicated the beginning of a capacity to engage with rather than be overwhelmed by raw emotional experiences.

TERMINATION PHASE IN A BIONIAN ORIENTATION

The ending of analysis is not a fixed point but a process of transformation. Rather than focusing on symptom reduction or achieving specific goals, a Bionian case ending would highlight the analysand's increased capacity for thinking and tolerating frustration and uncertainty. The analyst would describe how the patient has developed their ability to contain and process previously overwhelming emotional experiences. A Bionian case ending would likely discuss changes in the patient's relationship to truth and reality. The conclusion might explore how the analysand has moved from rigid certainties to a more flexible engagement with emotional truths, both pleasant and painful. The analyst might note an increased tolerance for "not-knowing" and openness to new realizations. The case conclusion would likely address transformations in the analytic relationship itself. It might describe how projective identifications have lessened, allowing for more genuine contact between analyst and analysand. The ending could explore how the patient has internalized the analytic function, becoming better able to reflect on their own experience.

A Bionian case study ending would likely avoid claims of "cure" or complete resolution. Instead, it might frame the ending as an opening to continued growth and discovery beyond the analysis. The analyst might describe how the patient has developed tools to continue their own emotional learning. The ending might touch on how the patient has grappled with existential realities like mortality, separation, and limitation. It could explore how facing these truths has led to a deeper engagement with life and relationships. Finally, a Bionian case ending would likely maintain some sense of mystery and open-endedness. It might acknowledge the unknowable aspects of the patient's future development and the ongoing nature of emotional growth. The ending could reflect on how both analyst and analysand have been changed by their encounter, while respecting the ultimately ineffable nature of the analytic experience.

Clinical example

Daniel, a successful architect in his late thirties, came to therapy presenting what he described as "a strange emptiness." His parents had fled Argentina during the military dictatorship when he was an infant, following the disappearance of his uncle—presumably murdered by the regime. Their trauma manifested as a peculiar emotional absence; they were physically present yet somehow not fully there.

Daniel functioned well professionally, yet his presence felt somewhat mechanical. In our early sessions, he described architectural projects with precision but seemed unable to inhabit the emotional space of our conversations. His dreams often involved empty buildings or incomplete structures.

The turning point came three years into treatment when he began designing a memorial for victims of political violence. He shared a dream: "I'm in a vast empty museum. All the exhibits are covered in white sheets. I keep walking through the halls, knowing there's something important underneath, but I can't lift the sheets. My hands pass through them like ghost hands."

Working with this dream revealed how Daniel had unconsciously covered over not just his own emotional life but also the unprocessed trauma inherited from his parents. His "ghost hands" reflected his struggle to grasp and connect with this buried emotional reality.

As our work drew to a close, Daniel presented another significant dream: "I'm in my childhood home, but the walls are made of glass. Through them, I can see both the Buenos Aires my parents left and the city where I grew up. The glass is both transparent and reflective—I can see through it, but also see myself."

In our final sessions, Daniel spoke of feeling both more solid and uncertain. "It's like I finally have permission to be haunted," he said, "not just by my parents' ghosts, but by my own living questions." The empty spaces in his psyche had transformed into the negative space in architecture—not just voids, but structural elements that shaped his emerging self.

The end of therapy wasn't marked by completion but by a new kind of incompleteness—one that could hold both presence and absence, knowing and not-knowing, in a living tension.

SUGGESTIONS FOR WRITING A CASE STUDY BASED ON BION'S THEORY

Dream-like memory analysis

When writing case studies, aim to capture the essence of "dream-like memory" that Bion described. Transcend traditional interpretative methods and engage in a form of waking dreaming during sessions. In your write-ups, convey the ethereal, shapeless qualities of the psychic reality that emerges in the therapeutic space. Rather than focusing solely on concrete events or dialogue, paint a picture of the emotional atmosphere and the subtle elements of your patient's inner world.

Let your mind enter a state of reverie while remaining fully present. Share the images, sensations, and emotions that arise as you absorb and process your patient's communications. Highlight moments where your ability to "dream" the session leads to deeper insights or unexpected connections.

As Ogden (2017) reminds us, "dreaming the session is not something one works at; rather, one tries not to get in its way" (p. 19). Each analyst must find their own way of dreaming each session with each patient. Let your case studies reflect your unique way of dreaming with each particular patient. Preserve the raw, unprocessed quality of these experiences, allowing readers to engage with the material in a more immediate and visceral way.

Basic approach to documentation

Writing case studies based on Bion and Ogden's approach to dreaming will be richer, more accurate, and more authentic when it includes the dimension of shared dreaming, spontaneous thoughts, and the process of making the conscious unconscious and back to conscious through careful interpretation.

The therapist's dreaming, as described by Ogden following Bion, constitutes a central key to writing rich and accurate case studies. When you allow yourselves to dream the session—that is, to transform conscious, rational experience into unconscious experience—you open a door to a rich world of unconscious thinking that contains multiple layers of meaning.

The spontaneous thoughts that arise in you during the session—thoughts about an argument with your spouse, song lyrics that come to mind, or childhood memories—are actually products of a joint creation between you and the patient. When you write the case study, you can integrate these experiences as an integral part of the clinical understanding, rather than as distractions to be ignored.

The process of dreaming the session allows you to view the experience from multiple vertices simultaneously—from the perspective of primary and secondary processes, from the viewpoint of mature symbol formation versus symbolic equation, and from the angle of adult construction of life events versus childhood construction. When you write the case study, you can document this multi-dimensionality and present the patient and the therapeutic process in all their complexity.

It is important to understand that not every "dream" is truly a therapeutic dream. Dreams that do not lead to psychic growth, such as dreams without associations or traumatic nightmares that repeat without change, are essentially "dreams that are not dreams." In writing the case study, you can distinguish between different types of dreams and document the difference between experiences that lead to psychological work and those that remain barren.

When a patient is unable to dream his experiences, you can use your own capacity for dreaming to assist him. In the case study, you can document how you dream together with the patient the dreams that were not dreamt or were partially dreamt. This process of shared dreaming is essentially the core of the analytic process, and you can describe how you contribute to developing the patient's capacity for dreaming.

Waking dreaming, which occurs in the treatment room primarily in the form of spontaneous thoughts of yours and the patient's, allows you to "catch the drift" of what is happening unconsciously at any given moment in the session. In the case study, you can include these experiences as part of the clinical understanding and describe how they contributed to understanding the unconscious dynamics.

The SCREAM framework

According to Giuseppe Civitarese (2023, p. 43), the SCREAM framework offers a useful structure for documenting different types of therapeutic interventions.

- Self-disclosure (rare but significant moments)
- Chorus (reflecting emotional truths)
- Reverie (your responsive daydreams)
- Emotion mapping (tracking affective shifts)
- Allucinosis (primitive mental states)
- Metaphor (capturing experience through imagery).

Show how different forms of intervention emerged from and impacted the therapeutic process.

Documenting core processes

Field perspective

Avoid falling into a simplistic "you-and-I" narrative structure. Instead of describing interactions as a series of actions and reactions between separate individuals ("the patient did this, I responded with that"), capture how the therapeutic field evolved as a shared dream space.

Container/contained relationship

When writing about therapeutic progress, emphasize the development of the patient's capacity to think rather than merely documenting insights or interpretations. Show how you tracked and supported the growth of their container (their ability to hold and process experience) rather than just focusing on content.

Structure your case study to demonstrate your careful attention to the patient's containment capacity. Show how you adjusted your interventions based on what the patient could tolerate and integrate at different stages of the treatment. Make explicit how you prioritized strengthening the container over filling it with content.

Beta element transformation

Pay special attention to the ongoing transformation of beta elements in the field. Rather than presenting therapy as a series of discrete interventions and responses, capture it as a continuous flow of emotional experience being processed in the shared space between you and your patient. Show how you monitored and participated in this ongoing process of transformation while acknowledging that you never had complete control over it.

Selected facts

Describe key moments when a selected fact emerged, bringing new understanding to the therapeutic process. Explain how these insights arose and how they contributed to the patient's growth. Discuss how the emergence of selected facts influenced your own understanding of the case and guided subsequent interventions.

Working with memory and desire

Suppression of desire

Wilfred Bion (2013) encourages therapists to reflect on the nature of desire and its effects on their work. He proposes this as a gradual experiment, urging careful consideration and slow implementation. The ultimate aim is to cultivate a more present, attentive, and unbiased therapeutic stance, allowing for deeper engagement with the patient's immediate experience and unconscious communications.

Remember that case writing itself should reflect this Bionian approach—not aiming for a perfect state of desire-free observation, which is impossible, but demonstrating the ongoing struggle and reflection involved in this work. Illustratte how even the struggles to suspend desire can lead to significant therapeutic understanding when properly examined and understood.

Handling memory

Bion cautions against relying too heavily on memory in psychoanalytic practice (2013). He suggests that memory often represents what we want to have happened, rather than what actually occurred. When writing a case, consider approaching the writing project with a fresh perspective, as if meeting the patient for the first time, while setting aside preconceptions based on previous sessions or theoretical understanding.

The therapist's development

Personal growth and learning

Include reflections on your own growth as an analyst. Discuss how the case challenged your thinking or preconceptions. Describe moments of uncertainty or confusion and how you worked through them.

Maintaining perspective

Throughout the case, strive to maintain what Bion called "patience"—a state of mind that tolerates uncertainty and avoids premature understanding. Your case should reflect the evolving, often ambiguous nature of the analytic process, demonstrating how meaning emerges gradually through the joint work of patient and analyst.

As Bion (2013) states:

> Now, here again I just listened to it, and I suppose I must have listened to it for a matter of months, and then something happened which I think is an accumulation of these perceptions, if that is what it is, this gradual build-up that I talked about—the interpretation that you don't give; you listen to it, and you listen to it, and you listen to it. I just listened to it. (p. 18)

Writing style and technique

Narrative approach

When describing interpretations in your case write-up, show both their content and the emotional context that made them possible. Demonstrate how the timing and depth of interpretations aligned with the patient's capacity to receive them.

Handling uncertainty

Resist the temptation to romanticize therapeutic uncertainty. While the analytic process inherently involves working with the unknown and unconscious processes, you must maintain clarity and trustworthiness in your reporting. Your task is to illuminate the therapeutic process, not to become lost in its mysteries. Present the uncertainties and complexities of the clinical work honestly, while maintaining your role as a credible narrator who can help readers understand the therapeutic journey, even when that journey involves exploring the unknown.

Remember to illustrate through clinical examples how seemingly individual experiences (like fear or inhibition) emerged as shared field phenomena, belonging to neither party exclusively but arising from the common unconscious layer of communication between two minds.

RECOMMENDED READING

The language of Bion: A dictionary of concepts, by Paulo Cesar Sandler. Routledge, 2005.

For clinicians writing case studies, having clear definitions and a solid understanding of Bion's complex concepts is crucial for articulating clinical material through a Bionian lens. Sandler's "The Language of Bion: A Dictionary of Concepts" is an essential resource for clinicians engaged in writing case studies within the Bionian tradition. What makes this dictionary particularly valuable is that it illustrates the evolution and interconnection of Bion's ideas rather than treating them as isolated concepts.

Five exemplary Bionian case studies

Negative capabilities, play and the negative, by Antonino Ferro. *American Journal of Psychoanalysis 81*, 351–360, 2011.

Antonino Ferro's case studies are the most creative, playful, and enjoyable to read in psychoanalytic literature. He has a unique way of engaging with Bion's ideas and has developed a rich theory explaining them. This paper is a Bionian case study demonstrating how to capture the emergence of "negative capability." Here you can read the marvelous lines on how "fantastical figures coming out of sleepers' minds (therapist and patient) play together, jumping about and yelling in an atmosphere which at times resembles something by Fellini."

". . . But at the same time and on another level . . .": Clinical applications in the Kleinian/ Bionian mode (Vol. 2), by James Grotstein. Karnac Books, 2009.

The book offers extensive clinical illustrations, complete session transcripts, and detailed explanations of the author's thought process, interpretations, reveries, and countertransference experiences. As Grotstein notes in his preface: "In Volume Two I describe in detail my impression of specifically how to understand and to interpret in an analytic session. The reader will note that I present clinical sessions in stenographic detail and display complete sessions . . . I go to great lengths to detail my private observations, reveries, and countertransferences as well as my thinking about how, when, and what should be interpreted." (p. XIV)

I recommend reading Clinical Example 2, Chapter 9, pages 113–133, on the Negative Therapeutic Reaction.

W. R. Bion's theories of mind: a contemporary introduction, by Annie Reiner. Routledge, 2023.

Through her vivid clinical illustrations, Annie Reiner demonstrates how to capture and describe the ineffable aspects of analytic experience that Bion emphasized—the moments of emotional truth, transformation, and contact with "O". Her case presentations effectively model how to write about these subtle psychoanalytic phenomena while preserving their alive, experiential quality. I recommend the clinical examples of Rosa and Rachel (pp. 58–62) on the "Royal Road to O."

Psychoanalytic field theory: A contemporary introduction, by Giuseppe Civitarese. Routledge, 2023.

Civitarese's book combines theoretical clarity with rich clinical illustrations that demonstrate how field theory concepts manifest in actual therapeutic work. Through detailed clinical examples, the book shows how to capture and write about the intersubjective unconscious field that emerges between analyst and patient, moving beyond traditional individual-focused case presentations to describe the shared emotional experience and unconscious communication that characterizes the analytic process. I highly recommend reading the case of Lori ("The cushion", pp. 70–73), on a patient who lied on a couch where the cushion was missing.

Flexibility of the psychoanalytic approach in the treatment of a suicidal patient: stubborn silences as "playing dead", by Ricardo Lombardi. *Psychoanalytic Dialogues 20*, 269–284, 2010.

Lombardi presents the case of Antonio, a suicidal patient who had previously undergone two unsuccessful analyses. The patient appeared emotionless, struggled with gambling addiction, and used silence as a defense mechanism. Through a flexible approach that emphasized being present in the here-and-now rather than reconstructing the past, this case study illustrates how to document the key elements of Bionian work: the analyst's use of reverie, working with beta elements, the transformation of emotional experience, and the development of thinking capacity.

REFERENCES

Aguayo, J. (2023). Attacks on linking and the creation of bizarre objects in contemporary psychoanalysis. *International Journal of Psychoanalysis, 104*(2), 287–305.

Bion, W. R. (1954). Notes on a theory of schizophrenia. *International Journal of Psychoanalysis, 35*, 113–118.

Bion, W. R. (1956). Development of schizophrenic thought. *International Journal of Psychoanalysis, 37*(4–5), 344–346.

Bion, W. R. (1962a). *Learning from experience*. Heinemann.

Bion, W. R. (1962b). A theory of thinking. *International Journal of Psychoanalysis, 43*(4–5), 306–310.

Bion, W. R. (1965). *Transformations*. Heinemann.

Bion, W. R. (1967a). *Second thoughts: Selected papers on psychoanalysis*. Heinemann.

Bion, W. R. (1967b). Notes on memory and desire. *Psychoanalytic Forum, 2*(3), 272–273.

Bion, W. R. (1970). *Attention and interpretation*. Tavistock Publications.

Bion, W. R. (1987). *Clinical seminars and four papers*. Fleetwood Press.

Bion, W. R. (2013). *The Los Angeles seminars*. Karnac Books.

Biran, H., & Pud, A. (2023). *Learning Bion: The elements of psychoanalysis—An interpretation of Learning from Experience*. Sifriat Tola'at Sfarim.

Britton, R., & Steiner, J. (1994). Interpretation: Selected fact or overvalued idea? *International Journal of Psychoanalysis, 75*(5–6), 1069–1078.

Cassorla, R. M. S. (2003). The transformation of beta elements and the work of dreaming. *International Journal of Psychoanalysis, 84*(4), 927–942.

Civitarese, G. (2022). *Psychoanalytic field theory: A contemporary introduction*. Routledge.

Civitarese, G. (2023). *Truth and the unconscious in psychoanalysis*. Routledge.

Ferro, A. (2011). Negative capabilities, play and the negative. *American Journal of Psychoanalysis, 71*(4), 351–360.

Ferro, A. (2018). *Torrential rains in my mind: Psychoanalysis, creativity and the analysand*. Routledge.

Grotstein, J. S. (2000). *Who is the dreamer who dreams the dream? A study of psychic presences*. Analytic Press.

Grotstein, J. S. (2009). *". . . But at the same time and on another level . . .": Clinical applications in the Kleinian/Bionian mode* (Vol. 2). Karnac Books.

Lombardi, R. (2010). Flexibility of the psychoanalytic approach in the treatment of a suicidal patient: Stubborn silences as "playing dead". *Psychoanalytic Dialogues, 20*(3), 269–284.

Meltzer, D. (1983). *Dream-life: A re-examination of the psychoanalytic theory and technique*. Clunie Press.

Ogden, T. H. (2012). Creative readings of classic psychoanalytic works. *International Journal of Psychoanalysis, 93*(2), 299–318.

Ogden, T. H. (2017). *The analytic third: Intersubjectivity and the analytic process*. Routledge.

Reiner, A. (2022). The capacity to bear the "no-thing": Bion's concept of negative capability in clinical practice. *Psychoanalytic Review, 109*(3), 245–268.

Reiner, A. (2023). *W. R. Bion's theories of mind: A contemporary introduction.* Routledge.

Sandler, J. (1988). *Projection, identification, projective identification.* International Universities Press.

Sandler, P. C. (2005). *The language of Bion: A dictionary of concepts.* Routledge.

Sapienza, A. (2001). The role of analytic intuition in understanding beta elements. *International Journal of Psychoanalysis, 82*(4), 715–732.

Symington, J. (1996). *The analytic experience: Lectures from the Tavistock.* Free Association Books.

CHAPTER 8

A case study in the spirit of Donald Winnicott

....

THE GREATEST CHALLENGES

Writing a case study in Winnicott's tradition becomes challenging precisely because his theoretical work defies systematic organization. Unlike the Kleinian tradition, which builds rigorous, structured frameworks, Winnicott's approach is intentionally fluid and resistant to definitive conceptualization (Elkins, 2015). Tair Caspi (2018) has described Winnicott as someone who wrote simple words about complex things and conveyed them in everyday language, almost devoid of psychoanalytic jargon, regarding the emotional development inherent in the infant. Jan Abram (2007) argued that Winnicott's ability to evoke a clinical psychoanalytic experience within the analytic couple led to the creation of a unique psychoanalytic language through a conversational and spontaneous style that fosters an intuitive understanding of the essence of his words. She added that Winnicott opposed technical psychoanalytic language in order to give his thinking vitality.

His work is characterized by:

- Conceptual improvisation rather than systematic theory-building
- Willingness to contradict himself within the same text
- Prioritizing exploratory thinking over establishing fixed definitions
- Leaving intellectual spaces between ideas intentionally unresolved.

These qualities emerge from Winnicott's fundamental belief that psychological experience cannot be captured through rigid theoretical structures. His writing style mirrors his therapeutic approach—adaptive, responsive, and fundamentally open-ended.

Winnicott did not intend for us to follow him and treat "the Winnicott way." He did not want people to become "Winnicottians." He wanted therapists to look in the directions he looked and find their own unique ways.

DOI: 10.4324/9781003538578-11

For a clinician writing a case study, this means abandoning traditional academic narrative models. The document must transform into a living text that preserves uncertainty, captures therapeutic nuance, and resists the impulse to provide conclusive explanations. The case study becomes less a scientific report and more a phenomenological exploration of psychological transformation. The challenge lies in representing a therapeutic process that is inherently improvisational, where meaning emerges through subtle, often pre-verbal interactions that resist straightforward linguistic representation.

How does one convey in prose the nuanced interplay of attunement between analyst and patient, or the subtle shifts in the analytic "holding environment" that Winnicott saw as crucial?

Indeed, the case study writer confronts the limitations of language itself in conveying the pre-verbal, somatic, and intersubjective dimensions of human experience that Winnicott placed at the center of his theory and practice. The task becomes one of evoking rather than explaining, of creating a literary equivalent to Winnicott's "holding environment" that allows the reader to engage with the clinical material in their own way.

The challenge extends to being "surprised" by patients and cultivating an inevitable creative "messiness" in the analytic process. A case study that appears too neatly packaged, too assured in its interpretations, would betray the spirit of Winnicott's approach. The writer must discover ways to convey tentativeness, leaving space for ambiguity and multiple meanings.

In essence, writing a case study in the spirit of Winnicott requires as much literary sensibility as clinical acumen—an ability to navigate the transitional space between poetry and prose, between showing and telling. The challenge, and the art, lies in finding ways to articulate what cannot ultimately be captured in words—to give form to the formless without violating its essential nature.

If all this seems daunting or even impossible, take heart. While Winnicott's unique writing style offers valuable inspiration, clinicians need not attempt to replicate his distinctive voice. Instead of trying to imitate Winnicott, each writer should discover their own playful style that aligns with their capabilities and authentic writing self—their own way of being "Winnicottian." This might involve using simpler language, being more direct in describing clinical interactions, or finding personal metaphors that feel natural. The key is to preserve the spirit of Winnicott's approach—the emphasis on genuine human connection and allowing space for ambiguity—while developing one's own clinical voice. A case study can be "Winnicottian" in its underlying values and observations without mimicking his particular literary style.

RELATED CONCEPTS

Holding environment, environmental failure, omnipotence, true and false self, primary maternal preoccupation, transitional space, transitional object, good enough mother, regression, fear of breakdown, hate in countertransference, surviving the patient's attacks, transition from object relating to object use.

THERAPEUTIC ATMOSPHERE

Surprising and unconventional, exceptionally intuitive, with an extraordinary connection to the patient's perspective. Winnicott himself created a friendly, warm, informal atmosphere and openly expressed affection towards his patients.

THERAPY GOAL

According to Winnicott, the aim of psychoanalytic treatment is to facilitate the patient's journey toward authenticity and aliveness. Winnicott conceptualized psychic health as the capacity to feel real, to experience one's true self, and to engage creatively with the world (Winnicott, 1965).

When writing about treatment goals in a psychodynamic case study from Winnicott's perspective, it is important to emphasize the focus on enabling the patient's journey toward authenticity and emotional aliveness.

The central aim of the treatment is to facilitate the emergence of the true self and to promote a genuine connection with one's experiences. In your written case, highlight how this process extends beyond mere symptom relief or gaining insights, framing it as an exploration of the patient's capacity to engage creatively with life. This can involve discussing the ways in which the patient's past experiences have shaped their current sense of self and their ability to engage with the outer world.

In the narrative, illustrate the role of the analytic setting as a reliable and supportive environment that allows the patient to regress to earlier developmental stages. Describe specific instances where the patient expresses feelings of dependence or vulnerability, reflecting their regression during the therapeutic process. Many patients confront traumatic events or periods in their lives that were not fully experienced at the time, leaving an emotional imprint. During therapy, they have the opportunity to re-experience these moments. This offers a chance to encounter the trauma in a supportive environment, one that fosters safety and containment. By detailing these dynamics, you highlight how the treatment space provides an opportunity for the patient to address developmental failures and the fear of disintegration that often accompanies unresolved trauma, thus facilitating a sense of holding that was absent during the original traumatic event.

> In Winnicott's framework, emphasize the importance of play as a therapeutic goal. Document instances where the patient engages in creative expression within the therapy setting. Observe how these moments mark a reconnection with their authentic subjectivity. Highlight how fostering a playful attitude enables the patient to navigate the complexities of their inner and outer realities, thus enhancing their capacity for meaning-making.

CAPTURING TRANSFORMATION: WRITING ABOUT CHANGE IN WINNICOTT'S FRAMEWORK

In Winnicott's approach, therapeutic change unfolds through a delicate balance of presence and absence, intervention and restraint. The case writer attuned to this process must cultivate a prose style that mirrors the therapist's stance—present yet unobtrusive, attentive yet non-impinging.

The narrative becomes a holding environment, allowing the reader to experience the gradual emergence of the patient's true self without prematurely closing off meaning. Central to this approach is the therapist's capacity for what we might call "active waiting"—a state of alert receptivity that enables the patient to use the therapist in unexpected ways. The case study must convey the texture of these silences, the weight of what remains unsaid.

Change occurs through the accumulation of moments where the patient feels genuinely seen and held without being invaded or controlled. The writer's challenge is to evoke this quality of attunement without resorting to heavy-handed explanation. In describing the therapeutic process, the clinician should capture how the patient's aggression or apparent resistance may actually attempt to establish the therapist as a "usable object" that can withstand attack without retaliation or collapse. This requires a narrative voice that remains non-judgmental and open to multiple meanings, reflecting the therapist's stance of "holding" rather than blaming. The written case should also address the paradoxical nature of change. Progress often emerges from the patient's growing capacity to simply "be" in the presence of another. The writer must find ways to convey how the therapist's non-demanding presence allows the patient to access more vital and authentic modes of being. This may involve describing subtle shifts in the patient's manner of relating or moments of spontaneity that signal the true self emerging.

DEMONSTRATIONS OF CLINICAL PHENOMENA

Unobtrusive presence

The therapist's presence is unobtrusive, emphasizing their ability to create a holding environment without imposing on the patient. This approach allows the patient to feel supported and contained while having space to explore their own thoughts and feelings, facilitating genuine self-discovery growth.

Clinical example

Leny entered my office for our first session with a nervous energy that seemed to fill the room. He paced back and forth, his eyes darting around as if searching for an escape route. When I invited him to sit, he chose the chair farthest from me, perching on its edge as if ready to bolt at any moment. As he began to speak, his words came out in a rapid, almost incoherent stream. He told me about his recent promotion at work, which should have been cause for celebration. Instead, it had triggered a series of panic attacks and insomnia that left him feeling constantly on edge. He mentioned, almost as an afterthought, that his father had passed away unexpectedly two months ago—"It was sudden, but these things happen, right?" In those early sessions, any attempt I made to interject or ask a question was met with an immediate change in subject, as if Leny was afraid of where a moment's pause might lead his thoughts. I quickly learned that my role was to be a silent, steady presence rather than an active participant in our sessions. As the weeks progressed, I noticed that Leny's frenetic energy seemed to diminish slightly in my presence. He began to sit further back in his chair, though his fingers still drummed restlessly on the armrests. The silences between his words grew longer, and I sensed that he was allowing himself, perhaps for the first time, to simply be still. During one particularly quiet session, I was reminded of nights spent with my older daughter when she was a teenager, sitting in companionable silence as she worked through her own anxieties about the future. I recalled how, over time, the tension in her shoulders would ease, and her breathing would slow to match mine. I realized that what Leny needed from me was not unlike what my daughter had needed during those late nights—a calm, unwavering presence to anchor him as he navigated the stormy seas of his grief and anxiety. My role was to provide a safe harbor, a space where he could gradually allow himself to feel the emotions he had been so frantically trying to outrun. As I sat with Leny, I felt myself becoming attuned to his rhythm—the cadence of his speech, the pattern of his breath. I was willing to be the steady ground beneath his feet, the silent witness to his struggle, for as long as he needed me to be. In this shared silence, I sensed we were forging a connection that words alone could not capture—a holding environment where healing could begin to take root.

Hate in the countertransference

Winnicott (1951) distinguishes between subjective countertransference and objective countertransference—where the analyst's hate reactions are based on actual observations of the patient's personality and behavior. He argues that objective hate, when properly recognized and contained, can serve a legitimate therapeutic function, especially with psychotic or antisocial patients who may actually need to experience the analyst's hatred to progress therapeutically.

It is important to note that Winnicott believed that at certain stages of analysis, the patient seeks the analyst's hate, and that objective hate is necessary (Winnicott, 1975). If the patient seeks objective or justified hate, they must be able to attain it; otherwise, they cannot feel they can achieve objective love. They can only believe they are loved after reaching the stage of being hated. In Winnicott's therapeutic approach, "objective hate" is a constructive force aimed at growth and development, not destruction.

The writing should demonstrate how hateful feelings were recognized, contained, and utilized therapeutically rather than denied or minimized. The case should illustrate specific clinical moments where hate emerged, how it was understood objectively, and its role in the therapeutic process. When relevant, authors should describe how the patient's need for the analyst's hatred manifested in the therapeutic relationship and how this understanding informed clinical interventions.

Clinical example

Sirote (2015) presents an unusual case in which he confesses his hatred to the patient. He describes a patient named Rafael, who is addicted to drugs and sex and consistently misses appointments without canceling in advance, simply leaving Sirote waiting for him. When Sirote tries to explore the reasons for his absence and suggests possible explanations, Rafael denies everything and shrugs, saying he simply didn't feel like coming.

Sirote explains that they enter into a sadomasochistic relationship pattern where he tries to offer possibilities. At the same time, Rafael dismissively rejects them, usually with a malicious smile that betrays his denied hostility. Sirote felt his frustrations accumulating and his anger escalating. He says Rafael aroused his sadism and projected his own into him.

According to Sirote, his interventions became rigid and desperate. Finally, when Rafael stared at him with yellow eyes and asked if Sirote simply didn't like him, Sirote was stunned. He describes this as a therapist's worst nightmare—the patient you don't like asking if you hate them.

After a long, apprehensive pause, Sirote admits to Rafael that he doesn't like him. This confession has a profound impact on Rafael, who becomes pale and stammers, revealing that this is the first time in 18 years that he's heard such honesty from a therapist.

Sirote reports that Rafael felt hurt, resentful, and shattered, but also relieved. Rafael confessed that he had asked this question to every therapist he had ever worked with, but Sirote was the first to be completely honest with him.

Sirote concludes by referencing Winnicott's paper "Hate in the Countertransference" (1975), suggesting that when hatred is acknowledged and dealt with, love becomes safer and more grounded.

Preferring silence over interpretation

Winnicott viewed clinical interpretation with deep skepticism. A case study writer must be cautious of premature interpretations that stem from the analyst's need for psychological comfort rather than true attunement to the patient's experience.

The key risks include:

- Using theory as a defense against uncertainty
- Generating interpretations to manage the analyst's anxiety
- Prioritizing theoretical frameworks over authentic patient experiences
- Rushing to "know" instead of remaining in a state of receptive not-knowing.

A Winnicottian case study should embrace uncertainty, resist premature theoretical closure, and document the therapeutic process as a dynamic, improvisational space where meaning emerges gradually and nonlinearly. The writer must be willing to tolerate ambiguity and track the subtle, often pre-verbal interactions that constitute genuine psychological transformation.

The goal is not to impose a predetermined narrative, but to create a textual space that reflects the fluid, responsive nature of the therapeutic encounter.

Clinical example

The patient consistently dismissed and cynically regarded the idea that the therapist's holiday had any effect on him. In the first session after a long break, the patient recounted that his wife was sad because only a handful of classmates attended their son's birthday party. He tried to convince her that the child didn't notice since he showed joy and cheerfulness during the party. I was almost tempted to interpret for the patient the parallel between this story and the conflict within him: one part feeling sadness over my departure for vacation while the other part dismisses and flattens the experience. However, something made me hesitate with the interpretation. I sensed that for a moment, the childlike voice emerged from that disconnected area where it resided, and an interpretation might be too intrusive and spoil this significant moment.

Regression

Regression to dependence represents a return to a state reminiscent of primary narcissism, where the individual and environment exist in a paradoxical unity—the environment holds the individual who simultaneously has no awareness of it as separate (Winnicott, 1955).

When documenting cases, clinicians should focus on creating and maintaining a reliable holding environment that enables therapeutic regression. Case studies should detail the subtle ways patients move towards dependency, including changes in their ability to maintain boundaries, shifts in their need for the therapist's presence, and variations in their capacity to symbolize experience. It is crucial to document how the clinical setting facilitates what Winnicott termed the "royal road" back to the true self, noting specific moments when patients display increased vulnerability and dependency alongside signs of emerging authenticity and creativity. Clinicians should record both the challenges and opportunities that arise in holding the regression, paying particular attention to countertransference reactions that might signal the patient's early environmental failures. The case should illustrate how this carefully held regression ultimately serves as a pathway for therapeutic growth, allowing patients to reconnect with their true selves and resume creative psychological development.

> It's important to note that not all patients undergo regression in therapy and that regression has become an almost mythical concept. Often, patients have come to me wanting to experience regression in psychoanalytic therapy, only to be quite disappointed to find that while they underwent other significant changes, they did not experience regression to what Winnicott termed the "total dependency" state (Winnicott, 1965). The concept of regression in therapy has been somewhat romanticized, leading to unrealistic expectations among patients and therapists.

Regression is not a universal or guaranteed aspect of psychoanalytic treatment. Each patient's therapeutic journey is unique, and forcing a predetermined psychological trajectory can be counterproductive.

Therefore, avoid the temptation to impose or narratively construct regression as a mandatory therapeutic experience. Instead, remain attuned to the patient's authentic process of psychological unfolding, respecting their rhythm of growth and self-discovery.

Clinical example

Ruth, a woman in her forties, married with children, mentally healthy, and generally functioning, developed a deep dependence on therapy after three years of analysis. In sessions, she often closes her eyes and reports a pleasant feeling of floating in the air without any fear of falling. This can last the entire session. To avoid disrupting the continuity of treatment, Ruth continued to come to me even during the COVID lockdown.

During this phase, I was concerned about infection as Ruth met clients in her room as part of her work. One day, immediately after one of the lockdowns, Ruth entered my room and sneezed. Without thinking, I automatically moved my chair far away from her. I acted reflexively, driven by anxiety rather than clinical thinking. She must have recognized the fear and recoil, as if she were a virus threatening to infect me.

Ruth reacted with shock and offense. She refused to lie on the couch and remained standing by the entrance door. Her face was pale. Finally, after recovering, and 20 minutes had already passed, she threw herself in despair with a thud onto the couch and sobbed. In the previous session, she thought something about her had repulsed me and made me want to distance myself. She hoped that my request to distance was related to her, so the event would be under her control and she could fix it. The immediate response was just the beginning of a more extensive deterioration in her functioning. In the weeks that followed, Ruth showed increasing signs of ego disintegration. She began experiencing difficulties maintaining her usual work routine, often going blank during conversations with clients. Her speech in sessions became notably different—sometimes stilted and overly formal, as if reading from a script, while at other times she struggled to form coherent sentences or follow others' speech.

The regression deepened as frozen memories from her early relationship with her hostile mother emerged. Ruth began experiencing severe primary anxiety, manifesting in an inability to focus on basic tasks. She developed a pattern of artificial congeniality in her professional life, clearly designed to keep others at a distance and prevent them from noticing her deteriorating state. During sessions, she would frequently lose affect entirely, a defensive measure against overwhelming feelings, only to be followed by periods of intense emotional flooding.

The regression was particularly evident in her heightened sensitivity to any perceived rejection. Minor changes in my tone or slight delays in responding would trigger immediate breakdowns in her functioning. She would often go blank, unable to verbalize her experience, suggesting access to pre-verbal trauma. Her associations increasingly centered around early childhood experiences, but these would emerge through disturbing transformations in her way of being rather than through coherent narratives.

Despite my attempts to repair the rupture, Ruth continued to struggle with basic ego functions. Simple daily tasks became overwhelming, and she reported increasing difficulty remembering recent events or maintaining her usual professional boundaries. What began as a single rupture in the therapeutic relationship had activated a profound regression, revealing the depth of her early trauma and the fragility of her adult functioning when early developmental wounds were triggered.

I felt that many weeks of analysis had gone to waste and that I could never fix it. In the end, I said to her: "I was afraid of getting infected with coronavirus. I didn't appreciate how much this would hurt you, and I was wrong." Somehow, we managed to overcome this.

Fear of breakdown

In Winnicott's (1974) view, a breakdown signifies the collapse of a defense organization established to shield the individual from an inconceivable, psychotic condition. Potentially underlying this state are what he termed "primitive agonies," such as the torment of disintegration, perpetual descent, disintegration of psychosomatic cohesion, dissolution of self-awareness, and the capacity to engage with objects. When the infantile ego cannot encompass these agonies, the infant fails to incorporate the experience into the realm of "personal omnipotence"—thus, it remains beyond the compulsion to repeat.

A clinician aiming to write a case that includes fear of breakdown faces several challenges in capturing the essence of Winnicott's complex concept. The writer must convey the paradoxical nature of this fear, as it relates to an event that has already occurred yet is experienced as a future threat. This requires a narrative that holds temporal ambiguity without losing coherence. The clinician must articulate the ineffable nature of primitive agonies, which by definition exist beyond the realm of representational thought. This demands a prose style that evokes the unthinkable without resorting to cliché or oversimplification. Additionally, the clinician must grapple with how to depict the patient's experience of timelessness and spacelessness that often accompanies fear of breakdown, requiring a narrative that can convey altered states of consciousness.

Clinical example

When Nathan was 4 years old, his father died by suicide, and his mother, overwhelmed by her own grief and depression, became emotionally unavailable. Young Nathan was suddenly left without his father's playful presence and his mother's warmth, forced to become "a brave little man," as his mother would say. Nathan, after three years of analysis, is in a constant state of depression. He has no passion for his wife, newborn son, or work. He seems to be stuck in his own labyrinth without a map. He perceives his wife as dependent and "clingy." Nathan feels that she constantly wants romantic gestures and expressions of love from him, which he has no intention or desire to give her. According to him, if he only had enough strength, he would leave her. Towards his son, he feels no affection or special emotion and tends to think that other parents who speak enthusiastically about their baby are exaggerating or lying. At most, Nathan finds the baby "cute." In analysis, he doesn't miss a single session but complains of boredom. He often glances at his watch to calculate how much time is left until the end of the session.

He often remains silent or talks about innovations in electronics. Shortly before the birth, his wife forced him to bring a puppy into the house. He felt intense resentment towards the puppy for a reason he can't explain. The puppy seemed ridiculous to him when it stuck out its tongue and licked his wife. When he was forced to take the puppy out for walks, he would run it intentionally to exhaust it and stopped only when the puppy, which followed him everywhere, was breathing heavily from the effort. Sometimes, he would unleash it and hide, enjoying seeing the puppy whining and searching for its lost owners. On one of the times he unleashed it, the puppy ran into the road, was run over, and died. As a result, the patient fell into a severe depression. Except for analysis and his work, he hardly left the house. It seemed he had lost interest in life. He didn't talk much about the dog, as if the puppy's death was just a trigger that activated an earlier loss that already had a life of its own.

He was so deeply depressed that I feared he wouldn't have the strength to come to me or that he might harm himself to stop the suffering. In treating Nathan during his severe breakdown following the dog's death, I maintained a careful therapeutic silence, creating space for his own thoughts and feelings to emerge. Rather than rushing to interpret or connect his current crisis to his childhood trauma of losing his father and first dog, I allowed his grief and depression to fill the analytic space. When Nathan barely spoke, staring blankly or discussing electronics, I refrained from redirecting him, understanding that even these seemingly disconnected communications were part of his process of gradually approaching his overwhelming affect.

Only after several weeks, when Nathan's profound despair began to find its voice in the safety of the analytic space, did his emotions start bridging between his present loss and the buried childhood trauma. Nathan himself began making subtle connections—a fleeting memory of his childhood dog, a fragment of recollection about his father. As these associations emerged naturally through his affect rather than through my interpretations, the therapeutic space became a container where both past and present grief could finally be experienced and processed.

My role was primarily to hold this space, allowing Nathan's psyche to move at its own pace from the immediate crisis of the puppy's death to the deeper layers of his original losses. When I did speak, it was mainly to acknowledge the depth of his pain rather than to make connections he wasn't yet ready to consciously hold. My "holding in silence" allowed Nathan to gradually find his own path through his breakdown, leading to a more authentic connection with his buried emotions and traumatic history.

Playfulness and creativity in therapy

Winnicott views creativity and play as fundamental forces in psychological development, not merely as defensive mechanisms. In therapy, creative moments emerge in various forms: when patients find new words for old feelings, during spontaneous play with ideas, or in moments of genuine surprise and discovery. These creative breakthroughs often occur when rigid defenses give way to flexible exploration.

When writing about these therapeutic moments, clinicians should craft narratives that mirror the lively quality of such experiences. The writing should embody creative flow while balancing theoretical understanding with vivid clinical examples. Rather than simply describing events, clinical writing should evoke the experience of creative discovery, capturing both the subtle interplay between silence and speech and the moments of mutual surprise between therapist and patient. This approach allows readers to engage with the material in their own creative way, making the clinical writing function as a transitional space where multiple meanings can coexist and new understandings can emerge.

There are specific markers that signal creative moments in therapy that clinicians should attend to in their writing: when patients discover fresh language for longstanding emotional patterns, during playful exploration of ideas and meanings, in moments of shared surprise or discovery between patient and therapist, when defensive rigidity yields to more flexible engagement, during collaborative meaning-making, when silence shifts from defensive to productive, when humor emerges and patients can laugh at themselves or with the therapist, when patients allow themselves to play with imagination and fantasy, and when patients find novel perspectives on past experiences. These moments represent the emergence of genuine therapeutic creativity and deserve particular attention in clinical writing.

Clinical example

Patient: "You're breathing heavily today, is it because I'm tiring you out?"

Therapist: "I didn't notice that."

Patient: "Are you saying I'm making this up?"

Therapist: "I didn't say that; I said I didn't notice it."

Patient: "You're not self-aware enough. Have you ever been in therapy?" (The therapist and patient laugh)

Therapist: "You know I have; it's part of every therapist's training."

Patient: "Tell me who you went to because they did a really poor job." (The therapist and patient laugh)

Use of an object

Winnicott's (1969) concept of object usage marks a shift in infant development, wherein the object is recognized as independent from the infant's projections. This process involves destructive impulses directed towards the object and its survival without retaliation.

This achievement signifies several important developmental milestones: the infant's understanding that objects continue to exist even when not present (object permanence), the ability to maintain a stable internal image of caregivers (object constancy), the capacity for symbolic thinking, and the crucial differentiation between internal and external reality. When the infant acknowledges the caregiver as external, they simultaneously recognize their own separate self. This is also when fantasy life truly begins, as the distinction between internal and external reality becomes established.

Challenges for clinicians writing about object usage include conveying the paradoxical nature of destruction and survival. Distinguishing object usage from earlier stages of object relations is crucial. Illustrating the shift from fantasy-based relating to reality-based object usage necessitates careful explanation. Articulating the implications of object usage for later psychological development enriches the clinical description.

The clinician must find a way to represent the patient's growing capacity for concern and reparation, which often follows successful use of the object, without oversimplifying this complex emotional process.

Clinical example

The patient is an 18-year-old female soldier in active service who was orphaned by her parents and currently lives with her aunt and uncle. Her aunt is ill and has to be away from home for hospitalizations. After completing basic training, she was assigned as a clerk in the headquarters, performing a tedious job that did not satisfy her. Her mental stability was shaken after her younger brother left home for boarding school. Since then, she often erupts in anger at her unit mates. Small, trivial matters, such as someone placing the stapler in a different location instead of its designated spot, cause her to lose her temper, scream, and even curse. Her commanders keep her in the unit solely because she is dedicated to her work and shows great commitment to every task. In the unit, she feels isolated and disliked. In therapy, she is careful to be polite and quiet, as if fearing that the storm she is experiencing will consume her only close and empathetic relationship.

One day, after a two-week vacation during which we hadn't met, she arrived in tears and told me that the sink in their bathroom had fallen and that she would have to buy a new one. After asking her how she planned to address this (an incorrect response, which treated the fallen sink as something needing a solution rather than as a symbolic event), an intense wave of anger filled the room.

She shouted: "How can I afford this? Where will I get the money from? You come up with it!!" She stood up, her face red, and continued to shout as she approached me, waving her hands in anger. This lasted for ten minutes. It seemed like she had lost control. I felt the need to protect myself from her anger. There was no option but to create more physical distance between us. Yet, I remained frozen in my seat, facing her shouting.

The first thought that crossed my mind was that her outburst related to the extended break in therapy and that she likely felt I had abandoned her. Eventually, she took one of the potted plants from the windowsill and angrily smashed it at my feet. The shards of the pot, the soil, and the exposed seedling with roots scattered across the room, some landing on my shoes and the hem of my pants.

After that, the shouting ceased. Stunned and silent, she sat back down, her head bowed. After a few minutes, she began to sob with rhythmic, whimpering breaths. She reminded me of a hungry puppy left alone. It seemed she didn't even notice my presence.

I said to her: "I am so, so sorry."

This was when the patient finally recognized my presence in the room again. She lifted her head but still didn't dare look at me. After remaining silent for a few minutes, she asked if she would need to pay for the damage she had caused. I replied that I appreciated her desire to make amends. I suggested we clean up the pot shards together, and we did so with vigorous efficiency. She continued to be silent.

In the next session, she returned calmer but didn't look at me. "I'm sure you hate me," she said.

I told her that it was unbearable for her to feel that I knew how much she hated me and wanted to hurt me, and she probably believed her hatred had destroyed our relationship.

I told her that I felt her anger and frustration, which impacted me deeply. I realized that my vacation had made her feel as if the aspects of therapy that involve holding, washing things, and cleaning had fallen and shattered, and that she hated me for it. I assured her that now that I'm back and there are no breaks in the near future, I will do everything possible to ensure therapy becomes regular and safe in her life again.

THE TERMINATION PHASE IN WINNICOTT'S APPROACH

In Winnicott's theory, therapy ends when the patient achieves emotional growth, a cohesive sense of self, and the capacity to live creatively and authentically. The process involves internalizing the analytic object, allowing the patient to integrate the therapeutic relationship and process, which enables them to manage their emotional life independently. Termination also occurs when the patient displays the capacity for play and creativity, bridging their inner and outer realities meaningfully.

A key aspect of this process is resolving dependency. During therapy, some patients regresses to a state of dependence, which is addressed until they transition to relative independence. Another important milestone is the ability to use the object—relating to others as separate and real individuals while acknowledging their survival of the patient's destructive impulses. This fosters trust and a sense of reality.

The end of therapy also signifies the integration of the "true self," as opposed to living under the dominance of a "false self." This reconnection with authenticity enables genuine living. Furthermore, therapy concludes when the patient develops emotional resilience and self-regulation, reflected in their "capacity to be alone" without excessive reliance on the therapist.

The timing of termination is highly individualized, occurring when both therapist and patient mutually recognize that therapeutic goals have been achieved.

In summary, therapy ends when the patient has reached emotional maturity, independence, and the ability to navigate life's relationships and challenges creatively and authentically. The therapist remains attuned to the patient's unique journey, ensuring that termination feels natural and appropriate. In practice, termination rarely unfolds with such seamless resolution.

In writing a clinical case study in Winnicott's spirit, the therapist encounters the complex challenge of conveying the depth of the therapeutic process and the significance of its conclusion. A comprehensive account should include detailed references to turning points that signify substantial change in the patient, the emotional and practical preparation for termination, significant interactions during the final sessions, and the emotional responses of both participants to the impending separation.

An in-depth case study reflects the complexities of the mourning process that accompanies termination and sheds light on how the patient internalizes the therapeutic relationship as an inner resource. The writing highlights the strengths that developed in the patient alongside ongoing areas of vulnerability, while also reflecting the therapist's experiences—satisfaction with the patient's progress alongside concerns and doubts.

Not every therapeutic termination unfolds ideally. Some patients leave therapy abruptly, with unresolved tensions or without a clear sense of emotional integration. Even in these cases, a sensitive case study can reveal the value of the partial process and the seeds sown for future growth. Such endings can still be understood through Winnicott's concept of the "true self" and the holding environment, even when the process appears fragmented or seemingly incomplete.

Writing about the termination of therapy is not merely technical documentation but the creation of a narrative that reflects the profound human encounter that took place—two people connected, learned, grew, and ultimately parted. Such writing becomes part of the clinical conversation itself, inviting reflection on the therapeutic bond, its transformations, and the enduring traces it leaves in both analyst and patient.

Clinical example

Gwen had grown up in the shadow of an older sister who had died in infancy. Her mother, unable to fully mourn this loss, had unconsciously sought to recreate her lost child in Gwen. This dynamic had profoundly shaped Gwen's sense of self, leading to a pervasive feeling of inauthenticity and a deep-seated fear of disappointing others.

As we approached the end of our work, Gwen shared a vivid dream: "I'm in a house with many rooms. In each room, I find a mirror, but my reflection is always slightly different. In the final room, I see no reflection at all. Instead, the mirror becomes a window, and through it, I see a garden I've never seen before. A child is playing there, laughing. I feel a mix of longing and fear."

This dream beautifully encapsulated Gwen's journey. The changing reflections symbolized her growing awareness of her multifaceted nature, moving beyond the rigid false self she had constructed. The mirror becoming a window illustrated her emerging capacity to see beyond her habitual self-perceptions. The unseen garden and the laughing child represented aspects of her true self that had remained hidden.

The termination process itself became crucial. Gwen's fear of disappointing me by ending therapy echoed her lifelong pattern of prioritizing others' needs. In our last meeting, she spoke of feeling more "real and alive" than ever. The end of therapy was not a completion, but a transition into a new phase of exploration.

To my surprise, Gwen contacted me three months later in deep depression. Our seemingly smooth farewell had triggered an early trauma, reawakening her identification with her deceased sister. She revealed intense feelings of resentment, feeling abandoned despite having initiated the resumption herself. Her reluctance to express these feelings had contributed to her depression.

I realized I had missed subtle signs of her unprocessed grief, perhaps colluding with her false self's need to please me by performing a "good ending." We agreed to resume therapy for another year. This unexpected continuation focused on exploring the fantasy of the "perfect ending" and working through the grief that had been suppressed for so long.

As we approached our second termination, Gwen's demeanor was markedly different. She was more grounded, able to acknowledge both positive and negative feelings about ending. She spoke of feeling "unfinished, but ready"—capturing her newfound ability to tolerate imperfection and ongoing growth.

In our final session, Gwen expressed gratitude for navigating the difficult emotions, acknowledging that the "messy" ending had ultimately been more healing than the idealized one. Gwen's journey highlighted the complex, nonlinear nature of therapeutic change and the importance of addressing rather than avoiding difficult emotions.

SUGGESTIONS FOR WRITING A CASE STUDY BASED ON WINNICOTT'S THEORY

Winnicott encouraged intellectual autonomy and prioritized spontaneous expression, which results in non-conformity to any "school of thought." Paradoxically, this openness has become the hallmark of adherence to a "Winnicott School."

However, case studies written using Winnicott's approach are identifiable and share common characteristics. The following suggestions aim to clarify the nature of these characteristics but do not constitute a recipe for writing a Winnicott-style case study.

Patrick Casement (2019) offers a suggestion that I wholeheartedly embrace: instead of applying Winnicott, find him within your therapeutic work. Instead of mechanically applying Winnicott's ideas, try to discover them in your own therapeutic work. In other words, rather than asking, "What would Winnicott do?", listen to and experience your patient and the relationship between you. Notice how Winnicott's principles—such as potential space, holding, containment, playfulness, and the exploration of the true self—emerge naturally within your sessions. In this sense, Winnicott is not something you "apply," but rather something that is "revealed" through the therapeutic dialogue itself.

To write a psychodynamic case study based on Winnicott's approach, consider incorporating the following guiding principles:

Emphasize the holding environment

Focus on how the therapeutic setting provides a holding environment for the patient. Describe how the therapist's presence creates a sense of safety and containment, allowing the patient to explore their vulnerabilities and emotional states without fear of intrusion or judgment. Show how the holding environment respects the patient's unique rhythm of discovery and integration.

Highlight experiential therapy

Since Winnicott's approach is primarily experiential, prioritize the patient's lived experiences and the therapeutic atmosphere over verbal interpretations. Detail how the therapist's intuitive and empathetic engagement facilitates the patient's self-exploration and self-discovery.

Explore true and false self dynamics

Discuss the patient's journey toward discovering their true self, often hidden beneath a false self constructed as a defense against early environmental failures. Illustrate how the therapy supports the patient in expressing their authentic self and integrating previously denied aspects of their identity.

USE INTERPRETATIONS SPARINGLY

Interpretations should be used judiciously, ensuring they do not close off exploration or overwhelm the patient. Focus on creating a space where the patient can project and work through their feelings, allowing for spontaneous growth and insight. Honor the patient's cadence to the greatest extent possible, facilitating their autonomous discoveries at an opportune moment. Winnicott particularly emphasized this aspect in his later years:

> If only we can wait, the patient arrives at understanding creatively and with immense joy, and I now enjoy this joy more than I used to enjoy the sense of having been clever. I think I interpret mainly to let the patient know the limits of my understanding. The principle is that the patient and only the patient has the answers.
>
> *Winnicott, 1971, p. 117.*

Regression to dependence

When regression to dependence occurs, it is significant and deserves careful attention in case studies. Depicting these experiences is challenging because they fundamentally shake the foundations of therapy.

The usual therapeutic frame and techniques may temporarily lose effectiveness, and the therapist might feel like they're navigating uncharted waters. Converting this sense of uncertainty and instability is important when writing about such cases.

Describe how the familiar landmarks of therapy—the setting, the therapeutic alliance, the usual interventions—suddenly seem insufficient or even counterproductive. Detail your own struggles as a therapist to find new ways of being present and responsive when your usual tools fail you.

At the same time, emphasize that this uncomfortable destabilization can be a crucial part of the therapeutic process for some patients. It may allow for a deeper level of work and healing that wouldn't be possible otherwise. The task in writing the case study is to capture both the peril and the potential of these moments, showing how the very disruption of therapy can, paradoxically, lead to its deepest successes.

Course of treatment

The emergence of the true self is a gradual process that unfolds over an extended period of therapeutic work. First, you must describe how you established a stable, predictable environment where the patient can develop a sense of safety. In the initial stages of treatment, consider outlining the paranoid-schizoid anxieties and their associated defenses that serve to shield the true self from direct contact with both the individual and the external world.

As you write your case study, detail the slow erosion of these protective barriers, facilitated by your consistent presence and the unwavering reliability of the therapeutic setting. With regressive patients, illustrate how this gradual process enabled a regression to dependence, allowing the most deeply traumatized aspects of the patient to resurface. Describe the transition as anxieties related to intrusion and the dissolution of subjective boundaries gradually diminished, opening the possibility for the patient to reveal themselves to you and eventually develop trust.

Throughout your case study, weave in examples of both progress and setbacks, demonstrating how these fluctuations contributed to the overall process of strengthening the patient's true self.

Atmosphere and non-verbal communication

Pay particular attention to silences—their texture, duration, and emotional resonance. Some silences feel pregnant with possibility, others heavy with dread, while still others carry a peaceful quality of shared being.

Note how the patient's emergence occurs not only through words but through the therapist's embodied presence—the way they hold the space through their breathing, posture, and energetic availability. Describe how your voice modulates to meet the patient's emotional state—perhaps softening to contain anxiety, finding a rhythm that soothes, or maintaining a steady tone that anchors. Document the subtle shifts in the patient's own non-verbal communication—a relaxing of held tension, a new openness in their gaze, a different way of inhabiting the therapeutic space.

Detail your internal experience as you contain primitive anxieties and fragmented states. How do you maintain your own grounding while remaining attuned to chaos? Include moments when the melody of the interaction—its rhythm, tone, and musicality—becomes more significant than the content of what is said.

Attend especially to those precious moments when hope begins to glimmer through the therapeutic atmosphere—perhaps in a spontaneous gesture, a new way of playing with words, or simply a quality of ease in shared silence. These are the moments when your reliable, nonintrusive presence has helped create conditions where something new can safely unfold.

RECOMMENDED READING

Five exemplary Winnicottian case studies

Withdrawal and Regression, by Donald Winnicott. In *Through Paediatrics to Psycho-Analysis,* pp. 255–261. Karnac Books, 1954/1992.

This case study describes the treatment of a schizoid-depressive patient, focusing on moments of withdrawal and regression during therapy sessions, where Winnicott highlights the therapist's capacity to promptly and accurately contain and respond to these states.

Infantile neurosis as a false-self organization, by Masud Khan. *Psychoanalytic Quarterly 40,* 245–263, 1971.

Masud Khan's case describes a patient who developed religious obsessions and precocious mental functioning as a false self defense against early environmental failures and threats of annihilation. This paper provides an excellent model for documenting how environmental provisions shape development, how defensive organizations emerge, and how the analyst's authentic presence, rather than technical interpretation, facilitates therapeutic change. As one of Winnicott's closest associates, Khan masterfully illustrates key Winnicottian concepts including true/false self, maternal provision, and the impact of early environmental failure through detailed clinical material that emphasizes the therapeutic relationship over interpretation.

The logic of play in psychoanalysis, by Michael Parsons. *International Journal of Psychoanalysis 80,* 871–884, 1999.

Michael Parsons is undoubtedly one of the most engaging and insightful case study writers, offering a sharp, clear-eyed perspective that is rich in imagination and playfulness. This article examines the crucial role of play in psychoanalysis, focusing on patients grappling with trust, self-expression, and creativity.

To experience Winnicott's spirit, it is beneficial to read two canonical papers written by his former patients, who were also seasoned analysts—Harry Guntrip and Margaret Little. These first-hand accounts of being in analysis with Winnicott deliver unique insights into his clinical approach and practice.

My experience of analysis with Fairbairn and Winnicott: How complete a result does psychoanalytic therapy achieve?, by Harry Guntrip. *International Journal of Psychoanalysis 77,* 739–754, 1996.

Guntrip's memoir offers clinicians a rare and invaluable insight into Winnicott's perspective on the analytic process, providing a unique window into the long-term effects of psychoanalysis beyond the treatment room.

Here is a short excerpt:

"'You too have a good breast,' Winnicott tells Guntrip, 'You've always been able to give more than take. I'm good for you but you're good for me. Doing your analysis is almost the most reassuring thing that happens to me. The chap before you makes me feel I'm no good at all. You don't have to be good for me. I don't need it and can cope without it, but in fact you are good for me.'" (p. 750)

Psychotic anxieties and containment: A personal record of an analysis with Winnicott, by Margaret I. Little, M. R. C. Psych. Jason Aronson, 1990.

This memoir provides a candid and detailed account of the author's psychoanalytic journey with three distinct analysts. While Margaret Little's work with Winnicott forms the narrative's core, her earlier experiences with a Jungian analyst and with Ella Freeman Sharpe provide crucial context. These earlier analyses serve as a powerful contrast, highlighting what made Winnicott's approach so revolutionary and effective.

REFERENCES

Abram, J. (2007). *The language of Winnicott: A dictionary of Winnicott's use of words* (2nd ed.). Karnac Books.

Casement, P. (2006). *Learning from life: Becoming a psychoanalyst.* Routledge.

Casement, P. (2019). *Learning Along the Way: Further Reflections on Psychoanalysis and Psychotherapy.* Routledge.

Caspi, T. (2018). Towards psychoanalytic contribution to linguistic metaphor theory. *International Journal of Psychoanalysis, 99*(5), 1186–1211.

Elkins, J. (2015). Winnicott's anti-systematic approach to psychoanalytic theory. *International Journal of Psychoanalysis, 96*(4), 1013–1034.

Guntrip, H. (1996). My experience of analysis with Fairbairn and Winnicott: How complete a result does psychoanalytic therapy achieve? *International Journal of Psychoanalysis, 77*(4), 739–754.

Khan, M. M. R. (1971). Infantile neurosis as a false-self organization. *Psychoanalytic Quarterly, 40*(2), 245–263.

Little, M. I. (1990). *Psychotic anxieties and containment: A personal record of an analysis with Winnicott.* Jason Aronson.

Parsons, M. (1999). The logic of play in psychoanalysis. *International Journal of Psychoanalysis, 80*(5), 871–884.

Sirote, A. (2015). The Patient Who Had Me Committed: A Mutually Influential Relationship Between Patient and Analyst in the Context of a Broadening Analytic Frame. *Psychoanalytic Perspectives, 12*(1), 1–14.

Winnicott, D. W. (1951). Transitional objects and transitional phenomena. *International Journal of Psychoanalysis, 34*(2), 89–97.

Winnicott, D. W. (1954/1992). Withdrawal and regression. In *Through paediatrics to psycho-analysis* (pp. 255–261). Karnac Books.

Winnicott, D. W. (1955). Clinical varieties of transference. *International Journal of Psychoanalysis, 36*(6), 386–388.

Winnicott, D. W. (1965). *The maturational processes and the facilitating environment.* Hogarth Press.

Winnicott, D. W. (1969). The use of an object and relating through identifications. *International Journal of Psychoanalysis, 50*(4), 711–716.

Winnicott, D. W. (1971). *Playing and reality.* Tavistock Publications.

Winnicott, D. W. (1974). Fear of breakdown. *International Review of Psychoanalysis, 1,* 103–107.

Winnicott, D. W. (1975). Hate in the countertransference. *International Journal of Psychoanalysis, 56*(1), 11–17.

CHAPTER 9

A case study in the spirit
of Heinz Kohut

....

THE GREATEST CHALLENGES

Writing case studies from a self psychology perspective requires clinicians to make fundamental shifts in observing and documenting therapeutic work compared to object relations and Kleinian approaches. Instead of focusing on uncovering unconscious phantasies or interpreting internal object relationships, the clinician must describe how the therapeutic relationship strengthens the patient's self-structure through compensatory selfobject experiences.

This perspective aligns more closely with the "trauma healing" tradition (see chapter 2) than truth-seeking approaches. It emphasizes the reparative power of the therapeutic relationship over the discovery of unconscious content. In this respect, it shares common ground with Winnicott's ideas, though it lacks the deep roots in Kleinian object relations theory.

When documenting clinical material, the focus shifts from describing internal objects and their dynamics to depicting self-cohesion and fragmentation. The writing must demonstrate how empathic understanding facilitates growth, emphasizing the healing aspect of the therapeutic relationship itself rather than insights gained through interpretation.

Selfobject transferences (mirroring, idealizing, twinship) should be depicted as compensatory experiences rather than manifestations of early object relationships or unconscious phantasies. Progress is highlighted through the development of self-cohesion and vitality, not merely through working through conflicts or achieving integration of split object relations.

The core challenge for clinicians is to maintain an experience-near quality in their writing while clearly grounding it in self psychology concepts, differentiating this approach from both classical and contemporary object relations models. This requires a delicate balance between describing the healing power of the therapeutic relationship and avoiding the implication that therapy is merely about gratifying needs or providing a corrective emotional experience.

An additional complexity in writing self psychology case studies stems from the evolution and diversification of the theory itself. Since Kohut's original formulation, self psychology has developed multiple branches and variations. Some writers may choose to ground their

DOI: 10.4324/9781003538578-12

work in classical Kohutian theory, focusing primarily on subjective experience and the three main selfobject transferences. Others might align with contemporary relational self psychology. Writers can also draw from versions that integrate infant research and neurobiology findings or from approaches that expand the concept of selfobject experiences to include a wider range of relational phenomena. The theoretical stance chosen will naturally shape how the case material is understood and presented, particularly regarding the balance between interpretation and the provision of selfobject experiences. There is no single "correct" version of self psychology to follow. Each writer must thoughtfully select and articulate their theoretical framework while maintaining an experience-near quality in their clinical writing.

RELATED CONCEPTS

Selfobject, selfobject needs, transmuting internalization, grandiose self, mirroring, idealization, twinship experience, empathic failure, empathy, narcissism.

THERAPEUTIC ATMOSPHERE

In reading self psychology case studies, a unique therapeutic atmosphere emerges characterized by several central features:

An atmosphere of unconditional acceptance and psychological safety. The first impression from these texts is of a completely protected space. This atmosphere allows the patient to bring all parts of the self—the wounded, angry, and despairing parts—without fear of criticism or judgment. The therapist is seen as a containing figure who enables full expression of narcissistic vulnerability.

A quality of extreme gentleness and caution. The reading experience has almost surgical precision in handling emotions. The therapist appears as someone who understands they are engaging with an extremely delicate psychological structure; therefore, every word and every response is carefully considered.

An experience of echo and emotional attunement. The reader senses an atmosphere of perfect emotional synchrony. The therapist is perceived as someone who manages to "step into the patient's shoes" in an almost mystical way. This feeling of deep understanding arises not from intellectual analysis, but from complete emotional attunement.

A quality of repair and nourishment. The atmosphere conveyed resembles a therapeutic space that acts like a "psychological greenhouse"—a place where wounded parts of the self can flourish and develop. The therapist is experienced as a consistent source of healthy narcissistic nourishment, someone who provides precisely what the patient needs.

THERAPY GOAL

According to Kohut, the fundamental aim of therapy is to help patients transform archaic narcissistic needs into more mature forms of self-regulation and relationships. Treatment focuses on shifting from primitive merger needs with selfobjects to more flexible, age-appropriate forms of connection and support. When writing case studies from this perspective, clinicians should document the gradual transformation in the patient's selfobject needs and relationships. The case narrative should trace how initially rigid and demanding narcissistic needs begin to evolve through the therapeutic relationship. Writers should illustrate specific moments when archaic merger needs surface in the treatment and then carefully describe how these shift toward more mature forms of connection. The writing should capture both subtle and significant shifts in how the patient relates to the therapist as a selfobject—from early experiences of desperately needed merger to more nuanced forms of connection. Clinicians should document examples of how patients gradually develop the capacity to maintain their sense of self even when experiencing temporary disconnection or disappointment in relationships. The written case should demonstrate how therapeutic progress manifests through the patient's growing ability to form and sustain mature selfobject relationships with the therapist and in broader life.

CAPTURING TRANSFORMATION: WRITING ABOUT CHANGE IN KOHUT'S FRAMEWORK

According to Kohut, this therapeutic process unfolds in two main movements: a deep immersion in empathy and understanding of the patient's nuclear self, followed by a phase of working through and understanding via interpretation. Dealing with empathic failures is also central to the treatment (Kohut, 1984).

When writing case studies from this perspective, clinicians should structure their narratives to reflect this two-phase process. Begin by describing the extended period of empathic attunement, illustrating how you worked to deeply understand the patient's core self, their aspirations, and their potential, even when obscured by trauma or developmental arrests.

Then, document pivotal moments of empathic failure and repair. Describe specific instances where breaks in empathic attunement occurred, and detail both the patient's emotional response (whether rage, withdrawal, or wishes to terminate) and your own response of acknowledging the failure without defensiveness. Show how these ruptures created opportunities to connect present disappointments with early childhood experiences of unmet selfobject needs.

> The written case should demonstrate how each empathic failure and repair cycle contributed to the patient's growth. Illustrate how your interpretations evolved from simple acknowledgment of feelings to deeper connections between present and past experiences. Document how the patient gradually developed new psychological structures through this process, showing concrete examples of how their relationship patterns and self-regulation capacities matured over time.

It is also crucial to emphasize the central role of emotional validation in the therapeutic process. As therapists, you should describe how you deeply understood and acknowledged your patient's emotional world. Show how you validated their experiences and feelings, even when these seemed irrational or distorted from an external perspective.

RELATIONAL SELF PSYCHOLOGY

Relational self psychology (Magid, Fosshage, & Shane, 2021) represents an evolution of Kohut's original self psychology theory into a more intersubjective, two-person model. Key aspects include a shift from viewing the analyst as primarily providing selfobject functions to recognizing the mutual influence and co-creation occurring between analyst and patient. There is a greater emphasis on the analyst's subjectivity and how it impacts the therapeutic relationship, rather than merely focusing on the patient's experience. The theory incorporates findings from infant research showing the bidirectional nature of mother-infant interactions, which are applied to the analytic relationship (Lachmann & Beebe, 1995). Change is conceptualized as occurring through ongoing cycles of attunement, disruption, and repair in the therapeutic relationship, rather than solely through interpretation and insight. The self is viewed as an emergent, fluid process of self-organization rather than a fixed structure. Ideas from dynamic systems theory are integrated to understand therapeutic change as involving complex, nonlinear processes. Overall, relational self psychology aims to preserve core self psychological concepts while expanding the theory to account for intersubjective, relational, and systemic factors in development and therapeutic change. When writing a case study from a relational self psychology perspective, therapists should aim to highlight the mutual influence and co-creation that occur between therapist and patient. This can be accomplished by describing instances where the therapist's subjectivity and experiences shape the therapeutic process, illustrating how the patient's and therapist's subjective experiences interact and influence one another, and demonstrating the bidirectional nature of the therapeutic relationship. Therapists should also emphasize the importance of attunement, disruption, and repair in the therapeutic process. This can be achieved by providing examples of moments of attunement between therapist and patient, outlining instances of disruption or misattunement in the therapeutic relationship, and illustrating the process of repair and how it contributes to therapeutic change. Furthermore, case studies should focus on the emergence of the self as a fluid process of self-organization rather than a fixed structure. Therapists can demonstrate this by tracking changes in the patient's sense of self over time and highlighting how these changes are influenced by the therapeutic relationship and other relational experiences. Integrating ideas from dynamic systems theory can help therapists conceptualize therapeutic change as a complex, nonlinear process. Case studies can illustrate this by describing the interplay of various factors, such as the patient's history, current relationships, and the therapeutic relationship, in shaping the patient's self-experience and promoting growth.

Clinical example

Jill, a 35-year-old artist, came to therapy struggling with creative blocks and intense self-criticism. As therapy progressed, I noticed that Jill seemed to crave unequivocal admiration and praise for her artwork.

During one session, Jill brought in a new painting, eagerly awaiting my response. I felt an intense pressure to provide effusive praise, which stirred a sense of resistance within me. I offered some warm words about the piece, but my tone was noticeably reserved.

Jill's reaction was immediate and intense. "You hate it, don't you?" she accused, her voice trembling with anger. "I thought you of all people would understand!"

Taken aback by the vehemence of Jill's response, I took a moment to reflect. I decided to share a bit of my experience.

"Jill, I can see how much my reaction has upset you," I began. "I want to be honest with you. It's difficult for me when you pressure me to respond in a certain way, and only in that way of admiration. It stirs up uncomfortable feelings in me and even resistance, as if you're not leaving it up to me how to respond."

Jill glared at me. "So you're saying the problem is me? That I'm too demanding?"

"No, that's not what I'm saying," I replied. "I think there's something more complex happening between us here. Perhaps we can explore this together?"

But Jill was already standing up, gathering her painting. "I don't need to sit here and listen to this," she said angrily. "I thought you were supposed to help me, not make me feel worse." She left the room, slamming the door behind her.

I sat there, stunned and confused. I felt the session had ended in disaster for both of us. I knew I would need to process what had happened and think about how to address this in our next session if Jill decided to return.

To my relief, Jill returned for our next session. She sat down, her posture tense and defensive. After a moment of uncomfortable silence, I decided to take a risk.

"Jill, I've been reflecting a lot on our last session," I began. "I want to share something with you. I realize that I have a personal difficulty when I feel pressured to provide unconditional praise. This is something I've struggled with for a long time, and it's related to my own history. I'm not comfortable going into the details, but I want you to know that my reaction wasn't just about you or your work."

Jill's expression softened slightly. "So . . . you have your own issues with this?"

"Yes," I replied. "I do. And I think what happened was a combination of your needs and my own personal challenge. I'm sorry I didn't handle it better in the moment."

This admission seemed to shift something between us. Jill leaned forward, her anger giving way to curiosity. "I never thought about how my demands might affect you," she said quietly.

From there, we began a more open dialogue about our therapeutic relationship. We explored Jill's need for validation and my struggles with feeling pressured, without delving into the specifics of my personal history. This conversation allowed us to examine how these dynamics played out not just in our sessions, but in Jill's other relationships as well.

Over the following weeks, our work deepened. Jill began to recognize her pattern of seeking external validation and how it impacted her creative process. I became more aware of my own triggers and how to navigate them more effectively in therapy.

This experience, while initially challenging, ultimately strengthened our therapeutic alliance. It opened up new avenues for exploration and growth, demonstrating how a therapist's judicious self-disclosure can enhance the therapeutic process when used to illuminate the relational dynamics at play and facilitate a deeper mutual understanding between therapist and patient.

This vignette embodies the principles of relational self psychology in several ways:

1. The therapist openly discusses their own subjectivity and emotional responses, acknowledging their "feelings of hesitation" and "fears of being intrusive," rather than presenting themselves as a neutral observer.
2. The case emphasizes the co-created nature of the therapeutic relationship, describing how both therapist and patient contribute to the dynamics: "we worked through this rupture," "our relational patterns were co-created."
3. The writing captures the nonlinear, complex nature of therapeutic change, acknowledging setbacks and ongoing challenges rather than presenting a neat narrative of progress.
4. The therapist candidly describes their own countertransference and struggles.

5. The description focuses on cycles of attunement, disruption, and repair in the therapeutic relationship, rather than just on interpretation and insight.
6. The writer maintains a stance of transparency about their own process, including moments of uncertainty.
7. The case study avoids presenting the therapist as an expert who merely provides selfobject functions, instead portraying the therapeutic relationship as a mutual journey of growth and discovery.

In essence, the writing style reflects the theoretical shift from a one-person to a two-person psychology, with the therapist's subjectivity and the co-created nature of the therapeutic relationship taking center stage in the narrative.

SELF PSYCHOLOGY AND THE SPIRITUAL DIMENSION

Today, self psychology has branched out in several directions. A central direction is represented by the "Human Spirit Buddhist Psychoanalytic Training Program" applied by The Israel Association for Self Psychology and the Study of Subjectivity (IASPS) in Israel. This approach integrates self psychology with Buddhist philosophy, incorporating yoga and meditation techniques into the curriculum, blending Eastern spiritual practices with Western psychological theory.

The aspirations of this group are to create, in Raanan Kulka's words, a super-infrastructure that will embrace the particular and the general within a universal matrix of total solidarity.

According to Raanan Kulka (2022), psychoanalysis, and particularly self psychology, contains a significant spiritual dimension. Kulka argues that Kohut's theory enables a transition from individual existence to a supra-personal existence of participation in the world—a movement from the emergence of the self towards dissolution and transcendence beyond the boundaries of time and space.

One of the transformations of narcissism according to Kohut is "cosmic" (Kohut, 1985)—when the self is cohesive enough to give up its personal narcissistic goals and undergoes transformation into an expanded self-state that merges with the world.

This perspective offers implications for writing psychodynamic case studies: writers should capture not only the patient's struggles with self-cohesion and narcissistic needs but also their journey toward transcendence and ethical development—moments when patients move beyond purely personal concerns toward a broader engagement with the world and others.

Clinical example

When Alexandra first entered my office, her presence embodied a striking contradiction. At 32, she was a successful orchestral violinist whose technical mastery was widely acclaimed; yet, she was plagued by what she called "an unbearable emptiness" after each performance. I would later understand this void as symbolizing a profound split between her artistic mastery and her capacity for authentic self-expression.

Alexandra's initial presentation centered on her inability to experience pleasure in music anymore—a particularly poignant complaint for a professional musician. She described feeling like "a perfectly programmed machine" during performances, disconnected from both the music and her audience. Although her technical execution remained flawless, she experienced increasing episodes of anxiety and depersonalization immediately after concerts.

Her family history revealed a childhood dominated by her father, a renowned music teacher, who transformed their home into what she called "a temple of technical perfection." Every mistake was met with cutting criticism, while technical achievements were celebrated with an intensity that, as she later realized, left no room for her own emotional experience of music.

The turning point in our work came unexpectedly during her third year of therapy. Alexandra had begun volunteering at a community music program for children with disabilities. During one session, she described working with a young student who struggled with basic rhythm. Instead of correcting his technique, she found herself simply playing along with his erratic tempo. "For the first time," she said, tears flowing, "I wasn't trying to achieve anything. We were just . . . making music together."

This moment exemplified the transformation from self-assertive narcissism to a more mature form of self-experience. Alexandra's ability to temporarily surrender her need for technical perfection allowed her to participate in what Kulka terms "the unified field of human experience."

The therapeutic process revealed how Alexandra's technical virtuosity, while impressive, had functioned as what Kohut calls a "defensive grandiose self"—a structure that protected her from the vulnerability of authentic emotional engagement. Our work involved not diminishing her technical mastery, but integrating it with her capacity for what she beautifully termed "musical empathy."

A shift occurred when Alexandra began experimenting with improvisation (Kohut, 1985)—something she had always avoided as too unpredictable. In these moments, she discovered a state where the self is cohesive enough to surrender individual control and merge with a larger artistic and human experience.

The transformation became evident in her professional life as well. During one session, she shared a review of her recent concert that noted a new quality in her playing—what the critic called "a rare combination of technical precision and emotional vulnerability." Alexandra's response was telling: "For the first time, I wasn't playing for the audience or for my father. I was playing with everyone in the hall."

This case illustrates how self psychology's spiritual dimension can illuminate the path from technical perfection to authentic artistic expression. Alexandra's journey wasn't about becoming a "better" musician in technical terms, but about developing what Kohut calls the capacity for mature transformation of narcissism—the ability to use her gifts not as a defensive structure but as a vehicle for genuine participation in the human experience of music.

As our work concluded, Alexandra had developed what she called "a new relationship with silence"—both in music and in life. Her technical mastery now served not as a shield but as a foundation for authentic self-expression and deep connection with others through music. This transformation exemplifies the movement from individual emergence to a state of transpersonal participation (Kulka, 2022), where personal achievement becomes a vehicle for universal connection.

The case demonstrates how self psychology's spiritual framework can help us understand psychological growth as the emergence of our inherent capacity for transcendent experience through authentic self-expression and connection with others.

DEMONSTRATIONS OF CLINICAL PHENOMENA

Transmuting internalization

Transmuting internalization refers to the gradual integration of the mutual interactions between therapist and patient into the fabric of the patient's personality. Start by providing a brief explanation of transmuting internalization. Describe how, through this process, the patient slowly internalizes aspects of the therapist's functions, particularly those related to selfobject needs. This enables the patient to develop and strengthen their own psychological structures that may have been underdeveloped or fragmented due to empathic failures in early life. The case study highlights the patient's progress from relying heavily on the therapist as an external selfobject to developing their own internal capacities for self-regulation, self-esteem, and a cohesive sense of identity. Use specific examples from therapy sessions to illustrate this growth. It is essential to emphasize that transmuting internalization is a rare and gradual process. It occurs through repeated cycles of empathic attunement, emotional validation, manageable empathic failures, and repair over an extended period. Clinicians should not give the impression that transmuting internalization is a frequent occurrence or that it happens in every therapy session.

Clinical example

The patient, an industrial engineer and mother of four, was 12 when her older sister died of cancer. Family life was shattered, and her devastated parents withdrew into themselves, never returning to the happy, sociable people she remembered before the tragedy. Nevertheless, her parents made a tremendous effort to "continue life as usual," rarely discussing their grief. Besides visiting the grave on the anniversary of the tragedy, her sister was hardly mentioned. An atmosphere of mourning pervaded everything, but it was hidden from the outside world as the family continued to pretend that it was "business as usual." When guests arrived or they visited others, the parents became more cheerful and open, but immediately after the event, they returned to being sad and withdrawn without acknowledging or discussing it. Towards the patient, they took care to fulfill their basic duties related to household management, ensured they attended parent-teacher meetings, and made sure she studied and prepared for exams; but beyond that, they showed no interest in her emotional world, invested no quality time in her, and focused solely on nurturing her academic abilities.

The only person who took an interest in her was her mother's brother, a 50-year-old bachelor and social worker, who made a point to visit them every week for years. She and her uncle developed a special bond. He would take her to the movies, plays, cafes, and even the opera. At every opportunity, he would marvel at her intelligence, diligence, and beauty, and she found herself looking forward to their meetings, yearning for touch and connection. She felt sexually attracted to him but wasn't sure how much he responded to her femininity. He helped her get through the depressing and dark years in her parents' home until she left to attend university.

She formed a good, pleasant, and cordial relationship in therapy and seemed to benefit greatly from it. However, at one of the meetings, something unusual happened. After not passing the interview, she discussed her failed attempt to land a job at an important and prestigious engineering firm. It was a position she wanted very much and had prepared for the tests and interview for many months. She said she was sad and spoke in a somber voice, but there was something different about her demeanor. She wore a crop top and short jeans, and it seemed she was flirting with me, trying to attract my attention. I found her very attractive, which filled me with great embarrassment. I chose to ignore these signs, and we continued to talk about her job search failure, her difficult feelings, and the other employment options she was considering.

In the next session, there was no trace of the provocative attire. She arrived looking very depressed, hunched over and broken. Nothing reminded me of the beautiful and attractive woman I had seen just two days before. She wore an oversized dress that hung carelessly on her, and her face was pale and expressionless. She said she had hesitated to come because she no longer felt the therapy was helping her. She looked desperate, like someone who had made a tremendous effort to swim in a stormy sea and had given up. Gradually, I understood what had happened between us: after not being accepted for the job, she could not bear such difficult feelings of rejection and failure. To deny them, she "opened" a seductive channel with me that was supposed to evoke my admiration and adoration for her femininity, liveliness, and youth, similar to the role her uncle played in her life. She desperately needed an admiring and sexually arousing response from me to erase the feelings of failure.

After I ignored her sexual hints and preferred to have a superficial conversation about the failure itself, she fell into an even deeper depression and was filled with a sense of despair.

Drawing on my empathic understanding towards her, I gently told her that I thought the failure to get the job had flooded her with difficult feelings.

"When you came to me, you were indeed depressed about not getting the job, but you dressed in a way that emphasized your sexuality and beauty. You wanted me to notice you, perhaps so you could forget the difficult feelings the failure evoked in you and compensate you. You wanted me to admire you, to tell you how beautiful you are. But I didn't react to your external appearance, and I didn't give you the recognition you so needed.

My ignoring you hurt you very much, and you felt even more desperate and depressed. You didn't get the comforting attention you so needed."

The patient responded to my words with a long silence. Her gaze became distant and sorrowful, and it was clear that something was shifting within her, silently. I understood that she was processing what I had said, and that my words had a profound impact on her. The stillness in the room was heavy with emotion, and I could sense the deep introspection she was experiencing. This silent, contemplative response seemed to indicate that she was connecting with the truth of my interpretation on a profound level, allowing herself to fully feel and acknowledge the complex emotions we had just explored together.

It seems that the interpretation helped restore the selfobject function that therapy served for her. My recognition of the empathic failure on my part in the treatment reinstated her sense of my ability to be a selfobject for her, as I understood her and allowed space for her distress. Thus, she could fully feel the sadness and depression stemming from the failure of not being accepted for the job. The crucial aspect was not the content of the interpretation, whether it was accurate or not, but her experience of me as a listening presence who could be with her and empathically acknowledge what she went through. The calmness and confidence with which my intervention was delivered, free from any hint of condemnation for her seductive behavior, enabled her to completely engage with a beneficial selfobject that offered her support.

As therapy progressed, the patient demonstrated a growing ability to regulate her emotions and maintain a stable sense of self-esteem, even in the face of disappointments and setbacks. She reported that she did not feel an intense need to rely on external validation to cope with difficult feelings, indicating that she had begun to internalize the selfobject functions provided by the therapist. This progress suggests that the patient experienced transmuting internalization, gradually developing her own internal capacities for self-regulation and self-esteem. The therapist's consistent empathic attunement, combined with the successful repair of minor empathic failures, allowed the patient to internalize the missing selfobject functions and strengthen her own psychological structures.

Self disorder in the preemergent phase (self-structure)

The concept of "Self Disorder" in the preemergent phase (Kohut, 1971) pertains to disturbances in the development of the self-structure before the emergence of a cohesive self. This phase occurs early in life, prior to the formation of a stable and cohesive self, typically before 18 months of age.

Key features of preemergent self disorders:

1. Trauma and early experiences: disturbances in this phase often arise from traumatic experiences or inadequate interactions with selfobjects during infancy. These disruptions affect the nascent self's ability to develop cohesion, vitality, and harmony.
2. Structural deficits: individuals with preemergent self disorders may experience severe anxiety, depression, rage, and shame. Their distorted self-image often includes feelings of being "unacceptably bad" or undesirable. These structural deficits become ingrained within the very fabric of their self-experience.
3. Therapeutic challenges: patients with preemergent self disorders often struggle with therapeutic processes due to their perception that affirmations by therapists confirm their distorted self-image. This can lead to negative therapeutic reactions and requires significant patience and empathy from clinicians.

When writing a case study inspired by Heinz Kohut's concept of self disorder in the preemergent phase, the clinician should focus on the patient's early developmental experiences and their impact on the formation of the self-structure. The preemergent phase is characterized by disturbances in the development of a cohesive self, often due to failures in empathic interactions with selfobjects during infancy. These disruptions can lead to severe psychopathologies, such as borderline states or psychosis, which are rooted in structural deficits of the self.

In describing the case, start with a comprehensive account of the patient's presenting issues, emphasizing symptoms such as pervasive feelings of shame, rage, and anxiety. Highlight any distorted self-image or feelings of being fundamentally "bad" or undesirable. The narrative should examine the patient's early relational dynamics with caregivers, pinpointing moments where empathic failures or traumatic experiences may have disrupted the development of a cohesive nuclear self.

Clinical example

James, a 42-year-old architect and father, presented with a profound sense of emptiness and disconnection that revealed deep-seated self disorders rooted in his earliest developmental experiences. From the moment he entered the analyst's office, a ritualistic behavior spoke volumes about his internal psychological state.

At the beginning of each session, James would methodically untie and retie his shoelaces. This seemingly mundane act was, in fact, a powerful metaphor for his psychological condition. With meticulous precision, he loosened the laces completely, allowing them to hang freely, then carefully reconstructed the knots—a physical enactment of his constant fear of disintegration and desperate attempts to maintain cohesion.

The shoe-tying ritual became a window into James's psychological landscape. Each untying represented a momentary dissolution of self, a literal and symbolic unraveling. The careful reknitting of the laces mirrored his ongoing struggle to construct and maintain a sense of internal stability. This repetitive performance, executed with almost mechanical precision at the start of every session, revealed the fragility of his sense of self and his deep-seated anxiety about potential psychological disintegration.

James's early relational history provided crucial context for understanding these self disorders. His mother, a high-ranking military officer, had been physically absent during his first six months of life, leaving him with a rotating cast of caregivers. Upon her return, she struggled with undiagnosed post-traumatic stress disorder, characterized by emotional unavailability and unpredictable emotional outbursts. His father, a civil engineer frequently absent due to work, was unable to provide the crucial selfobject experiences necessary for healthy self-development.

In the analytic space, James initially related to the analyst as a disembodied presence. His shoe-tying ritual served as a mechanism of control that allowed him to manage the anxiety of potential self-fragmentation. During sessions, he spoke in a monotone voice, rarely making eye contact, presenting a narrative that felt detached and impersonal—as if describing the life of a stranger.

As the analysis progressed, the significance of the shoe-tying ritual became increasingly apparent. Each meticulous knot represented James's attempt to bind together the disparate fragments of his psychological experience. The ritual was both a defense mechanism and a communication—a nonverbal expression of his internal struggle to maintain psychological coherence.

Dreams further illuminated James's fragmented self. Recurring nightmares featured buildings collapsing and bodies dissolving into mist, visceral representations of his fear of psychological disintegration. These images resonated deeply with his shoe-tying ritual—a constant negotiation between falling apart and pulling himself together.

The analyst's consistent, empathically attuned presence gradually enabled James to develop psychological structure through transmuting internalization. Slowly, the rigidity of his rituals began to soften. Moments of genuine emotional recognition emerged—fleeting, but increasingly substantial. James began to report feeling "more solid" after sessions, experiencing emotions with growing authenticity.

This case study exemplifies Kohut's understanding of self disorders, particularly in the preemergent phase. James's psychological journey illustrated the profound impact of early relational failures and the painstaking process of reconstructing a cohesive self when fundamental developmental experiences were disrupted.

Consolidations disorder (disturbances in selfobject experience)

The developmental trajectory of the self can be significantly impacted by traumatic experiences that occur after an initial, albeit temporary, establishment of self-cohesion but before its final consolidation into a robust and balanced entity (Wolf, 1994). Such traumas, while not completely derailing the self's development, can substantially impede its progress toward full cohesion and vitality. The resulting self-structure, though not entirely fragmented, remains vulnerable and susceptible to re-experiencing similar injurious events. To safeguard against such recurrences, the individual develops intricate defensive mechanisms. Although these protective structures are necessary for psychic survival, they often lead to heightened sensitivities that permeate the individual's daily life.

When describing a patient with a consolidation disorder, the clinician should highlight the specific traumatic experiences that occurred during this critical developmental period and how they have impacted the patient's sense of self.

The case study should also explore the intricate defensive mechanisms the patient has developed to protect against such recurrences. While these protective structures are essential for the patient's psychic survival, the clinician should clarify how they often lead to heightened sensitivities that affect the individual's daily life. These sensitivities can manifest as complex transference phenomena within the analytic setting and make the patient particularly vulnerable to common interpersonal slights and minor narcissistic injuries outside of therapy.

Clinical example

As Margaret's analyst, I found myself entangled in a complex transferential web that would ultimately reveal the deep fissures in her self-cohesion. In our fourth year of analysis, Margaret, a marketing executive known for orchestrating flawless product launches, arrived at our session in an unusual state of disarray. Her normally immaculate appearance was disheveled, and her characteristic composure was notably absent. She announced that her assistant of eight years, Lisa, had resigned unexpectedly.

I acknowledged her loss with what I thought was appropriate empathy, but my response proved catastrophically insufficient. Margaret sat in silence, methodically shredding a tissue in her lap. When I finally spoke, suggesting we explore her feelings about Lisa's departure, Margaret's response cut through the room: "You sound exactly like my father at my mother's funeral—perfectly appropriate, perfectly hollow."

This stark comparison startled me. In four years of analysis, Margaret had rarely spoken of her mother's death, which occurred when she was thirteen. Now, the story began to unfold with raw intensity. Her mother, a concert pianist, had suffered from bipolar disorder, alternating between periods of brilliant creativity and devastating withdrawal. Young Margaret had learned to navigate these swings, becoming expert at anticipating her mother's needs and adjusting her own emotional temperature to match her mother's state.

In the following sessions, Margaret's rage toward me intensified. "You're just like them—my father, the doctors, everyone who kept saying 'these things happen' when she died." Her voice trembled with fury. "Do you know what my father did two weeks after her funeral? He hired a 'household manager'—that's what he called her. Catherine. She reorganized everything, including my mother's sheet music. He said we needed to 'move forward.'"

The parallel between Lisa's resignation and these earlier losses now emerged with striking clarity. Margaret had transformed Lisa from an assistant into something far more significant—a stable, attentive presence who, like young Margaret with her mother, had learned to anticipate her needs perfectly. Lisa's departure had ripped open an old wound, but more importantly, it exposed my failure to recognize the depth of this loss—a failure that echoed her father's emotional absence.

In a particularly charged session, Margaret arrived wearing a pendant I had never seen before. When I commented on it, she touched it reflexively: "It was my mother's. She wore it to every performance." Her voice softened. "Lisa always noticed when I wore it. She knew what it meant." Then, with sudden bitterness: "But you—you've never noticed it before, have you? Four years, and you're just seeing it now."

This moment crystallized a crucial dynamic: my perceived failure to "notice" had activated Margaret's deepest fears about emotional attunement. In her world, not being noticed was equivalent to not existing. Her mother's bipolar disorder had created a pattern where Margaret's existence was alternately central and peripheral to her mother's awareness. Her father's emotional distance and quick replacement of her mother's presence had reinforced the message that feelings, like people, were replaceable.

The transferential storm intensified when I announced a two-week break for a vacation. Margaret's response was scathing: "Perfect timing, as always." She recalled how her father's business trips seemed to coincide with her mother's hospitalizations. In the sessions leading up to the break, Margaret began arriving late—first five minutes, then fifteen, and eventually thirty. When I interpreted this as her attempt to take control of our separations, she replied with chilling precision: "No, I'm teaching you what it feels like to wait for someone and not know if they're coming back."

This work with Margaret illustrates how early relational traumas can create complex templates for future relationships. Her hypersensitivity to abandonment wasn't merely a fear of loss; it was an intricate defensive structure built from repeated experiences of unstable attachment. The therapeutic process became a nuanced interplay of acknowledging these past wounds while carefully working through the transferential enactments they generated.

Through this crisis, Margaret began to articulate, for the first time, the full complexity of her relationship with her mother—both the exquisite attunement during good periods and the devastating absences. The transferential rupture surrounding Lisa's departure, painful as it was, opened a path to exploring these deeper patterns of loss and replacement in Margaret's life.

Margaret's case provides a compelling illustration of consolidation disorder, where trauma occurs after an initial establishment of self-cohesion but before its final consolidation. Her early development was shaped by her mother's bipolar disorder, creating a precarious foundation for self-cohesion. Margaret developed an initial self-structure organized around her extraordinary capacity to attune to her mother's fluctuating emotional states. However, the traumatic loss of her mother during early adolescence, followed by her father's emotional absence and his swift replacement of her mother's presence with a "household manager," disrupted this developmental trajectory at a critical juncture—before her self-structure could achieve robust consolidation.

The resulting pattern we see in Margaret's adult life—her exquisite sensitivity to perceived abandonment, her intense need for consistent attunement (as demonstrated in her relationship with Lisa), and her heightened reactions to any disruption in selfobject relationships—reflects this particular developmental timing. In the transference relationship, these protective structures became vividly apparent, particularly in her response to my conference absence and her sophisticated use of lateness to communicate her emotional experience.

Life curve disorders (disturbances of self experience)

Kohut's concept of life curve disorders focuses on disturbances (Wolf, 1994) that arise when individuals struggle to fulfill their core ambitions and ideals, established during the consolidation of the cohesive self. These disorders are distinct from earlier developmental issues, as they relate to the self's trajectory over time rather than to structural deficits.

Unlike classical psychoanalytic theory, which emphasizes childhood conflicts, self psychology recognizes that significant disturbances can emerge in later life stages, particularly in late middle age. This period serves as a critical juncture where individuals evaluate whether they have remained true to their innermost design. These disturbances manifest as a profound sense of hopelessness or depression, not rooted in guilt or self-aggression, but in the realization that one has failed to actualize their potential. The individual feels unable to rectify this perceived failure within their remaining lifespan. This perspective highlights self psychology's unique emphasis on the temporal aspect of self-development and fulfillment. It acknowledges that the self has a potential life curve from its establishment, and disruptions along this curve can lead to significant psychological distress, even if structural elements of the self remain intact.

For clinicians documenting a life curve disorder, it is crucial to approach the case narrative with a nuanced developmental perspective. The clinical description should meticulously trace the patient's life trajectory, paying special attention to pivotal moments where potential was either realized or foreclosed. Emphasize the patient's subjective experience of their life path, highlighting the gap between their idealized self-conception and their perceived actual achievements. Document not just external milestones, but also the internal narrative of hope, disappointment, and existential meaning-making.

Clinical example

At 52, Emily was a highly respected corporate lawyer, yet she approached analysis feeling profoundly unfulfilled and increasingly anxious about the direction of her life. Despite a successful career, she described feeling "hollow" and "inauthentic" in her interactions with others. As we delved deeper into Emily's history, a pattern began to emerge. From a young age, Emily had shown a remarkable affinity for the arts, particularly painting and music. Her childhood room had been filled with canvases and musical instruments, and she'd spent countless hours lost in creative pursuits. However, her parents, both successful professionals, had strongly discouraged these interests, viewing them as impractical hobbies rather than viable career paths. Under intense parental pressure, Emily pursued law, excelling academically and professionally. Yet, as she recounted her life story, I noticed a marked shift in her demeanor when discussing her abandoned artistic passions. Her voice would soften, her posture would relax, and a wistful smile would play at the corners of her mouth. It became clear that Emily's current distress was rooted in a profound deviation from her authentic life curve. The cohesive self that had formed in her youth had been built around her artistic ambitions and ideals. By choosing a path that aligned with her parents' expectations rather than her own inner design, Emily had unknowingly set herself on a trajectory that diverged sharply from her true potential for self-fulfillment.

This realization brought both clarity and pain. Emily began to experience intense periods of grief for the life she felt she had missed. She started to view her professional accomplishments, once a source of pride, as hollow victories that had come at the cost of her true calling. As our work progressed, Emily cautiously began to reintegrate artistic pursuits into her life. She joined a local choir and set up a small painting studio in her apartment. These activities, while initially anxiety-provoking, seemed to awaken something long dormant within her.

For the first time in our sessions, I witnessed moments of genuine joy and vitality. Emily's case powerfully illustrated Kohut's concept of life curve disorders. Her distress wasn't rooted in unresolved childhood conflicts or structural deficits in her self, but in the gradual realization that she had deviated from the trajectory laid out by her core ambitions and ideals. Our analytic work, therefore, focused not merely on uncovering repressed material or addressing early selfobject failures, but on helping Emily reconnect with her authentic self and explore ways to align her current life more closely with her innermost design.

Selfobject transference

Selfobject transference in psychoanalysis involves reactivating developmental selfobject needs within the analytic relationship, as the patient's archaic needs for mirroring, idealizing, and twinship are mobilized concerning the analyst. This projection is a complex blend of multiple elements: reactivated early childhood selfobject needs, current developmental needs appropriate to the patient's age and life stage, and specific needs that arise in response to the analyst and the therapeutic context. These transferences can manifest in various ways, including explicit or implicit expectations placed on the analyst or through defensive mechanisms aimed at suppressing these expectations. The concept underscores the multifaceted nature of the patient's emotional needs within the analytic relationship, reflecting both historical and present-day aspects of their psychological development and interpersonal dynamics. When documenting selfobject transference, clinicians should describe how the patient's early relational needs emerge and interact within the therapeutic relationship.

Clinical example

Maya has been in treatment for eighteen months. She is a 45-year-old environmental scientist who presents as an enigmatic figure of contradictions. She arrives at sessions wearing meticulously coordinated earth-toned outfits that she sews herself, yet her fingernails are perpetually stained with soil from her gardening experiments. Maya donates her hair to cancer patients every two years, leaving herself with an austere, straw-colored crop that she maintains using kitchen scissors. She carries a canvas bag filled with homemade granola bars that she offers to other patients in the waiting room, seemingly oblivious to their polite but bewildered responses.

What initially struck me about Maya was her profound self-sufficiency coupled with an almost desperate need for validation. She would arrive early to sessions, having walked the twelve miles from her home because she "doesn't trust machines," yet she would anxiously scan my face throughout our conversations for signs of approval or disapproval. Her voice carries a peculiar flatness that makes her seem distant, but her body language—arms crossed protectively over her chest—suggests someone defending against anticipated rejection.

Maya's selfobject needs manifested primarily through an intense idealizing transference. She would frequently comment on my "wisdom" and "insight," often attributing profound meaning to my most mundane observations. When I mentioned during one session that the autumn light was particularly beautiful that day, she spent the following week researching the psychological effects of seasonal lighting changes and returned with a detailed analysis of how my comment had "revolutionized" her understanding of mood regulation.

Her mirroring needs emerged more subtly. Maya would recount elaborate stories of her environmental activism—organizing community gardens, teaching children about sustainable living, and creating her own non-dairy ice cream from foraged ingredients—while maintaining her characteristic expressionless delivery. Yet I noticed how she would pause after each accomplishment, watching my face with an intensity that betrayed her need for acknowledgment. When I reflected her dedication to environmental causes, her entire posture would soften momentarily before returning to its defensive stance.

The twinship component of her selfobject transference was perhaps most poignant. Maya began bringing me articles about environmental research, always prefaced with comments like "I thought you might find this interesting" or "This reminded me of something you said." She started timing her arrivals to coincide with my lunch break, hoping to catch glimpses of what I ate, whether I recycled my containers, and how I moved through the world. She once mentioned, with uncharacteristic emotion, that she had purchased the same brand of pen I used during sessions because "it felt right in her hand."

Maya's defensive mechanisms around these needs were equally complex. She would often preemptively dismiss compliments with scientific explanations for her behaviors, as if to deflect the very mirroring she craved. "Dopamine response," she would mutter when I acknowledged her achievements. "Evolutionary adaptation," she would add when I commented on her generosity toward others.

Her relationship with vulnerability was particularly striking. Maya could discuss climate change data or soil composition with passionate detail, but when asked about her own emotional experiences, she would respond with the same flat affect she used to describe weather patterns. Yet beneath this scientific detachment, her selfobject needs pulsed with an almost childlike intensity—the same quality that led her to hand out granola bars to trick-or-treaters, genuinely believing they would be delighted by her homemade offerings.

The therapeutic work involved carefully attending to these layered selfobject needs while respecting her defensive structure. Maya's environmental activism, self-sufficiency, and social awkwardness all served as both expressions of and defenses against her fundamental need for connection and recognition. Her capacity to nurture others—through donated hair, home-made food, and environmental stewardship—reflected a profound empathy that she struggled to extend toward herself.

Maya's case illustrates how selfobject transferences can manifest through seemingly contra-dictory presentations. Her fierce independence masked deep longings for mirroring and ideali-zation, while her generosity toward others defended against acknowledging her own needs for care and recognition. The therapeutic challenge lay in creating space for these archaic needs to emerge safely within the analytic relationship, allowing Maya to experience the very connec-tion she simultaneously craved and feared.

Fragmented self

The term "fragmented self" (Kohut, 1971, p. 108) refers, in Kohut's self psychology, to a state in which a person's self is not cohesive or stable but is instead broken, discontinuous, and lacking inner unity. This state manifests as a person experiencing themselves as composed of parts that are not well connected, leading to feelings of disconnectedness, low self-worth, weakness, gloom, and sometimes a sense of emptiness and lack of meaning.

In a state of fragmented self, a person may experience extreme fluctuations between feelings of unrealistically high self-worth (grandiosity) and feelings of utter worthlessness, without the ability to experience both extremes simultaneously.

According to Kohut, the therapeutic goal is to help integrate the self, strengthen its cohesiveness, and enable the person to experience themselves as whole, stable, and mean-ingful. To effectively convey fragmentation states in clinical writing, begin with observable manifestations rather than theoretical assertions. Instead of stating "the patient experienced self-fragmentation," describe the specific changes you observed—perhaps how their usually meticulous appearance became disheveled, their speech patterns grew disorganized, or their typical self-assurance gave way to profound uncertainty.

These concrete details allow readers to witness the fragmentation process more vividly. When writing about bodily manifestations of fragmentation, capture both the physical symp-toms and the patient's struggle to understand them. Rather than simply listing hypochon-driacal concerns, illustrate how these bodily preoccupations connect to the patient's broader experience of disintegration. Demonstrate how these symptoms emerge in response to specific narcissistic injuries and resolve when empathic attunement is restored.

Clinical example

In our session following a week-long break, I immediately noticed a stark change in Rachel's demeanor. Usually meticulously groomed, she arrived wearing mismatched clothes, with unkempt hair and a visible tremor in her hands. As she sat down, her gaze darted nervously around the room, unable to meet my eyes.

"I don't know what's happening to me," Rachel began, her voice quavering. "Since our last session, since seeing you on the street and you not acknowledging me . . . I've felt like I'm falling apart. My thoughts are scattered, I can't concentrate at work, and I keep checking my body for signs of illness. Yesterday, I was convinced my left arm was detaching from my body."

Rachel continued, her speech becoming more fragmented: "I feel like . . . like I'm not real. Or maybe too real? Every sensation is overwhelming. I can't . . . I don't know how to be myself anymore."

I knew with certainty that I hadn't been on that street; I was in my office at the time she described. The easiest response would have been to correct this misperception, to offer her the comfort of objective reality. But I understood that her experience of being overlooked, whether factually accurate or not, carried a profound emotional truth that needed to be heard and understood.

"You felt invisible," I said softly, "as if even I, who should see you most clearly, had looked right through you."

Rachel's eyes filled with tears. "Yes," she whispered. "It was like . . . like when my mother would look at me but not really see me. She'd be physically present but somewhere else entirely. We've talked about this experience a million times, so why did you do it? You knew exactly what would happen."

By staying with her subjective experience rather than rushing to correct it, a deeper truth emerged. The street encounter, real or imagined, had activated a primal wound—the experience of being unseen, unacknowledged by vital selfobjects.

Sexualization as defense

Kohut viewed sexual behaviors as complex defensive mechanisms stemming from developmental disruptions. In his seminal work, he articulated a nuanced perspective on sexualization as a defense against self-fragmentation:

> When the child's self-assertive presence is not responded to by the mirroring selfobject, his healthy exhibitionism . . . will be given up, and isolated sexualized exhibitionistic preoccupations concerning single symbols of greatness (the urinary stream, feces, phallus) will take over. . . . That the perversion, i.e., the sexualized replica of the original healthy configuration, still contains fragments of the grandiose self . . . and of the idealized object . . . is to be understood as a vestige of one aspect of the original selfobject constellation.
>
> *Kohut, 1977, pp. 171–173.*

For clinicians writing about sexualization as a defense, illuminate how the sexual behavior represents a creative, albeit maladaptive, attempt to restore self-cohesion in the face of early relational traumas.

Clinical example

At 26, Jason sought therapy for compulsive sexual behaviors, particularly his obsession with large-breasted women and frequent visits to prostitutes. His sexual history was intimately connected to a profound early loss—his mother's death from an accident when he was seven years old.

In Jason's memory, she was a tender, soft and empathic presence—an almost mythical narrative of maternal connection that spoke more to his deepest emotional yearnings than to the uncertain realities of their actual relationship.

The most vivid memory from his early childhood was of shared baths, where he was fascinated by his mother's breasts and her physical warmth. As our therapeutic work unfolded, it became clear that Jason's sexual compulsions were intricate attempts to recreate and maintain a sense of self-cohesion in the face of fragmentation anxiety.

His fixation on large breasts emerged as a sexualized version of his yearning for the soothing presence of his lost mother. This compulsion manifested in particularly troubling ways during his daily commute. On the subway, Jason would find himself staring fixedly at women with large breasts, his gaze locked onto their chests in what he described as an almost trance-like state. He was painfully aware that his behavior made these women uncomfortable—many would shift uneasily in their seats or eventually move to different cars. The awareness that he was violating these women's privacy and personal space caused him significant distress, yet he felt powerless to control these urges. Later, these encounters would fuel his masturbation fantasies, providing temporary relief from his fragmentation anxiety.

The prostitutes provided a simulacrum of intimacy, allowing him to feel whole and connected momentarily. The breast became a "symbol of greatness," a fragment of his idealized lost mother, representing his attempts to restore the self-assertive presence disrupted by maternal loss. His compulsive staring on the subway and subsequent masturbation rituals served as desperate attempts to capture and internalize this soothing maternal presence.

Our therapeutic work focused on providing the empathic attunement and mirroring that Jason had missed in his early years. Through this process, we could gradually address not only his sexual compulsions but also the shame and self-loathing that accompanied his intrusive behaviors toward women in public spaces. As he began to see me as a reliable selfobject, his need for these sexualized forms of self-soothing gradually decreased.

Over time, Jason developed a more cohesive sense of self, becoming less reliant on sexualized defenses. He began forming more meaningful relationships and discovered healthier self-soothing mechanisms. While his attraction to large-breasted women persisted, it no longer dominated his life or relationships.

This case illuminates how seemingly perverse sexual behaviors can be understood as creative, albeit problematic, attempts at self-restoration in the face of early selfobject failures. By providing an empathic, supportive environment, we can help patients develop more robust self-structures and healthier ways to maintain self-cohesion.

THE TERMINATION PHASE IN KOHUT'S THEORY

When writing about the termination phase from a self psychological perspective, our focus should be on documenting the gradual transformation of selfobject needs and the development of self-cohesion. The key is to capture how archaic selfobject needs have evolved into more mature forms through transmuting internalization, while recognizing that some degree of selfobject responsiveness will always remain necessary.

Pay particular attention to describing how the patient has developed an increased capacity to maintain self-cohesion in the face of selfobject disappointments. Document specific instances where the patient demonstrates an enhanced ability to regulate self-states without falling into fragmentation. However, acknowledge that complete independence from selfobject needs is neither possible nor desirable; the goal is more flexible and mature ways of meeting these needs.

In documenting the therapeutic journey, highlight how repeated cycles of optimal frustration and empathic attunement have gradually strengthened the patient's self-structure. Describe concrete examples of how the patient has internalized the analyst's selfobject functions, developing more reliable internal sources of mirroring, idealization, and twinship. At the same time, note their growing capacity to seek out appropriate selfobject experiences in their relationships.

Focus on observable shifts in self-cohesion:

- More flexible utilization of selfobject experiences
- Increased capacity to restore self-cohesion after disruptions
- Greater tolerance for optimal frustration without self-depletion
- Development of more mature forms of idealization and mirroring needs.

Frame these developments within Kohut's concept of transmuting internalization: how the patient has gradually built internal structures through optimal responsiveness to selfobject needs. However, emphasize that this is an ongoing process. Some archaic selfobject needs may persist, requiring continued attention and empathic responsiveness.

Clinical example

Deborah, an 88-year-old museum curator, came to therapy after being asked for the first time to edit a chapter in a memorial book for her parents' Polish community. This project, which should have been an honor, triggered a deep psychological crisis. "My whole life I built a career on other people's Holocaust memories," she said in our first session, "but my own Holocaust always stayed locked away."

Deborah survived the war as an 8-year-old child hiding in the basement of a rural Polish family. Her parents perished in Auschwitz. She came to Israel as an orphan and grew up on a kibbutz, focusing on being "the perfect child"—her way of justifying her survival.

At 88, Deborah lived alone in a well-organized Tel Aviv apartment. Her relationship with her only son, a successful doctor, was polite but cold. "He always says I'm a strong mother," she shared, "but I'm not sure he actually sees me." Her daughter-in-law Ruth triggered particular tension in her. "She manages my life like I'm some charity project," Deborah complained bitterly, "and I don't know how to tell her that's not what I need."

My first empathic failure occurred when Deborah brought an old photograph of her parents. Instead of recognizing her need for idealization, I interpreted this as an attempt to "process grief." She withdrew immediately. "You don't understand," she said sharply, "this photo is what has sustained me for 70 years. I didn't come here to bury it."

The turning point came when Deborah received an invitation to speak at a Holocaust Remembrance Day ceremony. Instead of pride, she experienced profound fragmentation. "I stand there telling the story like a robot," she explained, "but inside I'm still an 8-year-old girl waiting for someone to tell her everything will be okay."

The selfobject transference developed in stages. Deborah sought mirroring and validation from me but also asked if I too sometimes felt like "a stranger in the world" as she did. When she sensed I didn't understand her precisely, she responded with rage that I came to understand was a protection of a vulnerable self, not mere aggression.

Toward the end of treatment, Deborah formed new connections with a group of survivors and found ways to integrate her personal story into her work. In our final session, she took out a small memorial pin. "Sometimes I still feel like I'm betraying my parents when I allow myself to feel good," she said, "but I've learned that memory doesn't have to mean suffering."

She asked to photograph the therapy room "in case I need to remember this feeling of safety." This request reflected a deep understanding that selfobject needs don't disappear; they mature and transform.

The therapy with Deborah showed me how, even at an advanced age, it's possible to develop new self-cohesion when selfobject needs receive empathic responses. Deborah not only developed better emotional stability but also a personal narrative that could contain both trauma and resilience.

The termination phase in Deborah's therapy vividly demonstrated the transition from fixation on archaic selfobject needs to greater flexibility—not an elimination of these needs, but their transformation into more mature and adaptive forms, while recognizing that the finality of therapy does not constitute an end to selfobject needs but rather the beginning of a new way of dealing with them.

SUGGESTIONS FOR WRITING A PSYCHODYNAMIC CASE STUDY BASED ON KOHUT'S SELF PSYCHOLOGY

Mapping selfobject needs

Present an in-depth analysis of the central selfobject needs identified in the patient. Examine how these needs manifest in attachment patterns, interpersonal relationships, and coping strategies. Measure the intensity of mirroring needs by assessing whether the patient frequently seeks validation and affirmation from others. Clinical example of termination does he experience profound narcissistic injury when this affirmation is absent? Investigate patterns of idealization—how does the patient relate to authority figures or individuals he admires? Is there a tendency toward absolute admiration that alternates with deep disappointment? Note expressions of twinship needs, the desire to feel similar to others, to belong, and to validate shared human experiences.

Document the developmental history of these needs, outlining when and how they developed and how early empathic failures influenced their formation. The analysis should be sensitive and precise, avoiding gross generalizations while preserving the unique complexity of the specific patient.

Transmuting internalization: From dependence to autonomy

Detail the therapeutic journey in which the patient undergoes the process of transmuting internalization—the central process identified by Kohut in healthy self-development. Describe identifiable stages in this process, from complete reliance on the therapist as a selfobject, through gradual internalization phases, to the construction of more stable internal structures. Demonstrate through specific therapeutic episodes how the patient gradually internalized functions initially provided by the therapist—for instance, the ability to self-soothe in stressful situations, regulate negative self-image, or create and maintain values and aspirations without requiring constant external approval.

It is essential to illustrate the complexity and dialectic of this process—this is not a simple linear progression, but a journey that includes regressions, sudden advancements, and periods of gradual integration.

Narcissistic expressions in therapy

Present an in-depth analysis of the narcissistic aspects of the patient's personality, avoiding judgmental labeling and maintaining the Kohutian understanding that narcissism is a vital developmental component, not merely pathology. Analyze the expressions of the grandiose self—are there fantasies of greatness and uniqueness? Does the patient struggle to accept limitations and flaws in himself? Examine the tendency for excessive idealization of others, as well as oscillations between absolute admiration and dismissal or contempt.

Describe the developmental history of these narcissistic patterns, how they were formed as defense mechanisms against experiences of vulnerability and worthlessness. Demonstrate how these patterns affect the patient's interpersonal relationships—does he find it challenging to see others as separate individuals with their own needs? Is there volatility in relationships that shifts between idealization and devaluation? Additionally, outline how narcissistic patterns have changed throughout therapy, demonstrating the development of nuance, emotional flexibility, and a more complex self-acceptance.

Fragmentation and emptiness: Encountering the fragmented self

Describe in detail the subjective experiences of fragmentation, inner emptiness, and lack of vitality that the patient brings to therapy. Provide an in-depth explanation connecting these experiences to persistent failures in meeting selfobject needs during early development. Has the patient described periods of profound meaninglessness? Were there moments when he felt a loss of inner continuity and cohesion? Outline the contexts and triggers for these fragmentation experiences—do they arise in response to interpersonal disappointments, criticism, or empathic failures?

Demonstrate how these experiences reflect the basic vulnerability of the self and relate to specific developmental deficits. For example, a patient who encountered failures in meeting idealization needs during childhood may experience fragmentation and a sense of directionlessness when someone he admires disappoints him. Document the changes in the frequency and intensity of fragmentation experiences throughout therapy, as well as the gradual development of the patient's ability to restore self-cohesion even after destabilizing events.

Empathic attunement: A bridge between two worlds

Describe in detail how your empathic attunement as a therapist contributed to the development of the patient's self. Document specific therapeutic episodes in which your empathic responsiveness offered a corrective experience, enabling the patient to achieve a deep understanding and acceptance of the injured and disconnected parts of himself. Were there moments when you recognized and addressed unspoken mirroring needs? How did the patient's experience shift following your response?

Additionally, present the challenges and obstacles faced in maintaining consistent empathic attunement—analyze empathic failures that occurred during therapy and the repair processes that facilitated the renewal of the therapeutic alliance. Outline the complex interplay between your empathic attunement and the development of the patient's capacity to regulate self-esteem and affect. Illustrate how, over time and in response to a consistently empathic therapeutic environment, the patient cultivated a more compassionate approach towards himself and learned to understand and accept his weaknesses and difficulties without experiencing profound narcissistic injury.

Optimal frustration

Present a clinical analysis of events in therapy where you applied the principle of optimal frustration—frustration that is gentle enough not to cause re-traumatization yet significant enough to enable growth and internalization. Describe cases where you needed to set boundaries, impose limitations, or disappoint the patient in ways that facilitated development. For instance, perhaps you refused a request to change the therapeutic framework, perhaps you withheld automatic approval and admiration, or perhaps you insisted that the patient face a certain challenge using his own resources.

Show the immediate responses to these frustrations—were there expressions of narcissistic rage, withdrawal, or disappointment? Subsequently, document the long-term processes that occurred following these experiences—how the patient gradually internalized the ability to cope with disappointments and frustrations, and how stronger self-structures were built over time. Use tangible examples to illustrate the connection between optimal frustration and the growth in self-cohesion as well as the ability to regulate negative affect.

The therapeutic relationship as a corrective selfobject

Present a comprehensive analysis of how the therapeutic relationship offered the patient opportunities for vital selfobject experiences that were missing in his early development. Analyze the types of transference that developed in therapy—did the patient establish a mirroring transference, where he expected you to affirm and reflect his uniqueness and worth? Did he develop an idealizing transference, where he perceived you as a strong and perfect figure he could rely on? Or perhaps he formed a twinship transference, where he sought a sense of partnership and basic similarity?

Describe how you engaged with these types of transference—not as resistance to be interpreted and overcome, but as legitimate expressions of developmental selfobject needs. Demonstrate how you provided the patient with corrective experiences that supplied what was missing—how you offered accurate mirroring where he had encountered distortion or absence, how you fostered idealization and a sense of security where he had experienced abandonment and instability, and how you created space for twinship and belonging where he had faced alienation and estrangement.

Signs of progress: A view of the changing self

Present signs of changes in the patient's self-cohesion throughout therapy. Use concrete and specific indicators—does the patient report fewer episodes of fragmentation and emptiness? Is he able to calm and soothe himself in stressful situations without resorting to narcissistic compensation strategies? Is he capable of bearing frustrations and interpersonal disappointments without losing a basic sense of self-worth?

Also examine the growing ability to pursue goals and realize aspirations. Is the patient now able to initiate projects and persist in them even when they require sustained effort? Is he able to experience enjoyment and inner satisfaction from his achievements, not just an empty pursuit of external approval? Analyze the development of the ability to maintain ideals and values flexibly—is the patient now able to strive for excellence without demanding absolute perfection? Can he maintain meaningful values even when the environment doesn't reinforce them? Integrate this analysis with an assessment of the patient's growing capacity to create and maintain meaningful interpersonal relationships, based on mutual empathy and not just on fulfilling narcissistic needs. Examine whether the patient has developed the ability to expand her sense of self beyond personal boundaries to include a commitment to others or broader humanitarian causes. Is she able to find meaning in contributing to others and society, not out of obligation or a need for approval, but from a sense of inner abundance and a genuine desire to share with the world?

This capacity reflects deep psychological maturity and the development of a strong and stable self that can extend beyond its private needs, finding satisfaction in enriching the lives of others and contributing to causes greater than the boundaries of the private self.

RECOMMENDED READING

Five exemplary self psychology case studies

The two analyses of Mr Z, by Heinz Kohut. *International Journal of Psychoanalysis, 60, 3,* 1979.

The famous case study by Heinz Kohut describes two different treatments of the same patient, conducted years apart. In the first analysis, Kohut treated the patient using a classical psychoanalytic approach, focusing on Oedipal conflicts and homosexual fears, but the treatment reached an impasse. In the second analysis, conducted after Kohut developed self psychology theory, he understood the same symptoms as expressions of unmet selfobject needs and early narcissistic vulnerabilities. The case dramatically demonstrates how the same clinical phenomena can be understood and treated in completely different ways, depending on the theoretical framework used by the therapist, and it became one of the foundational cases of self psychology.

Notably, the case provoked significant controversy when it was revealed that Kohut was not describing an actual patient but, in fact, writing an auto-therapeutic narrative about himself.

Treating the self: Elements of clinical self psychology, by Ernest Wolf. Guilford Press, 1988.

Wolf's detailed case presentations illustrate how to write about the patient's subjective experience and the analyst's empathic understanding. His careful attention to tracking shifts in self-states provides an excellent model for documenting cases.

Finding renee, by Lucyann Carlton. *International Journal of Psychoanalytic Self Psychology 1*, 199–218, 2006.

This case study describes a six-year psychoanalytic treatment of a severely traumatized woman who was raised by disturbed parents and experienced rape as an adolescent. She developed a deep therapeutic relationship through the sensitive use of dreams as a transitional space, demonstrating how a self psychology approach can effectively address trauma by creating a safe holding environment while respecting the patient's need for emotional protection and gradual self-disclosure.

Revisiting the negative therapeutic reaction: An example of comparative psychoanalysis, by Paul Ornstein. *International Journal of Psychoanalytic Self Psychology 10*, 118–127, 2015.

Ornstein's article presents a case study of Mr. K, illustrating how apparent "negative therapeutic reactions" can be reinterpreted as disruptions in selfobject transference, offering a comparative analysis between traditional psychoanalytic and self psychological perspectives. This comparison demonstrates how different theoretical frameworks can lead to vastly different interpretations and therapeutic approaches.

The fate of narcissistic rage in psychotherapy, by Anna Ornstein. *Psychoanalytic Inquiry 18*, 55–70, 1998.

This paper provides a detailed account of the therapeutic process, including the therapist's countertransference reactions, interpretive strategies, and the gradual transformation of the patient's narcissistic rage into more manageable emotions while demonstrating the application of self psychological concepts in clinical practice.

REFERENCES

Carlton, L. (2006). Finding Renee. *International Journal of Psychoanalytic Self Psychology 1*, 199–218.

Kohut, H. (1971). *The analysis of the self: A systematic approach to the psychoanalytic treatment of narcissistic personality disorders.* International Universities Press.

Kohut, H. (1977). *The restoration of the self.* International Universities Press.

Kohut, H. (1979). The Two Analyses of Mr Z. *International Journal of Psychoanalysis, 60,* 3–27.

Kohut, H. (1985). On courage. In C. Strozier (Ed.), *Self psychology and the humanities: Reflections on a new psychoanalytic approach* (pp. 5–50). W. W. Norton. (Original work published 1970)

Kulka, R. (2022). Self Psychology's Contribution to the Spiritual Dimension of Psychoanalysis. *Psychoanalytic Inquiry, 42,* 654–667.

Lachmann, F. M., & Beebe, B. (1995). Self psychology: Today. *Psychoanalytic Dialogues, 5*(3), 375–384.

Magid, B., Fosshage, J., & Shane, E. (2021). The emerging paradigm of relational self psychology: An historical perspective. *Psychoanalysis, Self, and Context*, 16(1), 1–23.

Ornstein, A. (1998). The fate of narcissistic rage in psychotherapy. *Psychoanalytic Inquiry*, 18(1), 55–70. https://doi.org/10.1080/07351699809534170

Ornstein, P. H. (2015). Revisiting the Negative Therapeutic Reaction: An Example of Comparative Psychoanalysis. *International Journal of Psychoanalytic Self Psychology*, 10(2), 118–127. https://doi.org/10.1080/15551024.2015.1005797

Sands, S. H. (1989). Chapter 6 Eating Disorders and Female Development: A Self-Psychological Perspective. *Progress in Self-Psychology*, 5, 75–103.

Wolf, E. S. (1988). *Treating the self: Elements of clinical self psychology*. Guilford Press.

Wolf, E. S. (1994). Varieties of disorders of the self. *British Journal of Psychotherapy*, 11(2), 198–208.

CHAPTER 10

A case study in the spirit of the relational approach

....

THE RELATIONAL REVOLUTION: TRANSFORMING PSYCHODYNAMIC CASE STUDIES

At the beginning of this chapter, I want to slightly deviate from the established order of previous chapters to share a few thoughts on the revolution brought about by the relational approach in written cases.

Case study writers owe as much to the relational approach as sailors do to the North Star: it guides and orients everything that follows. There is a clear distinction between the era before the relational approach and the one after it. The relational approach, championed by authors such as Stephen Mitchell, Phillip Bromberg, Adrienne Harris, Joyce Slochower, Jessica Benjamin, Muriel Dimen, Emanuel Ghent, Jill Salberg, Sue Grand, Lew Aron, Irwin Hoffman, Karen Maroda, Galit Atlas, Robert Grossmark, Jody Messler Davies, and many others, has fundamentally shaped our contemporary understanding of psychodynamic case studies. Their influence is so pervasive that it has become almost invisible in its ubiquity.

The relational approach was the first to fully embrace the twenty-first century, integrating into it as naturally as a fish in water. It provides a detailed analysis of the relationship between the individual and their socio-cultural environment, particularly as influenced by racial and gender issues. Future historians studying this era could gain insights from the case studies of relational writers just as effectively as from sociologists and historians, as their clinical work naturally captured the zeitgeist of the times.

It introduced several key elements that now define modern case studies: avoiding dry psychoanalytic jargon in favor of a vivid, conversational, opinionated, and sometimes enjoyable tone; emphasizing surprises and unexpected moments; seeking the therapist's inner truth; incorporating metaphors from cinema and literature; refining writing style to avoid pomposity; and portraying the therapist as humble, uncertain, and even hesitant in their knowledge.

DOI: 10.4324/9781003538578-13

The writing style has also evolved: relational therapists believe that the gap between the language of case studies and everyday speech should remain small. A striking freshness and informality are hallmarks of the relational style. Thus, contemporary psychodynamic case studies contain minimal heavy professional jargon, favoring simpler, narrative-driven, everyday language without sacrificing the emotional complexity of the cases. This shift reflects a broader movement toward accessibility and authenticity in clinical writing.

This approach has transformed case studies into dynamic, engaging narratives that inform and resonate on a deeper, more human level. It has bridged the gap between clinical observation and artistic expression, creating a new standard for understanding and communicating the intricacies of the therapeutic process.

Because the therapist's presence is felt through their writing, we sense the person behind the clinical observations. When we know something about the clinician writing the case, their clinical narrative becomes more credible and engaging.

The approach distances itself from anything that resembles therapeutic "technique" or theory-bound treatment (Grossman, 2014).

This theoretical shift has led to changes in clinical writing styles. Analysts began including their own experiences, reactions, and reflections in written cases. They have become more willing to discuss their personal responses, challenges faced in treatment, and the ways their own background and unresolved issues might influence the therapeutic process. While this hasn't meant complete self-disclosure, it has represented a meaningful move toward more balanced accounts that acknowledge both participants' contributions to the therapeutic relationship.

This evolution in clinical writing has helped create richer, more complete accounts of the therapeutic process while maintaining appropriate professional boundaries in how personal material is shared and discussed.

Relational therapists speak about themselves with openness, sometimes even with honesty that might embarrass some of their readers. But the important thing for them is to be true to themselves, distancing themselves from the image that has so tainted psychoanalysis of an all-knowing therapist who views their patients through the lens of someone else's theory.

The remarkable aspect is that the relational revolution has been so profound it has influenced case study writing across all schools of psychotherapy. Even the most traditional orientations could no longer revert to the dry, medical-reportorial style of the past.

In essence, the relational approach has transformed psychodynamic case studies into a form of creative nonfiction. They now possess the emotional resonance of memoir, the narrative drive of fiction, and the intellectual rigor of academic writing. The shock of this new wave has worn off, and many were reluctant to adopt it.

While this evocative writing style has its merits, it doesn't mean every clinician should embrace the relational approach of placing themselves at the center of the case study. Professional approaches to clinical writing are deeply personal and vary widely across theoretical orientations and individual comfort levels.

Not every clinician feels comfortable exposing their inner world, nor should they feel pressured to do so. Some therapists believe that professional boundaries require maintaining a certain distance, both in the therapeutic relationship and in their written work. Many feel that a more reserved, observational approach may best serve the commitment to the case.

The relational approach is not without its pitfalls. While many serious relational writers maintain a balanced and disciplined approach to case writing, some have swung too far in the opposite direction. Relational case studies are stories about excess: about excessive clinical documentation that blurs the line between professional insight and personal narrative; about therapists who, in their eagerness to demonstrate authentic connection, sometimes center their own emotional responses rather than the client's experience; and about the delicate balance between therapeutic presence and professional boundaries that effective relational work requires.

Some relational case studies can suffer from excessive self-disclosure and dramatic presentation, as if trying to make a powerful impression on readers. In an effort to distance themselves from the traditional "poker face" approach, some writers may overemphasize their own subjectivity at the expense of the patient's unique experience. The path from relationality to narcissism is short: if we make clinical understanding wholly dependent on the analyst's subjectivity, we might lose sight of the patient's separate mind.

Relational therapists are at their most appealing when they are fully engaged: navigating clinical complexities, wrestling with theoretical challenges, and facing the difficulties posed by the therapeutic encounter that they cannot pretend to control. Conversely, they are least appealing when they are at their most "authentic," yielding to unfiltered self-disclosure and excessive exposure of their personal lives. They risk displaying an infinite capacity for self-absorption, turning case studies into personal memoirs and shifting the focus from the patient's experience to their own internal drama. Without some professional distance, meaningful case studies cannot emerge—raw therapeutic experiences and emotional reactions may be present, but no coherent clinical narrative can take shape.

Yet, to their credit, they are acutely aware of these shortcomings (see Aron, Grand & Slochower, 2018). They demonstrate remarkable courage and openness in discussing these limitations, engaging in frank dialogues about the pitfalls of their approach both among themselves and with the broader psychoanalytic community. This self-reflective stance and willingness to critically examine their own tendencies set them apart and deepen their contribution to psychoanalytic thinking.

The challenge lies in finding the middle ground between the sterile, jargon-laden writing of traditional case studies and the sometimes overly dramatic self-disclosure of relational accounts. Your writing should strive to be emotionally authentic without being exhibitionistic, clinically precise without being dry, and personally engaged without overshadowing the patient's experience.

THE GREATEST CHALLENGES

If you're not used to reading relational case studies, you might feel overwhelmed at first. In nearly every case study, therapists recognize in themselves their own racism, blatant narcissism, envy, or even hatred and sexual fantasies towards their patients. Some even confess their sins to their patients and explain in detail the origins of these sins. Initially, you might think you've encountered an eccentric cult of therapists on a mission to purify their souls of various sins they assign to themselves that hinder their ability to be better therapists.

However, you will soon realize that behind this sometimes strange behavior lies a therapeutic method that redefines the therapeutic relationship. This approach arises from the core belief that therapists, like all humans, are subject to the same psychological afflictions that plague humanity as a whole: racism, aggression, narcissism, the desire for gratification, hatred of others, in-group preference, and more. The therapist operates unconsciously under hidden motives and must therefore maintain a constant and honest effort to self-examine. The patient, as an "other," can activate hidden needs or biases within the therapist, who, being susceptible to these influences, is inevitably affected by the patient. Only through rigorous self-examination can therapists truly understand and navigate these parallel processes occurring within the therapeutic relationship. Relational therapists are no longer secondary characters, hidden or downplayed, but primary actors taking center stage, as if focusing on the therapists' emotions and needs is the most natural thing in the world. Consider the following examples:

> Then Alice told me this: every week she had been stealing change from the pockets of my coat as it hung in the waiting room. With my change she bought candy, which she hid in her basement room.
>
> *Sue Grand, 2002, p. XIIII.*

Sam Gerson to his patient:

> There is something that I want to tell you. I had known since September that I would be out last Thursday and Friday, and I told all my patients about it back then except for you. Last Monday, when I realized that I hadn't yet said anything to you about this, I covered up my omission by saying that "Something unexpected had come up." I imagine you may have many reactions to this, but first, I'd like to ask you if you have any thoughts about why I acted this way.
>
> *Sam Gerson, 1996, p. 636.*

> My analyst betrayed her patient-lover first, but she also betrayed her other patients and ex-patients—including me. She undermined my professional ideal twice: by breaching sexual boundaries with her own patient and then by failing to honor the privileged nature of our relationship. I managed to sideline the fact that I had been both a witness and a victim. How difficult it is to metabolize this, even 30 years later.
>
> *Slochower, 2019, p. 198.*

These passages reveal how relational therapists position themselves as central figures in case studies, alongside their patients, with extraordinary boldness and impressive honesty. They are no longer figures who merely try to understand, interpret, help, or be present, but active partners at the center of the therapeutic stage, as if deeply examining their own feelings and needs constitutes a natural and essential part of the therapeutic process.

Perhaps most challengingly, the relational case writer must be willing to describe moments of enactment, impasse, and even failure in treatment. Rather than presenting a sanitized account of clinical mastery, the writer is called upon to explore the messiness of two subjectivities colliding and negotiating shared meaning. This level of transparency regarding the therapist's struggles and missteps can feel quite exposing. Ultimately, the written case aims to capture the co-constructed nature of the clinical encounter, with all its complexity and unpredictability. The writer must find a way to convey both participants' experiences while still crafting a coherent narrative. This requires considerable skill in balancing multiple perspectives and tolerating ambiguity.

When writing relational case studies, authors should be aware of certain common patterns that may limit their clinical presentations. Many relational case studies tend to follow a similar format: focusing primarily on dramatic interactions between therapist and patient, with development centered around singular events (Greenberg, 2001, p. 364). Writers might consider expanding beyond this pattern to include extended periods of slow and careful exploration through interpretations of the patient's motivations and unconscious dynamics. While the therapeutic relationship is crucial, overemphasizing relational dynamics should not come at the expense of exploring intrapsychic areas.

Notice that a fascinating phenomenon has developed in contemporary relational literature: the object relations patients from the works of the Kleinian tradition have seemingly vanished. You surely remember them—the intriguing cases from the writings of Klein and Bion, Joseph, Meltzer, and Rosenfeld, who were characterized by seeing strange objects, experiencing deep regressions, or teetering on the edge of psychosis. In their place, our contemporary literature appears to be populated almost exclusively by patients with style and good taste, possessing impressive expressive abilities and solid educational backgrounds.

One has to wonder: has our patient population genuinely transformed into a parade of highly functional individuals working through subtle relational nuances? Have the deeply disturbed patients simply found other therapeutic addresses? Or—and here's where it gets interesting—are we perhaps witnessing less a change in our patients and more a shift in our theoretical lenses? After all, might not the same patient who would have been described as "splitting" and "projecting bizarre objects" in a Kleinian case study now appear in a relational paper as "negotiating complex attachment patterns" and "working through early relational trauma"?

The mystery of the vanishing object-relations patient might say less about clinical reality and more about how our theoretical orientations influence what we observe—and choose to write about—in the consulting room.

> Let's confront the uncomfortable truth: there is remarkably little relational literature addressing work with schizophrenia, psychotic patients, OCD, eating disorders, or major depression. We rarely see relational case studies from psychiatric hospitals or acute care settings. Additionally, dreams have almost entirely disappeared from relational literature. Only recently have they received more nuanced treatment. What a loss!

This selective presentation creates a significant gap in our clinical literature. Authors should consider diversifying their case presentations to include work with more severely disturbed patients, focusing on primitive mental states and deep regression. The field would benefit from demonstrations of how relational theory can be meaningfully applied across the full spectrum of psychological functioning, including work with patients suffering from manic depression, schizophrenia, psychotic depression, and severe eating disorders.

RELATED CONCEPTS

Multiple self-states, two-person psychology, therapist's subjectivity, intersubjectivity, dissociation and trauma, enactment, context (including power relations, gender, and race), recognition, and submission.

THERAPEUTIC ATMOSPHERE

Relational therapists create a therapeutic environment characterized by an interactive and emotionally attuned approach. In the relational consulting room, dialogue takes precedence over monologue, with both parties actively engaging in the therapeutic discourse. The emphasis has shifted from interpretation to a more nuanced understanding of the emotional undercurrents within the therapeutic dyad (Mills, 2012, p. 98).

THERAPY GOAL

It's important to note that relational psychotherapy is not a unified school of thought but rather an approach that therapists develop from various theoretical orientations. Some relational therapists come from an object relations background, others from an interpersonal perspective, and still others from self psychology. Consequently, therapeutic goals can vary significantly among relational therapists, reflecting their primary theoretical orientations and clinical experiences.

While keeping this diversity in mind, some common therapeutic aims in relational psychotherapy include:

1. Developing mutual recognition in the intersubjective space: creating a space where the patient experiences themselves as seen and understood within the context of healing relationships, while rebuilding their capacity to perceive the therapist as a separate subject with an independent inner world. This includes processing transference-countertransference patterns that express historical recognition failures (Benjamin, 2017; Davies, 2012, p. 356).
2. Processing and conceptualizing enactments as a window into narcissistic wounds and early traumas: using repeated interactions between therapist and patient to expose and work through unconscious patterns of object relations, focusing on the shared "analytic field" as both a diagnostic and therapeutic tool (Grossmark, 2012, pp. 287–288; Davies, 2012, p. 357).
3. Reducing shame and transforming dissociation into integration: identifying shame as a central factor in emotional disconnection and encouraging the patient to experience "contained" emotional experiences through empathic recognition of narcissistic vulnerability. This is achieved through reflective interpretations that incorporate the therapist's subjectivity (Davies, 2012, p. 357; Grossmark, 2012, p. 297).
4. Creating "new relational experiences" through active analytic engagement: using "generative interventions" that enable the patient to experience alternative relational patterns to those familiar to them, emphasizing the therapist's proactive role in creating an imaginative space (Davies, 2012, pp. 663–664; Grossmark, 2012, p. 293).

However, these goals might be emphasized differently or conceptualized in various ways depending on the therapist's theoretical background. A relationally-oriented self psychologist might focus more on the development of self-cohesion through the therapeutic relationship, while a therapist with an object relations background might emphasize the working through of internalized object relations within the therapeutic dyad.

When writing case studies from a relational perspective, clinicians need to consider several key aspects:

The case study should capture not only the patient's internal world but also the intricate web of mutual influence between therapist and patient. This means documenting both participants' contributions to the therapeutic process, including the therapist's emotional responses, thoughts, and subjective experiences.

The writing style can reflect the therapist's personal theoretical integration, as the relational approach allows for the incorporation of various theoretical frameworks. There is no rigid template for case writing in the relational approach; rather, the writing should mirror the unique nature of each therapeutic relationship and the therapist's theoretical orientation.

This approach to case writing honors both the complexity of the therapeutic encounter and the uniqueness of each therapeutic relationship. Just as each therapeutic relationship is co-created by the specific individuals involved, each case study will reflect the unique perspective and style of the clinician-writer while maintaining professional standards and clarity.

CAPTURING TRANSFORMATION: WRITING ABOUT CHANGE IN THE RELATIONAL FRAMEWORK

1. Formation of an analytic field as a transformative agent: the field created between therapist and patient becomes an autonomous dynamic entity that contains the mutual projections of both participants. Change processes occur through the "flow of enactive engagement" that enables the expression of unprocessed self-states (Grossmark, 2012, pp. 291–292).
2. Mutual containment of unbearable feelings through recognition of dual subjectivity: the therapist uses their own experiences to identify and reflect back to the patient dissociative aspects of the self, while acknowledging that their conceptualization emerges from the encounter between two subjectivities (Davies, 2012, p. 661; Grossmark, 2012, p. 294).
3. Dismantling and reconstructing transference patterns through "vitalizing enactments": spontaneous and unplanned interactions (such as using metaphors or nonverbal interventions) create therapeutic breakthroughs by connecting to "dead" or disconnected parts of the psyche (Davies, 2012, p. 356; Grossmark, 2012, p. 297).
4. Using "evocative interventions" to enable safe regression: creating a "non-intrusive" therapeutic space that allows the patient to experience regression to early stages while receiving active guidance from the therapist, who helps mediate between nonverbal experience and symbolic conceptualization (Grossmark, 2012, p. 293; Davies, 2012, p. 663).

DEMONSTRATIONS OF CLINICAL PHENOMENA

Enactment

When writing about enactments in clinical case studies, it's important to capture both what Bass (2003) calls "big E" significant turning points and the "small e" ongoing patterns that constitute the therapeutic interaction. In a "small e" enactment, the therapist and patient unconsciously influence each other's behavior through their respective relational patterns and defenses. While this interaction reveals important dynamics, particularly around idealization and dependency, it doesn't fully demonstrate the more profound type of enactment central to relational theory.

Major Enactments typically involve the dramatic emergence of deeply dissociated, wounded self-states from both participants. These moments charge the therapeutic space with previously split-off trauma, creating interactions that feel overwhelming and uncontainable. In such cases, both the therapist and patient find themselves caught in powerful dynamics that touch their most profound wounds—dynamics that cannot be managed through ordinary clinical technique or conscious awareness alone. The case writer needs to capture these moments when dissociated self-states collide and previously inaccessible material suddenly emerges into the therapeutic relationship.

Aron and Atlas (2015) coined the term "generative enactment" to represent a forward-looking, constructive perspective on clinical enactments that emphasizes their potential for creating new possibilities and fostering psychological growth. Rather than viewing enactments primarily as repetitions of past patterns or defensive maneuvers, they highlight how enactments contain seeds of future development and transformation. This view shifts from seeing patients and analysts as passive objects determined by historical forces to viewing them as active subjects who unconsciously co-create opportunities for growth through their mutual participation. Like a rehearsal for future possibilities, generative enactments allow both participants to unconsciously anticipate, prepare for, and shape new ways of being and relating.

When writing relational case studies, clinicians should recognize and articulate how enactments present opportunities for growth and transformation instead of merely describing them as problematic patterns to be analyzed or interpreted. Cases should highlight the forward-looking, generative potential within clinical moments—demonstrating how apparent impasses or difficulties contain seeds of future development.

In describing enactments, consider including:

1. The continuous flow of enactive engagement rather than just isolated incidents. Illustrate how the enactment evolved over time and its role in the developmental journey of the therapeutic relationship (Aron & Atlas, 2015).
2. The interaction between dissociated self-states—both yours and your patient's. Explain how these aspects of both participants emerged and interacted in the therapeutic space.
3. Your own role and awareness within the enactment. Don't hesitate to acknowledge your conscious awareness of emerging feelings and conflicts. Document your decision-making process and internal reflections rather than portraying all significant moments as purely unconscious enactments.
4. The transformation process—how the enactment contributed to understanding and change. Illustrate how it dramatized both individual conflicts and the intersubjective field, creating opportunities for growth (Aron & Atlas, 2015).

When documenting enactments, strive for a balanced narrative that recognizes both the unconscious elements and your conscious therapeutic choices. Include your clinical reasoning and awareness while also acknowledging the complex intersubjective dynamics at play. Remember to demonstrate how the enactment served the therapeutic process rather than simply describing what occurred.

Be transparent about your role in the enactment without falling into either extreme of portraying yourself as completely unaware or entirely in control. Your written case should reflect the nuanced reality of therapeutic engagement while maintaining professional accountability and self-reflection.

Clinical example

Rachel, a 37-year-old physician, holds a senior position in a major healthcare system. Highly intelligent and accomplished, she rapidly advanced in her career, surpassing more senior candidates. Her facial expression conveys both determination and power, commanding respect and perhaps some fear from her colleagues. As the leader of a large team, she combines efficiency and success with emotional intelligence, managing to be both tough and sensitive in her role.

Rachel was born in Boston to Russian immigrant parents, both of whom were physicians. She was their only child. Her home life was marked by stark contrasts between her parents. While her mother was energetic at work, she was severely depressed at home—an ascetic woman who rejected all forms of pleasure and vitality, including art and entertainment. She wore colorless clothes and turned her depression into an ideology of denial and restraint.

Her father was the opposite—hedonistic, pleasure-seeking, and maintaining extramarital affairs. He would often come home late from shifts, drunk, playing jazz and insisting Rachel dance with him, moments she recalls with mixed feelings of excitement and disgust. The parents rarely communicated except for weekly arguments about his infidelities, during which he would eventually lash out, calling his wife a "broken robot" or a "boring corpse."

Both parents invested heavily in Rachel's intellectual development, praising her academic achievements and self-control. They appreciated that she was quiet and smart, never causing problems. While her mother's care was devoted but exhausted, her father displayed extreme emotional reactions—from uncontrollable joy to tears, as when Rachel fell seriously ill at 15.

Now, Rachel's main complaint centers on her profound loneliness. Her relationships with men are primarily sexual, beginning with passion but quickly fading when she finds them boring and routine, unable to maintain meaningful connections beyond physical attraction. "You're a woman too," she said to me pointedly, "so you must understand what I mean when I say that men just don't get it. They think sex is everything."

A month into analysis, Rachel became preoccupied with her deputy Nancy, who seemed to seek intimate moments with her and openly discussed her romantic relationships with women. Rachel believed Nancy is in love with her, triggering an intense reaction of disgust and recoil. She found herself obsessing over ways to fire Nancy, meticulously documenting her work errors yet avoiding direct confrontation. Rachel was troubled by the intensity of her own emotional response, noting that she had become as fixated on Nancy as Nancy appeared to be on her.

Rachel appealed to me from the first moment. She speaks her mind and, although it took me time to adjust to her direct style, in the first meeting, she sought to agree with me on the rules of the game that suited her. "With you, I'm not in a role, I'm paying you and that's all I owe you. I know psychologists well, all the tricks, and everything they say to patients to calm them down and make them feel good. With me, I ask that you only tell the truth to my face. I won't believe you if you fake it, and I'm excellent at detecting fakes."

I was a bit shocked by this provocative start. She didn't try to gain my favor or create a good atmosphere. I mumbled something about needing our relationship to be real and authentic, without faking, and of course, I also believe this is the best way to do therapy. But I felt bad about this response because it aligned with what she asked of me, and in this sense, I "faked" and failed the first test. She listened to my response, smiled, and seemed pleased, as if she understood that I had fallen into the trap she had set for me.

The events that followed happened at a dizzying pace. In almost every session, more or less towards the end, she would complain that she was hot and take off her shirt, under which was usually a black T-shirt. But when she did this, the undershirt also lifted, and so I was forced to watch her exposed breasts (sometimes she wore a bra and sometimes she came without). She moved casually and quickly, without looking at me or acknowledging that I was watching something akin to a short striptease show. It seemed to me that her exposed breasts lingered in view for a few seconds longer than the motion of stretching her undershirt should have taken, almost as if to ensure I saw enough, but I wasn't entirely sure about this.

I didn't understand if it was all in my head, or if she was exposing her breasts with full awareness that I was looking at her. I didn't know if I was allowed or forbidden to look. I thought that if she was doing this unintentionally, as if casually, without considering what I was seeing, it would be better not to peek since I had stumbled into a place I wasn't invited to and was intruding on her private space. However, doubts crept in that maybe she actually wanted me to see her body and that my gaze should be discreet, by stealing glances.

In the 70s I joined one of the groups where all the women were given mirrors and were asked to look at their vaginas apparently for the first time. The rationale was that once you saw yourself you can be yourself. My own history with body politics and self-examination collided with this clinical moment, making me acutely aware of the complex dynamics of seeing and being seen.

The fact that I knew every time she came to me that I was about to see her breasts disturbed my ability to concentrate on the content of the conversation. I felt my body reacting to her. I found myself waiting for the moment when she would take off her shirt. I found her chest to be attractive and appealing, especially the two nipples that looked like two magnificent and juicy crowns. I felt I was starting to go crazy because of Rachel's lack of awareness of the striptease show she was doing for me, and because I was enjoying stealing glances at her.

I find myself confronting parts of myself I've long kept separate—my own history of emotional unavailability and my learned patterns of maintaining professional distance as a defense against intimacy. The way I've split off my own neediness, my hunger for recognition, mirrors Rachel's splitting in uncanny ways. I realize that my "professional stance" of waiting and observing, which I've prided myself on, serves to protect me from acknowledging my own dissociated experiences of maternal emotional absence. Like Rachel, I too learned to wrap myself in layers—theoretical understanding, clinical distance, professional boundaries—all serving to keep my vulnerable parts safely disconnected.

My paralysis in the face of Rachel's exposure isn't just about ethical dilemmas or professional boundaries; it's about my own dissociated experience of wanting to be seen, desired, and emotionally touched while simultaneously fearing that very exposure. In my countertransference, I find myself oscillating between the emotionally unavailable mother and the excited, boundary-crossing father—unable to find a middle ground where authentic emotional and physical presence can safely coexist.

My thoughts continued: maybe she's aware of all the drama unfolding in my head? Maybe she's playing with me? Enjoying seeing me aroused? Imagining how my body is reacting to her intensely?

What should I do? If she's not aware of it, maybe I have an obligation to tell her that her body is exposed to me without her noticing? I must admit that a thought also crossed my mind that if I bring up the issue, everything will stop, and I'll never see her breasts again. My excitement and pleasure would come to an abrupt end. And if she's aware of it, maybe we need to open it all up and examine her response? On the other hand, opening up the subject could itself be interpreted as a sexual act, as a tempting invitation to examine, if only in fantasy, the potential sexual relationship that could exist between us? Do I really want the treatment to go in this direction? Is it right to introduce additional drama into her life beyond what exists between her and Nancy? And I had wonderings also about the meaning of the enactment: is she using me to feel my desire for her? Is she doing this with Nancy too? . . . Did she seduce Nancy to seduce her while she's seducing me to seduce her? Is she trying to ignite desire in the non-responsive mother?

In the following weeks Rachel sounded irritable, angry, and impatient with everything I said. She blocks every direction I try to lead to. She says she feels she could make better use of the money she's spending on therapy and is considering stopping it. At the same time, the undressings continue and it seems she's taking her time and dressing slowly so that the time I can watch her breasts is extended. I feel confused and overwhelmed, not understanding if she's trying to seduce me, or leave me, and again the dilemma arises for me that maybe it's all in my head. And if not, why am I not speaking up? Why am I not putting a stop to this? Why am I paralyzed?

After two weeks of such undressing, Rachel brings a dream:

"I'm in a massage room, waiting for a masseur to treat my wounded back. Instead, an older woman enters, wrapped in multiple layers of clothing despite the heat. She explains she's replacing the busy masseur and begins removing her layers, but never fully undresses, remaining in a white coat. I find myself unable to undress and feel disappointed—instead of the handsome masseur who would have admired my body, I'm stuck with this old woman. My back pain worsens as I doubt her ability to help me."

In associations to the dream, she connects the old woman to me and talks for the first time about her disappointment in me that I didn't manage to really touch her as she expected. Although she perceives me as a warm and smart woman and although she knows I care about her, she doesn't feel that I'm emotionally close to her and imagines that as soon as she leaves the room, I immediately forget about her and turn to my other occupations.

I see everything in her dream: that I was supposed to be a substitute for a close mother, desiring and touching, interested and in love, curious to explore the organs of the body of the baby born to her. All this underwent a sexual transformation and sexualization of a girl whose longings for her mother's touch, both emotional and physical, were not answered. Therefore, she turned to her father who offered her, as a substitute, uninhibited and tempting hedonism, but it also didn't fill the void created in the soul because the father was self-centered and not attentive to her needs, not managing to see her and be with her. Sexual relationships with men were supposed to fulfill this function, but they of course failed to do so.

In the dream, I too fail to fulfill this function. I'm described as an old and unattractive woman who replaces a handsome masseur, promising to be a suitable substitute but both of us struggle to remain naked and exposed. And most importantly—I'm wrapped in many layers and unwilling to undress.

Now I understand that she undresses so that I can see her in her nakedness and be close to her body, just as she would like to be close to my body.

I hesitate if this is the right time to expose her regular undressing in the sessions. How do I even bring up such a thing?

I decided to be very careful and talk about everything indirectly. "I think you're right that I am the old woman who appears in the dream. In the dream, you're disappointed that I appear instead of a handsome masseur who would know how to appreciate how beautiful your body is. I think you would want the old woman in the dream to be able to admire it too. That I could recognize and get excited about how beautiful and attractive you are."

Rachel answers: "Didn't you notice that every time I come here, I show you my breasts?"

The question I had been waiting so long to resolve caught me unprepared. So all this time she had been playing games with me, pretending to undress unintentionally? What should I say to her now? Maybe I should deny that I noticed it? But how can I be dishonest with her when she asks me to tell her the truth? I feel my body reacting, I'm blushing or turning pale as though blood is draining from my face. I feel as if I've been caught in the act of transgression, and I start to feel embarrassed and ashamed. I'm silent, trying to organize myself, to understand what happened here.

Slowly I manage to think. I understand that the primary needs underwent sexualization and are directed towards me.

It seems to me that from the moment Rachel came to me, she tried to be close to me. Even in her statement that we should be real with each other and that I shouldn't hide behind the professional facade was a call for a real relationship of closeness. But out of my fears and perhaps out of my attraction to her, I did not allow myself to be close to her. When she undressed in front of me, she was actually trying to overcome my empathic failure to admire her body and her sexuality and thus receive from me through the back door what she failed to receive through the main route. But I didn't respond to this either. I remained with many layers.

Finally, I say to her: "I think for a long time you've wanted me to respond to your beauty and your sexuality and for me to remove my unnecessary layers so we could be closer. Maybe when you didn't feel I was responding to you enough, you started to undress in the room. I noticed it, but I wasn't sure what the undressing meant and preferred to wait. This was a mistake because you experienced it as if I was ignoring your body. You felt me as distant, like your mother. I think you've been searching for the mother who would play with your body, enjoy it, love to touch you, admire you and your beauty all your life. You want to feel a vital mother who desires and hungers for contact with you. I could have been that, but I was too embarassed and missed something that was so important to you."

Rachel: "I feel relieved that it wasn't all in my head. You saw it all this time. And yes, I wanted so much for you to touch me. I wanted so much to be close to you."

Before my astonished eyes, this strong woman burst into heart-wrenching sobs, crying like a child. For the first time, I felt her beyond the masks we were both used to wearing. I touched the vulnerable, lost, lonely child who so longed for her mother to reach out to her and respond to her.

Suddenly, she transformed right before my eyes. I recognized the price she paid for projecting her deep yearning for connection onto her surroundings while refusing to allow herself to be needy, dependent, and vulnerable. Instead, she turned herself into an object of desire for those around her, acquiring more and more power to conceal her weakness, her loneliness, and her envy of others. Both Nancy and I fell into this trap: she seduced Nancy into loving her and then resented her for it; she seduced me to observe her body and react to it, and then perceived me as an old and redundant woman. I wonder how she would have reacted if she had been aware of the erotic feelings she stirred in me.

"I understand you, I see how sad you are," I gently told her.

The conversation led to a significant change. She cried a lot, feeling miserable and humiliated for being so exposed and needy. Two weeks after the conversation, she experienced a depressive episode that lasted several months and required medication. It was a period of intense mourning during which she had to face and ultimately let go of her lifelong fantasy of the nurturing mother she had always yearned for but never had.

Afterward, she recognized the change in herself, becoming more fragile and vulnerable. She spoke with empathy and tenderness about other people in her work environment.

She and Nancy became good friends, and although she did not surrender to Nancy sexually, it seemed that Nancy became relaxed and comfortable in her presence, happy with the new privilege of being Rachel's "bestie." It seems that the enactment that occurred in therapy allowed Rachel's archaic and early trauma to be revealed in treatment.

Enactment attempts to resolve early trauma that cannot be conceptualized in words. Therapeutic impasses, destructive repetitions, and existential relationship crises are opportunities for both the therapist and patient to resolve through dialogue. But dialogue is not enough. The therapist needs to reveal their humanity, vulnerability, and sometimes their helplessness within the therapy.

In this case, the enactment allowed not only Rachel's early trauma to surface but also forced me to confront my own dissociated experiences of emotional intimacy. My ability to finally acknowledge both her exposure and my witnessing of it came only after I could recognize and begin to integrate my own split-off experiences of wanting to be both emotionally present and professionally contained. The therapeutic breakthrough occurred when both of our dissociated self-states could meet and be acknowledged in the room.

The therapist's subjectivity

When writing clinical case studies from a relational perspective, clinicians should examine their own emotional reactions and internal conflicts that surfaced during treatment. As

Slochower (1996) notes, there are times when this subjective engagement must be carefully modulated: "During moments of holding, the patient must temporarily be protected from those aspects of the analyst's experience that would put into question the reality of the analyst's attunement" (p. 330). However, even in these moments of intense attunement, the analyst must sustain an internal awareness of the potential for more expansive, intersubjective engagement in the future.

Clinical example

Joyce Slochower (1996) describes a situation where, near the end of a session, her patient John passionately argues that, according to his watch, the session has not yet ended, even though, according to her watch, it's time to finish.

John is a patient who struggles deeply with dependency and expresses both longing and profound fear about leaning on the therapist. As the session approaches its end, Slochower moves to the front of her chair, signaling to John that the session is ending. In response, John looks at his watch and loudly claims that the session isn't over yet. Slochower checks her watch and confirms to herself that the session has indeed ended, but finds herself in a dilemma: on one hand, she wants to prove to John that she can be there for him—that is, emotionally available and attuned to his needs; on the other hand, she feels she has no choice but to set a boundary and end the session, because she too has needs and her own subjectivity. Another patient is waiting outside the room, and she has a busy day ahead.

Slochower chooses to tell John that, according to her watch, the session has indeed ended, but she understands that John has a different perception. She tries to acknowledge both perspectives: hers and John's. John, in response, stands up in protest and says, "It's not time," and leaves the room. Slochower is left with a sense of concern, but also with hope that recognizing both perspectives—hers and John's—might in the future enable a more complex therapeutic space, where there would be greater awareness of both their subjectivities.

Slochower's work with John demonstrates how relational therapists engage with their own subjectivity. Rather than canceling herself out for the patient's benefit or ignoring her own needs, Slochower tries to remain true to herself and her needs, while also recognizing and making space for John's subjectivity. She doesn't hide her perception about ending the session, but she also doesn't ignore John's feelings. She allows herself to be present, human, and imperfect, thus creating a space where both subjects—therapist and patient—can coexist, even if this creates tension or disagreement.

In this way, she creates a complex dialogue that accommodates both voices, allowing the patient to recognize the subjectivity of the other—of the therapist—as well.

Conflict and negative feelings

When writing clinical cases from a relational perspective, therapists should openly confront their negative feelings toward patients rather than minimizing or avoiding them. As Maroda (2022, pp. 89–119) notes, attempting to conceal or deny such feelings is not only futile but potentially harmful to the therapeutic process, as aggression will inevitably find alternative channels of expression.

The case should detail the therapist's internal process of navigating these emotions, including how they chose to address (or not address) these feelings with the patient. Writers should reflect on how their negative feelings illuminated important aspects of the patient's relational patterns and consider how working through these difficult emotions impacted the therapeutic relationship.

Clinical example

As an experienced therapist, I found myself grappling with increasing feelings of aversion towards my patient, Tom. He was more than just demanding; he had become unbearable. Tom constantly sought my admiration and attention, but it went far beyond that.

He repeatedly asked to extend our sessions and always claimed I was giving him too little time and attention. However, as our therapy progressed, his behavior became increasingly invasive and inappropriate.

Tom refused to end our sessions on time, often trying to stretch them indefinitely. Once, when I insisted we finish, he accused me of rushing him out for another patient. But that was merely the beginning.

He became obsessed with my personal life. Tom was convinced I had a lover who sent the beautiful flowers in my office. He'd spend entire sessions speculating about who this imaginary lover might be, describing in disturbing detail how he planned to tell my husband about this affair he'd concocted in his mind.

His invasiveness knew no bounds. He would try to sniff the air in the room, attempting to guess which perfume I was wearing. He'd comment on my clothing, hairstyle, and even how I sat. It felt like he was constantly trying to crawl under my skin.

In short, Tom's behavior went far beyond the usual challenges of therapy. I dreaded our sessions, counting the minutes until they were over.

Then came the day that changed everything. Tom arrived early for his session and encountered another one of my patients in the waiting room—a handsome young man. When Tom stormed into my office, I could see he was seething with jealousy. He demanded, "Tell me the truth! You prefer that guy over me, don't you? Be honest for once!"

I struggled to maintain my composure, exhausted by Tom's constant demands and accusations. Finally, I decided to take a risk and share my experience more directly.

"Tom, I notice that whenever you feel threatened, you become more demanding and accusatory. Right now, you're insisting I prefer another patient, just as you've insisted I must have a lover sending me flowers, or that I'm always rushing you out. I wonder if we can look at what's happening between us right now—how your fear of rejection leads you to become more aggressive, which actually pushes people away."

Tom's face reddened. "So now you're saying I'm pushing you away? That I'm the problem?"

"I'm saying that I feel attacked and cornered by you right now," I continued carefully. "And yes, if you weren't my patient, I might distance myself from someone who treats me this way. But you are my patient, and I believe understanding these patterns is crucial for your growth."

There was a long silence. Then Tom spoke, his voice quieter than usual. "You really mean that? About feeling attacked?"

"Yes, I do. And I imagine this isn't the first time your fear of rejection has led to behaviors that actually create what you fear most."

Tom slumped in his chair. "Maybe," he muttered. Then, with a hint of his usual intensity, "But at least you're finally being real with me."

This marked a turning point, but not an immediate transformation. In subsequent sessions, Tom continued to struggle with his invasive behaviors. He would slip back into old patterns of demanding attention and making inappropriate comments, but now we had a framework to discuss it. When he became intrusive, I could gently point out what was happening: "Tom, I notice you're focusing on my personal life again. What are you feeling right now?"

Sometimes he could reflect on these moments, acknowledging his anxiety about losing my attention. Other times, he would become defensive and angry, insisting I was rejecting him. The progress wasn't linear—there were sessions where he seemed to regress completely, demanding extensions and making accusations just as before.

At the depth of the dynamics that developed in the therapy room, one could discern Tom's unresolved Oedipal conflict expressed in its full intensity. His invasive and demanding behavior, together with his obsession with my personal life, reflected his failure to transition from dyadic to triangular relationships, as described by Ronald Britton (1998).

Tom's presentation of his demands in an aggressive rather than vulnerable manner made it easier for me to maintain my boundaries. His confrontational style implicitly demonstrated his resilience in handling my authentic response. Yet I remained concerned that my directness might have disrupted his tentative steps toward therapeutic dependence.

Our ongoing work together has involved constant negotiation between attunement and boundary-setting. I've come to understand that Tom needs to develop confidence in my ability to hold both his subjectivity and my own simultaneously—to be emotionally present while maintaining appropriate therapeutic boundaries. In this sense, our negotiations around these tensions may represent the core of our therapeutic work.

Mutual recognition

The term "mutual recognition" refers to a central concept in relational theory in psychoanalysis, primarily as developed in the writings of Jessica Benjamin (2017). Mutual recognition describes a state in which two subjects (for example, therapist and patient) recognize each other's subjectivity—that is, each of them is not only aware of the other's existence but also recognizes them as an independent subject with their own desires, feelings, and perspective. Mutual recognition is not a state of complete symmetry or constant harmony, but rather a dynamic process in which each party strives to recognize and be willing to be recognized by the other, while maintaining a separate identity.

Mutual recognition is not a "demand" or goal that can be imposed (Orange, 2010) but rather a possible outcome of good clinical work, and sometimes it occurs precisely as a reaction to situations of disruption or lack of mutual recognition. Mutual recognition does not eliminate the existence of other positions in human relationships—such as asymmetrical responsibility, care for the suffering other, or dialogical understanding—but rather coexists alongside them, and sometimes even in tension with them.

Clinical writing should illustrate how therapists navigate between different interventions—from offering interpretations to validating the patient's perspective as legitimate. Case material should document both successful and challenging moments in achieving mutual recognition, including instances where patients illuminate aspects of the therapist's experience that the therapist hadn't recognized. Writers should demonstrate how this mutual recognition develops over time, contributing to the patient's integration of dissociated experiences and development of new identifications.

Clinical example

In my work with Alex, a 32-year-old software engineer, I increasingly found myself frustrated by his pattern of occasional lateness to our sessions. About once a month, Alex would arrive 10–15 minutes late, often offering a casual explanation or sometimes no explanation at all. I had noticed this pattern but hadn't addressed it directly, choosing instead to simply start the session whenever he arrived.

During one session, after he had arrived late again, Alex suddenly said, "You know, I've noticed that whenever I'm late, you become much quieter during the session. It's like you're punishing me with silence." I was taken aback, initially wanting to deny his observation or defend my behavior. However, remembering the importance of self-reflection, I paused to consider his words.

As I explored Alex's perception, I realized he pointed out something I hadn't consciously acknowledged. It wasn't that I was intentionally punishing him, but rather that I was withdrawing emotionally in response to feeling disrespected or devalued. This reaction stemmed from my own childhood experiences of feeling ignored or dismissed when I expressed needs or feelings.

I shared with Alex, "You're right that something changes in me when you're late, but I don't think it's about punishment. I realize now that I feel hurt and perhaps devalued when you're late, and I react by withdrawing emotionally."

This disclosure led to a profound shift in our work. Alex, who had always struggled with passive-aggressive behavior in his relationships, began to see how his lateness might be a way of expressing anger or asserting control, much like he did in other areas of his life. He recalled how his mother would become emotionally distant when he disappointed her, much like he perceived me doing. This realization helped Alex understand his pattern of lateness as a way of testing boundaries and expressing unacknowledged anger.

As we explored this dynamic further, Alex admitted, "I think I've been trying to make you feel as powerless as I felt with my mother, without even realizing it. When you withdraw, it confirms my fear that people will abandon me if I'm not perfect." This insight opened up new avenues for us to explore Alex's relationships outside of therapy, where he often felt stuck in cycles of testing and disappointment.

Our exchange highlighted the relational approach's emphasis on mutual recognition and the co-construction of meaning. By acknowledging my own contribution to our dynamic, I modeled the self-reflection and vulnerability I was asking of Alex. This process allowed us to move beyond a simplistic interpretation of his lateness as mere resistance and into a more nuanced understanding of our intersubjective field. However, this approach also presented challenges.

At times, I questioned whether I had disclosed too much of my own emotional reactions, potentially shifting the focus away from Alex's issues. I also grappled with how to maintain appropriate boundaries while remaining authentic in my responses, especially concerning time management in our sessions. By recognizing and owning my contribution to our dynamic, I helped Alex see his own role more clearly. This process wasn't always smooth—there were sessions when Alex tested the boundaries further, arriving even later or canceling at the last minute, as if to see if I would abandon him. Yet, it was precisely these struggles that provided the richest material for our work together, illustrating the importance of both interpretation and recognition in the therapeutic process. As we continued to navigate this issue, both Alex and I became more aware of our patterns and more able to discuss them openly. This led to a more authentic and collaborative therapeutic relationship, where both of us could acknowledge our contributions to the dynamic without losing sight of Alex's primary role as the patient in need of help.

Self-disclosure

The relational approach recognizes the therapist's subjectivity as an integral part of the therapeutic process. In contrast to classical approaches that aspire to a neutral "blank slate," the relational approach views authenticity and mutual dialogue as central therapeutic tools. Kuchuck emphasizes that measured and goal-directed self-disclosure can disrupt rigid countertransference patterns and allow the patient to perceive the therapist as a subject with human complexity. However, significant dangers exist: shifting the therapeutic focus from the patient to the therapist, boundary confusion, and the reenactment of pathological patterns. Kuchuck (2009, 2021) particularly warns against disclosure arising from the therapist's unprocessed narcissistic needs and "reverse projective identification." Disclosure must be guided by the patient's needs rather than by the therapist's impulses.

First clinical example

After my father passed away, I took a week off for Shiva (mourning period). Despite my classical training making me hesitant about self-disclosure, I decided to tell some patients about my loss, following a colleague's advice that "they will notice it anyway." However, I was selective—choosing not to inform a patient whose mother was critically ill with cancer.

One particular patient, who often accused me of being robotic and lacking empathy, had lost both parents to cancer—her mother at age 5 and father at age 15. When I informed her about my father's death and absence, she responded suspiciously: "Why are you telling me this? Why is it important to you that I know this?" Her tone lacked any sympathy.

In our next session, she shared a dream: she was cycling in the mountains during a storm with black skies. Seeking shelter from intensifying rain and floods, she found a cave with an elderly bearded man inside. Though the cave looked warm and inviting, she grabbed a large branch for protection before approaching. As she neared, she noticed the man was missing a leg and using crutches. Realizing she wasn't in danger, she wondered if he would invite her in.

In her associations, she recognized how the vulnerable man in the cave represented me after my loss, and how her initial defensiveness mirrored her general approach to relationships. She experienced relief.

In this case, the self-disclosure allowed the patient to experience the therapist as a vulnerable and human person rather than an authoritative and threatening figure, opening a new pathway to intimacy that did not require defensiveness or aggression.

Second clinical example: Self-disclosure in bad taste

During a particularly charged session, as Michael discussed the tension with his partner about having children, I found myself leaning forward, recognizing the familiar queer dynamics of navigating parenthood within a same-sex relationship. "You know," I said, my voice softening, "as a gay man who's been through similar conversations, I understand the complexity."

I began to recount my own narrative—how I, too, had once believed children weren't for me. How I had been so certain, so resolute in my decision to remain childless. And then, the weight of my subsequent regret. I described the emptiness of my current life, the silence of my apartment, and the holidays spent alone. My eyes, I knew, were glistening with unshed tears.

"If I were in your partner's position," I told Michael, who was adamantly against having children, "I would feel heartbroken. Don't underestimate the desire for parenthood."

The room fell silent. Michael shifted uncomfortably, the therapeutic space now thick with my unprocessed grief, my personal narrative completely overshadowing his own struggle.

In that moment, I had transformed from his therapist to a cautionary tale, from a professional guide to a man broadcasting his deepest personal regret. This self-disclosure represents a profound breach of therapeutic boundaries and ethical practice. By sharing his deeply personal narrative of regret, the therapist has essentially hijacked the therapeutic session, turning it from a client-centered space of exploration and support into a platform for his own unresolved emotional wounds. The inappropriate sharing serves no clinical purpose for Michael, but instead burdens him with the therapist's emotional baggage, creating an uncomfortable power dynamic where the client is forced to manage the therapist's unprocessed grief (see also Kuchuch (2019) for a similar situation).

Dissociation

Philip Bromberg, a central relational theorist, conceptualizes the mind as composed of multiple self-states that maintain a creative dialectic among them. A healthy personality can move fluidly between different self-states while preserving what Bromberg terms "the healthy illusion of unitary selfhood" (Bromberg, 1996, p. 512). Unlike repression, dissociation happens when conflict becomes unbearable for the mind, leading certain self-states to become alienated from the person's experience of "me".

When writing clinical case studies from this perspective, therapists should emphasize the interplay between dissociated self-states as they manifest not only in the patient's narrative but also in the immediate therapeutic relationship through enactments. The writing should openly address the therapist's own dissociative processes and how these interact with the patient's dissociation, creating what Bromberg describes as collisions and negotiations

(Bromberg, 2011). This includes illustrating moments when the therapist becomes unaware of aspects of the patient they would rather not confront. These moments of mutual dissociation should be viewed not as therapeutic failures but as opportunities to better understand the patient's internal world.

The case should record the gradual transition from dissociation to the capacity for conflict, demonstrating how initially-sequestered self-states begin to communicate with one another through the therapeutic relationship. Special attention should be given to shame dynamics and how these manifest in the therapeutic relationship, including the therapist's own experiences of helplessness and their participation in the patient's shame dynamics.

Dreams and enactments in therapy should be underscored as vital avenues through which dissociated self-states attempt to find expression and integration. The case study should illustrate how the therapeutic process ultimately fosters the ability to hold multiple, even contradictory, perspectives simultaneously, leading to what Bromberg describes as "internal repair" (2011, p. 907).

Clinical example

Mary, a 35-year-old artist, had been in therapy with me for two years. I had repeatedly interpreted her pattern of self-sabotage in romantic relationships as a reenactment of her relationship with her emotionally unavailable father. Session after session, I would point out how she chose emotionally distant partners, while she politely but firmly disagreed, insisting that each relationship was different and that she was simply "unlucky in love."

During one session, as I was once again presenting my well-worn interpretation about her father, Mary interrupted me with unusual frustration, saying, "I hear what you're saying, but it feels like I'm caught between . . . between . . . a rock and a hard father." The malapropism—"hard father" instead of "hard place"—struck me so forcefully that I burst into uncontrollable laughter. As my laughter subsided, I felt mortified by my unprofessional reaction and looked at Rachel anxiously, expecting to find her hurt or angry.

To my surprise, Mary wasn't upset at all; she appeared confused by my reaction. When I explained the correct phrase "between a rock and a hard place," she looked at me blankly and said, "Is that what people say?" This led to a discussion about the idiom's meaning, and I found myself enthusiastically explaining how it originated from ancient Greek mythology's Scylla and Charybdis. As I elaborated on the metaphor of being trapped between two dangers, I became aware that I was speaking with unusual animation and engagement, quite different from my previous interpretive stance.

The real breakthrough came when Mary suddenly said, with a mix of irony and genuine insight, "So maybe I'm not just rejecting your interpretation—I'm actually caught between wanting to be daddy's good little girl and wanting to kill him off completely." I was taken aback by the stark honesty of her statement, which was so different from her usual careful responses. She then added, "And maybe you've been trying so hard to get me to see one side that I had to hold onto the other even more tightly."

This moment revealed how my persistent pushing of my "favorite" interpretation had actually reinforced Mary's dissociation rather than healing it. My unexpected laughter and shift from interpreter to engaged teacher had somehow created space for her dissociated self-states—the compliant daughter and the angry rebel—to emerge and interact. For months,

I had been dissociated from recognizing that my persistent pushing of my interpretation was actually reinforcing Mary's resistance. I was disconnected from the part of me that was aware of the anger my interpretations were arousing in her, insisting on "my truth" while avoiding dealing with her frustration.

Through her verbal slip and my surprisingly strong reaction, we had stumbled into a more authentic engagement that allowed these different aspects of her experience to coexist.

The therapeutic breakthrough came not from my carefully constructed interpretations but from a moment of genuine surprise and shared humanity. Mary's "hard father" slip opened up a space where dissociated self-states could begin to communicate with each other, leading to a more integrated understanding of her relationship patterns.

GENDER AND RACE ISSUES

Specifically regarding race, therapists should actively acknowledge and anticipate how race will shape the therapeutic relationship from the very first encounter, rather than attempting to dissociate from or avoid racial dynamics. Race unavoidably emerges as an influential factor in the therapeutic space, immediately highlighting similarities or differences between therapist and patient. When therapists try to distance themselves from racial dynamics, they risk compromising their ability to maintain effective therapeutic engagement when racial themes surface in the work (Suchet, 2007). By proactively recognizing their own position as "raced subjects" and preparing for how racial dynamics might manifest, therapists can better maintain their capacity to think and process when race-related material arises in the therapeutic encounter (Esprey, 2017).

Key principles in writing about gender and race issues:

- Recognizing identity as fluid and contextually negotiated
- Emphasizing the importance of therapists' self-reflection
- Exploring unconscious processes and societal power structures
- Avoiding normative solutions
- Embracing the complexity of intersecting identities.

The approach calls for clinical narratives that:

- Carefully document transferential and countertransferential dynamics
- Attend to cultural contexts and community expectations
- Examine how patients navigate multiple, sometimes conflicting, cultural identities
- Acknowledge the therapist's own positionality and biases.

First clinical example

Maya, a 15-year-old Black adolescent referred for self-harming behaviors, presented with profound conflicts about both her gender and racial identity. In our sessions, she struggled with deeply intertwined challenges: questioning her gender identity in a conservative Black community while simultaneously expressing desires to "become white." One particularly poignant session stands out in my memory. Maya discussed her envy of white students at school, especially the white boys, speaking with a mix of longing and shame about wanting to embody that particular intersection of whiteness and masculinity. In what I now recognize as a clumsy attempt to address the racial dynamics between us, I softly commented, "You know, I'm a white woman too." Maya's response was immediate and striking: "No, you're different. You're not like them—you understand." We quickly changed the subject, but that moment revealed layers of complexity in our therapeutic relationship. In that instant, I felt both relieved and troubled—relieved to be seen as "a different kind of white person," yet deeply uncomfortable with how this perception might be enabling both of us to avoid engaging with the real racial dynamics in the room. Was Maya's quick dismissal of my whiteness a way of protecting our relationship? Was my relief at being seen as "different" actually serving my own needs rather than Maya's therapeutic process? Looking back, I realize Maya might have been inviting me to join her in a kind of mutual disavowal—she would not see me as threateningly white if I would not see her as uncomfortably Black. My guilt and related discomfort, as well as my unconsciousness to the ways historical dynamics of power were being reenacted in our relationship, often sabotaged my ability to explore what was really happening between us.

These tensions remained actively present in our work, challenging both Maya's process of identity formation and my own assumptions about race, gender, and their intersections in the therapeutic relationship. My struggle to manage my guilt and culpability as a white, cisgender therapist often interfered with my ability to help Maya explore and integrate these complex aspects of her identity. I found myself questioning whether my responses were colored by my own racial and gender privilege guilt and whether this was preventing me from engaging authentically with Maya's struggles.

Second clinical example

As a gay white secular therapist working with Tariq, a deeply religious and conservative Muslim man grappling with his queer identity, I constantly faced the complexities of our differing worldviews. One of the most challenging aspects was listening to his expressions of internalized homophobia, deeply rooted in his religious beliefs. When he quoted religious texts condemning homosexuality or expressed disgust at gay relationships, I felt myself tensing up, struggling to maintain my therapeutic stance.

These moments forced me to confront a fundamental question: could I effectively help someone whose core beliefs were so radically different from my own? When Tariq spoke about homosexuality as a sin or a moral failing, I questioned whether I was the right therapist for him. As someone who had spent years advocating for LGBTQ+ rights, could I truly create a safe therapeutic space for someone with such opposing views?

The disconnect between our worldviews became even clearer when I realized that Tariq had specifically chosen me—a liberal, secular therapist—rather than seeking guidance from a religious leader. Yet this choice seemed to intensify rather than resolve his internal conflicts. The more I embodied a liberal, accepting stance toward his sexuality, the more he seemed to retreat and defend his conservative religious views. It was as if my very acceptance of his queer identity pushed him to more strongly identify with and advocate for his traditional religious perspective.

I often questioned whether a therapeutic relationship could be effective across such a vast cultural and ideological divide. How could I build genuine trust and understanding when our fundamental views on sexuality, religion, and identity were so distinct? These concerns became especially pressing when I realized that by agreeing to represent only the liberal, sexually accepting side of his experience, I had failed to help Tariq work toward a genuine integration of his religious and sexual identities.

This process compelled me to confront my own limitations and biases. Was my discomfort with his religious views preventing me from seeing the full complexity of his experience? Could I truly help him navigate this journey while carrying my own strong reactions to his beliefs? These questions didn't have easy answers, but wrestling with them became an essential part of our therapeutic work.

As I worked to create a space where Tariq could explore the complexity of his identities without judgment, I also embarked on my own journey of learning and self-reflection. This involved educating myself about Islam, seeking supervision to address my biases, and learning to sit with the discomfort of holding space for both his religious convictions and his sexual identity—even when those convictions included views I found personally challenging.

TERMINATION IN THE RELATIONAL APPROACH

Termination in psychoanalysis, particularly within a relational framework, is a profound and multilayered process that transcends a simple conclusion (Davies, 2005; Salberg, 2010). It is not a linear ending, but a complex emotional and psychological landscape where the deepest dynamics of the therapeutic relationship emerge in their most intricate form. Far from being a singular event, termination reveals multiple "series of endings" between the various self-other configurations that have developed throughout treatment, each with its own unique dynamic and need for closure.

Termination becomes a nuanced dialogue that reflects the unique intersubjective experience between two individuals, simultaneously highlighting both the progress achieved and the inherent challenges of separation. Jody Davies's (2005) work significantly enriches our understanding of the termination process by recognizing it as a "series of endings" between the multiple self-other dyads that have emerged throughout therapy. This necessitates acknowledging and working through the various relational configurations that have developed, each requiring its own form of closure. Davies underscores the critical role of the analyst's subjectivity and vulnerability, highlighting the challenges inherent in their emotional engagement during termination. The potential for patients to experience a sense of "seduction and abandonment" if the analyst's participation is not carefully managed emphasizes the analyst's responsibility to maintain awareness of their impact.

A crucial element of termination is the "de-idealization" of both patient and analyst, involving the acceptance of each other's imperfections and the relinquishing of fantasies about a perfect relationship. This process paves the way for a more realistic connection beyond the therapeutic setting. Davies also stresses the importance of working through unconscious enactments that may arise during termination, guiding the process from enactment to acknowledgment, interpretation, and ultimately, self-reflection for both participants. This facilitates deeper insight, fostering a more comprehensive understanding of relational patterns. Explicitly acknowledging the analyst's own mourning process during termination is another key contribution, recognizing how they have been touched and changed by the therapeutic work.

Unlike classical psychoanalytic writings that often depict termination as a neatly resolved conclusion, relational case studies recognize how termination resonates differently across various aspects of the psyche, with some finding resolution while others remain ongoing. This approach acknowledges that therapeutic endings, much like human relationships, are inherently incomplete and continue to evolve in both the patient's and therapist's internal worlds long after the formal conclusion of treatment. Thus, the case study becomes not a narrative of clean resolution but rather a testament to the intricate interweaving of multiple relational patterns.

The clinician encounters the challenge of articulating the intersubjective nature of the termination process, highlighting not only the patient's experience but also their own emotional responses, countertransference, and involvement in enactments. The writer must find a balance between professional objectivity and personal subjectivity, sharing enough of their own process without overshadowing the patient's experience.

Ultimately, writing about termination from a relational perspective requires clinicians to hold multiple truths simultaneously: the reality of endings alongside the lasting impact of the therapeutic relationship, the push for autonomy alongside the pull of attachment, and the universal human experience of loss alongside the unique co-created meaning within each dyad. It demands a narrative approach that is as layered, nuanced, and creatively vibrant as the termination process itself, concentrating not only on resolving conflicts but also on transforming unsatisfying relational patterns, aiding patients in developing new and more fulfilling ways of relating to others.

Clinical example

Over the years, my perspective on therapy termination has evolved significantly. I once firmly believed that therapy should continue as long as the patient was interested, viewing termination as the patient's exclusive right. Experience has taught me that this approach can perpetuate unhealthy patterns. I've learned to recognize patients who seek not growth but constant presence. They fear that leaving the therapist will lead to their emotional death and remain committed to continuing therapy not out of a desire for growth but from a fear of survival. This is a powerful illusion—a defense mechanism that keeps them tied to the therapeutic relationship long past its productive phase.

This dynamic presents a challenge: we must respect patients' fears while also recognizing when attachment has become growth-inhibiting. It's a nuanced interplay between providing support and encouraging autonomy. Part of our role is to help these patients recognize their strength and resilience, to help them see that they can thrive outside the therapeutic relationship.

This separation process can be a crucial step in their journey toward emotional independence. This understanding forced me to confront my own needs as a therapist. The idea of being reduced to a "breast" from whom someone feeds limitlessly, without recognition of my humanity, became difficult to accept. It's a limiting and sometimes objectifying role. I had to grapple with the guilt these feelings created and wondered whether my discomfort made me less empathetic as a therapist.

Helen's case brought these issues into sharp focus for me. She had been with me for 12 years. Her father, a failed businessman, left her and her mother when Helen was just seven years old, running off with his secretary. This abandonment shaped Helen's entire life. Her mother, bitter and heartbroken, never pursued another relationship, and her resentment was a constant presence in their home.

Helen grew up in an emotional vacuum, starved for the affection and validation her parents couldn't provide. Years later, Helen's father found success as a football coach, with his life revolving entirely around the sport. His passion for the game was all-consuming, leaving little room for anything—or anyone—else. He lived and breathed football, his eyes lighting up when discussing strategies or recounting memorable matches. But when it came to his daughter, that spark was conspicuously absent. He had no patience for what he perceived as weakness—tears, complaints, or requests for affection were met with thinly veiled disdain. "Toughen up," he'd say, his tone more suited to addressing a struggling player than a child seeking comfort. His world was one of harsh discipline and unyielding expectations, with no allowance for the gentler aspects of parenting.

When Helen first came to therapy, our work was incredibly productive. She delved into her past with courage, confronting the pain of her father's abandonment and her mother's emotional unavailability. We explored how these early experiences shaped her relationships and self-perception. Helen made significant strides, beginning to assert herself in her personal and professional life and even attempting to establish boundaries with her still-bitter mother.

However, as the years passed, our therapeutic relationship began to stagnate. Helen seemed to have reached a plateau, no longer pushing for growth but instead settling into a comfortable routine of weekly sessions. Our conversations became repetitive, circling the same themes without progression. I realized that I had become, for Helen, the stable, nurturing presence she had always craved—a role that, while initially healing, was now holding her back.

The decision to initiate termination was agonizing. I knew it would be painful for Helen, potentially triggering her deep-seated fears of abandonment. However, I also recognized that continuing our current pattern was not serving her best interests—or mine. The thought of maintaining this stagnant relationship indefinitely filled me with a sense of dread and resentment that I knew would ultimately compromise my ability to be an effective therapist.

When I broached the subject of ending our work together, Helen's reaction was intense. She cycled through anger, fear, and pleading. "You can't leave me too," she said, her voice breaking. "I need you." It was a moment of raw vulnerability that brought us back to the core of her struggles.

As we worked through the termination process, Helen suggested that we continue meeting less frequently—perhaps once a month or every few months. She presented it as a compromise, a way to maintain our connection while still moving towards independence. I found myself deeply conflicted about this proposal.

On one hand, I wanted to honor Helen's needs and fears. The idea of a gradual separation seemed kinder, less abrupt. But I also recognized it for what it likely was—an attempt to avoid true separation, to keep one foot in the door of our therapeutic relationship indefinitely.

Moreover, the thought of prolonging our relationship in this way filled me with a sense of dread. I realized I had reached my limit—emotionally and professionally—with this particular dynamic. The idea of seeing Helen sporadically for years to come, never fully separating, felt like it would be detrimental to both of us.

With a heavy heart, I explained to Helen why I didn't think continued, sporadic sessions would be beneficial. I tried to frame it in terms of her growth and independence, but I knew my words were hurting her. Her face crumpled, tears spilling down her cheeks. "So this is really it?" she asked, her voice small and broken.

The guilt I felt in that moment was almost overwhelming. I questioned whether I was making the right decision, whether I was failing Helen in some fundamental way. But I also knew that to continue would be a disservice to both of us.

Our final sessions were emotionally charged, filled with grief, anger, and moments of genuine connection. Helen oscillated between acceptance and renewed pleas to continue our work. I struggled to maintain appropriate boundaries while also providing the support she needed to navigate this transition.

As we discussed the end of our work together, an unexpected development occurred. Helen informed me that her family would be moving to another country due to her husband's job transfer. Suddenly, we had a concrete end date for our therapy, one that was beyond our control.

This turn of events left me with conflicting emotions. On one hand, I felt a sense of relief—the decision to end therapy was now out of my hands, dictated by external circumstances. I couldn't help but think that if I had not initiated the termination process earlier, it would have happened naturally, sparing Helen the pain of feeling rejected by me.

I was plagued by doubts. Had our difficult conversations about ending therapy been unnecessarily traumatic for Helen? Should I have taken a more gradual approach, perhaps spending a year slowly working towards termination? I found myself questioning every decision I had made in the process.

Our final session arrived, heavy with the weight of impending separation. Helen's eyes were red-rimmed, and her voice was thick with emotion as she spoke of her fears about moving to a new country, leaving behind not just therapy but everything familiar. I felt a deep sadness mixed with a lingering uncertainty about whether I had handled the termination process correctly. As Helen left my office for the last time, her parting words echoed in my mind: "I guess life makes the decisions for us sometimes."

The statement hung in the air, a bittersweet acknowledgment of the complex nature of endings and the unpredictability of life. Ultimately, I was left with the realization that there are rarely clean, perfect endings in therapy—or in life.

The termination process with Helen had been painful and imperfect, but it had also pushed both of us to confront important truths about attachment, growth, and the nature of the therapeutic relationship. While I may never be entirely certain that I made the right choices, I hope that our work together, including its difficult ending, will serve as a foundation for Helen's continued growth and resilience in her new life.

SUGGESTIONS FOR WRITING A CASE STUDY BASED ON THE RELATIONAL APPROACH

1. When writing a case study from a relational perspective, it is crucial to **go beyond the traditional focus on analysis and interpretation**. The clinician should strive to articulate the

unique and personal nature of the therapeutic relationship, emphasizing the specific contributions that extend beyond mere analysis. Pay particular attention to describing your proactive function as an analyst (Davies, 2018). This refers to what you actively provide to the patient beyond traditional analytic activities such as interpreting, understanding, or co-constructing meaning. Identify specific instances where you took proactive steps in therapy. What did you do or say that went beyond analysis or reflection? Consider how your proactive function was unique to this particular patient. How did it differ from your approach with others?

2. Acknowledge **and articulate your deep personal involvement in the therapeutic process.** Recognize that your interventions, interpretations, and capacity to hold and contain are not isolated actions, but co-constructed experiences involving both you and your patient. Emphasize how your unique personality, including your emotions, needs, vulnerabilities, and entire being, contributes to your specific encounters with this particular patient.

   Remember that you do not hold alone, contain alone, or interpret alone. Your patient is an active participant in creating and maintaining the therapeutic space. Crucially, bear in mind that every action you take in therapy is highly expressive and reveals much about who you are. Each intervention, each shift in your posture or tone of voice, is a window into your personality and your way of being with this particular patient.

3. **Do not shy away from conflicts with your patients.** When writing from a relational perspective, it is essential to embrace conflicts with patients as opportunities for growth and deeper understanding within the therapeutic process. Rather than avoiding or minimizing these inevitable tensions, therapists should explore them openly in their writing. Begin by acknowledging the conflict and delving into your own emotional responses, thoughts, and bodily sensations. Be honest about any discomfort, anger, or confusion you might feel. Look beyond surface-level explanations for your actions or reactions, considering how your personal history, biases, or desired self-image might influence your approach to the conflict. Remember that the therapist and patient contribute to the dynamic in relational therapy. Emphasize how working through the conflict led to new insights, personal growth, or improvements in the therapeutic relationship. This may include realizations about your own blind spots or biases.

4. **Feel free to draw upon diverse psychoanalytic theories** and concepts that best illuminate the patient's experience and the therapeutic process. Remember that being a relational therapist does not confine you to a single theoretical framework; rather, it emphasizes a particular way of engaging with the patient, characterized by deep self-reflection and an acute awareness of your subjectivity within the therapeutic relationship. Your case should highlight how you integrate various theoretical perspectives while maintaining a focus on the intersubjective nature of the therapeutic encounter and your reflexive participation in the process.

5. **Incorporate relevant self-disclosure thoughtfully.** Therapists must consider carefully the timing, content, and purpose of any self-disclosure, ensuring it serves the patient's best interests while maintaining the integrity of the therapeutic environment. When you choose to write about personal experiences or feelings, clarify your clinical rationale for doing so. Discuss how self-disclosure affects the power dynamics in the therapeutic

relationship and its impact on treatment. While your subjective experience is inherently part of the therapeutic process, ensure that every personal reflection, countertransference observation, or self-disclosure directly illuminates the clinical material and therapeutic relationship. Avoid using the case study as a platform for personal processing or self-centered discourse. The writer's presence should function as a careful guide, helping readers understand the clinical work without overshadowing the patient's story or the theoretical insights being conveyed.

6. **Detail significant enactments with depth.** Focus on the significant enactments that occurred during therapy. Describe these enactments in detail, explaining how they relate to the patient's early experiences and established relational patterns. Discuss the process of working through these enactments collaboratively with your patient. Pay particular attention to moments when emotionally intense enactments begin to settle. These are pivotal points where a sense of equality between therapist and patient often emerges. During pivotal moments in therapy, both the therapist and patient may experience a fleeting sense of having transcended the typical power dynamics inherent in their relationship. It's as if they've momentarily stepped into a realm where the usual hierarchical structures cease to exist. This transient illusion of absolute equality can be profoundly impactful. When this moment passes, as it inevitably does, therapist and patient find themselves back in the familiar asymmetrical relationship that defines the therapeutic setting. However, they return to this dynamic, which has changed due to their shared experience. The memory of that moment of perceived equality enriches their ongoing work together, potentially deepening their therapeutic alliance and opening new avenues for exploration and growth (Mark, 2018).

    Describe how, in these moments, the usual power dynamics and asymmetry of the therapeutic relationship seem to dissolve temporarily, creating what feels like a "radical" equality. In your description, highlight how this experience of equality becomes not just visible but experientially significant for both you and your patient. Explain how this shift in the relational dynamic contributes to the therapeutic process and potentially leads to new insights or changes in the patient's relational patterns.

7. **Address how sexuality, gender, and race impact therapeutic relationships.** When writing your case, consider the broader cultural context of your patient's experiences. Highlight how cultural forces and power differentials have shaped the context of your patient's problems. Reflect on how these cultural and societal factors influence not only the patient's individual and family context but also the therapeutic relationship itself. Your case should demonstrate an awareness of how these larger societal forces play a role in the patient's presenting issues and in the dynamics of therapy. Examine your own biases and blind spots related to these issues. Explore how sociocultural factors shape the patient's experience and the treatment.

8. **Calibrate and reflect on therapeutic excess.** In therapeutic work, the concept of "excess"—where the therapist goes beyond traditional therapeutic boundaries—represents a subtle tension between therapeutic necessity and potential risk. These moments of excess, whether manifesting as intense emotional involvement, greater self-disclosure, stronger countertransference reactions, or extended therapeutic contact, often arise naturally from the intimate nature of the therapeutic relationship. When writing relational case studies,

the written case should explore moments of "excess" with particular attention to their impact on both participants, describing not just what happened but how it felt, what it meant, and how it transformed the therapeutic relationship. Such writing requires a balance between professional insight and personal revelation, always focusing on how these interactions serve the therapeutic process while honestly examining the complex dynamics of the therapeutic relationship.

9. **Rethink psychoanalytic concepts through a relational lens.** When engaging with traditional psychoanalytic concepts, we must thoughtfully reexamine them through a relational lens, transforming them from a one-person perspective to a dialectic relationship between one- and two-person psychological frameworks. For instance, when writing about transference, projection, or regression, consider how these phenomena emerge within the mutual influence of the therapeutic dyad rather than simply residing within the patient. As Slochower (2021) emphasizes, concepts like regression need to be reconceptualized beyond the traditional view of a passive patient being held by an omniscient analyst. Instead, we must acknowledge the patient's active role and adult capacity to perceive, understand, and engage with the therapist as a real person.

RECOMMENDED READING

The analyst's vulnerability: Impact on theory and practice, by Karen Maroda. Routledge, 2021.

This book emphasizes that unconscious motivations and vulnerabilities, rooted in the analyst's own history, significantly influence therapeutic interventions and the analytic relationship. Maroda advocates for greater self-awareness and open dialogue, encouraging clinicians to recognize and accept their own needs and gratifications rather than deny them. By linking concepts such as enactment, mirror neurons, and therapeutic action to the analyst's personality structure, she challenges traditional tendencies toward passivity and idealization of harmony. Readers will gain invaluable insights into the relational approach, learning how embracing both analyst and patient humanity can enrich therapeutic work.

De-idealizing relational theory: A critique from within, by Lew Aron, Sue Grand, and Joyce Slochower (Eds.). Routledge, 2018.

This book focuses on the internal self-criticism of relational theory in psychoanalysis. The editors and authors seek to apply the principles of reflexivity and criticism that are central to psychoanalytic work to themselves, examining how the theoretical and clinical ideals of the relational approach may lead to blindness, extremism, and therapeutic obstacles.

Joyce Slochower's article addresses the dangers of "excessive relationality" and unrestrained self-disclosure, demonstrating how the ideal of mutuality can overshadow patients' (and sometimes therapists') need for protected space, privacy, and restraint. David Mark's article examines the use of self-disclosure as a tool for creating false equality, comparing different therapeutic styles. Articles by Corbett and Grossmark discuss the therapist's need for private space and the possibility of "unobtrusive" presence, particularly in situations where dialogue and interactivity might overwhelm or miss the patient's emotional needs.

Five exemplary relational case studies

You've got to suffer if you want to sing the Blues: Psychoanalytic reflections on guilt and self-pity, by Stephen Mitchell. *Psychoanalytic Dialogues 10*, 713–733, 2000.

This case study illustrates how Mitchell masterfully uses a clinical "mistake"—being 25 minutes late to a session—to explore deeper therapeutic themes around guilt, responsibility, and reparation. Rather than simply apologizing or waiving the fee, Mitchell engages with Ed's anger over being charged one-third of the session fee despite waiting in the cold. Their discussion reveals different approaches to handling guilt—Ed believes in symbolic gestures of reparation, while Mitchell argues that truly bearing guilt means sitting with the discomfort rather than trying to erase it through compensatory actions.

What makes this case particularly instructive is how Mitchell uses a clinical "failure" productively rather than defensively, demonstrating core relational principles about mutual influence, enactment, and working through conflicts in the therapeutic relationship itself. The writing conveys both the emotionality of the clinical moment and thoughtful theoretical reflection.

When the frame doesn't fit the picture, by Anthony Bass. *Psychoanalytic Dialogues 17*, 1–27, 2007.

The article exemplifies relational writing by illustrating how Bass's negotiation of frame issues with Helena, Roy, and Nicole became a shared process of growth and change, allowing both the analyst and the patients to evolve in their understanding through their struggles. Most notably, Bass openly discusses his own anxieties, blind spots, and transformations regarding fee arrangements and scheduling, demonstrating how the frame itself serves as a space for navigating relational dynamics.

God at an impasse: devotion, social justice, and the psychoanalytic subject; by Sue Grand. *Psychoanalytic Dialogues 23*, 449–463, 2013.

Sue Grand is undoubtedly one of the most compelling writers in the relational approach. Her case studies serve as guides for exploring and examining the world of relational case writing, offering depth, complexity, and a willingness to confront difficult questions. This case study focuses on treating a patient from a fundamentalist Christian migrant worker family who suffered severe childhood traumas of neglect, violence, and grueling physical labor.

The uniqueness of this case study stems from its challenge to classical psychoanalytic concepts. Grand emphasizes that traditional models of attachment and transference, which focus on the parent-child dyad, fail to explain the patient's collective experience as part of an oppressed group of children. The focus on traumatic fraternal bonds as foundational to establishing subjectivity highlights the limitations of traditional relational approaches. Furthermore, the article reveals the tension between the Jewish-secular psychoanalytic ethos and the patient's Christian faith, which views redemption after death as the solution to existential pain. This cultural-value divide becomes a central axis in the therapeutic impasse, underscoring the need to integrate ethical, spiritual, and political dimensions in understanding the subject.

The times we sizzle, and the times we sigh: The multiple erotics of arousal, anticipation, and release, by Jody Messler Davies. *Psychoanalytic Dialogues 16,* 665–686, 2006.

Since writing her classic paper "Love in the Afternoon" (1994), where she revealed her sexual fantasies to a patient, Jody Davies has become one of the most fascinating case writers, always addressing provocative topics and consistently knowing how to tell a story in the most captivating way. In this case study, Davies presents the story of Rose, a 75-year-old widow who enters analysis after experiencing her first orgasm with a new partner. The case explores Rose's sexual awakening and the complex interplay between her past and present relationships, her evolving sense of self, and her emerging erotic desires. Davies skillfully weaves together clinical material, theoretical insights, and her own experiences to illustrate the multifaceted nature of sexuality and desire in later life.

Touch me, know me: The enigma of erotic longing, by Galit Atlas. *Psychoanalytic Psychology, 32,* 123–139, 2015.

"I need to control myself as I listen and visualize what Ella is telling me. I try to recognize my moments of arousal and sexual associations, as well as my dissociation when it becomes overwhelming. I become more aware of our bodies when we sit in the same way, unclear who is imitating whom." Galit Atlas's case study of Ella provides a vivid and intimate portrayal of relational treatment, focusing on sexuality, longing, and the interplay between pragmatic and enigmatic aspects of human experience. Atlas describes her work with Ella, a young artist in her early thirties who struggles with intense distress, dysregulation, and a pattern of unfulfilling sexual encounters. The treatment spans several years, during which Atlas and Ella explore the patient's early attachment experiences, her relationship with her parents, and her sexual behaviors.

REFERENCES

Aron, L., & Atlas, G. (2015). Generative Enactment: Memories From the Future. *Psychoanalytic Dialogues, 25*(3), 309–324.

Aron, L., Grand, S., & Slochower, J. (Eds.). (2018). *De-Idealizing Relational Theory: A Critique From Within.* Routledge.

Atlas, G. (2015). Touch me, know me: The enigma of erotic longing. *Psychoanalytic Psychology, 32*(1), 123–139. https://doi.org/10.1037/a0037182

Bass, A. (2003). "E" Enactments in Psychoanalysis: Another Medium, Another Message. *Psychoanalytic Dialogues 13,* 657–675.

Bass, A. (2007). When the Frame Doesn't Fit the Picture. *Psychoanalytic Dialogues, 17*(1), 1–27. https://doi.org/10.1080/10481880701301022

Benjamin, J. (2017). *Beyond doer and done to: Recognition theory, intersubjectivity, and the third.* Routledge.

Britton, R. (1998). *Belief and Imagination—Explorations in Psychoanalysis.* Routledge.

Bromberg, P. M. (1996). Standing in the spaces: The multiplicity of self and the psychoanalytic relationship. *Contemporary Psychoanalysis, 32,* 509–535.

Bromberg, P. M. (2011). *The shadow of the tsunami and the growth of the relational mind.* Routledge.

Davies, J. M. (2005). Transformations of Desire and Despair: Reflections on the Termination Process from a Relational Perspective. *Psychoanalytic Dialogues, 15,* 779–805.

Davies, J. M. (2006). The Times We Sizzle, and the Times We Sigh: The Multiple Erotics of Arousal, Anticipation, and Release. *Psychoanalytic Dialogues, 16*(6), 665–686. https://doi.org/10.1080/10481880701357321

Davies, J. M. (2012). The "Once and future" focus of a relational psychoanalysis. *Psychoanalytic Dialogues, 22*(3), 355–359.

Davies, J. M. (2018). The "Rituals" of the Relational Perspective: Theoretical Shifts and Clinical Implications. *Psychoanalytic Dialogues, 28*(5), 651–669.

Esprey, Y. M. (2017). The Problem of Thinking in Black and White: Race in the South African Clinical Dyad. *Psychoanalytic Dialogues, 27*, 20–35.

Gerson, S. (1996). Neutrality, Resistance, and Self-Disclosure in an Intersubjective Psychoanalysis. *Psychoanalytic Dialogues, 6*, 623–645.

Grand, S. (2002). *The Reproduction of Evil: A Clinical and Cultural Perspective*. The Analytic Press.

Grand, S. (2013). God at an Impasse: Devotion, Social Justice, and the Psychoanalytic Subject. *Psychoanalytic Dialogues, 23*(4), 449–463. https://doi.org/10.1080/10481885.2013.810503

Greenberg, J. (2001). The Analyst's Participation: A New Look. *Journal of the American Psychoanalytic Association 49*, 359–381.

Grossman, L. (2014). Analytic technique: A reconsideration of the concept. *Psychoanalytic Review, 101*(3), 431–449.

Grossmark, R. (2012). The Flow of Enactive Engagement. *Contemporary Psychoanalysis, 48*(3), 287–300.

Kuchuck, S. (2009). Do Ask, Do Tell?: Narcissistic Need as a Determinant of Analyst Self-Disclosure. *Psychoanalytic Review, 96*(6), 1007–1024.

Kuchuck, S. (2021). *The Relational Revolution in Psychoanalysis and Psychotherapy*. Confer Books.

Mark, D. (2018). Forms of equality in relational psychoanalysis, In L. Aron, S. Grand, & J Slochower (Eds.), *De-Idealizing Relational Theory: A Critique From Within* (Chapter 4, pp. 80–101). Routledge.

Maroda, K. (2022). *The Analyst's Vulnerability: Impact on Theory and Practice*. Routledge.

Mills, J. P. (2012). *Conundrums: A critique of contemporary psychoanalysis*. Routledge.

Mitchell, S. A. (2000). You've Got to Suffer If You Want to Sing the Blues: Psychoanalytic Reflections on Guilt and Self-Pity. *Psychoanalytic Dialogues, 10*(5), 713–733. https://doi.org/10.1080/10481881009348578

Orange, D. M. (2010). *Thinking for clinicians: Philosophical resources for contemporary psychoanalysis and the humanistic psychotherapies*. Routledge.

Salberg, J. (Ed.). (2010). *Good enough endings: Breaks, interruptions, and terminations from contemporary relational perspectives*. Routledge.

Slochower, J. (1996). Holding and the Fate of the Analyst's Subjectivity. *Psychoanalytic Dialogues, 6*(3), 323–353.

Slochower, J. (2019). Don't Tell Anyone. *Psychoanalytic Psychology, 34*(2), 195–200.

Slochower, J. (2021). A Few Regrets. *Psychoanalytic Dialogues, 31*, 166–180.

Suchet, M. (2007). A relational encounter with race. *Psychoanalytic Dialogues, 14*, 423–438.

CHAPTER 11

Concluding remarks

The clinical case comes alive through art

....

The tradition of written case studies has its merits, but it may be time to broaden our approach to representing therapeutic experiences. Consider the potential impact of presenting a case through a curated selection of artworks that evoke the emotional journey of therapy, a choreographed dance piece expressing the dynamics between therapist and patient, a short film capturing key moments or themes from treatment, or a literary work that delves into the inner world of patient and therapist.

These alternative forms of representation could offer colleagues a visceral sense of the therapeutic experience that complements traditional case write-ups.

I thought about this when I recently saw Caravaggio's painting "Head of Medusa." It reminded me very much of how I experienced my patient Ruth. Ruth was always under terror and always had an expression of shock, fear, and horror. She was seized by such severe fits of rage and disgust at herself that it seemed her soul was producing an enormous amount of poison that she couldn't get rid of, as if she had snakes in her head. I felt that this picture described the patient better than any description I could write about her.

As the field of psychotherapy evolves, there may be growing recognition of the value in representing cases through multiple modalities. Written cases will likely remain important, but supplementing them with artistic representations could enrich our understanding of the therapeutic process and its profound impact on both patient and therapist.

Imagine that instead of presenting the treatment orally, you say to your group: "Want to feel what the treatment experience was like for me? It was like this," and then spread out a giant picture of Mark Rothko or Georg Baselitz, asking your colleagues to look at them quietly and with concentration. Or perhaps you show a dance performance, a Bergman film, or anything else that reflects the treatment experience. In this case, your colleagues would know little about the course of treatment and its development or about the background from which

DOI: 10.4324/9781003538578-14

the patient emerged, but they could understand a lot about how the treatment was experienced for you. Perhaps in the future, there will be room to represent therapeutic cases creatively in addition to written descriptions.

I wanted to convey that the psychodynamic case study should, in this sense, do to the viewer what a work of art does: convey an emotional experience that teaches them "the unique ability of art to recapture in one unit what overflows, eludes, vanishes, undermines, restored resilience. The victory of representation over destruction" (Anzieu & Monjauze, 2010/2002, p. 12). The possibility available to art in general and visual art in particular is to present the object of work differently from what is familiar and known to the observer.

Of course, pictures or books created by other artists cannot replace writing about case studies because only writing allows us to delve into the different layers of the case, learn from them, and share our insights with the community.

*

Meanwhile, we are left with the written case as the exclusive representative (along with oral case presentations) of the therapeutic process. "A large acquaintance with particulars makes us wiser than the possession of abstract formulas however deep," wrote William James in the preface to his "Varieties of Religious Experience."

James's assertion highlights why detailed case studies are essential to psychoanalytic knowledge. While theoretical abstractions offer frameworks, it is the intimate familiarity with individual cases—their complexities, nuances, and particularities—that fosters true clinical wisdom. Case studies capture the living reality of psychoanalytic work in ways that pure theory cannot. Indeed, this reality becomes even richer through the writing process itself.

As therapists engage in writing, they often find themselves re-analyzing and reinterpreting the therapeutic journey, uncovering new insights and understanding that may have remained hidden during the actual therapy. This "second analysis" through writing serves as a bridge, transforming the deeply personal experience of therapy into shared knowledge that contributes to the collective understanding of human psychology.

It is no coincidence that a guide on how to write case studies often overlaps with a potential guide on how to treat patients. This overlap reflects the intrinsic connection between documenting therapeutic experiences and the actual practice of therapy. Both activities involve similar skills and perspectives, such as careful observation, analysis, and reflection on the therapeutic journey. This parallel underscores the reciprocal relationship between clinical practice and its documentation, each informing and enhancing the other.

The evolution of case study writing reflects broader shifts in psychoanalytic theory and practice, serving as a barometer for changes in the field's understanding of the therapeutic relationship and process. As the discipline evolves, so too does the way clinicians narrate and interpret their experiences with patients.

Ultimately, successful case studies achieve a nuanced interplay between being "true" to the clinical material and being "good" narratives. This suggests that effective clinical writing is as much an art as a science, requiring technical proficiency, creative insight, and literary skills. Translating the therapeutic experience into written form offers unique potential for both clinical insight and professional development, allowing therapists to deepen their understanding of their work and contribute to the broader psychoanalytic discourse.

REFERENCES

Anzieu, D. & Monjauze, C. (2002). *Le groupe et l'inconscient*. Dunod.
James, William. (1902). *The Varieties of Religious Experience: A Study in Human Nature*. Preface, p. viii, Longmans, Green, and Co.

Index

". . . But at the same time and on another level . . .": Clinical applications in the Kleinian/ Bionian mode (Grotstein) 182

"A Clinical Contribution to the Analysis of a Perversion" (Jospeh) 156
Abram, Jan 185
achievement in therapy, discussing and summarizing 84–86, 150, 161
AI (artificial intelligence) tools and assistants 39–41, 171
Airas, Christel 91
alpha function, alpha elements 55, 57, 161, 164–166, 167, 168, 176
Altstein, Rachel 21
Alvarez, Anne 67
Amir, Dana 33, 119
"An Aspect of the Repetition Compulsion" (Joseph) 53–55
The Analyst's Vulnerability (Maroda) 257
analytic superego 141
"Analytic writing as a form of fiction" (Ogden) 20
anxiety 145; patient 34, 36, 49–50, 51, 81, 124, 145, 169; therapist (writing, fear of criticism) 23, 26
Aron, Lewis 122, 126, 129, 236
Atlas, Galit 236, 259
attacks on linking 55, 57, 168–169
Authenticity in the Psychoanalytic Encounter: The Work of Irma Brenman Pick (Pick, Davis, Shavit) 155

background history 48–50
Barber, Jacques P. 91, 102

Barros, Elias Rocha 45
Baselitz, Georg 261
Bass, Anthony 235–236, 258
Bernstein, S.B. 19n1
beta elements, beta element transformation 55, 57, 161, 164, 165, 166, 167, 176, 180
Bionian (Wilfred Bion) case studies 154–155; capturing transformation, change 162; challenges 159; clinical phenomena demonstrating 162–176; exemplary case studies, clinical examples 163, 164–165, 166–167, 169, 170, 171–172, 173–177, 182; psychodynamic formulations 55–58; related concepts 161; termination phase 176–177; therapeutic atmosphere 161; therapy goal focus 159; writing guidelines 177–181
Bionian (Wilfred Bion) case studies, clinical phenomena: alpha function, alpha elements 55, 57, 161, 164–166, 167, 168, 176, 179; analytic field, container development in 167–168, 182; attacks on linking 55, 57, 168–169; catastrophic change 170–172; container/ contained 55, 56–57, 162–163, 179; psychic growth 175–176; selected fact 172–175, 180; state of NO-THING 40–41, 169–170; therapist's transformative dream 165–167
Bionian (Wilfred Bion) case studies, clinical phenomena, writing guidelines/ recommendations 177–181; documentation approach 178–179; documenting core processes 179–180; dream-like memory analysis 177–178; fundamental principles 177–180; maintaining perspective 181; narrative approach, style 100, 102, 181; SCREAM framework 179; uncertainty

handling 180–181; working with memory and desire 161, 162, 180; writing style, technique 181

Bionian (Wilfred Bion) case studies, psychodynamic formulations 55–58; alpha function, alpha elements 55, 57, 161, 164–166; attacks on linking 55, 57; beta elements 55, 57, 161, 164; container/contained 55, 56–57, 162–163, 179; demonstration, example 55–58; frustration 55; key elements 54–58; projective identification 55, 57, 162, 164; psychotic personality part 55; reverie 55, 57; thinking apparatus 55, 57–58; transformations 55

Biran, H. 172

Bishop, Elisabeth 107

Boesky, Dale 45

Bollas, Christopher 29, 105–106

bonsai cultivation 43

breakdown 192–194

Brenman Pick, Irma 135, 140–142, 155

Britton, Ronald 23, 36–37, 148–150, 173, 244

Bromberg, Phillip 247–248

Bucci, Wilma 20–21

Busch, Fred 155n1

Cabaniss, Deborah L. 90

"Calamities and Secrets, the Power of the Fetish" (Rubin) 75

capturing transformation, change: Bion's framework 162; Klein's framework 136–137; Kohut's framework 205; relational approach framework 235; Winnicott's framework 187–188

Cardinal, Marie 25

Carlton, Lucyann 227

case journal 30–33, 31

Case studies in child and adolescent psychoanalysis (Airas) 91

case studies reading and research as training 34–39; example, detail perceptions (Odgen) 35–36; example, hidden complexities (Britton) 36–37; focused reading vs paralyzation 37–39; as genre internalizations 35; narrative structure and flow 37–38; theory–practice integration 38; therapist voice and presence 38

"Case" vs "case" distinction 3–4

Casement, Patrick 97, 198

cases study journal 30–33

Caspi, Tair 185

catastrophic change (Bion) 170–172

Chabert, Catherine 45

Challenges in case study writing; *see* writing challenges

characterizing the patient 106–110; deep noticing (unconscious expressions, body language) 107–109; example 109–110; factual information 106–107

Chekhov, Anton 103–104

Cherry, Sabrina 90

children: child patients case reports 88–90; countertransference in child psychotherapy cases 90; "general childhood situations" exploring (Klein) 152–153

choosing patients for case study 27–28

Civitarese, Giuseppe 8, 20, 167–168, 179, 182–183

clichés 40, 41, 114–116

"Clinical case studies in psychoanalytic and psychodynamic treatment" (Willemsen, Della Rosa, Kegerreis) 20, 91

clinical phenomena: Bion's framework 162–176; Klein's framework 142–148; Kohut's framework 210–221; relational approach framework 235–249; Winnicott's framework 188–196

Clinical psychoanalytic case studies with complex patients (Zachary) 91

Clinician's Thesaurus: The Guide to Conducting Interviews and Writing (Zuckerman) 91

Coltart, Nina 25–26

communication symphony 112–114

concealment–revelation paradox 17

confidentiality issues 121–128; colleague as author 123; composites 122; disguise 122, 123–125; Glen Gabbard's strategies 122–123; patient consent 122, 126–128

"Confidentiality and Consent Issues in Psychotherapy Case Reports" (Thomas-Anttila) 128–129

consent 122, 126–128

consolidations, consolidation disorder 214–216

container within the analytic field development 167–168, 182

container/contained concept (Bion) 55, 56–57, 162–163, 179

cosmic narcissism (Kohut) 208, 209

countertransference: analysis, case study discussion 87–88; child psychotherapy cases 90; cliché avoidance in writing 114–115; crisis phase, therapeutic relationship 76, 79; disruption (goal-directed self-disclosure) 246; hate in 189; Kleinian, Joseph approach, interpretation 133–134, 137, 138, 154–155; psychodynamic formulation component 51; silence, dead therapy periods 71; subjective vs objective 189; therapist's transformation stage 79; transference-countertransference dynamics and therapy shifts 67, 82, 106, 127, 134

course of treatment, phases structure 64–74; case study examples 64–67; challenges and value 64; chronological treatment division 68–70; milestone-based approach (artistic journey), Milner 64–66; phase division principles 69–70; thematic exploration (erotic imagination),

Stoller 66–67; therapy evolution through dreams 73–74; writing about silences/dead therapy periods 70–73; writing on each session 67–68; writing on themes or shifts 67; *see also* formal sections case study

course of treatment, plot axes 74–80; distrust-honeymoon-crisis-resolution 76–80; pendulum of treatment 74–75; *see also* formal sections case study

course of treatment, through interpretation 80–82

Crastnopol, M. 126

creativity: analytic process and therapy 186, 187, 194; case study as creative nonfiction genre 5, 11–13, 48, 230; creative destruction 29–30; creative expression (Winnicott's psychodynamic formulation) 58, 60; developing 167; responsible creativity 13, 16–19; as therapy goal 196

crisis phase, therapeutic relationship 28, 69, 77, 78–79, 80

cycles of resistance, progress and regression 69, 205

cyclical nature of therapeutic change 80, 206

Davids, M. F. 141, 155

Davies, Jody Messler 259

dead periods in therapy 70–72

death drive 52

defense mechanisms 52, 54–55, 70, 85, 114, 115, 144

De-Idealizing Relational Theory: A Critique From Within (Aron, Grand, Slochower) 257

Della Rosa, Elena 20, 91

depression: acute crisis, example 78; depressive position (Klein) 43, 52, 88, 134, 146–147, 150, 152; in psychodynamic formulations 51, 52, 58–59; reparation/manic reparation (Klein) 146–147

developmental arrests 61, 63–64

discussion section in case studies 86–88; example 87–88; guidelines 87; key elements 86–87; *see also* formal sections case study

disguise, confidentiality 121, 122, 123–126; betrayal 26; disguise vs invention 17; exaggerated 125; example 124; pseudonyms 110–111; recommendations, considerations 123, 124–125; thick 123; thin 125

"Disguise or Consent" (Gabbard) 128

distance, analytical/reflective 94, 95–96, 97–98, 99, 136, 138, 230–231, 238

distance-proximity and trust crisis dialectic 69

distrust phase, therapeutic relationship 77, 121

distrust-honeymoon-crisis-resolution 76–80; crisis phase 78–79; cyclical nature of therapeutic change 80; distrust phase 77; honeymoon phase 77–78; therapist's

transformation stage 79–80; *see also* course of treatment, plot axes

disturbances: self experience 216–217; selfobject experience 214–216; self-structure 212–214

documentation 12, 17, 39, 67–68, 141, 151, 178–179, 231, 262

Dora, case study (Freud) 34, 35, 104

Douglas, Carolyn J. 90

dreams: daydreams, erotic 66; disguise for confidentiality 123–125; documentation (Bion, Ogden) 178–179; dream-like memory analysis (Bionian) 177–179; dreamscape evolution example 73–74; Freudian interpretation 29; manic defenses 143, 144; negative therapy reactions 142; Oedipal triangle 149; reparation (Klein) 147; therapist's transformative dream 165–167; therapy evolution through dreams 18–19, 73–74, 76, 81; as turning points 76

Durban, Joshua 156

"Eating disorders and female development: A self psychological perspective" (Sands) 227

Eigen, Michael 16, 35, 100–101, 102, 117

enactment 28, 140, 174, 232, 234, 235–241, 248, 252

"Ending Analysis" (Joseph) 150

envy 52, 54–55, 57, 142–143, 153, 175, 250

erotic fantasy, imagination 66–67

Eshel, Ofra 71, 79

Etchegoyen, Ricardo Horacio 101–102

Ethical Considerations in Psychoanalytic Writing Revisited" (Aron) 129

exaggerated disguise 125

experiential therapy 198

external appearance and behavior 111–112

failure of case studies 44, 50

fantasy 51–52, 66, 96, 136, 139, 146–147, 154, 194

fantasy, clinical prose 15

"The fate of narcissistic rage in psychotherapy," (Ornstein) 227

fear of criticism 23–27; absolute differentiation approach 24; case distillation, editing and trimming challenges 24–25; internalized judgmental superego 24; publication anxiety, rejection fear 23; therapeutic dyad betrayal 26–27; therapy ambiguity vs explicatory writing needs 25–26

Ferro, Antonino 167–168, 182

field perspective 179

field theory, psychoanalytic 167–168, 182

"Finding Renee" (Carlton) 227

"Finding words" (Altstein) 21

"Flexibility of the psychoanalytic approach in the treatment of a suicidal patient" (Lombardi) 183 formal sections case study 5, 47–90; background history 48–50; child patients case reports 88–90; course of treatment (phases, plot axes) 64–74 (*see also* course of treatment); discussion section 86–88; psychodynamic formulations 50–64 (*see also* psychodynamic formulations); referral reasons 47–48; termination phase 82–86

Forrester, John 66–67

"Four domains of experience in the therapeutic discourse" (Bucci) 20–21

fragmented self concept (James) 213, 219–220

Freud as a Writer (Mahony) 118

Freud, Sigmund: case studies (Dora, Little Hans, Wolf Man) 34, 35, 66, 104, 128–129; depression 51; dream interpretation 29, 48, 66; free association 96; narrative style 98, 100–101; Oedipal complex 148; opening paragraphs, introduction 104–105; patient disguise 110, 123; psychic truth 41–42; self-analysis 21; *The Rat Man* 82; "Studies in Hysteria" 104–105; termination phase 82, 83

Gabbard, Glen 122–123, 128

gender issues 59, 110, 229, 249–251, 256

"general childhood situations" exploring (Klein) 152–153

generative enactment 236

Gerson, Sam 232

"God at an Impasse: Devotion, Social Justice, and the psychoanalytic subject" (Grand) 258

Govrin, Aner 11, 16, 100, 132

Grand, Sue 105, 111, 232, 257, 258

Graver, Ruth L. 90

Grossmark, Robert 111, 234, 235, 257

Grotstein, James 161, 182

Guntrip, Harry 201

"The Hands of the Living God" (Milner) 84–85

harsh superego, "psychoanalytic police" 24, 144–146

hate 189–190, 196

"Hate in the Countertransference" (Winnicot) 189–190

"Holding and Interpretation" (Winnicott) 67, 71, 82, 94

holding environment 58, 59, 64, 186, 188–189, 190, 197, 198

honeymoon phase, therapeutic relationship 69, 77–78, 80

humor 103

hybrid nature of case studies (creative nonfiction–medical reporting) 12, 13–16

"Infantile neurosis as a false-self organization" (Khan) 201

Introduction to the Work of Melanie Klein (Segal) 155

Isaacson, Walter 12–13

Joseph, Betty 53, 81–82, 107, 134, 137–139, 150, 153–154, 156

Kantrowitz, Judy Leopold 83, 126–127, 128

Keats, John 26

Kegerreis, Sue 20, 91

Khan, Masud 201

Klein, Melanie, case study Richard ("Narrative of a Child Analysis") 34, 48, 67, 82, 93

Kleinian case studies 51–55, 101, 133–157; achievement presenting 84–86, 150; Betty Joseph approach 137–140; capturing transformation, change in Klein's framework 136–137; challenges 133–135; clinical phenomena demonstrating 142–148; exemplary case studies, clinical examples 136–137, 139–140, 144, 146, 147, 150–151, 156–157; Irma Brenman Pick approach 140–142; narrative approaches, writing style 93, 94, 101; Oedipal triangle understanding 148–150; psychic truth 41–43, 133, 135; psychodynamic formulation 51–55; recommendations for writing 151–155; related concepts 134; session recording 67, 68; termination phase 82, 85, 150–151; therapeutic atmosphere 135; therapy goal 135–136

Kleinian case studies, clinical phenomena 142–148; envy 52, 54–55, 142–143, 150, 153; harsh superego 24, 144–146; manic defenses 54–55, 143; manic reparation 147–148, 149, 153; negative therapeutic reaction 142–143; reparation 146–147; splitting 144; symbolic equation 146

Kleinian case studies, writing guidelines/ recommendations 151–155; countertransference 154–155; "general childhood situations," developmental history 152–153; patient's response 154; transference and interpretation 153–154

Kleinian case studies, psychodynamic formulation 51–55; death drive and envy 52, 54–55; defense mechanisms 52, 54; demonstration example 52–55; integration of experiences 52, 54; key elements 52; Kleinian positions 52; object relations 52, 54–55; otherness recognition 52; pathological organization 52, 139; projective identification 52, 54, 88; symbolization capacity 52; unconscious fantasies 51–52, 154

Kohut, Heinz / self psychology case studies 203–227; capturing transformation, change 205; challenges 203–204; clinical phenomena 210–221, 221; exemplary case studies, clinical examples 206–208, 208–209, 210–212, 213–214, 214–216, 216–217, 217–219, 219–220, 220–221, 222–223, 226–227; individual framework selection 204; related concepts 204; relational self psychology 205–208; spiritual dimension 208–209; termination phase 221–222; therapeutic atmosphere 204; therapy goals 204; writing challenges 203–204; writing guidelines/recommendations case studies 223–226

Kohut, Heinz / self psychology, clinical phenomena 210–221; consolidations disorder 214–216; fragmented self 213, 219–220; life curve disorders 216–217; self disorder, preemergent phase (self-structure) 212–214; selfobject transference 217–219; sexualization as defense 220–221; transmuting internalization 210–212

Kuchuck, S. 246

Kulka, Raanan 208–209

The language of Bion: A dictionary of concepts (Paulo Cesar Sandler) 181

Levine 127

life curve disorders 216–217

linking, attacks on 55, 57, 168–169

Little, Margaret I. 200, 201

Little Hans, case study (Freud) 34, 35

"Live Presence: Psychoanalytic Psychotherapy with Autistic Children, Borderline Children, Children Affected by Deprivation, and Victims of Abuse" (Alvarez) 67

"The logic of play in psychoanalysis" (Parsons) 201

Lombardi, Ricardo 183

"Love in the Afternoon" (Davies) 259

Mahony, Patrick J. 21, 104, 118

"'Making a person': Clinical considerations regarding the interpretation of anxieties in the analyses of children on the autistic-psychotic spectrum" (Durban) 156

manic defenses 143

manic reparation 147–148, 149, 153

mapping selfobject needs 223

Maroda, Karen 242, 257

McWilliams, Nancy 90

Meltzer, Donald 156–157, 166

memory: complex, reconstructive character 28–29, 180; dream-like memory analysis (Bion) 177–178; limitations, selectivity 28–29, 180; memory and desire suspension (Bion) 161, 162, 180

metaphors 16–17, 30, 102, 108, 116–118, 179

Mills, J. P. 234

Milner, Marion 39, 64–67, 84–85

mistrust 77, 121; *see also* distrust-honeymoon-crisis-resolution

Mitchell, Stephen 258

"'The Music of What Happens' in Poetry and Psychoanalysis" (Ogden) 35–36, 45

"My experience of analysis with Fairbairn and Winnicott: How complete a result does psychoanalytic therapy achieve?" (Guntrip) 201

Naiburg, Suzi 119

narcissism, narcissistic expressions: case examples 81–82, 150–151, 208–209; compensation strategies, narcissistic rage 61, 226, 227; cosmic narcissism (Kohut) 208, 209; healthy narcissistic nourishment 204; narcissistic injuries, vulnerability 54, 61, 63–64, 69, 204, 234; pathology 138, 224; pattern 224; primary 175, 190; therapy goals 204, 208

narration 93–98, 96; direct quotes 94; first or third person 93–95; omniscience 97–98; tenses 95–96; tensions, profanity 95–96

"Narrative of a Child Analysis" (Klein) 82, 93

narrative style 98–103; Bion, Wilfred 100, 102, 181; choosing 99–102; as clinical sensibility expression 98–99; Eigen, Michael 100, 102; Etchegoyen, Ricardo Horacio 101–102; Freud, Sigmund 100–101; humor 103; Klein, Melanie 101; Parsons, Michael 101, 102; pragmatic 102; Sirote, Alan 101, 102; Stoller, Robert 100

negative capabilities 26, 182

"Negative capabilities, play and the negative" (Ferro) 182

negative therapeutic reaction 142–143

"no breast" experiences 55, 169

NO-THING, state of (Bion) 40–41, 169–170

nonfiction genre, case study as 5, 11–13, 48, 230

non-mutual treatment endings 83

"Notes on the Psycho-Analysis of the Super-Ego Conflict of an Acute Schizophrenic" (Rosenfeld) 155

object relations 24, 50, 52, 54, 65, 80, 87, 115, 153, 195, 203, 233–234, 234

Oedipal triangle 148–150

Oedipus complex, conflicts 151, 152, 244

Ogden, Thomas H. 7–8, 20, 35–36, 45, 104, 117, 159, 178

omniscience 97–98

"On the Word's Work" (Civitarese) 20, 179

opening paragraphs 103–106; Bollas, Christopher 105–106; Freud, Sigmund 104–105; function and challenges 103–104, 105–106; Grand, Sue 105; key considerations 106

Ornstein, Anna 227

Ornstein, Paul 227

Osler, William 13

Oz, Amos 39

Paikin, Henning 21, 24

paranoid-schizoid position 52, 147, 150, 152, 172, 200

parents 62–63; alpha function 164–165; family history as background history 48–50; reverie 56; working with 90

Parsons, Michael 77, 101, 102, 103, 201

past–present relationship analysis 153–154

pathological organization 52, 139

patience concept (Bion) 181

patient characterization 106–110; deep noticing (unconscious expressions, body language) 107–109; example 109–110; factual information 106–107

patient disguise, confidentiality 121, 122, 123–125; betrayal 26; disguise vs invention 17; exaggerated 125; example 124; pseudonyms 110–111; recommendations, considerations 123, 124–125; thick 123; thin 125

patient consent 122, 126–128

Perelberg, Rosine 156

personal growth/learning, therapist 180

perspective, maintaining 180

Phillips, Adam 84

playfulness in therapy 60, 194–195

poetry as writing inspiration 39

Poincaré, Jules-Henri 172

preemergent phase, preemergent self disorders 212–214

primary envy 175

primitive superego 144, 145

"The process with adult patients" (Meltzer) 156–157

projective identification 52, 54, 55, 57, 88, 162–163, 164, 166, 167, 246

proximity-distance and trust crises dialectic 69

pseudonym, patient's 110–111; *see also* patient disguise, confidentiality

psychic growth concept (Bion) 175–176

psychic truth as case mapping guide 41–43, 133, 135

Psychoanalytic diagnosis (McWilliams) 90

Psychoanalytic field theory (Civitarese) 182–183

Psychodynamic formulation (Cabaniss, Cherry, Douglas, Graver, Schwartz) 90

psychodynamic formulations 50–64; Bionian 55–58 (*see also* Bionian psychodynamic formulations); definition 50; key components 50–51; Kleinian 51–55 (*see also* Kleinian psychodynamic formulation); vs life event report 50–51; by school of thoughts, psychoanalytic theories 51; self psychology, Kohut 60–64 (*see also* self psychology, psychodynamic formulation); subjective vs objective character 51; Winnicott 58–60 (*see also* Winnicott's psychodynamic formulation);

Psychodynamic therapy: A guide to evidence-based practice (Summers, Barber, Zilcha-Mano) 91, 102

"Psychotic anxieties and containment: A personal record of an analysis with Winnicott" (Little) 201

Pud, O. 172

race issues 229, 249–251, 256

The Rat Man (Freud) 82

referral reasons 47–48

regression 69, 115, 162, 190–192, 199, 257

Reiner, Annie 182

relational approach to case studies 229–259; authenticity, self-disclosure (therapist) 230–231; capturing transformation, change 235; clinical phenomena 235–249; exemplary case studies, clinical examples 237–241, 242, 243–244, 245–246, 246–247, 248, 249–250, 252–254, 258–259; gender and race issues 249–251; related concepts 233; shortcoming, pitfalls 231; sources 234; therapeutic atmosphere 234; treatment goals 234; writing challenges 231–234; writing guidelines/recommendations case studies 254–257; writing style 230, 235

relational approach to case studies, clinical phenomena 235–249; conflicts, negative feelings 242–244; dissociation 247–249; enactment 235–241; mutual recognition 244–246; self-disclosure 246–247; therapist's subjectivity 241–242

relational revolution in case study writing 16, 229–231

relational self psychology 205–208

reparation 146–147, 149, 152, 153, 203

responsible creativity concept 5, 13, 16–19; clinical example 18–19; concealment–revelation paradox 17; function 17; guidelines 19; written case as therapeutic process continuation 17–18

reverie 55, 57, 162, 176, 178, 179

"Revisiting the negative therapeutic reaction: An example of comparative psychoanalysis" (Ornstein) 227

"The riddle of anxiety: Between the familiar and the unfamiliar" (Perelberg) 156

Riviere, Joan 135

Rosenfeld, Herbert 133, 156, 233

Roth, Merav 141

Rothko, Mark 261

Rubin, Margaret 75

Sandler, J. 163

Sandler, Paulo Cesar 172, 181

Sands, Susan H. 227

Schellekes, Alina 90–91

Schimmel, Harold 44
Schwartz, Anna R. 90
scientific perspective 91
SCREAM framework 179
"Second thoughts" Bion 172–173
Segal, Hanna 133, 135, 146, 153, 155
selected fact (Bion) 172–175, 180
self disorder, preemergent phase 212–214
self experience disturbances 216–217
self psychology, psychodynamic formulation
    60–64; demonstration, example 62–64;
    developmental arrests and narcissistic
    injuries 61, 63–64; key elements 61; self and
    selfobjects 61, 63; self-coherence and self-
    esteem regulation 61, 63; selfobject needs 61,
    63; transference and selfobject needs 61, 64;
    transmuting internalization 61, 63; treatment
    goals and interventions 61, 64
self-coherence 61, 63
self-esteem maintenance and regulation 61, 63,
    212, 225
selfobject experience disturbances 214–216
selfobject needs 61, 63, 64, 217, 218–219,
    221–222, 223
selfobject transferences 203–204, 217–219, 223
Semi, Antonio Alberto 21
"Sexual Excitement: Dynamics of Erotic Life"
    (Stoller) 66–67
sexualization 59, 66, 96, 149, 211, 220–221, 231,
    238–240
Shavit, N. 141, 155
Shepard, Sam 82–83
silence: active waiting, therapist's 187–188;
    companionable/shared, holding environment
    188–189, 193, 194, 200; dead periods in
    therapy 70–72; defensive vs productive 194;
    and non-verbal communication 112–113, 200;
    silence over interpretation 190
Sirote, Alan 189–190
Sirote, L. 101
Slochower, Joyce 232, 241–242, 257
Spillius, Elisabeth 142, 152
splitting 52, 54, 144
state of NO-THING (Bion) 40–41, 169–170
"Stations Along the Via Dolorosa Towards
    Good-Enough Endings" (Schellekes) 90–91
Steiner, John 173
Stimmel, B. 126
Stoller, Robert 66–67, 100, 110
storytelling, therapist as storyteller 5, 93–118,
    168; case enriching 116; characterizing the
    patient 106–110; clichés 114–116; external
    appearance and behavior 111–112; metaphors
    116–118; narration 93–98; opening
    paragraphs 103–106; patient pseudonym
    selection 110–111; punctuation vs precision

language 118; reading text aloud 118; style
    98–103; symphony of communication
    112–114
*Structure and spontaneity in clinical prose:
    A writer's guide for psychoanalysts and
    psychotherapists* (Naiburg) 119
"Studies in Hysteria" (Freud) 104–105
"Studium and Punctum in Psychoanalytic
    Writing: Reading Case Studies Through
    Roland Barthes" (Amir) 118–119
style, narrative; *see* narrative style
Summers, Richard F. 91, 102
superego 24, 141, 144–146
symbol formation 52, 65, 178
symbolic equation 52, 146, 178
symbolic thinking, symbolization capacity 52,
    55, 58, 166, 169–170
symbolization capacity 58
symphony of communication 112–114

termination phase 82–86; achievement presenting
    84–86; Bionian case studies 176–177; end of
    treatment myths and realities 83; example
    case 85–86; example excerpts 82–83; Kleinian
    case studies 82, 85, 150–151; Kohut' approach
    221–222; non-mutual endings 83; relational
    approach 251–254; Winnicott's theory
    196–198; writing approaches 83–84; *see also*
    formal sections case study
therapeutic atmosphere: Bionian framework 161;
    Kleinian framework 134; Kohut's framework
    204; relational approach framework 234;
    Winnicott's framework 186, 200
therapist's development 180–181
therapist's transformation stage 79–80
therapist's transformative dream 165–167
thick disguise 123
thin disguise 125
Thomas-Anttila, Jeremy 128–129
therapy/treatment goals: Bion's framework
    161; Klein's framework 135–136; Kohut's
    framework 204; relational approach
    framework 234; Winnicott's framework
    186–187
"The times we sizzle, and the times we sigh: The
    multiple erotic of arousal, anticipation, and
    release" (Davies) 259
timing of writing (during vs after treatment)
    28–29
tools and techniques 27–45; AI (artificial
    intelligence) 39–41, 171; case journal
    30–33; case studies reading/research 34–39;
    creative deconstruction and reconstruction
    29–30; failure reasons 44; finishing, case
    study endings 43; help from colleagues 34;
    patient choice 27–28; poetry reading 39;

psychic truth as mapping guide 41–42; timing of writing (during vs after treatment) 28–29; trauma healing as mapping guide 41–43, 203

"total situation," transference as 134

"Touch me, know me: The enigma of erotic longing" (Atlas) 259

training in case study writing 4

transference: analysis, case study discussion 86–88; cliché avoidance 114–115; crisis phase, therapeutic relationship 76; and dependence-independence dialectic 69; dismantling, reconstructing 235; Kleinian, Joseph approach, interpretation 133–134, 137, 153–154; psychodynamic formulation component 51; selfobject 203–204, 217–219, 223, 225; and selfobject needs 61; selfobject transference 217–219; transference-countertransference dynamics and therapy shifts 60, 67, 106, 127, 134; in trauma-handling approaches 42–43; types 225–226

transformations: beta elements, beta element transformation 55, 57, 161, 164, 165, 166, 167, 176, 180; Bion's framework 55, 161, 162, 176–177; capturing (*see* capturing transformation, change); enactment and 236; hallucinatory 55; Klein's framework 136–137; Kohut's framework 205, 208–209, 221–222; projective 55; relational approach framework 235; rigid 55; therapist's 79–80, 165–167; Winnicott's framework 187–188

transitional phenomena 58, 60

translation, case writing as 13, 18–19, 39, 262

transmuting internalization 61, 63, 210–212, 221–222, 224

trauma healing as case mapping guide 41–43, 203

Treating the self: Elements of clinical self psychology (Wolf) 227

true self 58, 60, 187–188, 196–197, 199–200

trust, trust crisis 69, 76–77, 121, 126, 196, 251; *see also* distrust-honeymoon-crisis-resolution

truth-focused work 41, 42

"The Two Analyses of Mr Z" (Kohut) 83, 226

"two-armed therapy" (Roth) 141

uncertainty, therapist's 26, 38, 79, 98, 104, 159, 162, 180–181, 190

unconscious fantasies 51–52, 136, 139, 154

unobtrusive therapist presence 188–189

Valéry, Paul 43

W. R. Bion's Theories of Mind: A Contemporary Introduction (Reiner) 182

"What Does the Presentation of Case Material Tell Us about What Actually Happened in an Analysis and How Does It Do This?" (Boesky, Barros, Chabert) 45

"When the frame doesn't fit the picture" (Bass) 258

"When the Sun Bursts: The Enigma of Schizophrenia" (Bollas) 105–106

Willemsen, Jochem 20, 91

Winnicott (Donald)-inspired case studies 58–60, 185–202; capturing transformation, change 187–188; challenges 185–186; clinical phenomena 188–196; exemplary case studies, clinical examples 188–189, 189–190, 191–192, 193, 194, 195–196, 197–198, 200–202; psychodynamic formulations 58–60; related concepts 186; termination phase 196–198; therapeutic atmosphere 186; therapy goal 187; writing challenges 185–186; writing guidelines, recommendations 198–200

Winnicott (Donald)-inspired case studies, clinical phenomena 188–196; breakdown, fear of 192–194; countertransference, hate in 189; object use 195–196; playfulness and creativity in therapy 194; regression 190–192; silence/uncertainty over premature interpretation 190; unobtrusive therapist presence 188–189

Winnicott (Donald)-inspired case studies, psychodynamic formulation 58–60; aggression 58, 60; demonstration, example 58–60; holding environment 58, 59; key elements 58; primary maternal preoccupation 58, 59; transitional objects, transitional space 58, 59; transitional phenomena, creativity, playfulness 58, 60; true self, false self 58, 60

Winnicott (Donald)-inspired case studies, writing guidelines/recommendations 198–200; atmosphere and non-verbal communication 200; course of treatment 199–200; experiential therapy highlighting 198; holding environment, emphasizing 198; sparing interpretation use 199; true and false self dynamics 199

"Withdrawal and Regression" (Winnicott) 200

Wolf, Ernest 227

Wolf Man, case study (Freud) 34, 66, 104, 128–129

Writing About Patients: Responsibilities, Risks, and Ramifications (Kantrowitz) 128

writing challenges 2–4; Bionian case studies 159–161; fear of criticism 23–27; hybrid nature of case studies (creative nonfiction–medical reporting) 12, 13–16; Kleinian case studies 133–135; Kohut's self psychology case studies 203–204; relational approach case studies

231–234; tools and techniques 27–45 (*see also* tools and techniques); Winnicott-guided case studies 185–186

writing guidelines/recommendations case studies: Bionian 177–181; Kleinian 151–155; Kohut's self psychology 223–226; relational psychodynamic 254–257; Winnicott guided 198–200

Writing in psychoanalysis (Piccioli, Rossi, Semi) 21

Yadlin-Gadot, S. 25

"You've got to suffer if you want to sing the Blues: Psychoanalytic reflections on guilt and selfpity" (Mitchell) 258

Zachary, Anne 91

Zilcha-Mano, Sigal 91, 102

Zuckerman, Edward L. 91

For Product Safety Concerns and Information please contact our EU
representative GPSR@taylorandfrancis.com
Taylor & Francis Verlag GmbH, Kaufingerstraße 24, 80331 München, Germany

www.ingramcontent.com/pod-product-compliance
Lightning Source LLC
Chambersburg PA
CBHW080130270326
41926CB00021B/4428